LYNCHBURG COLLEGE
SYMPOSIUM READINGS

CLASSICAL SELECTIONS ON GREAT ISSUES

SERIES TWO
VOLUME V

MAN AND SOCIETY

Gibbon
Macaulay
Spengler
Toynbee
More
Aristotle
Comte
Weber
Mill
Spencer
Veblen
Ward
Benedict
Ibsen

UNIVERSITY
PRESS OF
AMERICA

ii

SERIES TWO
SYMPOSIUM READINGS
Lynchburg College in Virginia

Compiled and Edited by the
following faculty members of Lynchburg College:

Kenneth E. Alrutz, Ph.D., University of Pennsylvania; Assistant Professor of English

Virginia B. Berger, M.A., Harvard University; Associate Professor of Music

Anne Marshall Bippus, Ed.D., University of Virginia; Associate Professor of Education

James L. Campbell, Ph.D., University of Virginia; Associate Professor of English

Robert L. Frey, Ph.D., University of Minnesota; Professor of History

James A. Huston, Ph.D., New York University; Dean of the College, Professor of History and International Relations

Shannon McIntyre Jordan, Ph.D., University of Georgia; Instructor in Philosophy

Jan G. Linn, D.Min., Christian Theological Seminary; Assistant Professor, College Chaplain

Peggy S. Pittas, M.A., Dalhousie University; Associate Professor of Psychology

Clifton W. Potter, Jr., Ph.D., University of Virginia; Professor of History

Julius A. Sigler, Ph.D., University of Virginia; Professor of Physics

Phillip H. Stump, Ph.D., University of California at Los Angeles; Assistant Professor of History

Thomas C. Tiller, Ph.D., Florida State University; Dean of Student Affairs, Professor of Education

iii

Copyright © 1982 by

University Press of America, Inc.

P.O. Box 19101, Washington, D.C. 20036

Printed in the United States of America

ISBN (Perfect): 0-8191-2253-X

ISBN   (Cloth): 0-8191-2296-3

Library of Congress Catalog Card Number: 81-71467

ACKNOWLEDGEMENTS

The following copyrighted materials have been used with the permission of the copyright holders:

From *The Decline of the West, Vol.1,* by Oswald Spengler. c. 1926, Alfred A. Knopf.

From *A Study of History, Vol.II,* by Arnold Toynbee. c.1957, Oxford University Press.

From *The Protestant Ethic and the Spirit of Capitalism,* by Max Weber, c.1952, Allen & Unwin, Inc.

From *Patterns of Culture* by Ruth Benedict. c.1959, Riverside Press.

The authors acknowledge with appreciation the permissions granted by these holders of the respective copyrights.

INTRODUCTION TO VOLUME V

What is society? Can any historical patterns in the development of societies be observed? The former query returns one full circle to the original unit in the Senior Symposium, "The Nature of Man"; while the latter is particularly tantalizing because it promises clues about how modern society developed and what may be its future. The linking of these two themes seldom occurred in human thought until the eighteenth century when Edward Gibbon, with unfailing energy, sought the nature of Rome's decline while neatly dividing history into ancient, medieval, and modern periods before rejecting his own era as a poor reflection of classical glory.

To nineteenth-century historians like Thomas Babington Macaulay, who first conceived the idea of writing social history, modern man had surpassed the ancients and stood at the threshold of the millennium. By the present century, many dissonant chords were to be heard in this symphony of progress. Oswald Spengler struck a very gloomy note when he predicted that the current age of progress is really the death throes of Western culture. More recently, Arnold Toynbee, in a similar study, has retreated from Spengler's extreme pessimism but without recovering Macaulay's optimism.

This tension seems to pervade all systematic studies of society; Comte, Spencer, Mill, and Ward echo Macaulay's optimism in varying degrees while Weber, Veblen, and Benedict issue more guarded judgments of Western society and the modern passion for accumulating wealth - an obsession which Sir Thomas More rejected in his ideal society, Utopia. But the central issues that concern man in society transcend time and the narrow confines of the West; concerns upon which Aristotle touched twenty-three centuries ago, and with which we still struggle today. Among the most interesting topics that will recur constantly in these readings are: the relationship of society and the individual social change, the roles of men and women in the family and society, the meaning of cultural symbols and institutions, and the importance of social order and hierarchy.

CONTENTS

Edward Gibbon,   THE DECLINE AND FALL OF THE ROMAN
                 EMPIRE

Oswald Spengler,   THE DECLINE OF THE WEST
                          (Trans. by Charles F. Atkinson)

Arnold Toynbee,   A STUDY OF HISTORY
                          (Abridged by D. C. Somervell)

1. In what ways did the polytheism of Rome contribute
   to the greatness of the empire?

2. What methods were used by the Romans to unite and
   absorb conquered nations?

3. Discuss the Romans' treatment of their slaves.

4. How did language and architecture influence Roman
   society?

5. What principal attributes of ancient Rome accounted
   for its greatness and what lessons may be learned
   by contemporary societies from Rome's example?

6. In order of importance, list the major reasons for
   the fall of the Roman Empire in the west as out-
   lined by Gibbon.

7. If we followed Spengler's ideas, this theme should
   probably be entitled "Man and Societies" rather
   than "Man and Society". Why, according to Spengler, does the study of history differ from the
   study of a natural science?

8. Spengler's approach to history is based on his view
   of the society of ancient Greece and Rome. What
   are the two prevalent views of this society which
   Spengler criticizes and why does he find them both
   wrong? Which of these views does Gibbon represent?
   What pattern of Western history does Spengler see
   in place of the tripartite ancient-medieval-modern
   pattern?

9.. What does Spengler mean by the terms "culture" and
   "civilization"? How is the "civilization" phase
   of a society both its fulfillment and its death?
   What is the significance and effect of money in
   this civilization phase? How does life in the

world-city of this phase differ from life in the earlier "culture" phase of the society?

10. What would Spengler say about Macaulay's enthusiastic depiction of the progress of modern England as evidenced by the growth and development of London? What does the future of our society hold in store, according to Spengler? Do you agree with Spengler's pessimistic outlook?

11. In seeking the sources of civilizations, Toynbee turns to myths concerned with encounters between two personalities, one or both of whom are superhuman. What are some of these stories?

12. The general plan of such myths is that a discordant factor is injected into a state of perfection and then requires action and suffering from which a resolution ensues. What problems of logic exist in such myths? Why are they not questioned?

13. In comparing the rise of Egyptian and Sudanese civilizations, Toynbee relies on the different choices made by these people when climatic changes occur. Explain their options and the results of the choice of each group.

14. For what reasons and by what process does an affiliate society break off from an older civilization?

15. What elements in his upbringing and occupations did Toynbee think were favorable to his being a historian?

16. According to Toynbee, what is the future of our society?

Edward Gibbon (1737-1794) completed his masterpiece, *The Decline and Fall of the Roman Empire*, in 1787. Although Gibbon's historical accuracy has been questioned and his discussion of Christianity attacked, the grace and stylistic elegance of his work is greatly admired. The following brief excerpts from this massive work are representative of Gibbon's analysis of the greatness of the Empire and the causes of its decline and fall.

THE DECLINE AND FALL

OF THE ROMAN EMPIRE

CHAPTER III.

OF THE CONSTITUTION OF THE ROMAN EMPIRE, IN THE AGE OF THE ANTONINES.

THE obvious definition of a monarchy seems to be that of a state, in which a single person, by whatsoever name he may be distinguished, is intrusted with the execution of the laws, the management of the revenue, and the command of the army. But, unless public liberty is protected by intrepid and vigilant guardians, the authority of so formidable a magistrate will soon degenerate into despotism. The influence of the clergy, in an age of superstition, might be usefully employed to assert the rights of mankind; but so intimate is the connection between the throne and the altar, that the banner of the church has very seldom been seen on the side of the people.* A martial nobility and stubborn commons, possessed of arms, tenacious of property, and collected into constitutional assemblies, form the only balance capable of preserving a free constitution against enterprises of an aspiring prince.

Every barrier of the Roman constitution had been levelled by the vast ambition of the dictator; every fence had been extirpated by the cruel hand of the triumvir. After the victory of Actium, the fate of the Roman world depended on the will of Octavianus, surnamed Cæsar, by his uncle's adoption, and afterwards Augustus, by the flattery of the senate. The conqueror was at the head of forty-four veteran legions,[1] conscious of their own strength, and of the

---

[1] Orosius, vi. 18.†

* Often enough in the ages of superstition, but not in the interest of the people or the state, but in that of the church, to which all others were subordinate. Yet the power of the pope has often been of great service in repressing the excesses of sovereigns, and in softening manners.—W. The history of the Italian republics proves the error of Gibbon, and the justice of his German t.anslator's comment.—M.

† Dion says twenty-five (or three), (lv. 23.) The united triumvirs had but forty-three. (Appian. Bell. Civ. iv. 3.) The testimony of Orosius is of little value when more certain may be had.—W. But all the legions, doubtless, submitted to Augustus after the battle of Actium.—M.

3

weakness of the constitution, habituated, during twenty years' civil war, to every act of blood and violence, and passionately devoted to the house of Cæsar, from whence alone they had received, and expected, the most lavish rewards. The provinces, long oppressed by the ministers of the republic, sighed for the government of a single person, who would be the master, not the accomplice, of those petty tyrants. The people of Rome, viewing, with a secret pleasure, the humiliation of the aristocracy, demanded only bread and public shows; and were supplied with both by the liberal hand of Augustus. The rich and polite Italians, who had almost universally embraced the philosophy of Epicurus, enjoyed the present blessings of ease and tranquillity, and suffered not the pleasing dream to be interrupted by the memory of their old tumultuous freedom. With its power, the senate had lost its dignity; many of the most noble families were extinct. The republicans of spirit and ability had perished in the field of battle, or in the proscription. The door of the assembly had been designedly left open, for a mixed multitude of more than a thousand persons, who reflected disgrace upon their rank, instead of deriving honor from it.[2]

The reformation of the senate was one of the first steps in which Augustus laid aside the tyrant, and professed himself the father of his country. He was elected censor; and, in concert with his faithful Agrippa, he examined the list of the senators, expelled a few members,* whose vices or whose obstinacy required a public example, persuaded near two hundred to prevent the shame of an expulsion by a voluntary retreat, raised the qualification of a senator to about ten thousand pounds, created a sufficient number of patrician families, and accepted for himself the honorable title of Prince of the Senate,† which had always been be-

---

[2] Julius Cæsar introduced soldiers, strangers, and half-barbarians into the senate (Sueton. in Cæsar. c. 77, 80.) The abuse became still more scandalous after his death.

---

* Of these Dion and Suetonius knew nothing.—W. Dion says the contrary, αὐτὸς μὲν οὐδένα αὐτῶν ἀπήλειψε.—M.

† But Augustus, then Octavius, was censor, and in virtue of that office, even according to the constitution of the free republic, could reform the senate, expel unworthy members, name the Princeps Senatûs, &c. That was called, as is well known, Senatum legere. It was customary, during the free republic, for the censor to be named Princeps Senatûs (S. Liv. l. xxvii. c. 11, l. xl. c. 51); and Dion expressly says, that this was done according to ancient usage. He was empowered by a decree of the senate (βουλῆς ἐπιτρεψάσης) to admit a number of families among the patricians. Finally, the senate was not the legislative power.—W.

stowed, by the censors, on the citizen the most eminent for his honors and services.[3] But whilst he thus restored the dignity, he destroyed the independence, of the senate. The principles of a free constitution are irrecoverably lost, when the legislative power is nominated by the executive.

Before an assembly thus modelled and prepared, Augustus pronounced a studied oration, which displayed his patriotism, and disguised his ambition. "He lamented, yet excused, his past conduct. Filial piety had required at his hands the revenge of his father's murder; the humanity of his own nature had sometimes given way to the stern laws of necessity, and to a forced connection with two unworthy colleagues: as long as Antony lived, the republic forbade him to abandon her to a degenerate Roman, and a barbarian queen. He was now at liberty to satisfy his duty and his inclination. He solemnly restored the senate and people to all their ancient rights; and wished only to mingle with the crowd of his fellow-citizens, and to share the blessings which he had obtained for his country." [4]

It would require the pen of Tacitus (if Tacitus had assisted at this assembly) to describe the various emotions of the senate; those that were suppressed, and those that were affected. It was dangerous to trust the sincerity of Augustus; to seem to distrust it was still more dangerous. The respective advantages of monarchy and a republic have often divided speculative inquirers; the present greatness of the Roman state, the corruption of manners, and the license of the soldiers, supplied new arguments to the advocates of monarchy; and these general views of government were again warped by the hopes and fears of each individual. Amidst this confusion of sentiments, the answer of the senate was unanimous and decisive. They refused to accept the resignation of Augustus; they conjured him not to desert the republic, which he had saved. After a decent resistance, the crafty tyrant submitted to the orders of the senate; and consented to receive the government of the provinces, and the general command of the Roman armies, under the well-known names of PROCONSUL and IMPERATOR.[5]

<hr/>

[3] Dion Cassius, l. liii. p. 693. Suetonius in August. c. 35.

[4] Dion (l. liii. p. 698) gives us a prolix and bombast speech on this great occasion. I have borrowed from Suetonius and Tacitus the general language of Augustus.

[5] Imperator (from which we have derived Emperor) signified under the republic no more than general, and was emphatically bestowed by the soldiers, when on the field of battle they proclaimed their victorious leader worthy of that title. When the Roman emperors assumed it in that sense, they placed it after their name, and marked how often they had taken it.

But he would receive them only for ten years. Even before the expiration of that period, he hoped that the wounds of civil discord would be completely healed, and that the republic, restored to its pristine health and vigor, would no longer require the dangerous interposition of so extraordinary a magistrate. The memory of this comedy, repeated several times during the life of Augustus, was preserved to the last ages of the empire, by the peculiar pomp with which the perpetual monarchs of Rome always solemnized the tenth years of their reign.[6]

Without any violation of the principles of the constitution, the general of the Roman armies might receive and exercise an authority almost despotic over the soldiers, the enemies, and the subjects of the republic. With regard to the soldiers, the jealousy of freedom had, even from the earliest ages of Rome, given way to the hopes of conquest, and a just sense of military discipline. The dictator, or consul, had a right to command the service of the Roman youth; and to punish an obstinate or cowardly disobedience by the most severe and ignominious penalties, by striking the offender out of the list of citizens, by confiscating his property, and by selling his person into slavery.[7] The most sacred rights of freedom, confirmed by the Porcian and Sempronian laws, were suspended by the military engagement. In his camp the general exercised an absolute power of life and death; his jurisdiction was not confined by any forms of trial, or rules of proceeding, and the execution of the sentence was immediate and without appeal.[8] The choice of the enemies of Rome was regularly decided by the legislative authority. The most important resolutions of peace and war were seriously debated in the senate, and solemnly ratified by the people. But when the arms of the legions were carried to a great distance from Italy, the generals assumed the liberty of directing them against whatever people, and in whatever manner, they judged most advantageous for the public service. It was from the success, not from the justice, of their enterprises, that they expected the honors of a triumph. In the use of victory, especially after they were no longer controlled by the com-

---

[6] Dion, l. liii. p. 703, &c.
[7] Livy Epitom. l. xiv. [c. 27.] Valer. Maxim. vi. 3.
[8] See, in the viiith book of Livy, the conduct of Manlius Torquatus and Papirius Cursor. They violated the laws of nature and humanity, but they asserted those of military discipline ; and the people, who abhorred the action, were obliged to respect the principle.

missioners of the senate, they exercised the most unbounded despotism. When Pompey commanded in the East, he rewarded his soldiers and allies, dethroned princes, divided kingdoms, founded colonies, and distributed the treasures of Mithridates. On his return to Rome, he obtained, by a single act of the senate and people, the universal ratification of all his proceedings.[9] Such was the power over the soldiers, and over the enemies of Rome, which was either granted to, or assumed by, the generals of the republic. They were, at the same time, the governors, or rather monarchs, of the conquered provinces, united the civil with the military character, administered justice as well as the finances, and exercised both the executive and legislative power of the state.

From what has been already observed in the first chapter of this work, some notion may be formed of the armies and provinces thus intrusted to the ruling hand of Augustus. But as it was impossible that he could personally command the legions of so many distant frontiers, he was indulged by the senate, as Pompey had already been, in the permission of devolving the execution of his great office on a sufficient number of lieutenants. In rank and authority these officers seemed not inferior to the ancient proconsuls; but their station was dependent and precarious. They received and held their commissions at the will of a superior, to whose *auspicious* influence the merit of their actions was legally attributed.[10] They were the representatives of the emperor. The emperor alone was the general of the republic, and his jurisdiction, civil as well as military, extended over all the conquests of Rome. It was some satisfaction, however, to the senate, that he always delegated his power to the members of their body. The imperial lieutenants were of consular or prætorian dignity; the legions were commanded by senators, and the præfecture of Egypt was the only important trust committed to a Roman knight.

[9] By the lavish but unconstrained suffrages of the people, Pompey had obtained a military command scarcely inferior to that of Augustus. Among the extraordinary acts of power executed by the former, we may remark the foundation of twenty-nine cities, and the distribution of three or four millions sterling to his troops. The ratification of his acts met with some opposition and delays in the senate. See Plutarch, Appian, Dion Cassius, and the first book of the epistles to Atticus.

[10] Under the commonwealth, a triumph could only be claimed by the general, who was authorized to take the Auspices in the name of the people. By an exact consequence, drawn from this principle of policy and religion, the triumph was reserved to the emperor; and his most successful lieutenants were satisfied with some marks of distinction, which, under the name of triumphal honors, were invented in their favor.

7

Within six days after Augustus had been compelled to accept so very liberal a grant, he resolved to gratify the pride of the senate by an easy sacrifice. He represented to them, that they had enlarged his powers, even beyond that degree which might be required by the melancholy condition of the times. They had not permitted him to refuse the laborious command of the armies and the frontiers; but he must insist on being allowed to restore the more peaceful and secure provinces to the mild administration of the civil magistrate. In the division of the provinces, Augustus provided for his own power and for the dignity of the republic. The proconsuls of the senate, particularly those of Asia, Greece, and Africa, enjoyed a more honorable character than the lieutenants of the emperor, who commanded in Gaul or Syria. The former were attended by lictors, the latter by soldiers.* A law was passed, that wherever the emperor was present, his extraordinary commission should supersede the ordinary jurisdiction of the governor; a custom was introduced, that the new conquests belonged to the imperial portion; and it was soon discovered that the authority of the *Prince*, the favorite epithet of Augustus, was the same in every part of the empire.

In return for this imaginary concession, Augustus obtained an important privilege, which rendered him master of Rome and Italy. By a dangerous exception to the ancient maxims, he was authorized to preserve his military command, supported by a numerous body of guards, even in time of peace, and in the heart of the capital. His command, indeed, was confined to those citizens who were engaged in the service by the military oath; but such was the propensity of the Romans to servitude, that the oath was voluntarily taken by the magistrates, the senators, and the equestrian order, till the homage of flattery was insensibly converted into an annual and solemn protestation of fidelity.

Although Augustus considered a military force as the firmest foundation, he wisely rejected it as a very odious instrument of government. It was more agreeable to his

* This distinction is without foundation. The lieutenants of the emperor, who were called Propraetors, whether they had been praetors or consuls, were attended by six lictors; those who had the right of the sword, (of life and death over the soldiers.—M.) bore the military habit (paludamentum) and the sword. The provincial governors commissioned by the senate, who, whether they had been consuls or not, were called Proconsuls, had twelve lictors when they had been consul-, and six only when they had but been praetors. The provinces of Africa and Asia were only given to ex-consuls. See, on the Organization of the Provinces, Dion, liii. 12, 16. Strabo, xvii. 840.—W.

8

temper, as well as to his policy, to reign under the venerable names of ancient magistracy, and artfully to collect, in his own person, all the scattered rays of civil jurisdiction. With this view, he permitted the senate to confer upon him, for his life, the powers of the consular [11] and tribunitian offices,[12] which were, in the same manner, continued to all his successors. The consuls had succeeded to the kings of Rome, and represented the dignity of the state. They superintended the ceremonies of religion, levied and commanded the legions, gave audience to foreign ambassadors, and presided in the assemblies both of the senate and people. The general control of the finances was intrusted to their care; and though they seldom had leisure to administer justice in person, they were considered as the supreme guardians of law, equity, and the public peace. Such was their ordinary jurisdiction; but whenever the senate empowered the first magistrate to consult the safety of the commonwealth, he was raised by that decree above the laws, and exercised, in the defence of liberty, a temporary despotism.[13] The character of the tribunes was, in every respect, different from that of the consuls. The appearance of the former was modest and humble; but their persons were sacred and inviolable. Their force was suited rather for opposition than for action. They were instituted to defend the oppressed, to pardon offences, to arraign the enemies of the people, and, when they judged it necessary, to stop, by a single word, the whole machine of government. As long as the republic subsisted, the dangerous influence, which either the consul or the tribune might derive from their respective jurisdiction, was diminished by several important restrictions. Their authority expired with the year in which they were elected; the former office was divided between two, the latter among ten persons; and, as both in their private and public interest they were averse to each other, their mutual conflicts contributed, for the most part, to strengthen rather than to

[11] Cicero (de Legibus, iii. 3) gives the consular office the name of *Regia potestas;* and Polybius (l. vi. c. 3) observes three powers in the Roman constitution. The monarchical was represented and exercised by the consuls.

[12] As the tribunitian power (distinct from the annual office) was first invented by the dictator Cæsar, (Dion, l. xliv. p. 384.) we may easily conceive, that it was given as a reward for having so nobly asserted, by arms, the sacred rights of the tribunes and people. See his own Commentaries, de Bell. Civil. l. i.

[13] Augustus exercised nine annual consulships without interruption. He then most artfully refused that magistracy, as well as the dictatorship, absented himself from Rome, and waited till the fatal effects of tumult and faction forced the senate to invest him with a perpetual consulship. Augustus, as well as his successors, affected, however, to conceal so invidious a title.

destroy the balance of the constitution.* But when the consular and tribunitian powers were united, when they were vested for life in a single person, when the general of the army was, at the same time, the minister of the senate and the representative of the Roman people, it was impossible to resist the exercise, nor was it easy to define the limits, of his imperial prerogative.

To these accumulated honors, the policy of Augustus soon added the splendid as well as important dignities of supreme pontiff, and of censor. By the former he acquired the management of the religion, and by the latter a legal inspection over the manners and fortunes, of the Roman people. If so many distinct and independent powers did not exactly unite with each other, the complaisance of the senate was prepared to supply every deficiency by the most ample and extraordinary concessions. The emperors, as the first ministers of the republic, were exempted from the obligation and penalty of many inconvenient laws : they were authorized to convoke the senate, to make several motions in the same day, to recommend candidates for the honors of the state, to enlarge the bounds of the city, to employ the revenue at their discretion, to declare peace and war, to ratify treaties ; and by a most comprehensive clause, they were empowered to execute whatsoever they should judge advantageous to the empire, and agreeable to the majesty of things private or public, human or divine.[14]

When all the various powers of executive government were committed to the *Imperial magistrate*, the ordinary magistrates of the commonwealth languished in obscurity, without vigor, and almost without business. The names and forms of the ancient administration were preserved by Augustus with the most anxious care. The usual number of consuls, prætors, and tribunes,[15] were annually invested

[14] See a fragment of a Decree of the Senate, conferring on the Emperor Vespasian all the powers granted to his predecessors, Augustus, Tiberius, and Claudius. This curious and important monument is published in Gruter's Inscriptions, No. ccxlii.†

[15] Two consuls were created on the Calends of January ; but in the course of the year others were substituted in their places, till the annual number seems to have amounted to no less than twelve. The prætors were usually sixteen or eighteen, (Lipsius in Excurs. D. ad Tacit. Annal. l. i.) I have not mentioned the

* The note of M. Guizot on the tribunitian power applies to the French translation rather than to the original. The former has, maintenir la balance toujours égale, which implies much more than Gibbon's general expression. The note belongs rather to the history of the Republic than that of the Empire.—M.

† It is also in the editions of Tacitus by Ryck, (Annal. p. 420, 421,) and Ernesti, (Excurs. ad lib. iv. 6 ;) but this fragment contains so many inconsistencies, both in matter and form, that its authenticity may be doubted.—W.

with their respective ensigns of office, and continued to discharge some of their least important functions. Those honors still attracted the vain ambition of the Romans ; and the emperors themselves, though invested for life with the powers of the consulship, frequently aspired to the title of that annual dignity, which they condescended to share with the most illustrious of their fellow-citizens.[16] In the election of these magistrates, the people, during the reign of Augustus, were permitted to expose all the inconveniences of a wild democracy. That artful prince, instead of discovering the least symptom of impatience, humbly solicited their suffrages for himself or his friends, and scrupulously practised all the duties of an ordinary candidate.[17] But we may venture to ascribe to his councils the first measure of the succeeding reign, by which the elections were transferred to the senate.[18] The assemblies of the people were forever abolished, and the emperors were delivered from a dangerous multitude, who, without restoring liberty, might have disturbed, and perhaps endangered, the established government.

By declaring themselves the protectors of the people, Marius and Cæsar had subverted the constitution of their country. But as soon as the senate had been humbled and disarmed, such an assembly, consisting of five or six hundred persons, was found a much more tractable and useful instrument of dominion. It was on the dignity of the senate that Augustus and his successors founded their new empire ; and they affected, on every occasion, to adopt the language and principles of Patricians. In the administration of their own powers, they frequently consulted the great national

Ædiles or Quæstors. Officers of the police or revenue easily adapt themselves to any form of government. In the time of Nero, the tribunes legally possessed the right of *intercession*, though it might be dangerous to exercise it. (Tacit. Annal. xvi. 26.) In the time of Trajan, it was doubtful whether the tribuneship was an office or a name, (Plin. Epist. i. 23.)

[16] The tyrants themselves were ambitious of the consulship. The virtuous princes were moderate in the pursuit, and exact in the discharge of it. Trajan revived the ancient oath, and swore before the consul's tribunal that he would observe the laws, (Plin. Panegyric. c. 64.)

[17] Quoties Magistratuum Comitiis interesset. Tribus cum candidatis suis circuibat: supplicabatque more solemni. Ferebat et ipse suffragium in tribubus, ut unus e populo. Suetonius in August. c. 56.

[18] Tum primum Comitia e campo ad patres translata sunt. Tacit. Annal. i. 15. The word *primum* seems to allude to some faint and unsuccessful efforts which were made towards restoring them to the people.*

---

* The emperor Caligula made the attempt : he restored the Comitia to the people, but, in a short time, took them away again. Suet. in Caio. c. 16. Dion. lix. 9, 20. Nevertheless, at the time of Dion, they preserved still the form of the Comitia. Dion. lviii. 20.—W.

council, and *seemed* to refer to its decision the most important concerns of peace and war. Rome, Italy, and the internal provinces, were subject to the immediate jurisdiction of the senate. With regard to civil objects, it was the supreme court of appeal; with regard to criminal matters, a tribunal, constituted for the trial of all offences that were committed by men in any public station, or that affected the peace and majesty of the Roman people. The exercise of the judicial power became the most frequent and serious occupation of the senate; and the important causes that were pleaded before them afforded a last refuge to the spirit of ancient eloquence. As a council of state, and as a court of justice, the senate possessed very considerable prerogatives; but in its legislative capacity, in which it was supposed virtually to represent the people, the rights of sovereignty were acknowledged to reside in that assembly. Every power was derived from their authority, every law was ratified by their sanction. Their regular meetings were held on three stated days in every month—the Calends, the Nones, and the Ides. The debates were conducted with decent freedom; and the emperors themselves, who gloried in the name of senators, sat, voted, and divided with their equals.

To resume, in a few words, the system of the Imperial government, as it was instituted by Augustus, and maintained by those princes who understood their own interest and that of the people, it may be defined an absolute monarchy disguised by the forms of a commonwealth. The masters of the Roman world surrounded their throne with darkness, concealed their irresistible strength, and humbly professed themselves the accountable ministers of the senate, whose supreme decrees they dictated and obeyed.[19]

The face of the court corresponded with the forms of the administration. The emperors, if we except those tyrants whose capricious folly violated every law of nature and decency, disdained that pomp and ceremony which might offend their countrymen, but could add nothing to their real power. In all the offices of life, they affected to

[19] Dion Cassius (l. liii. p. 703-714) has given a very loose and partial sketch of the Imperial system. To illustrate and often to correct him, I have meditated Tacitus, examined Suetonius, and consulted the following moderns: the Abbé de la Bleterie, in the Mémoires de l'Académie des Inscriptions, tom. xix. xxi. xxiv. xxv. xxvii. Beaufort, République Romaine, tom. i. p. 255-275. The Dissertations of Noodt and Gronovius, *de lege Regia*, printed at Leyden, in the year 1731. Gravina de Imperio Romano, p. 479-544 of his Opuscula. Maffei, Verona Illustrata, p. i. p. 245, &c.

confound themselves with their subjects, and maintained with them an equal intercourse of visits and entertainments. Their habit, their palace, their table, were suited only to the rank of an opulent senator. Their family, however numerous or splendid, was composed entirely of their domestic slaves and freedmen.[20] Augustus or Trajan would have blushed at employing the meanest of the Romans in those menial offices, which, in the household and bedchamber of a limited monarch, are so eagerly solicited by the proudest nobles of Britain.

The deification of the emperors [21] is the only instance in which they departed from their accustomed prudence and modesty. The Asiatic Greeks were the first inventors, the successors of Alexander the first objects, of this servile and impious mode of adulation.* It was easily transferred from the kings to the governors of Asia; and the Roman magistrates very frequently were adored as provincial deities, with the pomp of altars and temples, of festivals and sacrifices.[22] It was natural that the emperors should not refuse what the proconsuls had accepted; and the divine honors which both the one and the other received from the provinces, attested rather the despotism than the servitude of Rome. But the conquerors soon imitated the vanquished nations in the arts of flattery; and the imperious spirit of the first Cæsar too easily consented to assume, during his lifetime, a place among the tutelar deities of Rome. The milder temper of his successor declined so dangerous an

[20] A weak prince will always be governed by his domestics. The power of slaves aggravated the shame of the Romans; and the senate paid court to a Pallas or a Narcissus. There is a chance that a modern favorite may be a gentleman.

[21] See a treatise of Vandale de Consecratione Principium. It would be easier for me to copy, than it has been to verify, the quotations of that learned Dutchman.

[22] See a dissertation of the Abbé Mongault in the first volume of the Academy of Inscriptions.

* This is inaccurate. The successors of Alexander were not the first deified sovereigns: the Egyptians had deified and worshipped many of their kings; the Olympus of the Greeks was peopled with divinities who had reigned on earth; finally, Romulus himself had received the honors of an apotheosis (Tit. Liv. i. 16) a long time before Alexander and his successors. It is also an inaccuracy to confound the honors offered in the provinces to the Roman governors, by temples and altars, with the true apotheosis of the emperors; it was not a religious worship, for it had neither priests nor sacrifices. Augustus was severely blamed for having permitted himself to be worshipped as a god in the provinces, (Tac. Ann. i. 10;) he would not have incurred that blame if he had only done what the governors were accustomed to do.—G. from W. M. Guizot has been guilty of a still greater inaccuracy in confounding the deification of the living with the apotheosis of the dead emperors. The nature of the king-worship of Egypt is still very obscure; the hero-worship of the Greeks very different from the adoration of the "præsens numen" in the reigning sovereign.—M.

ambition, which was never afterwards revived, except by the madness of Caligula and Domitian. Augustus permitted indeed some of the provincial cities to erect temples to his honor, on condition that they should associate the worship of Rome with that of the sovereign; he tolerated private superstition, of which he might be the object;[23] but he contented himself with being revered by the senate and the people in his human character, and wisely left to his successor the care of his public deification. A regular custom was introduced, that on the decease of every emperor who had neither lived nor died like a tyrant, the senate by a solemn decree should place him in the number of the gods; and the ceremonies of his apotheosis were blended with those of his funeral.† This legal, and, as it should seem, injudicious profanation, so abhorrent to our stricter principles, was received with a very faint murmur,[24] by the easy nature of Polytheism; but it was received as an institution, not of religion, but of policy. We should disgrace the virtues of the Antonines by comparing them with the vices of Hercules or Jupiter. Even the characters of Cæsar or Augustus were far superior to those of the popular deities. But it was the misfortune of the former to live in an enlightened age, and their actions were too faithfully recorded to admit of such a mixture of fable and mystery, as the devotion of the vulgar requires. As soon as their divinity was established by law, it sunk into oblivion, without contributing either to their own fame, or to the dignity of succeeding princes.

In the consideration of the Imperial government, we have frequently mentioned the artful founder, under his well-known title of Augustus, which was not, however, conferred upon him till the edifice was almost completed. The obscure name of Octavianus he derived from a mean family, in the little town of Aricia.‡ It was stained with the blood

23 Jurandasque tuum per nomen ponimus aras, says Horace to the emperor himself, and Horace was well acquainted with the court of Augustus.*
24 See Cicero in Philippic. i. 6. Julian in Cæsaribus. Inque Deûm templis jurabit Roma per umbras, is the indignant expression of Lucan; but it is a patriotic, rather than a devout indignation.

* The good princes were not those who alone obtained the honors of an apotheosis; it was conferred on many tyrants. See an excellent treatise of Schæpflin, de Consecratione Imperatorum Romanorum, in his Commentationes historicæ et criticæ. Bâle, 1741, p. 184.—W.
† The curious satire the ἀποκολυντωσις, in the works of Seneca, is the strongest remonstrance of profaned religion.—M.
‡ Octavius was not of an obscure family, but of a considerable one of the equestrian order. His father, C. Octavius, who possessed great property, had been prætor, governor of Macedonia, adorned with the title of Imperator, and

14

of the proscription; and he was desirous, had it been possible, to erase all memory of his former life. The illustrious surname of Cæsar he had assumed, as the adopted son of the dictator; but he had too much good sense, either to hope to be confounded, or to wish to be compared, with that extraordinary man. It was proposed in the senate to dignify their minister with a new appellation; and after a serious discussion, that of Augustus was chosen, among several others, as being the most expressive of the character of peace and sanctity, which he uniformly affected.[25] *Augustus* was therefore a personal, *Cæsar* a family distinction. The former should naturally have expired with the prince on whom it was bestowed; and however the latter was diffused by adoption and female alliance, Nero was the last prince who could allege any hereditary claim to the honors of the Julian line. But, at the time of his death, the practice of a century had inseparably connected those appellations with the Imperial dignity, and they have been preserved by a long succession of emperors, Romans, Greeks, Franks, and Germans, from the fall of the republic to the present time. A distinction was, however, soon introduced. The sacred title of Augustus was always reserved for the monarch, whilst the name of Cæsar was more freely communicated to his relations; and from the reign of Hadrian, at least, was appropriated to the second person in the state, who was considered as the presumptive heir of the empire.*

The tender respect of Augustus for a free constitution which he had destroyed can only be explained by an attentive consideration of the character of that subtle tyrant.

---

[25] Dion Cassius, l. liii. p. 710, with the curious Annotations of Reimar.

---

was on the point of becoming consul when he died. His mother, Attia, was daughter of M. Attius Balbus, who had also been prætor. M. Anthony reproached Octavius with having been born in Aricia, which, nevertheless, was a considerable municipal city: he was vigorously refuted by Cicero. Philip. iii. c. 6.—W. Gibbon probably meant that the family had but recently emerged into notice.—M.

* The princes who by their birth or their adoption belonged to the family of the Cæsars, took the name of Cæsar. After the death of Nero, this name designated the Imperial dignity itself, and afterwards the appointed successor. The time at which it was employed in the latter sense, cannot be fixed with certainty. Bach (Hist. Jurisprud. Rom. 304) affirms from Tacitus, H. i. 15, and Suetonius, Galba 17, that Galba conferred on Piso Licinianus the title of Cæsar, and from that time the term had this meaning: but these two historians simply say that he appointed Piso his successor, and do not mention the word Cæsar. Aurelius Victor (in Traj. 348, ed. Artzen) says that Hadrian first received this title on his adoption; but as the adoption of Hadrian is still doubtful, and besides this, as Trajan, on his death-bed, was not likely to have created a new title for his successor, it is more probable that Ælius Verus was the first who was called Cæsar, when adopted by Hadrian. Spart. in Ælio Vero, 102.—W.

15

A cool head, an unfeeling heart, and a cowardly disposition, prompted him at the age of nineteen to assume the mask of hypocrisy, which he never afterwards laid aside. With the same hand, and probably with the same temper, he signed the proscription of Cicero, and the pardon of Cinna. His virtues, and even his vices, were artificial; and according to the various dictates of his interest, he was at first the enemy, and at last the father, of the Roman world.[26] When he framed the artful system of the Imperial authority, his moderation was inspired by his fears. He wished to deceive the people by an image of civil liberty, and the armies by an image of civil government.

I. The death of Cæsar was ever before his eyes. He had lavished wealth and honors on his adherents; but the most favored friends of his uncle were in the number of the conspirators. The fidelity of the legions might defend his authority against open rebellion; but their vigilance could not secure his person from the dagger of a determined republican; and the Romans, who revered the memory of Brutus,[27] would applaud the imitation of his virtue. Cæsar had provoked his fate, as much by the ostentation of his power, as by his power itself. The consul or the tribune might have reigned in peace. The title of king had armed the Romans against his life. Augustus was sensible that mankind is governed by names; nor was he deceived in his expectation, that the senate and people would submit to slavery, provided they were respectfully assured that they still enjoyed their ancient freedom. A feeble senate and enervated people cheerfully acquiesced in the pleasing illusion, as long as it was supported by the virtue, or even by the prudence, of the successors of Augustus. It was a motive of self-preservation, not a principle of liberty, that animated the conspirators against Caligula, Nero, and Domitian. They attacked the person of the tyrant, without aiming their blow at the authority of the emperor.

[26] As Octavianus advanced to the banquet of the Cæsars, his color changed like that of the chameleon; pale at first, then red, afterwards black, he at last assumed the mild livery of Venus and the Graces (Cæsars, p. 309). This image, employed by Julian in his ingenious fiction, is just and elegant; but when he considers this change of character as real, and ascribes it to the power of philosophy, he does too much honor to philosophy and to Octavianus.

[27] Two centuries after the establishment of monarchy, the emperor Marcus Antoninus recommends the character of Brutus as a perfect model of Roman virtue.*

* In a very ingenious essay, Gibbon has ventured to call in question the preëminent virtue of Brutus. Misc. Works, iv. 95.—M.

There appears, indeed, *one* memorable occasion, in which the senate, after seventy years of patience, made an ineffectual attempt to resume its long-forgotten rights. When the throne was vacant by the murder of Caligula, the consuls convoked that assembly in the Capitol, condemned the memory of the Cæsars, gave the watchword *liberty* to the few cohorts who faintly adhered to their standard, and during eight-and-forty hours acted as the independent chiefs of a free commonwealth. But while they deliberated, the prætorian guards had resolved. The stupid Claudius, brother of Germanicus, was already in their camp, invested with the Imperial purple, and prepared to support his election by arms. The dream of liberty was at an end; and the senate awoke to all the horrors of inevitable servitude. Deserted by the people, and threatened by a military force, that feeble assembly was compelled to ratify the choice of the prætorians, and to embrace the benefit of an amnesty, which Claudius had the prudence to offer, and the generosity to observe.[28]

II. The insolence of the armies inspired Augustus with fears of a still more alarming nature. The despair of the citizens could only attempt, what the power of the soldiers was, at any time, able to execute. How precarious was his own authority over men whom he had taught to violate every social duty! He had heard their seditious clamors; he dreaded their calmer moments of reflection. One revolution had been purchased by immense rewards; but a second revolution might double those rewards. The troops professed the fondest attachment to the house of Cæsar; but the attachments of the multitude are capricious and inconstant. Augustus summoned to his aid whatever remained in those fierce minds of Roman prejudices; enforced the rigor of discipline by the sanction of law; and, interposing the majesty of the senate between the emperor and the army, boldly claimed their allegiance, as the first magistrate of the republic.[29]

During a long period of two hundred and twenty years, from the establishment of this artful system to the death of Commodus, the dangers inherent to a military government

---

[28] It is much to be regretted that we have lost the part of Tacitus which treated of that transaction. We are forced to content ourselves with the popular rumors of Josephus, and the imperfect hints of Dion and Suetonius.

[29] Augustus restored the ancient severity of discipline. After the civil wars, he dropped the endearing name of Fellow-Soldiers, and called them only Soldiers (Sueton. in August. c. 25). See the use Tiberius made of the Senate in the mutiny of the Pannonian legions, (Tacit. Annal. i.)

were, in a great measure, suspended. The soldiers were seldom roused to that fatal sense of their own strength, and of the weakness of the civil authority, which was, before and afterwards, productive of such dreadful calamities. Caligula and Domitian were assassinated in their palace by their own domestics : * the convulsions which agitated Rome on the death of the former were confined to the walls of the city. But Nero involved the whole empire in his ruin. In the space of eighteen months, four princes perished by the sword; and the Roman world was shaken by the fury of the contending armies. Excepting only this short, though violent eruption of military license, the two centuries from Augustus to Commodus passed away unstained with civil blood, and undisturbed by revolutions. The emperor was elected by *the authority of the senate* and *the consent of the soldiers.*[30] The legions respected their oath of fidelity ; and it requires a minute inspection of the Roman annals to discover three inconsiderable rebellions, which were all suppressed in a few months, and without even the hazard of a battle.[31]

In elective monarchies, the vacancy of the throne is a moment big with danger and mischief. The Roman emperors, desirous to spare the legions that interval of suspense, and the temptation of an irregular choice, invested their designed successor with so large a share of present power, as should enable him, after their decease, to assume the remainder, without suffering the empire to perceive the change

[30] These words seem to have been the constitutional language. See Tacit. Annal. xiii. 4.†
[31] The first was Camillus Scribonianus, who took up arms in Dalmatia against Claudius, and was deserted by his troops in five days ; the second, L. Antonius, in Germany, who rebelled against Domitian ; and the third, Avidius Cassius, in the reign of M. Antoninus. The two last reigned but a few months, and were cut off by their own adherents. We may observe, that both Camillus and Cassius colored their ambition with the design of restoring the republic ; a task, said Cassius, peculiarly reserved for his name and family.

* Caligula perished by a conspiracy formed by the officers of the praetorian troops, and Domitian would not, perhaps, have been assassinated without the participation of the two chiefs of that guard in his death.—W.
† This panegyric on the soldiery is rather too liberal. Claudius was obliged to purchase their consent to his coronation : the presents which he made, and those which the praetorians received on other occasions, considerably embarrassed the finances. Moreover, this formidable guard favored, in general, the cruelties of the tyrants. The distant revolts were more frequent than Gibbon thinks : already, under Tiberius, the legions of Germany would have seditiously constrained Germanicus to assume the Imperial purple. On the revolt of Claudius Civilis, under Vespasian, the legions of Gaul murdered their general, and offered their assistance to the Gauls who were in insurrection. Julius Sabinus made himself be proclaimed emperor, &c. The wars, the merit, and the severe discipline of Trajan, Hadrian, and the two Antonines, established, for some time, a greater degree of subordination.—W.

of masters. Thus Augustus, after all his fairer prospects had been snatched from him by untimely deaths, rested his last hopes on Tiberius, obtained for his adopted son the censorial and tribunitian powers, and dictated a law, by which the future prince was invested with an authority equal to his own, over the provinces and the armies.[32] Thus Vespasian subdued the generous mind of his eldest son. Titus was adored by the eastern legions, which, under his command, had recently achieved the conquest of Judæa. His power was dreaded, and, as his virtues were clouded by the intemperance of youth, his designs were suspected. Instead of listening to such unworthy suspicions, the prudent monarch associated Titus to the full powers of the Imperial dignity; and the grateful son ever approved himself the humble and faithful minister of so indulgent a father.[33]

The good sense of Vespasian engaged him indeed to embrace every measure that might confirm his recent and precarious elevation. The military oath and the fidelity of the troops had been consecrated, by the habits of a hundred years, to the name and family of the Cæsars; and although that family had been continued only by the fictitious rite of adoption, the Romans still revered, in the person of Nero, the grandson of Germanicus, and the lineal successor of Augustus. It was not without reluctance and remorse, that the prætorian guards had been persuaded to abandon the cause of the tyrant.[34] The rapid downfall of Galba, Otho, and Vitellius taught the armies to consider the emperors as the creatures of *their* will, and the instruments of *their* license. The birth of Vespasian was mean; his grandfather had been a private soldier, his father a petty officer of the revenue;[35] his own merit had raised him, in an advanced age, to the empire; but his merit was rather useful than shining, and his virtues were disgraced by a strict and even sordid parsimony. Such a prince consulted his true interest by the association of a son, whose more splendid and amiable character might turn the public attention from the obscure origin to the future glories of the Flavian house. Under the mild administration of Titus, the Roman world enjoyed a transient

<hr/>

[32] Velleius Paterculus, l. ii. c. 121. Sueton. in Tiber. c. 20.
[33] Sueton. in Tit. c. 6. Plin. in Præfat. Hist. Natur.
[34] This idea is frequently and strongly inculcated by Tacitus. See Hist. i. 5, 16, ii. 76.
[35] The emperor Vespasian, with his usual good sense, laughed at the genealogists, who deduced his family from Flavius, the founder of Reate (his native country), and one of the companions of Hercules. Suet. in Vespasian, c. 12.

felicity, and his beloved memory served to protect, above fifteen years, the vices of his brother Domitian.

Nerva had scarcely accepted the purple from the assassins of Domitian, before he discovered that his feeble age was unable to stem the torrent of public disorders, which had multiplied under the long tyranny of his predecessor. His mild disposition was respected by the good; but the degenerate Romans required a more vigorous character, whose justice should strike terror into the guilty. Though he had several relations, he fixed his choice on a stranger. He adopted Trajan, then about forty years of age, and who commanded a powerful army in the Lower Germany; and immediately, by a decree of the senate, declared him his colleague and successor in the empire.[36] It is sincerely to be lamented, that whilst we are fatigued with the disgustful relation of Nero's crimes and follies, we are reduced to collect the actions of Trajan from the glimmerings of an abridgment, or the doubtful light of a panegyric. There remains, however, one panegyric far removed beyond the suspicion of flattery. Above two hundred and fifty years after the death of Trajan, the senate, in pouring out the customary acclamations on the accession of a new emperor, wished that he might surpass the felicity of Augustus and the virtue of Trajan.[37]

We may readily believe, that the father of his country hesitated whether he ought to intrust the various and doubtful character of his kinsman Hadrian with sovereign power. In his last moments, the arts of the empress Plotina either fixed the irresolution of Trajan, or boldly supposed a fictitious adoption;[38] the truth of which could not be safely disputed, and Hadrian was peaceably acknowledged as his lawful successor. Under his reign, as has been already mentioned, the empire flourished in peace and prosperity. He encouraged the arts, reformed the laws, asserted military discipline, and visited all his provinces in person. His vast and active genius was equally suited to the most enlarged views, and the minute details of civil policy. But the ruling passions of his soul were curiosity and vanity. As they prevailed, and as they were attracted by different

[36] Dion, l. lxviii. p. 1121. Plin. Secund. in Panegyric.
[37] Felicior Augusto, MELIOR TRAJANO. Eutrop. viii. 5.
[38] Dion (l. lxix. p. 1249) affirms the whole to have been a fiction, on the authority of his father, who, being governor of the province where Trajan died, had very good opportunities of sifting this mysterious transaction. Yet Dodwell (Prælect. Camden. xvii.) has maintained that Hadrian was called to the certain hope of the empire, during the lifetime of Trajan.

20

objects, Hadrian was, by turns, an excellent prince, a ridiculous sophist, and a jealous tyrant. The general tenor of his conduct deserved praise for its equity and moderation. Yet in the first days of his reign he put to death four consular senators, his personal enemies, and men who had been judged worthy of empire; and the tediousness of a painful illness rendered him, at last, peevish and cruel. The senate doubted whether they should pronounce him a god or a tyrant; and the honors decreed to his memory were granted to the prayers of the pious Antoninus.[39]

The caprice of Hadrian influenced his choice of a successor. After revolving in his mind several men of distinguished merit, whom he esteemed and hated, he adopted Ælius Verus, a gay and voluptuous nobleman, recommended by uncommon beauty to the lover of Antinous.[40] But whilst Hadrian was delighting himself with his own applause, and the acclamations of the soldiers, whose consent had been secured by an immense donative, the new Cæsar [41] was ravished from his embraces by an untimely death. He left only one son. Hadrian commended the boy to the gratitude of the Antonines. He was adopted by Pius; and, on the accession of Marcus, was invested with an equal share of sovereign power. Among the many vices of this younger Verus, he possessed one virtue; a dutiful reverence for his wiser colleague, to whom he willingly abandoned the ruder cares of empire. The philosophic emperor dissembled his follies, lamented his early death, and cast a decent veil over his memory.

As soon as Hadrian's passion was either gratified or disappointed, he resolved to deserve the thanks of posterity, by placing the most exalted merit on the Roman throne. His discerning eye easily discovered a senator about fifty years of age, blameless in all the offices of life; and a youth of about seventeen, whose riper years opened a fair prospect of every virtue: the elder of these was declared the son and successor of Hadrian, on condition, however, that he himself should immediately adopt the younger. The two Antonines (for it is of them that we are now speaking) governed the Roman world forty-two years, with the same invariable

[39] Dion (l. lxx. p. 1171). Aurel. Victor.
[40] The deification of Antinous, his medals, statues, temples, city, oracles, and constellation are well known, and still dishonor the memory of Hadrian. Yet we may remark, that of the first fifteen emperors, Claudius was the only one whose taste in love was entirely correct. For the honors of Antinous, see Spanheim, Commentaire sur les Cæsars de Julien, p. 80.
[41] Hist. August. p. 13. Aurelius Victor in Epitom.

spirit of wisdom and virtue. Although Pius had two sons,[42] he preferred the welfare of Rome to the interest of his family, gave his daughter Faustina in marriage to young Marcus, obtained from the senate the tribunitian and proconsular powers, and with a noble disdain, or rather ignorance of jealousy, associated him to all the labors of government. Marcus, on the other hand, revered the character of his benefactor, loved him as a parent, obeyed him as his sovereign,[43] and, after he was no more, regulated his own administration by the example and maxims of his predecessor. Their united reigns are possibly the only period of history in which the happiness of a great people was the sole object of government.

Titus Antoninus Pius has been justly denominated a second Numa. The same love of religion, justice, and peace, was the distinguishing characteristic of both princes. But the situation of the latter opened a much larger field for the exercise of those virtues. Numa could only prevent a few neighboring villages from plundering each other's harvests. Antoninus diffused order and tranquillity over the greatest part of the earth. His reign is marked by the rare advantage of furnishing very few materials for history; which is, indeed, little more than the register of the crimes, follies, and misfortunes of mankind. In private life, he was an amiable, as well as a good man. The native simplicity of his virtue was a stranger to vanity or affectation. He enjoyed with moderation the conveniences of his fortune, and the innocent pleasures of society;[44] and the benevolence of his soul displayed itself in a cheerful serenity of temper.

The virtue of Marcus Aurelius Antoninus was of a

---

[42] Without the help of medals and inscriptions, we should be ignorant of this fact, so honorable to the memory of Pius.*

[43] During the twenty-three years of Pius's reign, Marcus was only two nights absent from the palace, and even those were at different times. Hist. August. p. 25.

[44] He was fond of the theatre, and not insensible to the charms of the fair sex. Marcus Antoninus, i. 16. Hist. August. pp. 20, 21. Julian in Cæsar.

---

* Gibbon attributes to Antoninus Pius a merit which he either did not possess, or was not in a situation to display. 1. He was adopted only on the condition that he would adopt, in his turn, Marcus Aurelius and L. Verus. 2. His two sons died children, and one of them, M. Galerius, alone, appears to have survived, for a few years, his father's coronation. Gibbon is also mistaken, when he says (note 42) that "without the help of medals and inscriptions, we should be ignorant that Antoninus had two sons." Capitolinus says expressly (c. 1), Filii mares duo, duæ fœminæ; we only owe their names to the medals. Pagi. Cont. Baron, i. 33, edit. Paris.—W.

severer and more laborious kind.[45] It was the well-earned harvest of many a learned conference, of many a patient lecture, and many a midnight lucubration. At the age of twelve years he embraced the rigid system of the Stoics, which taught him to submit his body to his mind, his passions to his reason; to consider virtue as the only good, vice as the only evil, all things external as things indifferent.[46] His meditations, composed in the tumult of a camp, are still extant; and he even condescended to give lessons of philosophy, in a more public manner than was perhaps consistent with the modesty of a sage, or the dignity of an emperor.[47] But his life was the noblest commentary on the precepts of Zeno. He was severe to himself, indulgent to the imperfection of others, just and beneficent to all mankind. He regretted that Avidius Cassius, who excited a rebellion in Syria, had disappointed him, by a voluntary death,* of the pleasure of converting an enemy into a friend; and he justified the sincerity of that sentiment by moderating the zeal of the senate against the adherents of the traitor.[48] War he detested, as the disgrace and calamity of human nature; ‡ but when the necessity of a just defence called upon him to take up arms, he readily exposed his person to eight winter campaigns on the frozen banks of the Danube, the severity of which was at last fatal to the weakness of his constitution. His memory was revered by a grateful posterity, and above a century after his death,

[45] The enemies of Marcus charged him with hypocrisy, and with a want of that simplicity which distinguished Pius and even Verus (Hist. August. 6, 34). This suspicion, unjust as it was, may serve to account for the superior applause bestowed upon personal qualifications in preference to the social virtues. Even Marcus Antoninus has been called a hypocrite; but the wildest skepticism never insinuated that Cæsar might possibly be a coward, or Tully a fool. Wit and valor are qualifications more easily ascertained than humanity or the love of justice.

[46] Tacitus has characterized, in a few words, the principles of the portico: Doctores sapientiæ secutus est, qui sola bona quæ honesta, mala tantum quæ turpia; potentiam, nobilitatem, cæteraque extra animum, neque bonis neque malis adnumerant. Tacit. Hist. iv. 5.

[47] Before he went on the second expedition against the Germans, he read lectures of philosophy to the Roman people, during three days. He had already done the same in the cities of Greece and Asia. Hist. August. in Cassio, c. 3.

[48] Dion, l. lxxi. p. 1190. Hist. August. in Avid. Cassio.†

* Cassius was murdered by his own partisans. Vulcat. Gallic. in Cassio, c. 7. Dion, lxxi. c. 27.—W.

† See one of the newly-discovered passages of Dion Cassius. Marcus wrote to the senate, who urged the execution of the partisans of Cassius. "I entreat and beseech you to preserve my reign unstained by senatorial blood. None of your order must perish either by your desire or mine." Mai. Fragm. Vatican. ii. p. 224.—M.

‡ Marcus would not accept the services of any of the barbarian allies who crowded to his standard in the war against Avidius Cassius. "Barbarians," he said, with wise but vain sagacity, "must not become acquainted with the dissensions of the Roman people." Mai. Fragm. Vatican. i. 224.—M.

many persons preserved the image of Marcus Antoninus among those of their household gods.[49]

If a man were called to fix the period in the history of the world during which the condition of the human race was most happy and prosperous, he would, without hesitation, name that which elapsed from the death of Domitian to the accession of Commodus. The vast extent of the Roman empire was governed by absolute power, under the guidance of virtue and wisdom. The armies were restrained by the firm but gentle hand of four successive emperors, whose characters and authority commanded involuntary respect. The forms of the civil administration were carefully preserved by Nerva, Trajan, Hadrian, and the Antonines, who delighted in the image of liberty, and were pleased with considering themselves as the accountable ministers of the laws. Such princes deserved the honor of restoring the republic, had the Romans of their days been capable of enjoying a rational freedom.

The labors of these monarchs were overpaid by the immense reward that inseparably waited on their success; by the honest pride of virtue, and by the exquisite delight of beholding the general happiness of which they were the authors. A just but melancholy reflection imbittered, however, the noblest of human enjoyments. They must often have recollected the instability of a happiness which depended on the character of a single man. The fatal moment was perhaps approaching, when some licentious youth, or some jealous tyrant, would abuse, to the destruction, that absolute power, which they had exerted for the benefit of their people. The ideal restraints of the senate and the laws might serve to display the virtues, but could never correct the vices, of the emperor. The military force was a blind and irresistible instrument of oppression; and the corruption of Roman manners would always supply flatterers eager to applaud, and ministers prepared to serve, the fear or the avarice, the lust or the cruelty, of their masters.

These gloomy apprehensions had been already justified by the experience of the Romans. The annals of the emperors exhibit a strong and various picture of human nature, which we should vainly seek among the mixed and doubtful characters of modern history. In the conduct of those monarchs we may trace the utmost lines of vice and virtue; the most exalted perfection, and the meanest degeneracy of

[49] Hist. August. in Marc. Antonin. c. 18.

our own species. The golden age of Trajan and the Antonines had been preceded by an age of iron. It is almost superfluous to enumerate the unworthy successors of Augustus. Their unparalleled vices, and the splendid theatre on which they were acted, have saved them from oblivion. The dark, unrelenting Tiberius, the furious Caligula, the feeble Claudius, the profligate and cruel Nero, the beastly Vitellius,[50] and the timid, inhuman Domitian, are condemned to everlasting infamy. During fourscore years (excepting only the short and doubtful respite of Vespasian's reign)[51] Rome groaned beneath an unremitting tyranny, which exterminated the ancient families of the republic, and was fatal to almost every virtue and every talent that arose in that unhappy period.

Under the reign of these monsters, the slavery of the Romans was accompanied with two peculiar circumstances, the one occasioned by their former liberty, the other by their extensive conquests, which rendered their condition more completely wretched than that of the victims of tyranny in any other age or country. From these causes were derived, 1. The exquisite sensibility of the sufferers; and, 2. The impossibility of escaping from the hand of the oppressor.

I. When Persia was governed by the descendants of Sefi, a race of princes whose wanton cruelty often stained their divan, their table, and their bed, with the blood of their favorites, there is a saying recorded of a young nobleman, that he never departed from the sultan's presence, without satisfying himself whether his head was still on his shoulders. The experience of every day might almost justify the scepticism of Rustan.[52] Yet the fatal sword, suspended above him by a single thread, seems not to have disturbed the slumbers, or interrupted the tranquillity, of the Persian. The monarch's frown, he well knew, could level him with the dust; but the stroke of lightning or apoplexy might be equally fatal; and it was the part of a wise man to forget the inevitable calamities of human life

---

[50] Vitellius consumed in mere eating at least six millions of our money in about seven months. It is not easy to express his vices with dignity, or even decency. Tacitus fairly calls him a hog, but it is by substituting for a coarse word a very fine image. "At Vitellius, umbraculis hortorum abditus, ut ignava animalia, quibus si cibum suggeras, jacent torpentque, præterita, instantia, futura, pari oblivione dimiserat. Atque illum nemore Aricino desidem et marcentem," &c. Tacit. Hist. iii. 36, ii. 95. Sueton. in Vitell. c. 13. Dion Cassius, l. lxv. p. 1062.

[51] The execution of Helvidius Priscus, and of the virtuous Eponina, disgraced the reign of Vespasian.

[52] Voyage de Chardin en Perse, vol. iii. p. 293.

25

in the enjoyment of the fleeting hour. He was dignified
with the appellation of the king's slave; had, perhaps, been
purchased from obscure parents, in a country which he had
never known; and was trained up from his infancy in the
severe discipline of the seraglio.[53] His name, his wealth,
his honors, were the gift of a master, who might, without
injustice, resume what he had bestowed. Rustan's knowledge, if he possessed any, could only serve to confirm his
habits by prejudices. His language afforded not words for
any form of government, except absolute monarchy. The
history of the East informed him that such had ever been
the condition of mankind.[54] The Koran, and the interpreters of that divine book, inculcated to him that the sultan was the descendant of the prophet, and the vicegerent
of heaven; that patience was the first virtue of a Mussul-
man, and unlimited obedience the great duty of a subject.

The minds of the Romans were very differently prepared
for slavery. Oppressed beneath the weight of their own
corruption and of military violence, they for a long while
preserved the sentiments, or at least the ideas, of their free-
born ancestors. The education of Helvidius and Thrasea,
of Tacitus and Pliny, was the same as that of Cato and
Cicero. From Grecian philosophy, they had imbibed the
justest and most liberal notions of the dignity of human
nature, and the origin of civil society. The history of their
own country had taught them to revere a free, a virtuous,
and a victorious commonwealth; to abhor the successful
crimes of Cæsar and Augustus; and inwardly to despise
those tyrants whom they adored with the most abject flattery. As magistrates and senators, they were admitted
into the great council, which had once dictated laws to the
earth, whose name still gave a sanction to the acts of the
monarch, and whose authority was so often prostituted to
the vilest purposes of tyranny. Tiberius, and those emperors who adopted his maxims, attempted to disguise their
murders by the formalities of justice, and perhaps enjoyed
a secret pleasure in rendering the senate their accomplice
as well as their victim. By this assembly, the last of the
Romans were condemned for imaginary crimes and real

[53] The practice of raising slaves to the great offices of state is still more common among the Turks than among the Persians. The miserable countries of
Georgia and Circassia supply rulers to the greatest part of the East.
[54] Chardin says, that European travellers have diffused among the Persians
some ideas of the freedom and mildness of our governments. They have done
them a very ill office.

virtues. Their infamous accusers assumed the language of independent patriots, who arraigned a dangerous citizen before the tribunal of his country ; and the public service was rewarded by riches and honors.[55] The servile judges professed to assert the majesty of the commonwealth, violated in the person of its first magistrate,[56] whose clemency they most applauded when they trembled the most at his inexorable and impending cruelty.[57] The tyrant beheld their baseness with just contempt, and encountered their secret sentiments of detestation with sincere and avowed hatred for the whole body of the senate.

II. The division of Europe into a number of independent states, connected, however, with each other by the general resemblance of religion, language, and manners, is productive of the most beneficial consequences to the liberty of mankind. A modern tyrant, who should find no resistance either in his own breast, or in his people, would soon experience a gentle restraint from the example of his equals, the dread of present censure, the advice of his allies, and the apprehension of his enemies. The object of his displeasure, escaping from the narrow limits of his dominions, would easily obtain, in a happier climate, a secure refuge, a new fortune adequate to his merit, the freedom of complaint, and perhaps the means of revenge. But the empire of the Romans filled the world, and when that empire fell into the hands of a single person, the world became a safe and dreary prison for his enemies. The slave of Imperial despotism. whether he was condemned to drag his gilded chain in Rome and the senate, or to wear out a life of exile on the barren rock of Seriphus, or the frozen banks of the Danube, expected his fate in silent despair.[58] To resist was

[55] They alleged the example of Scipio and Cato (Tacit. Annal. iii. 66). Marcellus Epirus and Crispus Vibius had acquired two millions and a half under Nero. Their wealth, which aggravated their crimes, protected them under Vespasian. See Tacit. Hist. iv. 43. Dialog. de Orator. c. 8. For one accusation, Regulus, the just object of Pliny's satire, received from the senate the consular ornaments and a present of sixty thousand pounds.

[56] The crime of *majesty* was formerly a treasonable offence against the Roman people. As tribunes of the people, Augustus and Tiberius applied it to their own persons, and extended it to an infinite latitude.*

[57] After the virtuous and unfortunate widow of Germanicus had been put to death, Tiberius received the thanks of the senate for his clemency. She had not been publicly strangled ; nor was the body drawn with a hook to the Gemoniæ, where those of common malefactors were exposed. See Tacit. Annal. vi. 25. Sueton. in Tiberio, c. 53.

[58] Seriphus was a small rocky island in the Ægean Sea. the inhabitants of which were despised for their ignorance and obscurity. The place of Ovid's

* It was Tiberius, not Augustus, who first took in this sense the words crimen læsæ majestatis. Bachii Trajanus, 27.—W.

27

THE DECLINE AND FALL

fatal, and it was impossible to fly. On every side he was encompassed with a vast extent of sea and land, which he could never hope to traverse without being discovered, seized, and restored to his irritated master. Beyond the frontiers, his anxious view could discover nothing, except the ocean, inhospitable deserts, hostile tribes of barbarians, of fierce manners and unknown language, or dependent kings, who would gladly purchase the Emperor's protection by the sacrifice of an obnoxious fugitive.[59] "Wherever you are," said Cicero to the exiled Marcellus, "remember that you are equally within the power of the conqueror."[60]

exile is well known, by his just, but unmanly lamentations. It should seem that he only received an order to leave Rome in so many days, and to transport himself to Tomi. Guards and jailers were unnecessary.

[59] Under Tiberius, a Roman knight attempted to fly to the Parthians. He was stopped in the straits of Sicily; but so little danger did there appear in the example, that the most jealous of tyrants disdained to punish it. Tacit. Annal. vi. 14.

[60] Cicero ad Familiares, iv. 7.

GENERAL OBSERVATIONS ON THE FALL OF THE ROMAN EMPIRE IN THE WEST.

The Greeks, after their country had been reduced into a province, imputed the triumphs of Rome, not to the merit, but to the FORTUNE, of the republic. The inconstant goddess, who so blindly distributes and resumes her favors, had *now* consented (such was the language of envious flattery) to resign her wings, to descend from her globe, and to fix her firm and immutable throne on the banks of the Tiber.[1] A wiser Greek, who has composed, with a philosophic spirit, the memorable history of his own times, deprived his countrymen of this vain and delusive comfort, by opening to their view the deep foundations of the greatness of Rome.[2] The fidelity of the citizens to each other, and to the state, was confirmed by the habits of education, and the prejudices of religion. Honor, as well as virtue, was the principle of the republic; the ambitious citizens labored to deserve the solemn glories of a triumph; and the ardor of the Roman youth was kindled into active emulation, as often as they beheld the domestic images of their ancestors.[3] The temperate struggles of the patricians and plebeians had finally established the firm and equal balance of the constitution; which united the freedom of popular assemblies, with the authority and wisdom of a senate, and the executive powers of a regal magistrate. When the consul displayed the standard of the republic, each citizen bound himself, by the obligation of an oath, to draw his sword in the cause of his country, till he had discharged the sacred duty by a military service of ten years. This wise institution continually poured into the field the rising generations of freemen and

[1] Such are the figurative expressions of Plutarch (Opera, tom. ii. p. 318, edit. Wechel), to whom, on the faith of his son Lamprias (Fabricius, Bibliot, Græc. tom. iii. p. 341), I shall boldly impute the malicious declamation, περὶ τῆς Ῥωμαιων τυχης. The same opinions had prevailed among the Greeks two hundred and fifty years before Plutarch; and to confute them, is the professed intention of Polybius (Hist. l. i. p. 90, edit. Gronov. Amstel. 1670).
[2] See the inestimable remains of the sixth book of Polybius, and many other parts of his general history, particularly a digression in the seventeenth book, in which he compares the phalanx and the legion.
[3] Sallust, de Bell. Jugurthin. c. 4. Such were the generous professions of P. Scipio and Q. Maximus. The Latin historian had read, and most probably transcribes, Polybius, their contemporary and friend.

soldiers; and their numbers were reenforced by the warlike and populous states of Italy, who, after a brave resistance, had yielded to the valor, and embraced the alliance, of the Romans. The sage historian, who excited the virtue of the younger Scipio, and beheld the ruin of Carthage,[4] has accurately described their military system; their levies, arms, exercises, subordination, marches, encampments; and the invincible legion, superior in active strength to the Macedonian phalanx of Philip and Alexander. From these institutions of peace and war, Polybius has deduced the spirit and success of a people, incapable of fear, and impatient of repose. The ambitious design of conquest, which might have been defeated by the seasonable conspiracy of mankind, was attempted and achieved; and the perpetual violation of justice was maintained by the political virtues of prudence and courage. The arms of the republic, sometimes vanquished in battle, always victorious in war, advanced with rapid steps to the Euphrates, the Danube, the Rhine, and the Ocean; and the images of gold, or silver, or brass, that might serve to represent the nations and their kings, were successively broken by the *iron* monarchy of Rome.[5]

The rise of a city, which swelled into an empire, may deserve, as a singular prodigy, the reflection of a philosophic mind. But the decline of Rome was the natural and inevitable effect of immoderate greatness. Prosperity ripened the principle of decay; the causes of destruction multiplied with the extent of conquest; and as soon as time or accident had removed the artificial supports, the stupendous fabric yielded to the pressure of its own weight. The story of its ruin is simple and obvious; and instead of inquiring *why* the Roman empire was destroyed, we should rather be surprised that it had subsisted so long. The victorious legions, who, in distant wars, acquired the vices of strangers and mercenaries, first oppressed the freedom of the republic, and afterwards violated the majesty of the purple. The emperors, anxious for their personal safety and the public

---

[4] While Carthage was in flames, Scipio repeated two lines of the Iliad, which express the destruction of Troy, acknowledging to Polybius, his friend and protector (Polyb. in Excerpt. de Virtut. et Vit. tom. ii. pp. 1455-1465), that while he recollected the vicissitudes of human affairs, he inwardly applied them to the future calamities of Rome (Appian. in Libycis, p. 136, edit. Toll).

[5] See Daniel. ii. 31-40. "And the fourth kingdom shall be strong as *iron*; forasmuch as iron breaketh in pieces and subdueth a l things." The remainder of the prophecy (the mixture of iron and *clay*) was accomplished, according to St. Jerom, in his own time. Sicut enim in principio nihil Romano Imperio fortius et durius, it a in fine rerum nihil imbecillius: quum et in bellis civilibus et adversus diversas nationes, aliarum gentium barbararum auxilio indigemus (Opera, tom. v. p. 572).

peace, were reduced to the base expedient of corrupting the discipline which rendered them alike formidable to their sovereign and to the enemy; the vigor of the military government was relaxed, and finally dissolved, by the partial institutions of Constantine; and the Roman world was overwhelmed by a deluge of Barbarians.

The decay of Rome has been frequently ascribed to the translation of the seat of empire; but this History has already shown, that the powers of government were *divided*, rather than *removed*. The throne of Constantinople was erected in the East; while the West was still possessed by a series of emperors who held their residence in Italy, and claimed their equal inheritance of the legions and provinces. This dangerous novelty impaired the strength, and fomented the vices, of a double reign: the instruments of an oppressive and arbitrary system were multiplied; and a vain emulation of luxury, not of merit, was introduced and supported between the degenerate successors of Theodosius. Extreme distress, which unites the virtue of a free people, imbitters the factions of a declining monarchy. The hostile favorites of Arcadius and Honorius betrayed the republic to its common enemies; and the Byzantine court beheld with indifference, perhaps with pleasure, the disgrace of Rome, the misfortunes of Italy, and the loss of the West. Under the succeeding reigns, the alliance of the two empires was restored; but the aid of the Oriental Romans was tardy, doubtful, and ineffectual; and the national schism of the Greeks and Latins was enlarged by the perpetual difference of language and manners, of interests, and even of religion. Yet the salutary event approved in some measure the judgment of Constantine. During a long period of decay, his impregnable city repelled the victorious armies of Barbarians, protected the wealth of Asia, and commanded, both in peace and war, the important straits which connect the Euxine and Mediterranean Seas. The foundation of Constantinople more essentially contributed to the preservation of the East, than to the ruin of the West.

As the happiness of a *future* life is the great object of religion, we may hear without surprise or scandal, that the introduction, or at least the abuse, of Christianity, had some influence on the decline and fall of the Roman empire. The clergy successfully preached the doctrines of patience and pusillanimity: the active virtues of society were discouraged; and the last remains of military spirit were buried in

31

the cloister: a large portion of public and private wealth was consecrated to the specious demands of charity and devotion; and the soldiers' pay was lavished on the useless multitudes of both sexes, who could only plead the merits of abstinence and chastity.* Faith, zeal, curiosity, and the more earthly passions of malice and ambition, kindled the flame of theological discord : the church, and even the state, were distracted by religious factions, whose conflicts were sometimes bloody, and always implacable ; the attention of the emperors was diverted from camps to synods; the Roman world was oppressed by a new species of tyranny ; and the persecuted sects became the secret enemies of their country. Yet party spirit, however pernicious or absurd, is a principle of union as well as of dissension. The bishops, from eighteen hundred pulpits, inculcated the duty of passive obedience to a lawful and orthodox sovereign ; their frequent assemblies, and perpetual correspondence, maintained the communion of distant churches ; and the benevolent temper of the gospel was strengthened, though confined, by the spiritual alliance of the Catholics. The sacred indolence of the monks was devoutly embraced by a servile and effeminate age; but if superstition had not afforded a decent retreat, the same vices would have tempted the unworthy Romans to desert, from baser motives, the standard of the republic. Religious precepts are easily obeyed, which indulge and sanctify the natural inclinations of their votaries ; but the pure and genuine influence of Christianity may be traced in its beneficial, though imperfect, effects on the Barbarian proselytes of the North. If the decline of the Roman empire was hastened by the conversion of Constantine, his victorious religion broke the violence of the fall, and mollified the ferocious temper of the conquerors.

This awful revolution may be usefully applied to the instruction of the present age. It is the duty of a patriot to prefer and promote the exclusive interest and glory of his native country: but a philosopher may be permitted to enlarge his views, and to consider Europe as one great republic, whose various inhabitants have attained almost the same level of politeness and cultivation. The balance of power will continue to fluctuate, and the prosperity of our own, or the neighboring kingdoms, may be alternately ex-

* It might be a curious speculation, how far the purer morals of the genuine and more active Christians may have compensated, in the population of the Roman empire, for the secession of such numbers into inactive and unproductive celibacy.—M.

alted or depressed; but these partial events cannot essentially injure our general state of happiness, the system of arts, and laws, and manners, which so advantageously distinguish, above the rest of mankind, the Europeans and their colonies. The savage nations of the globe are the common enemies of civilized society; and we may inquire, with anxious curiosity, whether Europe is still threatened with a repetition of those calamities, which formerly oppressed the arms and institutions of Rome. Perhaps the same reflections will illustrate the fall of that mighty empire, and explain the probable causes of our actual security.

I. The Romans were ignorant of the extent of their danger, and the number of their enemies. Beyond the Rhine and Danube, the Northern countries of Europe and Asia were filled with innumerable tribes of hunters and shepherds, poor, voracious, and turbulent; bold in arms, and impatient to ravish the fruits of industry. The Barbarian world was agitated by the rapid impulse of war; and the peace of Gaul or Italy was shaken by the distant revolutions of China. The Huns, who fled before a victorious enemy, directed their march towards the West; and the torrent was swelled by the gradual accession of captives and allies. The flying tribes who yielded to the Huns assumed in *their* turn the spirit of conquest; the endless column of Barbarians pressed on the Roman empire with accumulated weight; and, if the foremost were destroyed, the vacant space was instantly replenished by new assailants. Such formidable emigrations can no longer issue from the North; and the long repose, which has been imputed to the decrease of population, is the happy consequence of the progress of arts and agriculture. Instead of some rude villages, thinly scattered among its woods and morasses, Germany now produces a list of two thousand three hundred walled towns: the Christian kingdoms of Denmark, Sweden, and Poland, have been successively established; and the Hanse merchants, with the Teutonic knights, have extended their colonies along the coast of the Baltic, as far as the Gulf of Finland. From the Gulf of Finland to the Eastern Ocean, Russia now assumes the form of a powerful and civilized empire. The plough, the loom, and the forge, are introduced on the banks of the Volga, the Oby, and the Lena; and the fiercest of the Tartar hordes have been taught to tremble and obey. The reign of independent Barbarism is now contracted to a narrow span; and the remnant of Calmucks or Uzbecks, whose forces may be almost numbered, cannot seriously excite the apprehensions of the great republic of Europe.[5] Yet this apparent security should not tempt us to forget, that new enemies, and unknown dangers, may *possibly* arise from some obscure people, scarcely visible in the map of the world. The Arabs or Saracens, who spread their conquests from India to Spain, had languished in poverty and contempt, till Mahomet breathed into those savage bodies the soul of enthusiam.

II. The empire of Rome was firmly established by the singular and perfect coalition of its members. The subject nations, resigning the hope, and even the wish, of independence, embraced the character of Roman citizens; and the provinces of the West were reluctantly torn by the Barbarians from the bosom of their mother country.[7] But this union was purchased by the loss of national freedom and military spirit; and the servile provinces, destitute of life and motion, expected their safety from the mercenary troops and governors, who were directed by the orders of a distant court. The happiness of a hundred millions depended on the personal merit of one or two men, perhaps children, whose minds were corrupted by education, luxury, and despotic power. The deepest wounds were inflicted on the empire during the minorities of the sons and grandsons of Theodosius; and after those incapable princes seemed to attain the age of manhood, they abandoned the church to the bishops, the state to the eunuchs, and the provinces to the Barbarians. Europe is now divided into twelve powerful, though unequal kingdoms, three respectable commonwealths, and a variety of smaller, though independent, states: the chances of royal and ministerial talents are multiplied, at least, with the number of its rulers; and a Julian, or Semiramis, may reign in the North, while Arcadius and Honorius again slumber on the thrones of the South. The abuses of tyranny are restrained by the mutual influence of fear and shame; republics have acquired order and stability;

[5] The French and English editors of the Genealogical History of the Tartars have subjoined a curious, though imperfect, description of their present state. We might question the independence of the Calmucks, or Eluths, since they have been recently vanquished by the Chinese, who, in the year 1759, subdued the Lesser Bucharia, and advanced into the country of Bandakshan, near the sources of the Oxus (Mémoires sur les Chinois, tom. i. pp. 325-400). But these conquests are precarious, nor will I venture to insure the safety of the Chinese empire.

[7] The prudent reader will determine how far this general proposition is weakened by the revolt of the Isaurians, the independence of Britain and Armorica, the Moorish tribes, or the Bagaudæ of Gaul and Spain (vol. i. p. 328, vol. iii. p. 315, vol. iii. pp. 372, 480).

monarchies have imbibed the principles of freedom, or, at least, of moderation; and some sense of honor and justice is introduced into the most defective constitutions by the general manners of the times. In peace, the progress of knowledge and industry is accelerated by the emulation of so many active rivals; in war, the European forces are exercised by temperate and undecisive contests. If a savage conqueror should issue from the deserts of Tartary, he must repeatedly vanquish the robust peasants of Russia, the numerous armies of Germany, the gallant nobles of France, and the intrepid freemen of Britain; who, perhaps, might confederate for their common defence. Should the victorious Barbarians carry slavery and desolation as far as the Atlantic Ocean, ten thousand vessels would transport beyond their pursuit the remains of civilized society; and Europe would revive and flourish in the American world, which is already filled with her colonies and institutions.[8]

III. Cold, poverty, and a life of danger and fatigue, fortify the strength and courage of Barbarians. In every age they have oppressed the polite and peaceful nations of China, India, and Persia, who neglected, and still neglect, to counterbalance these natural powers by the resources of military art. The warlike states of antiquity, Greece, Macedonia, and Rome, educated a race of soldiers; exercised their bodies, disciplined their courage, multiplied their forces by regular evolutions, and converted the iron, which they possessed, into strong and serviceable weapons. But this superiority insensibly declined with their laws and manners; and the feeble policy of Constantine and his successors armed and instructed, for the ruin of the empire, the rude valor of the Barbarian mercenaries. The military art has been changed by the invention of gunpowder; which enables man to command the two most powerful agents of nature, air and fire. Mathematics, chemistry, mechanics, architecture, have been applied to the service of war; and the adverse parties oppose to each other the most elaborate modes of attack and of defence. Historians may indignantly observe, that the preparations of a siege would found and maintain a flourishing colony;[9] yet we cannot be displeased, that the

---

[8] America now contains about six millions of European blood and descent: and their numbers, at least in the North, are continually increasing. Whatever may be the changes of their political situation, they must preserve the manners of Europe; and we may reflect with some pleasure, that the English language will probably be diffused over an immense and populous continent.

[9] On avoit fait venir (for the siege of Turin) 140 pièces de canon; et il est à remarquer que chaque gros canon monté revient à environ 2000 écus : il y avoit

subversion of a city should be a work of cost and difficulty; or that an industrious people should be protected by those arts, which survive and supply the decay of military virtue. Cannon and fortifications now form an impregnable barrier against the Tartar horse; and Europe is secure from any future irruption of Barbarians; since, before they can conquer, they must cease to be barbarous. Their gradual advances in the science of war would always be accompanied, as we may learn from the example of Russia, with a proportionable improvement in the arts of peace and civil policy; and they themselves must deserve a place among the polished nations whom they subdue.

Should these speculations be found doubtful or fallacious, there still remains a more humble source of comfort and hope. The discoveries of ancient and modern navigators, and the domestic history, or tradition, of the most enlightened nations, represent the *human savage*, naked both in mind and body, and destitute of laws, of arts, of ideas, and almost of language.[10] From this abject condition, perhaps the primitive and universal state of man, he has gradually arisen to command the animals, to fertilize the earth, to traverse the ocean, and to measure the heavens. His progress in the improvement and exercise of his mental and corporeal faculties[11] has been irregular and various; infinitely slow in the beginning, and increasing by degrees with redoubled velocity: ages of laborious ascent have been followed by a moment of rapid downfall; and the several climates of the globe have felt the vicissitudes of light and darkness. Yet the experience of four thousand years should enlarge our hopes, and diminish our apprehensions: we cannot determine to what height the human species may aspire in their advances towards perfection; but it may safely be pre-

100,000 boulets; 106,000 cartouches d'une façon, et 300,000 d'une autre; 21,000 bombes; 27,700 grenades, 15,000 sacs à terre, 30,000 instruments pour la pionnage; 1,200,000 livres de poudre. Ajoutez à ces munitions, le plomb, le fer, et le fer-blanc, les cordages, tout ce qui sert aux mineurs, le souphre, le salpêtre, les outils de toute espèce. Il est certain que les frais de tous ces préparatifs de destruction suffiroient pour fonder et pour faire fleurir la plus nombreuse colonie. Voltaire, Siècle de Louis XIV. c. xx. in his Works, tom. xi. p. 391.

[10] It would be an easy, though tedious, task, to produce the authorities of poets, philosophers and historians. I shall therefore content myself with appealing to the decisive and authentic testimony of Diodorus Siculus (tom. i. l. i. pp. 11, 12, l. iii. p. 184. &c., edit. Wesseling). The Icthyophagi, who in his time wandered along the shores of the Red Sea, can only be compared to the natives of New Holland (Dampier's Voyages, vol. i. pp. 464–469). Fancy, or perhaps reason, may still suppose an extreme and absolute state of nature far below the level of these savages, who had acquired some arts and instruments.

[11] See the learned and rational work of the president Goguet, de l'Origine des Loix, des Arts, et des Sciences. He traces from facts, or conjectures (tom. i. pp. 147–337, edit. 12mo.), the first and the most difficult steps of human invention.

sumed, that no people, unless the face of nature is changed, will relapse into their original barbarism. The improvements of society may be viewed under a threefold aspect. 1. The poet or philosopher illustrates his age and country by the efforts of a *single* mind ; but those superior powers of reason or fancy are rare and spontaneous productions ; and the genius of Homer, or Cicero, or Newton, would excite less admiration, if they could be created by the will of a prince, or the lessons of a preceptor. 2. The benefits of law and policy, of trade and manufactures, of arts and sciences, are more solid and permanent : and *many* individuals may be qualified, by education and discipline, to promote, in their respective stations, the interest of the community. But this general order is the effect of skill and labor : and the complex machinery may be decayed by time, or injured by violence. 3. Fortunately for mankind, the more useful, or at least, more necessary arts, can be performed without superior talents, or national subordination ; without the powers of *one*, or the union of *many*. Each village, each family, each individual, must always possess both ability and inclination to perpetuate the use of fire [12] and of metals ; the propagation and service of domestic animals ; the methods of hunting and fishing ; the rudiments of navigation ; the imperfect cultivation of corn, or other nutritive grain ; and the simple practice of the mechanic trades. Private genius and public industry may be extirpated ; but these hardy plants survive the tempest, and strike an everlasting root into the most unfavorable soil. The splendid days of Augustus and Trajan were eclipsed by a cloud of ignorance ; and the Barbarians subverted the laws and palaces of Rome. But the scythe, the invention or emblem of Saturn, [13] still continued annually to mow the harvests of Italy ; and the human feasts of the Læstrigons [14] have never been renewed on the coast of Campania.

Since the first discovery of the arts, war, commerce, and religious zeal have diffused, among the savages of the Old

[12] It is certain, however strange, that many nations have been ignorant of the use of fire. Even the ingenious natives of Otaheite, who are destitute of metals, have not invented any earthen vessels capable of sustaining the action of fire, and of communicating the heat to the liquids which they contain.

[13] Plutarch. Quæst. Rom. in tom. ii. p. 275. Macrob. Saturnal. l. i. c. 8. p. 152, edit. London. The arrival of Saturn (of his religious worship) in a ship, may indicate, that the savage coast of Latium was first discovered and civilized by the Phœnicians.

[14] In the ninth and tenth books of the Odyssey, Homer has embellished the tales of fearful and credulous sailors, who transformed the cannibals of Italy and Sicily into monstrous giants.

and New World, these inestimable gifts : they have been successively propagated ; they can never be lost. We may therefore acquiesce in the pleasing conclusion, that every age of the world has increased, and still increases, the real wealth, the happiness, the knowledge, and perhaps the virtue, of the human race.[15]

[15] The merit of discovery has too often been stained with avarice, cruelty, and fanaticism ; and the intercourse of nations has produced the communication of disease and prejudice. A singular exception is due to the virtue of our own times and country. The five great voyages, successively undertaken by the command of his present Majesty, were inspired by the pure and generous love of science and of mankind. The same prince, adapting his benefactions to the different stages of society, has founded a school of painting in his capital ; and has introduced into the islands of the South Sea the vegetables and animals most useful to human life.

Although he earned a doctorate in Greek history, Oswald Spengler (1880-1936) never held a university post, but taught in high school or pursued his writing as a private scholar in his home in Munich, Germany. Although very conservative and anti-democratic, he repudiated Nazism.   His work is provocative and often eccentric, and has stimulated much discussion.

THE DECLINE OF THE WEST

x

Our narrower task, then, is primarily to determine, from such a world-survey, the state of West Europe and America as at the epoch of 1800–2000 — to establish the chronological position of this period in the ensemble of Western culture-history, its significance as a chapter that is in one or other guise necessarily found in the biography of every Culture, and the organic and symbolic meaning of its political, artistic, intellectual and social expression-forms.

Considered in the spirit of analogy, this period appears as chronologically parallel — "contemporary" in our special sense — with the phase of Hellenism, and its present culmination, marked by the World-War, corresponds with the transition from the Hellenistic to the Roman age. *Rome*, with its rigorous realism — uninspired, barbaric, disciplined, practical, Protestant, *Prussian* — will always give us, working as we must by analogies, the key to understanding our own future. The *break of destiny that we express by hyphening the words "Greeks=Romans" is occurring for us also, separating that which is already fulfilled from that which is to come.* Long ago we might and should have seen in the "Classical" world a development which is the complete counterpart of our own Western development, differing indeed from it in every detail of the surface but entirely similar as regards the inward power driving the great organism towards its end. We might have found the constant *alter ego* of our own actuality in establishing the correspondence, item by item, from the "Trojan War" and the Crusades, Homer and the Nibelungenlied, through Doric and Gothic, Dionysian movement and Renaissance, Polycletus and John Sebastian Bach, Athens and Paris, Aristotle and Kant, Alexander and Napoleon, to the world-city and the imperialism common to both Cultures.

Unfortunately, this requires an interpretation of the picture of Classical history very different from the incredibly one-sided, superficial, prejudiced, limited picture that we have in fact given to it. We have, in truth been only too conscious of our near relation to the Classical Age, and only too prone in consequence to unconsidered assertion of it. Superficial similarity is a great snare, and our entire Classical study fell a victim to it as soon as it passed from the (admittedly masterly) ordering and critique of the discoveries to the interpretation of their spiritual meaning. That close inward relation in which we conceive ourselves to stand towards the Classical, and which leads us to think that we are its pupils and successors (whereas in reality we are simply its adorers), is a venerable prejudice which ought at last to be put aside. The whole religious-philosophical, art-historical and social-critical work of the 19th Century has been necessary to enable us, not to *understand* Æschylus, Plato, Apollo and Dionysus, the Athenian state and Cæsarism (which we are far indeed from doing), but to begin to realize, once and for all, how immeasurably alien and distant these things are from our inner selves — more alien, maybe, than Mexican gods and Indian architecture.

Our views of the Græco-Roman Culture have always swung between two extremes, and our standpoints have invariably been defined for us by the "ancient-mediæval-modern" scheme. One group, public men before all else — economists, politicians, jurists — opine that "present-day mankind" is making excellent progress, assess it and its performances at the very highest value and measure everything earlier by its standards. There is no modern party that has not weighed up Cleon, Marius, Themistocles, Catiline, the Gracchi, according to its own principles. On the other hand we have the group of artists, poets, philologists and philosophers. These feel themselves to be out of their element in the aforesaid present, and in consequence choose for themselves in this or that past epoch a standpoint that is in its way just as absolute and dogmatic from which to condemn "to-day." The one group looks upon Greece as a "not yet," the other upon modernity as a "nevermore." Both labour under the obsession of a scheme of history which treats the two epochs as part of the same straight line.

In this opposition it is the two souls of Faust that express themselves. The danger of the one group lies in a clever superficiality. In its hands there remains finally, of all Classical Culture, of all reflections of the Classical soul, nothing but a bundle of social, economic, political and physiological facts, and the rest is treated as "secondary results," "reflexes," "attendant phenomena." In the books of this group we find not a hint of the mythical force of Æschylus's choruses, of the immense mother-earth struggle of the early sculpture, the Doric column, of the richness of the Apollo-cult, of the real depth of the Roman Emperor-worship. The other group, composed above all of belated romanticists — represented in recent times by the three Basel professors Bachofen, Burckhardt and Nietzsche — succumb to the usual dangers of ideology. They lose themselves in the clouds of an antiquity that is really no more than the image of their own sensibility in a philological mirror. They rest their case upon the only evidence which they consider worthy to support it, viz., the relics of the old literature, yet there never was a Culture so incompletely represented for us by its great writers.[1] The first group, on the other hand, supports itself principally upon the humdrum material of law-sources, inscriptions and coins (which Burckhardt and Nietzsche, very much to their own loss, despised) and subordinates thereto, often with little or no sense of truth and fact, the surviving literature. Consequently, even in point of critical foundations, neither group takes the other seriously. I have never heard that Nietzsche and Mommsen had the smallest respect for each other.

But neither group has attained to that higher method of treatment which reduces this opposition of criteria to ashes, although it was within their power to do so. In their self-limitation they paid the penalty for taking over the causality-principle from natural science. Unconsciously they arrived at a pragmatism that sketchily copied the world-picture drawn by physics and, instead of revealing, obscured and confused the quite other-natured forms of history. They had no better expedient for subjecting the mass of historical material to critical and normative examination than to consider one complex of phenomena as being primary and causative and the rest as being secondary, as being consequences or effects. And it was not only the matter-of-fact school that resorted to this method. The romanticists did likewise, for History had not revealed even to their dreaming gaze its specific logic; and yet they *felt* that

---

[1] This is conclusively proved by the selection that determined survival, which was governed not by mere chance but very definitely by a deliberate tendency. The Atticism of the Augustan Age, tired, sterile, pedantic, back-looking, conceived the hall-mark "classical" and allowed only a very small group of Greek works up to Plato to bear it. The rest, including the whole wealth of Hellenistic literature, was rejected and has been almost entirely lost. It is this pedagogue's anthology that has survived (almost in its entirety) and so fixed the imaginary picture of "Classical Antiquity" alike for the Renaissance Florentine and for Winckelmann, Hölderlin, and even Nietzsche.

[In this English translation, it should be mentioned, the word "Classical" has almost universally been employed to translate the German *antike*, as, in the translator's judgment, no literal equivalent of the German word would convey the specific meaning attached to *antike* throughout the work, "antique," "ancient" and the like words having for us a much more general connotation. — Tr.]

42

there was an immanent necessity in it to determine this somehow, rather than turn their backs upon History in despair like Schopenhauer.

XI

Briefly, then, there are two ways of regarding the Classical — the materialistic and the ideological. By the former, it is asserted that the sinking of one scale-pan has its cause in the rising of the other, and it is shown that this occurs invariably (truly a striking theorem); and in this juxtaposing of cause and effect we naturally find the social and sexual, at all events the purely political, facts classed as causes and the religious, intellectual and (so far as the materialist tolerates them as facts at all) the artistic as effects. On the other hand, the ideologues show that the rising of one scale-pan follows from the sinking of the other, which they are able to prove of course with equal exactitude; this done, they lose themselves in cults, mysteries, customs, in the secrets of the strophe and the line, throwing scarcely a side-glance at the commonplace daily life — for them an unpleasant consequence of earthly imperfection. Each side, with its gaze fixed on causality, demonstrates that the other side either cannot or will not understand the true linkages of things and each ends by calling the other blind, superficial, stupid, absurd or frivolous, oddities or Philistines. It shocks the ideologue if anyone deals with Hellenic finance-problems and instead of, for example, telling us the deep meanings of the Delphic oracle, describes the far-reaching money operations which the Oracle priests undertook with their accumulated treasures. The politician, on the other hand, has a superior smile for those who waste their enthusiasm on ritual formulæ and the dress of Attic youths, instead of writing a book adorned with up-to-date catchwords about antique class-struggles.

The one type is foreshadowed from the very outset in Petrarch; it created Florence and Weimar and the Western classicism. The other type appears in the middle of the 18th Century, along with the rise of civilized,[1] economic-megalopolitan[2] politics, and England is therefore its birthplace (Grote). At bottom, the opposition is between the conceptions of culture-man and those of civilization-man, and it is too deep, too essentially human, to allow the weaknesses of *both standpoints alike* to be seen or overcome.

The materialist himself is on this point an idealist. He too, without wishing or desiring it, has made his views dependent upon his wishes. In fact all our finest minds without exception have bowed down reverently before the picture of the Classical, abdicating in this one instance alone their function of unrestricted criticism. The freedom and power of Classical research are always

---

[1] As will be seen later, the words *zivilisierte* and *Zivilisation* possess in this work a special meaning. — *Tr.*

[2] English not possessing the adjective-forming freedom of German, we are compelled to coin a word for the rendering of *grossstädtisch*, an adjective not only frequent but of emphatic significance in the author's argument. — *Tr.*

hindered, and its data obscured, by a certain almost religious awe. In all history there is no analogous case of one Culture making a passionate cult of the memory of another. Our devotion is evidenced yet again in the fact that since the Renaissance, a thousand years of history have been undervalued so that an ideal "Middle" Age may serve as a link between ourselves and antiquity. We Westerners have sacrificed on the Classical altar the purity and independence of our art, for we have not dared to create without a side-glance at the "sublime exemplar." We have projected our own deepest spiritual needs and feelings on to the Classical picture. Some day a gifted psychologist will deal with this most fateful illusion and tell us the story of the "Classical" that we have so consistently reverenced since the days of Gothic. Few theses would be more helpful for the understanding of the Western soul from Otto III, the first victim of the South, to Nietzsche, the last.

Goethe on his Italian tour speaks with enthusiasm of the buildings of Palladio, whose frigid and academic work we to-day regard very sceptically: but when he goes on to Pompeii he does not conceal his dissatisfaction in experiencing "a strange, half-unpleasant impression," and what he has to say on the temples of Pæstum and Segesta — masterpieces of Hellenic art — is embarrassed and trivial. Palpably, when Classical antiquity in its full force met him face to face, he did not recognize it. It is the same with all others. Much that was Classical they chose not to see, and so they saved their inward image of the Classical — which was in reality the background of a life-ideal that they themselves had created and nourished with their heart's blood, a vessel filled with their own world-feeling, a phantom, an idol. The audacious descriptions of Aristophanes, Juvenal or Petronius of life in the Classical cities — the southern dirt and riff-raff, terrors and brutalities, pleasure-boys and Phrynes, phallus worship and imperial orgies — excite the enthusiasm of the student and the dilettante, who find the same realities in the world-cities of to-day too lamentable and repulsive to face. "In the cities life is bad; there are too many of the lustful." — *also sprach Zarathustra*. They commend the state-sense of the Romans, but despise the man of to-day who permits himself any contact with public affairs. There is a type of scholar whose clarity of vision comes under some irresistible spell when it turns from a frock-coat to a toga, from a British football-ground to a Byzantine circus, from a transcontinental railway to a Roman road in the Alps, from a thirty-knot destroyer to a trireme, from Prussian bayonets to Roman spears — nowadays, even, from a modern engineer's Suez Canal to that of a Pharaoh. He would admit a steamengine as a symbol of human passion and an expression of intellectual force if it were Hero of Alexandria who invented it, not otherwise. To such it seems blasphemous to talk of Roman central-heating or book-keeping in preference to the worship of the Great Mother of the Gods.

But the other school sees *nothing but* these things. It thinks it exhausts the essence of this Culture, alien as it is to ours, by treating the Greeks as simply equivalent, and it obtains its conclusions by means of simple factual substitutions, ignoring altogether the Classical *soul*. That there is not the slightest inward correlation between the things meant by "Republic," "freedom," "property" and the like then and there and the things meant by such words here and now, it has no notion whatever. It makes fun of the historians of the age of Goethe, who honestly expressed their own political ideals in classical history forms and revealed their own personal enthusiasms in vindications or condemnations of lay-figures named Lycurgus, Brutus, Cato, Cicero, Augustus — but it cannot itself write a chapter without reflecting the party opinion of its morning paper.

It is, however, much the same whether the past is treated in the spirit of Don Quixote or in that of Sancho Panza. Neither way leads to the end. In sum, each school permits itself to bring into high relief that part of the Classical which best expresses its own views — Nietzsche the pre-Socratic Athens, the economists the Hellenistic period, the politicians Republican Rome, poets the Imperial Age.

Not that religious and artistic phenomena are more primitive than social and economic, any more than the reverse. For the man who in these things has won his unconditional freedom of outlook, beyond *all* personal interests whatsoever, there is no dependence, no priority, no relation of cause and effect, no differentiation of value or importance. That which assigns relative ranks amongst the individual detail-facts is simply the greater or less purity and force of their form-language, their symbolism, beyond all questions of good and evil, high and low, useful and ideal.

XII

Looked at in this way, the "Decline of the West" comprises nothing less than the problem of *Civilization*. We have before us one of the fundamental questions of all higher history. What is Civilization, understood as the organic-logical sequel, fulfilment and finale of a culture?

For every Culture has *its own* Civilization. In this work, for the first time the two words, hitherto used to express an indefinite, more or less ethical, distinction, are used in a *periodic* sense, to express a strict and necessary *organic succession*. The Civilization is the inevitable *destiny* of the Culture, and in this principle we obtain the viewpoint from which the deepest and gravest problems of historical morphology become capable of solution. Civilizations are the most external and artificial states of which a species of developed humanity is capable. They are a conclusion, the thing-become succeeding the thing-becoming, death following life, rigidity following expansion, intellectual age and the stone-built, petrifying world-city following mother-earth and the spiritual childhood of Doric and Gothic. They are an end, irrevocable, yet by inward necessity reached again and again.

So, for the first time, we are enabled to understand the Romans as the *successors* of the Greeks, and light is projected into the deepest secrets of the late-Classical period. What, but this, can be the meaning of the fact — which can only be disputed by vain phrases — that the Romans were barbarians who did not *precede* but *closed* a great development? Unspiritual, unphilosophical, devoid of art, clannish to the point of brutality, aiming relentlessly at tangible successes, they stand between the Hellenic Culture and nothingness. An imagination directed purely to practical objects — they had religious laws governing godward relations as they had other laws governing human relations, but there was no specifically Roman saga of gods — was something which is not found at all in Athens. In a word, Greek *soul* — Roman *intellect;* and this antithesis is the differentia between Culture and Civilization. Nor is it only to the Classical that it applies. Again and again there appears this type of strong-minded, completely non-metaphysical man, and in the hands of this type lies the intellectual and material destiny of each and every "late" period. Such are the men who carried through the Babylonian, the Egyptian, the Indian, the Chinese, the Roman Civilizations, and in such periods do Buddhism, Stoicism, Socialism ripen into definitive world-conceptions which enable a moribund humanity to be attacked and re-formed in its intimate structure. *Pure* Civilization, as a historical process, consists in a progressive *taking-down* of forms that have become inorganic or dead.

The transition from Culture to Civilization was accomplished for the Classical world in the 4th, for the Western in the 19th Century. From these periods onward the great intellectual decisions take place, not as in the days of the Orpheus-movement or the Reformation in the "whole world" where not a hamlet is too small to be unimportant, but in three or four world-cities that have absorbed into themselves the whole content of History, while the old wide landscape of the Culture, become merely provincial, serves only to feed the cities with what remains of its higher mankind.

World-city and province [1] — the two basic ideas of every civilization — bring up a wholly new form-problem of History, the very problem that we are living through to-day with hardly the remotest conception of its immensity. In place of a world, there is a *city, a point,* in which the whole life of broad regions is collecting while the rest dries up. In place of a type-true people, born of and grown on the soil, there is a new sort of nomad, cohering unstably in fluid masses, the parasitical city dweller, traditionless, utterly matter-of-fact, religionless, clever, unfruitful, deeply contemptuous of the countryman and especially that highest form of countryman, the country gentleman. This is a very great stride towards the inorganic, towards the end — what does it signify? France and England have already taken the step and Germany is beginning to do so. After Syracuse, Athens, and Alexandria comes Rome. After Madrid,

[1] See Vol. II, pp. 117 et seq.

Paris, London come Berlin and New York. It is the destiny of whole regions that lie outside the radiation-circle of one of these cities — of old Crete and Macedon and to-day the Scandinavian North [1] — to become "provinces."

Of old, the field on which the opposed conception of an epoch came to battle was some world-problem of a metaphysical, religious or dogmatic kind, and the battle was between the soil-genius of the countryman (noble, priest) and the "worldly" patrician genius of the famous old small towns of Doric or Gothic springtime. Of such a character were the conflicts over the Dionysus religion — as in the tyranny of Kleisthenes of Sikyon [2] — and those of the Reformation in the German free cities and the Huguenot wars. But just as these cities overcame the country-side (already it is a purely civic world-outlook that appears in even Parmenides and Descartes), so in turn the world-city overcame them. It is the common intellectual process of later periods such as the Ionic and the Baroque, and to-day — as in the Hellenistic age which at its outset saw the foundation of artificial, land-alien Alexandria — Culture-cities like Florence, Nürnberg, Salamanca, Bruges and Prag, have become provincial towns and fight inwardly a lost battle against the world-cities. The world-city means cosmopolitanism in place of "home," [3] cold matter-of-fact in place of reverence for tradition and age, scientific irreligion as a fossil representative of the older religion of the heart, "society" in place of the state, natural instead of hard-earned rights. It was in the conception of *money* as an inorganic and abstract magnitude, entirely disconnected from the notion of the fruitful earth and the primitive values, that the Romans had the advantage of the Greeks. Thenceforward any high ideal of life becomes largely a question of money. Unlike the Greek stoicism of Chrysippus, the Roman stoicism of Cato and Seneca presupposes a private income; [4] and, unlike that of the 18th Century, the social-ethical sentiment of the 20th, if it is to be realized at a higher level than that of professional (and lucrative) agitation, is a matter for millionaires. To the world-city belongs not a folk but a mass. Its uncomprehending hostility to all the traditions representative of the Culture (nobility, church, privileges, dynasties, convention in art and limits of knowledge in science), the keen and cold intelligence that confounds the wisdom of the peasant, the new-fashioned naturalism that in relation to all matters of sex and society goes back far beyond Rousseau and Socrates to quite primitive instincts and conditions, the reappear-

---

[1] One cannot fail to notice this in the development of Strindberg and especially in that of Ibsen, who was never quite at home in the civilized atmosphere of his problems. The motives of "Brand" and "Rosmersholm" are a wonderful mixture of innate provincialism and a theoretically-acquired megalopolitan outlook. Nora is the very type of the provincial derailed by reading.

[2] Who forbade the cult of the town's hero Adrastos and the reading of the Homeric poems, with the object of cutting the Doric nobility from its spiritual roots (c. 560 B.C.).

[3] A profound word which obtains its significance as soon as the barbarian becomes a culture-man and loses it again as soon as the civilization-man takes up the motto "*Ubi bene, ibi patria.*"

[4] Hence it was that the first to succumb to Christianity were the Romans who could *not afford* to be Stoics. See Vol. II, pp. 607 et seq.

ance of the *panem et circenses* in the form of wage-disputes and football-grounds — all these things betoken the definite closing-down of the Culture and the opening of a quite new phase of human existence — anti-provincial, late, futureless, but quite inevitable.

This is what has to be *viewed*, and viewed not with the eyes of the partisan, the ideologue, the up-to-date novelist, not from this or that "standpoint," but in a high, time-free perspective embracing whole millenniums of historical world-forms, if we are really to comprehend the great crisis of the present.

To me it is a symbol of the first importance that in the Rome of Crassus — triumvir and all-powerful building-site speculator — the Roman people with its proud inscriptions, the people before whom Gauls, Greeks, Parthians, Syrians afar trembled, lived in appalling misery in the many-storied lodging-houses of dark suburbs,[1] accepting with indifference or even with a sort of sporting interest the consequences of the military expansion: that many famous old-noble families, descendants of the men who defeated the Celts and the Samnites, lost their ancestral homes through standing apart from the wild rush of speculation and were reduced to renting wretched apartments; that, while along the Appian Way there arose the splendid and still wonderful tombs of the financial magnates, the corpses of the people were thrown along with animal carcases and town refuse into a monstrous common grave — till in Augustus's time it was banked over for the avoidance of pestilence and so became the site of Mæcenas's renowned park; that in depopulated Athens, which lived on visitors and on the bounty of rich foreigners, the mob of parvenu tourists from Rome gaped at the works of the Periclean age with as little understanding as the American globe-trotter in the Sistine Chapel at those of Michelangelo, every removable art-piece having ere this been taken away or bought at fancy prices to be replaced by the Roman buildings which grew up, colossal and arrogant, by the side of the low and modest structures of the old time. In such things — which it is the historian's business not to praise or to blame but to consider morphologically — there lies, plain and immediate enough for one who has learnt to see, an *idea*.

For it will become manifest that, from this moment on, all great conflicts of world-outlook, of politics, of art, of science, of feeling will be under the influence of this one opposition. What is the hall-mark of a politic of Civilization to-day, in contrast to a politic of Culture yesterday? It is, for the Classical rhetoric, and for the Western journalism, both serving that abstract which represents the power of Civilization — *money*.[2] It is the money-spirit which

---

[1] In Rome and Byzantium, lodging-houses of six to ten stories (with street-widths of ten feet at most!) were built without any sort of official supervision, and frequently collapsed with all their inmates. A great part of the *cives Romani*, for whom *panem et circenses* constituted all existence, possessed no more than a high-priced sleeping-berth in one of the swarming ant-hills called *insula*. (Pohlmann, *Aus Altertum und Gegenwart*, 1911, pp. 199 ff.)

[2] See Vol. II, 577.

penetrates unremarked the historical forms of the people's existence, often without destroying or even in the least disturbing these forms — the form of the Roman state, for instance, underwent very much less alteration between the elder Scipio and Augustus than is usually imagined. Though forms subsist, the great political parties nevertheless cease to be more than reputed centres of decision. The decisions in fact lie elsewhere. A small number of superior heads, whose names are very likely not the best-known, settle everything, while below them are the great mass of second-rate politicians — rhetors, tribunes, deputies, journalists — selected through a provincially-conceived franchise to keep alive the illusion of popular self-determination. And art? Philosophy? The ideals of a Platonic or those of a Kantian age had for the higher mankind concerned a general validity. But those of a Hellenistic age, or those of our own, are valid exclusively for the brain of the Megalopolitan. For the villager's or, generally, the nature-man's world-feeling our Socialism — like its near relation Darwinism (how utterly un-Goethian are the formulæ of "struggle for existence" and "natural selection"!), like its other relative the woman-and-marriage problem of Ibsen, Strindberg, and Shaw, like the impressionistic tendencies of anarchic sensuousness and the whole bundle of modern longings, temptations and pains expressed in Baudelaire's verse and Wagner's music — are simply non-existent. The smaller the town, the more unmeaning it becomes to busy oneself with painting or with music of these kinds. To the Culture belong gymnastics, the tournament, the agon, and to the Civilization belongs Sport. This is the true distinction between the Hellenic palæstra and the Roman circus.[1] Art itself becomes a sport (hence the phrase "art for art's sake") to be played before a highly-intelligent audience of connoisseurs and buyers, whether the feat consist in mastering absurd instrumental tone-masses and taking harmonic fences, or in some *tour de force* of colouring. Then a new fact-philosophy appears, which can only spare a smile for metaphysical speculation, and a new literature that is a necessity of life for the megalopolitan palate and nerves and both unintelligible and ugly to the provincials. Neither Alexandrine poetry nor *plein-air* painting is anything to the "people." And, then as now, the phase of transition is marked by a series of scandals only to be found at such moments. The anger evoked in the Athenian populace by Euripides and by the "Revolutionary" painting of Apollodorus, for example, is repeated in the opposition to Wagner, Manet, Ibsen, and Nietzsche.

It is possible to understand the Greeks without mentioning their economic relations; the Romans, on the other hand, can *only* be understood through these. Chæronea and Leipzig were the last battles fought about an idea. In the First Punic War and in 1870 economic motives are no longer to be overlooked. Not

---

[1] German gymnastics, from the intensely provincial and natural forms imparted to it by Jahn, has since 1813 been carried by a very rapid development into the sport category. The difference between a Berlin athletic ground on a big day and a Roman circus was even by 1914 very slight.

49

till the Romans came with their practical energy was slave-holding given that big collective character which many students regard as the die-stamp of Classical economics, legislation and way of life, and which in any event vastly lowered both the value and the inner worthiness of such free labour as continued to exist side by side with gang-labour. And it was not the Latin, but the Germanic peoples of the West and America who developed out of the steam-engine a big industry that transformed the face of the land. The relation of these phenomena to Stoicism and to Socialism is unmistakable. Not till the Roman Cæsarism — foreshadowed by C. Flaminius, shaped first by Marius, handled by strong-minded, large-scale men of fact — did the Classical World learn the *pre-eminence of money*. Without this fact neither Cæsar, nor "Rome" generally, is understandable. In every Greek is a Don Quixote, in every Roman a Sancho Panza factor, and these factors are dominants.

After being educated in the classics, London-born Arnold J. Toynbee (1889-1975) served from 1915 to 1919 on the staff of the Foreign Office. While working with his wife on the voluminous *Survey of International Affairs* which was published annually, Toynbee began the task of writing his *A Study of History* which appeared from 1934 to 1954 and has become one of the most widely known world histories in modern times. This excerpt is taken from the two volume abridgement of *A Study of History* done by D.C. Somervell with the approval of Toynbee.

II. THE GENESES OF CIVILIZATIONS

IV. THE PROBLEM AND HOW NOT TO SOLVE IT

(1) *The Problem Stated*

Of our twenty-three 'civilized' societies sixteen are affiliated to previous civilizations but six have emerged direct from primitive life. Primitive societies existing to-day are static, but it is clear that they must originally have been dynamically progressive. Social life is older than the human race itself; it is found among insects and animals, and it must have been under the aegis of primitive societies that sub-man rose to the level of man—a greater advance than any civilization has as yet achieved. However, primitive societies, as we know them, are static. The problem is: why and how was this primitive 'cake of custom' broken?

(2) *Race*

The factor that we are looking for must be some special quality in the human beings who started civilizations or some special features of their environment at the time or some interaction between the two. The first of these views, namely, that there is some innately superior race, e.g. the Nordic Race, in the world, which is responsible for the creation of civilizations, is examined and rejected.

(3) *Environment*

The view that certain environments, presenting easy and comfortable conditions of life, provide the key to an explanation of the origin of civilizations is examined and rejected.

V. CHALLENGE AND RESPONSE

(1) *The Mythological Clue*

The fallacy in the two views already examined and rejected is that they apply the procedure of sciences which deal with material things to a problem that is really spiritual. A survey of the great myths in which the wisdom of the human race is enshrined suggests the possibility that man achieves civilization, not as a result

52

of superior biological endowment or geographical environment, but as a response to a challenge in a situation of special difficulty which rouses him to make a hitherto unprecedented effort.

(2) *The Myth applied to the Problem*

Before the dawn of civilization the Afrasian Steppe (the Sahara and the Arabian Desert) was a well-watered grassland. The prolonged and progressive desiccation of this grassland presented its habinitants with a challenge to which they responded in various ways. Some stood their ground and changed their habits, thus evolving the Nomadic manner of life. Others shifted their ground southwards, following the retreating grassland to the tropics, and thus preserved their primitive way of life—which they are still living today. Others entered the marshes and jungles of the Nile Valley and—faced with the challenge that it presented—set to work to drain it, and these evolved the Egyptiac civilization.

The Sumeric civilization originated in the same way and from the same causes in the Tigris–Euphrates Valley, and the Indus culture in the Indus Valley.

The Shang culture originated in the Yellow River Valley. The nature of the challenge which started it is unknown, but it is clear that the conditions were severe rather than easy.

The Mayan civilization arose in answer to the challenge of a tropical forest; the Andean in answer to that of a bleak plateau.

The Minoan civilization arose in answer to the challenge of the sea. Its founders were refugees from the desiccating coasts of Africa who took to the water and settled in Crete and other Aegean islands. They did not, in the first instance, come from the nearer mainlands of Asia or Europe.

In the cases of the affiliated civilizations the challenge that brought them into existence must have come primarily not from geographical factors but from their human environment, i.e. from the 'dominant minorities' of the societies to which they are affiliated. A dominant minority is, by definition, a ruling class that has ceased to lead and has become oppressive. To this challenge the internal and external proletariats of the failing civilization respond by seceding from it and thereby laying the foundations of a new civilization.

VI. THE VIRTUES OF ADVERSITY

The explanation of the geneses of civilizations given in the last chapter rests on the hypothesis that it is difficult rather than easy conditions that produce these achievements. This hypothesis is now brought nearer to proof by illustrations taken from localities where civilization once flourished but subsequently failed and where the land has reverted to its original condition.

What was once the scene of the Mayan civilization is now again tropical forest.

The Indic civilization in Ceylon flourished in the rainless half of the island. This is now entirely barren, though the ruins of the Indic irrigation system remain as evidence of the civilization that once flourished here.

The ruins of Petra and Palmyra stand on small oases in the Arabian Desert.

Easter Island, one of the remotest spots in the Pacific, is proved by its statues to have been once a centre of the Polynesian civilization.

New England, whose European colonists have played a predominant part in the history of North America, is one of the bleakest and most barren parts of that continent.

The Latin townships of the Roman Campagna, till recently a malarial wilderness, made a great contribution to the rise of the Roman Power. Contrast the favourable situation and poor performance of Capua. Illustrations are also drawn from Herodotus, the Odyssey, and the Book of Exodus.

The natives of Nyasaland, where life is easy, remained primitive savages down to the advent of invaders from a distant and inclement Europe.

VII. THE CHALLENGE OF THE ENVIRONMENT

(1) *The Stimulus of Hard Countries*

A series of pairs of contiguous environments is adduced. In each case the former is the 'harder' country and has also had the more brilliant record as an originator of one form or other of civilization: the Yellow River Valley and the Yangtse Valley; Attica and Boeotia; Byzantium and Calchedon; Israel, Phoenicia, Philistia; Brandenburg and the Rhineland; Scotland and England; the various groups of European colonists in North America.

(2) *The Stimulus of New Ground*

We find that 'virgin soil' produces more vigorous responses than land which has already been broken in and thus rendered 'easier' by previous 'civilized' occupants. Thus, if we take each of the affiliated civilizations, we find that it has produced its most striking early manifestations in places outside the area occupied by the 'parent' civilization. The superiority of the response evoked by new ground is most strikingly illustrated when the new ground has to be reached by a sea-passage. Reasons for this fact are given, and also for the phenomenon that the drama develops in homelands and epic in overseas settlements.

(3) *The Stimulus of Blows*

Various examples from Hellenic and Western history are given to illustrate the point that a sudden crushing defeat is apt to stimulate the defeated party to set its house in order and prepare to make a victorious response.

(4) *The Stimulus of Pressures*

Various examples show that peoples occupying frontier positions, exposed to constant attack, achieve a more brilliant development than their neighbours in more sheltered positions. Thus the 'Osmanlis, thrust up against the frontier of the East Roman Empire, fared better than the Qaramanlis to the east of them; Austria had a more brilliant career than Bavaria thanks to being exposed to the prolonged assault of the Ottoman Turks. The situation and fortunes of the various communities in Britain between the fall of Rome and the Norman Conquest are examined from this point of view.

(5) *The Stimulus of Penalizations*

Certain classes and races have suffered for centuries from various forms of penalization imposed upon them by other classes or races who have had the mastery over them. Penalized classes or races generally respond to this challenge of being excluded from certain opportunities and privileges by putting forth exceptional energy and showing exceptional capacity in such directions as are left open to them—much as the blind develop exceptional sensitiveness of hearing. Slavery is perhaps the heaviest of penalizations, but out of the hordes of slaves imported into Italy from the Eastern Mediterranean during the last two centuries B.C. there arose a 'freedmen' class which proved alarmingly powerful. From this slave world, too, came the new religions of the internal proletariat, among them Christianity.

The fortunes of various groups of conquered Christian peoples under 'Osmanli rule are examined from the same standpoint—particularly the case of the Phanariot Greeks. This example and that of the Jews are used to prove that so-called racial characteristics are not really racial at all but are due to the historical experiences of the communities in question.

(1) *Enough and Too Much*

Can we say simply: the sterner the challenge the finer the response? Or is there such a thing as a challenge too severe to evoke a response? Certainly some challenges which have defeated one or more parties that have encountered them have ultimately provoked a victorious response. For example, the challenge of expanding Hellenism proved too much for the Celts but was victoriously answered by their successors the Teutons. The 'Hellenic intrusion' into the Syriac world evoked a series of unsuccessful Syriac responses—the Zoroastrian, the Jewish (Maccabaean), the Nestorian, and the Monophysite—but the fifth response, that of Islam, was successful.

(2) *Comparisons in Three Terms*

None the less, it can be proved that challenges can be too severe: i.e. the *maximum* challenge will not always produce the *optimum* response. The Viking emigrants from Norway responded splendidly to the severe challenge of Iceland but collapsed before the severer challenge of Greenland. Massachusetts presented European colonists with a severer challenge than 'Dixie' and evoked a better response, but Labrador, presenting a severer challenge still, proved too much for them. Other examples follow: e.g. the stimulus of blows can be too severe, especially if prolonged, as in the effect of the Hannibalic War on Italy. The Chinese are stimulated by the social challenge involved in emigrating to Malaya but are defeated by the severer social challenge of a white man's country, e.g. California. Finally, varying degrees of challenge presented by civilizations to neighbouring barbarians are reviewed.

(3) *Two Abortive Civilizations*

This section is a continuation of the argument of the last example in the preceding section. Two groups of barbarians on the frontiers of Western Christendom in the first chapter of its history were so stimulated that they began to evolve rival civilizations of their own which were, however, nipped in the bud, namely the Far Western Celtic Christians (in Ireland and Iona) and the Scandinavian Vikings. These two cases are considered and the consequences that might have ensued if these rivals had not been swallowed and absorbed by the Christian civilization radiating from Rome and the Rhineland.

(4) *The Impact of Islam on the Christendoms*

On Western Christendom the effect of this impact was wholly good, and Western culture in the Middle Ages owed much to Muslim Iberia. On Byzantine Christendom the impact was excessive and evoked a crushing re-erection of the Roman Empire.

XII. THE PROSPECTS OF THE WESTERN CIVILIZATION

XXXIX. THE NEED FOR THIS INQUIRY

The ensuing inquiry marked a departure from the standpoint, adopted and hitherto maintained throughout this *Study*, of treating all the civilizations known to history synoptically. The departure is justified by the facts that the Western society is the only one surviving that is not manifestly in disintegration, that in many respects it had become world-wide, and that its prospects were, in fact, the prospects of a 'Westernizing world'.

XL. THE INCONCLUSIVENESS OF *A PRIORI* ANSWERS

There was no reason for supposing, on pseudo-scientific grounds, that, because all other civilizations had perished or were perishing, the West was bound to go the same way. Emotional reactions, such as 'Victorian' optimism and 'Spenglerian' pessimism, were equally void of cogency as evidence.

XLI. THE TESTIMONY OF THE HISTORIES OF THE CIVILIZATIONS

(1) *Western Experiences with Non-Western Precedents*

What light do our previous studies of breakdowns and disintegrations throw on our present problem? We have noted war and militarism as being the most potent cause of the breakdown of a society. The West has so far wrestled unsuccessfully with this disease. On the other hand it has achieved unprecedented successes in other directions: e.g. the abolition of slavery; the growth of democracy and education. The West also now displays the ominous division into dominant minority and internal and external proletariats. On the other hand, some remarkable successes have been achieved in coping with the problems of a diversity of internal proletariats within the Westernizing world.

(2) *Unprecedented Western Experiences*

The mastery of Man over non-human nature and the accelerating rapidity of social change are both without parallel in the histories of earlier civilizations. The plan of the following chapters is indicated.

XLII. TECHNOLOGY, WAR, GOVERNMENT

(1) *Prospects of a Third World War*

Characteristics of the United States of America and of the Soviet Union, and of the attitude of the rest of the human race towards each of them.

(2) *Towards a Future World Order*

The prospects of the human race compared with Heyerdahl's raft, *Kon-tiki*, on approaching the reef. A future World Order would inevitably be something very different from the present United Nations Organization. The qualifications of the American nation for leadership are discussed.

XLIII. TECHNOLOGY, CLASS-CONFLICT, AND EMPLOYMENT

(1) *The Nature of the Problem*

The triumphs of modern technology had led to an unprecedented demand for 'freedom from want'; but would Mankind be prepared to pay the price required for the satisfaction of this demand?

(2) *Mechanization and Private Enterprise*

Modern technology had entailed a mechanization, or regimentation, not only of the manual workers, but also of their employers (nationalization, &c.), of the civil service ('red tape'), and of the politicians (party discipline). The working-class organs of resistance (trade unions) had required further regimentation. The authors of the Industrial Revolution, on the other hand, had come out of a non-regimented society.

(3) *Alternative Approaches to Social Harmony*

The American, the Russian, and the West European, especially the British, approaches analysed and compared.

(4) *Possible Costs of Social Justice*

Social life impossible without some measure both of personal liberty and of social justice. Technology tilts the balance in favour of the latter. What, in an age when the death-rate was being lowered by preventive medicine, were going to be the consequences of an uncontrolled 'personal liberty' to propagate the human species? The prospects of a Great Famine ahead are discussed, and the conflicts that it seemed likely to engender.

(5) *Living happy ever after?*

Suppose that the World Society found a successful solution of all these problems, would the human race thenceforth 'live happy ever after'? No, because 'original sin' is born again in every child that comes into the World.

XIII. CONCLUSION

XLIV. HOW THIS BOOK CAME TO BE WRITTEN

The writer, born into the age of the Late Victorian optimism, and encountering the First World War in early manhood, was struck by the parallels between the experience of his own society in his own lifetime and those of the Hellenic society, a study of which had provided the staple of his education. This raised in his mind the questions: Why do civilizations die? Is the Hellenic civilization's fate in store for the Modern West? Subsequently his inquiries were extended to include the breakdowns and disintegrations of the other known civilizations, as further evidence for throwing light on his questions. Finally, he proceeded to investigate the geneses and growths of civilizations, and so this *Study of History* came to be written.

Thomas Babington Macaulay, HISTORY OF ENGLAND

1. Macaulay speaks of the delusion which leads one
    generation to overrate the happiness of preceding
    generations. Do you feel this delusion exists to-
    day?

2. In what ways was Macaulay's prediction of how twen-
    tieth-century England might view nineteenth-century
    England basically accurate?

3. The country gentleman of seventeenth-century Eng-
    land was described as being "gross, uneducated, and
    untravelled." Why then is he referred to as a gen-
    tleman?

4. Contrast seventeenth-century London with nineteenth-
    century London.

5. Macaulay stated that "Never was an Englishman more
    at home than when he took his ease in his inn."
    What part did the inns play in the social life of
    the Englishman? Did this also apply to the women
    of that day? How can you account for the popular-
    ity of today's "English pubs" which seem to be
    spreading throughout the United States?

Thomas Babington Macaulay's *The History of England from the Accession of James II,* in four valumes, is vivid, colorful, and written in a readable, lively style. This is considered to be his greatest work and represents one of the first examples of social history. The readings selected are from the third chapter of Volume I and illustrate how Macaulay has been able to weave social, economic, and intellectual facts into the fabric of his account of political and military events.

CHAPTER III.

I INTEND, in this chapter, to give a description of the state in which England was at the time when the crown passed from Charles the Second to his brother. Such a description, composed from scanty and dispersed materials, must necessarily be very imperfect. Yet it may perhaps correct some false notions which would make the subsequent narrative unintelligible or uninstructive.

If we would study with profit the history of our ancestors, we must be constantly on our guard against that delusion which the well known names of families, places, and offices naturally produce, and must never forget that the country of which we read was a very different country from that in which we live. In every experimental science there is a tendency towards perfection. In every human being there is a wish to ameliorate his own condition. These two principles have often sufficed, even when counteracted by great public calamities and by bad institutions, to carry civilisation rapidly forward. No ordinary misfortune, no ordinary misgovernment, will do so much to make a nation wretched, as the constant progress of physical knowledge and the constant effort of every man to better himself will do to make a nation prosperous. It has often been found that profuse expenditure, heavy taxation, absurd commercial restrictions, corrupt tribunals, disastrous wars, seditions, persecutions, conflagrations, inundations, have not been able to destroy capital so fast as the exertions of private citizens have been able to create it. It can easily be proved that, in our own land, the national wealth has, during at least six centuries, been almost uninterruptedly increasing; that it was greater under the Tudors than under the Plantagenets; that it was greater under the Stuarts than under the Tudors; that, in spite of battles, sieges, and confiscations, it was greater on the day of the Restoration than on the day when the Long Parliament met; that, in spite of maladministration, of extravagance, of public bankruptcy, of two costly and unsuccessful wars, of the pestilence and of the fire, it was greater on the day of the death of Charles the Second than on the day of his Restoration. This progress, having continued during many ages, became at length, about the middle of the eighteenth century, portentously rapid, and has proceeded, during the nineteenth, with accelerated velocity. In consequence partly of our geographical and partly of our moral position, we have, during several generations, been exempt from evils which have elsewhere impeded the efforts and destroyed the fruits of industry. While every part of the Continent, from Moscow to Lisbon, has been the theatre of bloody and devastating wars, no hostile standard has been seen here but as a trophy. While revolutions have taken place all around us, our government has never once been subverted by violence. During more than a hundred years there has been in our island no tumult of sufficient importance to be called an insurrection; nor has the law been once borne down either by popular fury or by regal tyranny : public credit has been held sacred : the administration of justice has been pure : even in times which might by Englishmen be justly called evil times, we have enjoyed what almost every other nation in the world would have considered as an ample measure of civil and religious freedom. Every man has felt entire confidence that the state would protect him in the possession of what had been earned by his diligence and hoarded by his selfdenial. Under the benignant influence of peace and liberty, science has

CHAP.
III.

Great
change in
the state
of England
since 1685.

flourished, and has been applied to practical purposes on a scale never before known. The consequence is that a change to which the history of the old world furnishes no parallel has taken place in our country. Could the England of 1685 be, by some magical process, set before our eyes, we should not know one landscape in a hundred or one building in ten thousand. The country gentleman would not recognise his own fields. The inhabitant of the town would not recognise his own street. Every thing has been changed, but the great features of nature, and a few massive and durable works of human art. We might find out Snowdon and Windermere, the Cheddar Cliffs and Beachy Head. We might find out here and there a Norman minster, or a castle which witnessed the wars of the Roses. But, with such rare exceptions, every thing would be strange to us. Many thousands of square miles which are now rich corn land and meadow, intersected by green hedgerows, and dotted with villages and pleasant country seats, would appear as moors overgrown with furze, or fens abandoned to wild ducks. We should see straggling huts built of wood and covered with thatch, where we now see manufacturing towns and seaports renowned to the farthest ends of the world. The capital itself would shrink to dimensions not much exceeding those of its present suburb on the south of the Thames. Not less strange to us would be the garb and manners of the people, the furniture and the equipages, the interior of the shops and dwellings. Such a change in the state of a nation seems to be at least as well entitled to the notice of a historian as any change of the dynasty or of the ministry.*

* During the interval which has elapsed since this chapter was written, England has continued to advance rapidly in material prosperity. I have left my text nearly as it originally stood; but I have added a few notes which may enable the reader to form some notion of the progress which has been made during the last nine years; and, in ge-

The progress of this great change can nowhere be more clearly traced than in the Statute Book. The number of enclosure acts passed since King George the Second came to the throne exceeds four thousand. The area enclosed under the authority of those acts exceeds, on a moderate calculation, ten thousand square miles. How many square miles, which were formerly uncultivated or ill cultivated, have, during the same period, been fenced and carefully tilled by the proprietors, without any application to the legislature, can only be conjectured. But it seems highly probable that a fourth part of England has been, in the course of little more than a century, turned from a wild into a garden.

Even in those parts of the kingdom which at the close of the reign of Charles the Second were the best cultivated, the farming, though greatly improved since the civil war, was not such as would now be thought skilful. To this day no effectual steps have been taken by public authority for the purpose of obtaining accurate accounts of the produce of the English soil. The historian must therefore follow, with some misgivings, the guidance of those writers on statistics whose reputation for diligence and fidelity stands highest. At present an average crop of wheat, rye, barley, oats, and beans, is supposed considerably to exceed thirty millions of quarters. The crop of wheat would be thought wretched if it did not exceed twelve millions of quarters. According to the computation made in the year 1696 by Gregory King, the whole quantity of wheat, rye, barley, oats, and beans, then annually grown in the kingdom, was somewhat less than ten millions of quarters. The wheat, which was then cultivated only on the strongest clay, and consumed only by those who were in easy circumstances, he estimated at less than two millions of quarters. Charles Davenant, an acute and well informed though most unprincipled and rancorous politician, differed from King as to some of the items of the account, but came to nearly the same general conclusions.*

The rotation of crops was very imperfectly understood. It was known, indeed, that some vegetables lately introduced into our island, particularly the turnip, afforded excellent nutriment in winter to sheep and oxen: but it was not yet the practice to feed cattle in this manner. It was therefore by no means easy to keep them alive during the season when the grass is scanty. They were killed and salted in great numbers at the beginning of the cold weather; and, during several months, even the gentry tasted scarcely any fresh animal food, except game and river fish, which were consequently much more important articles in housekeeping than at present. It appears from the Northumberland Household Book that, in the reign of Henry the Seventh, fresh meat was never eaten even by the gentlemen attendant on a great Earl, except during the short interval between Midsummer and Michaelmas. But in the course of two centuries an improvement had taken place; and under Charles the Second it was not till the beginning of November that families laid in their stock of salt provisions, then called Martinmas beef.†

The sheep and the ox of that time were diminutive when compared with the sheep and oxen which are now driven to our markets.‡ Our native horses, though

* King's Natural and Political Conclusions. Davenant on the Balance of Trade.

† See the Almanacks of 1684 and 1685.

‡ See Mr. M'Culloch's Statistical Account of the British Empire, Part III. chap. i. sec. 6.

serviceable, were held in small esteem, and fetched low prices. They were valued, one with another, by the ablest of those who computed the national wealth, at not more than fifty shillings each. Foreign breeds were greatly preferred. Spanish jennets were regarded as the finest chargers, and were imported for purposes of pageantry and war. The coaches of the aristocracy were drawn by grey Flemish mares, which trotted, as it was thought, with a peculiar grace, and endured better than any cattle reared in our island the work of dragging a ponderous equipage over the rugged pavement of London. Neither the modern dray horse nor the modern race horse was then known. At a much later period the ancestors of the gigantic quadrupeds, which all foreigners now class among the chief wonders of London, were brought from the marshes of Walcheren; the ancestors of Childers and Eclipse from the sands of Arabia. Already, however, there was among our nobility and gentry a passion for the amusements of the turf. The importance of improving our studs by an infusion of new blood was strongly felt; and with this view a considerable number of barbs had lately been brought into the country. Two men whose authority on such subjects was held in great esteem, the Duke of Newcastle and Sir John Fenwick, pronounced that the meanest hack ever imported from Tangier would produce a finer progeny than could be expected from the best sire of our native breed. They would not readily have believed that a time would come when the princes and nobles of neighbouring lands would be as eager to obtain horses from England as ever the English had been to obtain horses from Barbary.[*]

* King and Davenant as before; The Duke of Newcastle on Horsemanship; Gentleman's Recreation, 1686. The " dappled Flanders mares " were marks of greatness in the time of Pope, and even later.   The vulgar proverb, that the grey mare is the better horse, originated, I suspect, in the preference generally given to the grey mares of Flanders over the finest coach horses of England.

The increase of vegetable and animal produce, though great, seems small when compared with the increase of our mineral wealth. In 1685 the tin of Cornwall, which had, more than two thousand years before, attracted the Tyrian sails beyond the pillars of Hercules, was still one of the most valuable subterranean productions of the island. The quantity annually extracted from the earth was found to be, some years later, sixteen hundred tons, probably about a third of what it now is.* But the veins of copper which lie in the same region were, in the time of Charles the Second, altogether neglected, nor did any landowner take them into the account in estimating the value of his property. Cornwall and Wales at present yield annually near fifteen thousand tons of copper, worth near a million and a half sterling; that is to say, worth about twice as much as the annual produce of all English mines of all descriptions in the seventeenth century.† The first bed of rock salt had been discovered in Cheshire not long after the Restoration, but does not appear to have been worked till much later. The salt which was obtained by a rude process from brine pits was held in no high estimation. The pans in which the manufacture was carried on exhaled a sulphurous stench; and, when the evaporation was complete, the substance which was left was scarcely fit to be used with food. Physicians attributed the scorbutic and pulmonary complaints which were common among the English to this unwholesome condiment. It was therefore seldom used by the upper and middle classes; and there was a regular and considerable importation from France. At present our springs and mines not only supply our own immense

* See a curious note by Tonkin, in Lord De Dunstanville's edition of Carew's Survey of Cornwall.

† Borlase's Natural History of Cornwall, 1758. The quantity of copper now produced, I have taken from parliamentary returns. Davenant, in 1700, estimated the annual produce of all the mines of England at between seven and eight hundred thousand pounds.

CHAP.
III.

demand, but send annually more than seven hundred millions of pounds of excellent salt to foreign countries.*

Far more important has been the improvement of our iron works. Such works had long existed in our island, but had not prospered, and had been regarded with no favourable eye by the government and by the public. It was not then the practice to employ coal for smelting the ore; and the rapid consumption of wood excited the alarm of politicians. As early as the reign of Elizabeth there had been loud complaints that whole forests were cut down for the purpose of feeding the furnaces: and the parliament had interfered to prohibit the manufacturers from burning timber. The manufacture consequently languished. At the close of the reign of Charles the Second, great part of the iron which was used in this country was imported from abroad; and the whole quantity cast here annually seems not to have exceeded ten thousand tons. At present the trade is thought to be in a depressed state if less than a million of tons are produced in a year.†

One mineral, perhaps more important than iron itself, remains to be mentioned. Coal, though very little used in any species of manufacture, was already the ordinary fuel in some districts which were fortunate enough to possess large beds, and in the capital, which could easily be supplied by water carriage. It seems reasonable to believe that at least one half of the quantity then extracted from the pits was consumed in London. The consumption of London seemed to the writers of that age enormous, and was often mentioned by them as a proof of the greatness of the imperial city. They

* Philosophical Transactions, No. 53. Nov. 1669, No. 66. Dec. 1670, No. 103. May 1674, No. 156. Feb. 168¾.

† Yarranton, England's Improvement by Sea and Land, 1677; Porter's Progress of the Nation. See also a remarkably perspicuous history, in small compass, of the English iron works, in Mr. M‘Culloch's Statistical Account of the British Empire.

scarcely hoped to be believed when they affirmed that two hundred and eighty thousand chaldrons, that is to say, about three hundred and fifty thousand tons, were, in the last year of the reign of Charles the Second, brought to the Thames. At present three millions and a half of tons are required yearly by the metropolis; and the whole annual produce cannot, on the most moderate computation, be estimated at less than thirty millions of tons.*

While these great changes have been in progress, the rent of land has, as might be expected, been almost constantly rising. In some districts it has multiplied more than tenfold. / In some it has not more than doubled. It has probably, on the average, quadrupled.

Of the rent, a large proportion was divided among the country gentlemen, a class of persons whose position and character it is most important that we should clearly understand; for by their influence and by their passions the fate of the nation was, at several important conjunctures, determined.

We should be much mistaken if we pictured to ourselves the squires of the seventeenth century as men bearing a close resemblance to their descendants, the county members and chairmen of quarter sessions with whom we are familiar. The modern country gentleman generally receives a liberal education, passes from a distinguished school to a distinguished college, and has ample opportunity to become an excellent scholar. He has generally seen something of foreign countries. A considerable part of his life has generally been passed in the capital; and the refinements of the capital follow him into the country. There is perhaps no class of

* See Chamberlayne's State of England, 1684, 1687 ; Angliæ Metropolis, 1691 ; M'Culloch's Statistical Account of the British Empire, Part III. chap. ii. (edition of 1847). In 1845 the quantity of coal brought into London appeared, by the parliamentary returns, to be 3,460,000 tons. (1848.) In 1854 the quantity of coal brought into London amounted to 4,378,000 tons. (1857.)

dwellings so pleasing as the rural seats of the English gentry. In the parks and pleasure grounds, nature, dressed yet not disguised by art, wears her most alluring form. In the buildings, good sense and good taste combine to produce a happy union of the comfortable and the graceful. The pictures, the musical instruments, the library, would in any other country be considered as proving the owner to be an eminently polished and accomplished man. A country gentleman who witnessed the revolution was probably in receipt of about a fourth part of the rent which his acres now yield to his posterity. He was, therefore, as compared with his posterity, a poor man, and was generally under the necessity of residing, with little interruption, on his estate. To travel on the Continent, to maintain an establishment in London, or even to visit London frequently, were pleasures in which only the great proprietors could indulge. It may be confidently affirmed that of the squires whose names were then in the Commissions of Peace and Lieutenancy not one in twenty went to town once in five years, or had ever in his life wandered so far as Paris. Many lords of manors had received an education differing little from that of their menial servants. The heir of an estate often passed his boyhood and youth at the seat of his family with no better tutors than grooms and gamekeepers, and scarce attained learning enough to sign his name to a Mittimus. If he went to school and to college, he generally returned before he was twenty to the seclusion of the old hall, and there, unless his mind were very happily constituted by nature, soon forgot his academical pursuits in rural business and pleasures. His chief serious employment was the care of his property. He examined samples of grain, handled pigs, and, on market days, made bargains over a tankard with drovers and hop merchants. His chief pleasures were commonly derived from field sports and from an unrefined sensuality. His language and pronunciation were such as we should now expect to hear only from the most ignorant clowns. His oaths, coarse jests, and scurrilous terms of abuse, were uttered with the broadest accent of his province. It was easy to discern, from the first words which he spoke, whether he came from Somersetshire or Yorkshire. He troubled himself little about decorating his abode, and, if he attempted decoration, seldom produced any thing but deformity. The litter of a farmyard gathered under the windows of his bedchamber, and the cabbages and gooseberry bushes grew close to his hall door. His table was loaded with coarse plenty; and guests were cordially welcomed to it. But, as the habit of drinking to excess was general in the class to which he belonged, and as his fortune did not enable him to intoxicate large assemblies daily with claret or canary, strong beer was the ordinary beverage. The quantity of beer consumed in those days was indeed enormous. For beer then was to the middle and lower classes, not only all that beer now is, but all that wine, tea, and ardent spirits now are. It was only at great houses, or on great occasions, that foreign drink was placed on the board. The ladies of the house, whose business it had commonly been to cook the repast, retired as soon as the dishes had been devoured, and left the gentlemen to their ale and tobacco. The coarse jollity of the afternoon was often prolonged till the revellers were laid under the table.

It was very seldom that the country gentleman caught glimpses of the great world; and what he saw of it tended rather to confuse than to enlighten his understanding. His opinions respecting religion, government, foreign countries and former times, having been derived, not from study, from observation, or from conversation with enlightened companions, but from such traditions as were current in his own small circle, were the opinions of a child He adhered to them, however, with the obstinacy which is generally found in ignorant men accustomed to be fed with flattery. His animosities were numerous and bitter. He hated Frenchmen and Italians, Scotchmen and Irishmen, Papists and Presbyterians, Independents and Baptists, Quakers and Jews. Towards London and Londoners he felt an aversion which more than once produced important political effects. His wife and daughter were in tastes and acquirements below a housekeeper or a stillroom maid of the present day. They stitched and spun, brewed gooseberry wine, cured marigolds, and made the crust for the venison pasty.

From this description it might be supposed that the English esquire of the seventeenth century did not materially differ from a rustic miller or alehouse keeper of our time. There are, however, some important parts of his character still to be noted, which will greatly modify this estimate. Unlettered as he was and unpolished, he was still in some most important points a gentleman. He was a member of a proud and powerful aristocracy, and was distinguished by many both of the good and of the bad qualities which belong to aristocrats. His family pride was beyond that of a Talbot or a Howard. He knew the genealogies and coats of arms of all his neighbours, and could tell which of them had assumed supporters without any right, and which of them were so unfortunate as to be greatgrandsons of aldermen. He was a magistrate, and, as such, administered gratuitously to those who dwelt around him a rude patriarchal justice, which, in spite of innumerable blunders and of occasional acts of tyranny, was yet better than no justice at all. He was an officer of the trainbands; and his military dignity, though it might move the mirth of gallants who had served a campaign in Flanders, raised his character in his own eyes and in the eyes of his neighbours. Nor indeed was his soldiership justly a subject of derision.

In every county there were elderly gentlemen who had seen service which was no child's play. One had been knighted by Charles the First, after the battle of Edge-hill. Another still wore a patch over the scar which he had received at Naseby. A third had defended his old house till Fairfax had blown in the door with a petard. The presence of these old Cavaliers, with their old swords and holsters, and with their old stories about Goring and Lunsford, gave to the musters of militia an earnest and warlike aspect which would otherwise have been wanting. Even those country gentlemen who were too young to have themselves exchanged blows with the cuirassiers of the Parliament had, from childhood, been surrounded by the traces of recent war, and fed with stories of the martial exploits of their fathers and uncles. Thus the character of the English esquire of the seventeenth century was compounded of two elements which we seldom or never find united. His ignorance and uncouthness, his low tastes and gross phrases, would, in our time, be considered as indicating a nature and a breeding thoroughly plebeian. Yet he was essentially a patrician, and had, in large measure, both the virtues and the vices which flourish among men set from their birth in high place, and used to respect themselves and to be respected by others. It is not easy for a generation accustomed to find chivalrous sentiments only in company with liberal studies and polished manners to image to itself a man with the deportment, the vocabulary, and the accent of a carter, yet punctilious on matters of genealogy and precedence, and ready to risk his life rather than see a stain cast on the honour of his house. It is however only by thus joining together things seldom or never found together in our own experience, that we can form a just idea of that rustic aristocracy which constituted the main strength of the armies of Charles the First, and which

74

long supported, with strange fidelity, the interest of his descendants.

The gross, uneducated, untravelled country gentleman was commonly a Tory: but, though devotedly attached to hereditary monarchy, he had no partiality for courtiers and ministers. He thought, not without reason, that Whitehall was filled with the most corrupt of mankind, and that of the great sums which the House of Commons had voted to the crown since the Restoration part had been embezzled by cunning politicians, and part squandered on buffoons and foreign courtesans. His stout English heart swelled with indignation at the thought that the government of his country should be subject to French dictation. Being himself generally an old Cavalier, or the son of an old Cavalier, he reflected with bitter resentment on the ingratitude with which the Stuarts had requited their best friends. Those who heard him grumble at the neglect with which he was treated, and at the profusion with which wealth was lavished on the bastards of Nell Gwynn and Madam Carwell, would have supposed him ripe for rebellion. But all this ill humour lasted only till the throne was really in danger. It was precisely when those whom the sovereign had loaded with wealth and honours shrank from his side that the country gentlemen, so surly and mutinous in the season of his prosperity, rallied round him in a body. Thus, after murmuring twenty years at the misgovernment of Charles the Second, they came to his rescue in his extremity, when his own Secretaries of State and the Lords of his own Treasury had deserted him, and enabled him to gain a complete victory over the opposition; nor can there be any doubt that they would have shown equal loyalty to his brother James, if James would, even at the last moment, have refrained from outraging their strongest feeling. For there was one institution, and one only, which they prized even more than hereditary

75

monarchy; and that institution was the Church of England. Their love of the Church was not, indeed, the effect of study or meditation. Few among them could have given any reason, drawn from Scripture or ecclesiastical history, for adhering to her doctrines, her ritual, and her polity; nor were they, as a class, by any means strict observers of that code of morality which is common to all Christian sects. But the experience of many ages proves that men may be ready to fight to the death, and to persecute without pity, for a religion whose creed they do not understand, and whose precepts they habitually disobey.*

The rural clergy were even more vehement in Tory- ism than the rural gentry, and were a class scarcely less important. It is to be observed, however, that the individual clergyman, as compared with the individual gentleman, then ranked much lower than in our days. The main support of the Church was derived from the tithe; and the tithe bore to the rent a much smaller ratio than at present. King estimated the whole income of the parochial and collegiate clergy at only four hundred and eighty thousand pounds a year; Davenant at only five hundred and forty-four thousand a year. It is certainly now more than seven times as great as the larger of these two sums. The average rent of the land has not, according to any estimate, increased proportionally. It follows that the rectors and vicars must have been, as compared with the neighbouring knights and squires, much poorer in the seventeenth than in the nineteenth century.

The place of the clergyman in society had been completely changed by the Reformation. Before that event, ecclesiastics had formed the majority of the

* My notion of the country gen- must leave my description to the tleman of the seventeenth century judgment of those who have studied has been derived from sources too the history and the lighter literature numerous to be recapitulated. I of that age.

The position of London, relatively to the other towns of the empire, was, in the time of Charles the Second, far higher than at present. For at present the population of London is little more than six times the population of Manchester or of Liverpool. In the days of Charles the Second the population of London was more

than seventeen times the population of Bristol or of Norwich. It may be doubted whether any other instance can be mentioned of a great kingdom in which the first city was more than seventeen times as large as the second. There is reason to believe that, in 1685, London had been, during about half a century, the most populous capital in Europe. The inhabitants, who are now at least nineteen hundred thousand, were then probably little more than half a million.* London had in the world only one commercial rival, now long ago outstripped, the mighty and opulent Amsterdam. English writers boasted of the forest of masts and yardarms which covered the river from the Bridge to the Tower, and of the stupendous sums which were collected at the Custom House in Thames Street. There is, indeed, no doubt that the trade of the metropolis then bore a far greater proportion than at present to the whole trade of the country; yet to our generation the honest vaunting of our ancestors must appear almost ludicrous. The shipping which they thought incredibly great appears not to have exceeded seventy thousand tons. This was, indeed, then more than a third of the whole tonnage of the kingdom, but is now less than a fourth of the tonnage of Newcastle, and is nearly equalled by the tonnage of the steam vessels of the Thames. The customs of London amounted, in 1685, to about three hundred and thirty thousand pounds a year. In our time the net duty paid annually, at the same place, exceeds ten millions.†

Whoever examines the maps of London which were

---

* According to King, 530,000. (1848.) In 1851 the population of London exceeded 2,300,000. (1857.)

† Macpherson's History of Commerce; Chalmers's Estimate; Chamberlayne's State of England, 1684. The tonnage of the steamers belonging to the port of London was, at the end of 1847, about 60,000 tons. The customs of the port, from 1842 to 1845, very nearly averaged 11,000,000l. (1848.) In 1854 the tonnage of the steamers of the port of London amounted to 138,000 tons, without reckoning vessels of less than fifty tons. (1857.)

published towards the close of the reign of Charles the Second will see that only the nucleus of the present capital then existed. The town did not, as now, fade by imperceptible degrees into the country. No long avenues of villas, embowered in lilacs and laburnums, extended from the great centre of wealth and civilisation almost to the boundaries of Middlesex and far into the heart of Kent and Surrey. In the east, no part of the immense line of warehouses and artificial lakes which now stretches from the Tower to Blackwall had even been projected. On the west, scarcely one of those stately piles of building which are inhabited by the noble and wealthy was in existence; and Chelsea, which is now peopled by more than forty thousand human beings, was a quiet country village with about a thousand inhabitants.* On the north, cattle fed, and sportsmen wandered with dogs and guns, over the site of the borough of Marylebone, and over far the greater part of the space now covered by the boroughs of Finsbury and of the Tower Hamlets. Islington was almost a solitude; and poets loved to contrast its silence and repose with the din and turmoil of the monster London.† On the south the capital is now connected with its suburb by several bridges, not inferior in magnificence and solidity to the noblest works of the Cæsars. In 1685, a single line of irregular arches, overhung by piles of mean and crazy houses, and garnished, after a fashion worthy of the naked barbarians of Dahomy, with scores of mouldering heads, impeded the navigation of the river.

Of the metropolis, the City, properly so called, was the most important division. At the time of the Restoration it had been built, for the most part, of wood and plaster; the few bricks that were used were ill

The City.

* Lyson's Environs of London. The baptisms at Chelsea, between 1680 and 1690, were only forty-two a year.

† Cowley, Discourse of Solitude.

The centre of Lincoln's Inn Fields was an open space where the rabble congregated every evening, within a few yards of Cardigan House and Winchester House, to hear mountebanks harangue, to see bears dance, and to set dogs at oxen. Rubbish was shot in every part of the area. Horses were exercised there. The beggars were as noisy and importunate as in the worst governed cities of the Continent. A Lincoln's Inn mumper was a proverb. The whole fraternity knew the arms and liveries of every charitably disposed grandee in the neighbourhood, and, as soon as his lordship's coach and six appeared, came hopping and crawling in crowds to persecute him. These disorders lasted, in spite of many accidents, and of some legal proceedings, till, in the reign of George the Second, Sir Joseph Jekyll, Master of the Rolls, was knocked down and nearly killed in the middle of the square. Then at length palisades were set up, and a pleasant garden laid out.*

Saint James's Square was a receptacle for all the offal and cinders, for all the dead cats and dead dogs of Westminster. At one time a cudgel player kept the ring there. At another time an impudent squatter settled himself there, and built a shed for rubbish under the windows of the gilded saloons in which the first magnates of the realm, Norfolk, Ormond, Kent, and Pembroke, gave banquets and balls. It was not till these nuisances had lasted through a whole generation, and till much had been written about them, that

---

* London Spy ; Tom Brown's Comical View of London and Westminster ; Turner's Propositions for the employing of the Poor. 1678 ; Daily Courant and Daily Journal of June 7. 1733 ; Case of Michael v. Allestree, in 1676, 2 Levinz, p. 172. Michael had been run over by two horses which Allestree was breaking in Lincoln's Inn Fields. The declaration set forth that the defendant "porta deux chivals ungovernable en un coach, et improvide, incaute, et absque debita consideratione ineptitudinis loci la eux drive pur eux faire tractable et apt pur un coach, quels chivals, pur ceo que, per leur ferocite, ne poient estre rule, curre sur le plaintiff et le noie."

the inhabitants applied to Parliament for permission to CHAP.
put up rails, and to plant trees.* III.

When such was the state of the region inhabited by
the most luxurious portion of society, we may easily
believe that the great body of the population suffered
what would now be considered as insupportable grievances. The pavement was detestable: all foreigners
cried shame upon it. The drainage was so bad that
in rainy weather the gutters soon became torrents.
Several facetious poets have commemorated the fury
with which these black rivulets roared down Snow Hill
and Ludgate Hill, bearing to Fleet Ditch a vast tribute
of animal and vegetable filth from the stalls of butchers
and greengrocers. This flood was profusely thrown to
right and left by coaches and carts. To keep as far
from the carriage road as possible was therefore the
wish of every pedestrian. The mild and timid gave the
wall. The bold and athletic took it. If two roisterers
met, they cocked their hats in each other's faces, and
pushed each other about till the weaker was shoved
towards the kennel. If he was a mere bully he sneaked
off, muttering that he should find a time. If he was
pugnacious, the encounter probably ended in a duel
behind Montague House.†

The houses were not numbered. There would indeed
have been little advantage in numbering them; for of
the coachmen, chairmen, porters, and errand boys of
London, a very small proportion could read. It was
necessary to use marks which the most ignorant could

---

* Stat. 12 Geo. I. c. 25.; Commons' Journals, Feb. 25. March 2.
172⅚; London Gardener, 1712;
Evening Post, March 23. 1731. I
have not been able to find this number of the Evening Post; I therefore quote it on the faith of Mr.
Malcolm, who mentions it in his
History of London.

† Lettres sur les Anglois, written
early in the reign of William the
Third; Swift's City Shower; Gay's
Trivia. Johnson used to relate a
curious conversation which he had
with his mother about giving and
taking the wall.

CHAP.
III.

understand. The shops were therefore distinguished by painted or sculptured signs, which gave a gay and grotesque aspect to the streets. The walk from Charing Cross to Whitechapel lay through an endless succession of Saracens' Heads, Royal Oaks, Blue Bears, and Golden Lambs, which disappeared when they were no longer required for the direction of the common people.

When the evening closed in, the difficulty and danger of walking about London became serious indeed. The garret windows were opened, and pails were emptied, with little regard to those who were passing below. Falls, bruises, and broken bones were of constant occurrence. For, till the last year of the reign of Charles the Second, most of the streets were left in profound darkness. Thieves and robbers plied their trade with impunity: yet they were hardly so terrible to peaceable citizens as another class of ruffians. It was a favourite amusement of dissolute young gentlemen to swagger by night about the town, breaking windows, upsetting sedans, beating quiet men, and offering rude caresses to pretty women. Several dynasties of these tyrants had, since the Restoration, domineered over the streets. The Muns and Tityre Tus had given place to the Hectors, and the Hectors had been recently succeeded by the Scourers. At a later period arose the Nicker, the Hawcubite, and the yet more dreaded name of Mohawk.* The machinery for keeping the peace was utterly contemptible. There was an Act of Com-

Police of
London.

---

* Oldham's Imitation of the 3rd Satire of Juvenal, 1682; Shadwell's Scourers, 1690. Many other authorities will readily occur to all who are acquainted with the popular literature of that and the succeeding generation. It may be suspected that some of the Tityre Tus, like good Cavaliers, broke Milton's windows shortly after the Restoration. I am confident that he was thinking of those pests of London when he dictated the noble lines,—

" And in luxurious cities, when the noise
Of riot ascends above their loftiest towers,
And injury and outrage, and when night
Darkens the streets, then wander forth
    the sons
Of Belial, flown with insolence and
    wine."

81

mon Council which provided that more than a thousand watchmen should be constantly on the alert in the city, from sunset to sunrise, and that every inhabitant should take his turn of duty. But this Act was negligently executed. Few of those who were summoned left their homes; and those few generally found it more agreeable to tipple in alehouses than to pace the streets.*

It ought to be noticed that, in the last year of the reign of Charles the Second, began a great change in the police of London, a change which has perhaps added as much to the happiness of the body of the people as revolutions of much greater fame. An ingenious projector, named Edward Heming, obtained letters patent conveying to him, for a term of years, the exclusive right of lighting up London. He undertook, for a moderate consideration, to place a light before every tenth door, on moonless nights, from Michaelmas to Lady Day, and from six to twelve of the clock. Those who now see the capital all the year round, from dusk to dawn, blazing with a splendour beside which the illuminations for La Hogue and Blenheim would have looked pale, may perhaps smile to think of Heming's lanterns, which glimmered feebly before one house in ten during a small part of one night in three. But such was not the feeling of his contemporaries. His scheme was enthusiastically applauded, and furiously attacked. The friends of improvement extolled him as the greatest of all the benefactors of his city. What, they asked, were the boasted inventions of Archimedes, when compared with the achievement of the man who had turned the nocturnal shades into noon day? In spite of these eloquent eulogies the cause of darkness was not left undefended. There were fools in that age who opposed the introduction of what was called the new light as strenuously as fools in our age have op-

* Seymour's London.

posed the introduction of vaccination and railroads, as
strenuously as the fools of an age anterior to the dawn
of history doubtless opposed the introduction of the
plough and of alphabetical writing. Many years after
the date of Heming's patent there were extensive districts in which no lamp was seen.*

White-
friars.
We may easily imagine what, in such times, must have
been the state of the quarters of London which were
peopled by the outcasts of society. Among those
quarters one had attained a scandalous preeminence.
On the confines of the City and the Temple had been
founded, in the thirteenth century, a House of Carmelite
Friars, distinguished by their white hoods. The precinct of this house had, before the Reformation, been a
sanctuary for criminals, and still retained the privilege
of protecting debtors from arrest. Insolvents consequently were to be found in every dwelling, from cellar
to garret. Of these a large proportion were knaves and
libertines, and were followed to their asylum by women
more abandoned than themselves. The civil power was
unable to keep order in a district swarming with such
inhabitants; and thus Whitefriars became the favourite
resort of all who wished to be emancipated from the
restraints of the law. Though the immunities legally
belonging to the place extended only to cases of debt,
cheats, false witnesses, forgers, and highwaymen found
refuge there. For amidst a rabble so desperate no peace
officer's life was in safety. At the cry of "Rescue,"
bullies with swords and cudgels, and termagant hags with
spits and broomsticks, poured forth by hundreds; and the
intruder was fortunate if he escaped back into Fleet Street,
hustled, stripped, and pumped upon. Even the warrant
of the Chief Justice of England could not be executed
without the help of a company of musketeers. Such
relics of the barbarism of the darkest ages were to be

* Angliæ Metropolis, 1690, Sect. 17. entitled, "Of the new lights";
Seymour's London.

found within a short walk of the chambers where Somers was studying history and law, of the chapel where Tillotson was preaching, of the coffee house where Dryden was passing judgment on poems and plays, and of the hall where the Royal Society was examining the astronomical system of Isaac Newton.*

Each of the two cities which made up the capital of England had its own centre of attraction. In the metropolis of commerce the point of convergence was the Exchange; in the metropolis of fashion the Palace. But the Palace did not retain its influence so long as the Exchange. The Revolution completely altered the relations between the Court and the higher classes of society. It was by degrees discovered that the King, in his individual capacity, had very little to give; that coronets and garters, bishoprics and embassies, lordships of the Treasury and tellerships of the Exchequer, nay, even charges in the royal stud and bedchamber, were really bestowed, not by him, but by his advisers. Every ambitious and covetous man perceived that he would consult his own interest far better by acquiring the dominion of a Cornish borough, and by rendering good service to the ministry during a critical session, than by becoming the companion, or even the minion, of his prince. It was therefore in the antechambers, not of George the First and of George the Second, but of Walpole and of Pelham, that the daily crowd of courtiers was to be found. It is also to be remarked that the same Revolution, which made it impossible that our Kings should use the patronage of the state merely for the purpose of gratifying their personal predilections, gave us several Kings unfitted by their education and habits to be gracious and affable hosts. They had been born and bred on the Continent. They never felt themselves at home in our island. If they spoke our language,

* Stowe's Survey of London; London Spy; Stat. 8 & 9 Gul. III. Shadwell's Squire of Alsatia; Ward's cap. 27.

they spoke it inelegantly and with effort. Our national character they never fully understood. Our national manners they hardly attempted to acquire. The most important part of their duty they performed better than any ruler who had preceded them: for they governed strictly according to law: but they could not be the first gentlemen of the realm, the heads of polite society. If ever they unbent, it was in a very small circle where hardly an English face was to be seen; and they were never so happy as when they could escape for a summer to their native land. They had indeed their days of reception for our nobility and gentry; but the reception was mere matter of form, and became at last as solemn a ceremony as a funeral.

Not such was the court of Charles the Second. Whitehall, when he dwelt there, was the focus of political intrigue and of fashionable gaiety. Half the jobbing and half the flirting of the metropolis went on under his roof. Whoever could make himself agreeable to the prince, or could secure the good offices of the mistress, might hope to rise in the world without rendering any service to the government, without being even known by sight to any minister of state. This courtier got a frigate, and that a company; a third, the pardon of a rich offender; a fourth, a lease of crown land on easy terms. If the King notified his pleasure that a briefless lawyer should be made a judge, or that a libertine baronet should be made a peer, the gravest counsellors, after a little murmuring, submitted.* Interest, therefore, drew a constant press of suitors to the gates of the palace; and those gates always stood wide. The King kept open house every day, and all day long, for the good society of London, the extreme Whigs only excepted. Hardly any gentleman had any difficulty in

* See Sir Roger North's account of the way in which Wright was made a judge, and Clarendon's ac- count of the way in which Sir George Savile was made a peer.

making his way to the royal presence. The levee was exactly what the word imports. Some men of quality came every morning to stand round their master, to chat with him while his wig was combed and his cravat tied, and to accompany him in his early walk through the Park. All persons who had been properly introduced might, without any special invitation, go to see him dine, sup, dance, and play at hazard, and might have the pleasure of hearing him tell stories, which indeed he told remarkably well, about his flight from Worcester, and about the misery which he had endured when he was a state prisoner in the hands of the canting meddling preachers of Scotland. Bystanders whom His Majesty recognised often came in for a courteous word. This proved a far more successful kingcraft than any that his father or grandfather had practised. It was not easy for the most austere republican of the school of Marvel to resist the fascination of so much good humour and affability: and many a veteran Cavalier in whose heart the remembrance of unrequited sacrifices and services had been festering during twenty years, was compensated in one moment for wounds and sequestrations by his sovereign's kind nod, and "God bless you, my old friend!"

Whitehall naturally became the chief staple of news. Whenever there was a rumour that any thing important had happened or was about to happen, people hastened thither to obtain intelligence from the fountain head. The galleries presented the appearance of a modern club room at an anxious time. They were full of people inquiring whether the Dutch mail was in, what tidings the express from France had brought, whether John Sobiesky had beaten the Turks, whether the Doge of Genoa was really at Paris. These were matters about which it was safe to talk aloud. But there were subjects concerning which information was asked and given in whispers. Had Halifax got the better of Rochester?

Was there to be a Parliament? Was the Duke of York really going to Scotland? Had Monmouth really been summoned from the Hague? Men tried to read the countenance of every minister as he went through the throng to and from the royal closet. All sorts of auguries were drawn from the tone in which His Majesty spoke to the Lord President, or from the laugh with which His Majesty honoured a jest of the Lord Privy Seal; and in a few hours the hopes and fears inspired by such slight indications had spread to all the coffee houses from St. James's to the Tower.*

The coffee houses.

The coffee house must not be dismissed with a cursory mention. It might indeed at that time have been not improperly called a most important political institution. No Parliament had sat for years. The municipal council of the City had ceased to speak the sense of the citizens. Public meetings, harangues, resolutions, and the rest of the modern machinery of agitation had not yet come into fashion. Nothing resembling the modern newspaper existed. In such circumstances the coffee houses were the chief organs through which the public opinion of the metropolis vented itself.

The first of these establishments had been set up, in the time of the Commonwealth, by a Turkey merchant, who had acquired among the Mahometans a taste for their favourite beverage. The convenience of being able to make appointments in any part of the town, and of being able to pass evenings socially at a very small charge, was so great that the fashion spread fast. Every man of the upper or middle class went daily to his coffee house to learn the news and to discuss it.

---

* The sources from which I have drawn my information about the state of the court are too numerous to recapitulate. Among them are the Despatches of Barillon, Van Citters, Ronquillo, and Adda, the Travels of the Grand Duke Cosmo, the works of Roger North, the Diaries of Pepys, Evelyn, and Teonge, and the Memoirs of Grammont and Reresby.

Every coffee house had one or more orators to whose
eloquence the crowd listened with admiration, and who soon became, what the journalists of our time have been called, a fourth Estate of the realm. The Court had long seen with uneasiness the growth of this new power in the state. An attempt had been made, during Danby's administration, to close the coffee houses. But men of all parties missed their usual places of resort so much that there was an universal outcry. The government did not venture, in opposition to a feeling so strong and general, to enforce a regulation of which the legality might well be questioned. Since that time ten years had elapsed, and during those years the number and influence of the coffee houses had been constantly increasing. Foreigners remarked that the coffee house was that which especially distinguished London from all other cities; that the coffee house was the Londoner's home, and that those who wished to find a gentleman commonly asked, not whether he lived in Fleet Street or Chancery Lane, but whether he frequented the Grecian or the Rainbow. Nobody was excluded from these places who laid down his penny at the bar. Yet every rank and profession, and every shade of religious and political opinion, had its own head quarters. There were houses near Saint James's Park where fops congregated, their heads and shoulders covered with black or flaxen wigs, not less ample than those which are now worn by the Chancellor and by the Speaker of the House of Commons. The wig came from Paris; and so did the rest of the fine gentleman's ornaments, his embroidered coat, his fringed gloves, and the tassel which upheld his pantaloons. The conversation was in that dialect which, long after it had ceased to be spoken in fashionable circles, continued, in the mouth of Lord Foppington, to excite the mirth of theatres.* The atmosphere was like

* The chief peculiarity of this words, the O was pronounced like dialect was that, in a large class of A. Thus Lord was pronounced

B B

that of a perfumer's shop. Tobacco in any other form than that of richly scented snuff was held in abomination. If any clown, ignorant of the usages of the house, called for a pipe, the sneers of the whole assembly and the short answers of the waiters soon convinced him that he had better go somewhere else. Nor, indeed, would he have had far to go. For, in general, the coffee rooms reeked with tobacco like a guardroom; and strangers sometimes expressed their surprise that so many people should leave their own firesides to sit in the midst of eternal fog and stench. Nowhere was the smoking more constant than at Will's. That celebrated house, situated between Covent Garden and Bow Street, was sacred to polite letters. There the talk was about poetical justice and the unities of place and time. There was a faction for Perrault and the moderns, a faction for Boileau and the ancients. One group debated whether Paradise Lost ought not to have been in rhyme. To another an envious poetaster demonstrated that Venice Preserved ought to have been hooted from the stage. Under no roof was a greater variety of figures to be seen. There were Earls in stars and garters, clergymen in cassocks and bands, pert Templars, sheepish lads from the Universities, translators and index makers in ragged coats of frieze. The great press was to get near the chair where John Dryden sate. In winter that chair was always in the warmest nook by the fire; in summer it stood in the balcony. To bow to the Laureate, and to hear his opinion of Racine's last tragedy or of Bossu's treatise on epic poetry, was thought a privilege. A pinch from his snuff box was an honour sufficient to turn the head of a young enthusiast. There were coffee houses where the first medical men might be consulted. Doctor John Radcliffe, who, in

Lard. See Vanbrugh's Relapse. Lord Sunderland was a great master of this court tune, as Roger North calls it; and Titus Oates affected it in the hope of passing for a fine gentleman. Examen, 77. 254.

the year 1685, rose to the largest practice in London, came daily, at the hour when the Exchange was full, from his house in Bow Street, then a fashionable part of the capital, to Garraway's, and was to be found, surrounded by surgeons and apothecaries, at a particular table. There were Puritan coffee houses where no oath was heard, and where lankhaired men discussed election and reprobation through their noses; Jew coffee houses where darkeyed money changers from Venice and from Amsterdam greeted each other; and Popish coffee houses where, as good Protestants believed, Jesuits planned, over their cups, another great fire, and cast silver bullets to shoot the King.*

These gregarious habits had no small share in forming the character of the Londoner of that age. He was, indeed, a different being from the rustic Englishman. There was not then the intercourse which now exists between the two classes. Only very great men were in the habit of dividing the year between town and country. Few esquires came to the capital thrice in their lives. Nor was it yet the practice of all citizens in easy circumstances to breathe the fresh air of the fields and woods during some weeks of every summer. A cockney, in a rural village, was stared at as much as if he had intruded into a Kraal of Hottentots. On the other hand, when the lord of a Lincolnshire or Shropshire manor appeared in Fleet Street, he was as easily distinguished from the resident population as a Turk or a Lascar. His dress, his gait, his accent, the

---

* Lettres sur les Anglois; Tom Brown's Tour; Ward's London Spy; The Character of a Coffee House, 1673; Rules and Orders of the Coffee House, 1674; Coffee Houses vindicated, 1675; A Satyr against Coffee; North's Examen, 138.; Life of Guildford, 152.; Life of Sir Dudley North, 149.; Life of Dr. Radcliffe, published by Curll in 1715. The liveliest description of Will's is in the City and Country Mouse. There is a remarkable passage about the influence of the coffee house orators in Halstead's Succinct Genealogies, printed in 1685.

manner in which he gazed at the shops, stumbled into the gutters, ran against the porters, and stood under the waterspouts, marked him out as an excellent subject for the operations of swindlers and banterers. Bullies jostled him into the kennel. Hackney coachmen splashed him from head to foot. Thieves explored with perfect security the huge pockets of his horseman's coat, while he stood entranced by the splendour of the Lord Mayor's show. Moneydroppers, sore from the cart's tail, introduced themselves to him, and appeared to him the most honest friendly gentlemen that he had ever seen. Painted women, the refuse of Lewkner Lane and Whetstone Park, passed themselves on him for countesses and maids of honour. If he asked his way to St. James's, his informants sent him to Mile End. If he went into a shop, he was instantly discerned to be a fit purchaser of every thing that nobody else would buy, of secondhand embroidery, copper rings, and watches that would not go. If he rambled into any fashionable coffee house, he became a mark for the insolent derision of fops and the grave waggery of Templars. Enraged and mortified, he soon returned to his mansion, and there, in the homage of his tenants and the conversation of his boon companions, found consolation for the vexations and humiliations which he had undergone. There he was once more a great man, and saw nothing above himself except when at the assizes he took his seat on the bench near the Judge, or when at the muster of the militia he saluted the Lord Lieutenant.

Difficulty of travelling.
The chief cause which made the fusion of the different elements of society so imperfect was the extreme difficulty which our ancestors found in passing from place to place. Of all inventions, the alphabet and the printing press alone excepted, those inventions which abridge distance have done most for the civilisation of our species. Every improvement of the means of locomotion

benefits mankind morally and intellectually as well as materially, and not only facilitates the interchange of the various productions of nature and art, but tends to remove national and provincial antipathies, and to bind together all the branches of the great human family. In the seventeenth century the inhabitants of London were, for almost every practical purpose, farther from Reading than they now are from Edinburgh, and farther from Edinburgh than they now are from Vienna.

The subjects of Charles the Second were not, it is true, quite unacquainted with that principle which has, in our own time, produced an unprecedented revolution in human affairs, which has enabled navies to advance in face of wind and tide, and brigades of troops, attended by all their baggage and artillery, to traverse kingdoms at a pace equal to that of the fleetest race horse. The Marquess of Worcester had recently observed the expansive power of moisture rarefied by heat. After many experiments he had succeeded in constructing a rude steam engine, which he called a fire water work, and which he pronounced to be an admirable and most forcible instrument of propulsion.* But the Marquess was suspected to be a madman, and known to be a Papist. His inventions, therefore, found no favourable reception. His fire water work might, perhaps, furnish matter for conversation at a meeting of the Royal Society, but was not applied to any practical purpose. There were no railways, except a few made of timber, on which coals were carried from the mouths of the Northumbrian pits to the banks of the Tyne.† There was very little internal communication by water. A few attempts had been made to deepen and embank the natural streams, but with slender success. Hardly a single navigable canal had been even projected. The English of that day were in the habit

* Century of Inventions, 1663, No. 68.
† North's Life of Guildford, 136.

of talking with mingled admiration and despair of the immense trench by which Lewis the Fourteenth had made a junction between the Atlantic and the Mediterranean. They little thought that their country would, in the course of a few generations, be intersected, at the cost of private adventurers, by artificial rivers making up more than four times the length of the Thames, the Severn, and the Trent together.

Badness of
the roads. It was by the highways that both travellers and goods generally passed from place to place; and those highways appear to have been far worse than might have been expected from the degree of wealth and civilisation which the nation had even then attained. On the best lines of communication the ruts were deep, the descents precipitous, and the way often such as it was hardly possible to distinguish, in the dusk, from the unenclosed heath and fen which lay on both sides. Ralph Thoresby, the antiquary, was in danger of losing his way on the great North road, between Barnby Moor and Tuxford, and actually lost his way between Doncaster and York.[*] Pepys and his wife, travelling in their own coach, lost their way between Newbury and Reading. In the course of the same tour they lost their way near Salisbury, and were in danger of having to pass the night on the plain.[†] It was only in fine weather that the whole breadth of the road was available for wheeled vehicles. Often the mud lay deep on the right and the left; and only a narrow track of firm ground rose above the quagmire.[‡] At such times obstructions and quarrels were frequent, and the path was sometimes blocked up during a long time by carriers, neither of whom would break the way. It happened, almost every day, that coaches stuck fast, until a team of cattle could be procured from some neighbouring farm, to tug them out of the slough. But in bad seasons the traveller had to

[*] Thoresby's Diary, Oct. 21. 1680, Aug. 3. 1712.
[†] Pepys's Diary, June 12. and 16. 1668.
[‡] Ibid. Feb. 28. 1660.

encounter inconveniences still more serious. Thoresby, who was in the habit of travelling between Leeds and the capital, has recorded, in his Diary, such a series of perils and disasters as might suffice for a journey to the Frozen Ocean or to the Desert of Sahara. On one occasion he learned that the floods were out between Ware and London, that passengers had to swim for their lives, and that a higgler had perished in the attempt to cross. In consequence of these tidings he turned out of the high road, and was conducted across some meadows, where it was necessary for him to ride to the saddle skirts in water.* In the course of another journey he narrowly escaped being swept away by an inundation of the Trent. He was afterwards detained at Stamford four days, on account of the state of the roads, and then ventured to proceed only because fourteen members of the House of Commons, who were going up in a body to Parliament with guides and numerous attendants, took him into their company.† On the roads of Derbyshire, travellers were in constant fear for their necks, and were frequently compelled to alight and lead their beasts.‡ The great route through Wales to Holyhead was in such a state that, in 1685, a viceroy, going to Ireland, was five hours in travelling fourteen miles, from Saint Asaph to Conway. Between Conway and Beaumaris he was forced to walk great part of the way; and his lady was carried in a litter. His coach was, with much difficulty, and by the help of many hands, brought after him entire. In general, carriages were taken to pieces at Conway, and borne, on the shoulders of stout Welsh peasants, to the Menai Straits.§ In some parts of Kent and Sussex, none but

---

* Thoresby's Diary, May 17. 1695.

† Ibid. Dec. 27. 1708.

‡ Tour in Derbyshire, by J. Browne, son of Sir Thomas Browne,

1662. Cotton's Angler, 1676.

§ Correspondence of Henry Earl of Clarendon, Dec. 30. 1685, Jan. 1. 1686.

the strongest horses could, in winter, get through the bog, in which, at every step, they sank deep. The markets were often inaccessible during several months. It is said that the fruits of the earth were sometimes suffered to rot in one place, while in another place, distant only a few miles, the supply fell far short of the demand. The wheeled carriages were, in this district, generally pulled by oxen.* When Prince George of Denmark visited the stately mansion of Petworth in wet weather, he was six hours in going nine miles; and it was necessary that a body of sturdy hinds should be on each side of his coach, in order to prop it. Of the carriages which conveyed his retinue several were upset and injured. A letter from one of the party has been preserved, in which the unfortunate courtier complains that, during fourteen hours, he never once alighted, except when his coach was overturned or stuck fast in the mud.†

One chief cause of the badness of the roads seems to have been the defective state of the law. Every parish was bound to repair the highways which passed through it. The peasantry were forced to give their gratuitous labour six days in the year. If this was not sufficient, hired labour was employed, and the expense was met by a parochial rate. That a route connecting two great towns, which have a large and thriving trade with each other, should be maintained at the cost of the rural population scattered between them is obviously unjust; and this injustice was peculiarly glaring in the case of the great North road, which traversed very poor and thinly inhabited districts, and joined very rich and populous districts. Indeed it was not in the power of the parishes of Huntingdonshire to mend a highway worn by the constant traffic between the West Riding

---

* Postlethwaite's Dict., Roads; History of Hawkhurst, in the Bibliotheca Topographica Britannica. † Annals of Queen Anne, 1703, Appendix, No. 3.

of Yorkshire and London. Soon after the Restoration this grievance attracted the notice of Parliament; and an act, the first of our many turnpike acts, was passed, imposing a small toll on travellers and goods, for the purpose of keeping some parts of this important line of communication in good repair.* This innovation, however, excited many murmurs; and the other great avenues to the capital were long left under the old system. A change was at length effected, but not without much difficulty. For unjust and absurd taxation to which men are accustomed is often borne far more willingly than the most reasonable impost which is new. It was not till many toll bars had been violently pulled down, till the troops had in many districts been forced to act against the people, and till much blood had been shed, that a good system was introduced.† By slow degrees reason triumphed over prejudice; and our island is now crossed in every direction by near thirty thousand miles of turnpike road.

On the best highways heavy articles were, in the time of Charles the Second, generally conveyed from place to place by stage waggons. In the straw of these vehicles nestled a crowd of passengers, who could not afford to travel by coach or on horseback, and who were prevented by infirmity, or by the weight of their luggage, from going on foot. The expense of transmitting heavy goods in this way was enormous. From London to Birmingham the charge was seven pounds a ton; from London to Exeter twelve pounds a ton.‡ This was about fifteen pence a ton for every mile, more by a third than was afterwards charged on turnpike roads, and fifteen times what is now demanded by railway companies. The cost of conveyance amounted to a pro-

---

* 15 Car. II. c. 1.
  † The evils of the old system are strikingly set forth in many petitions which appear in the Commons' Journal of 172⅚. How fierce an opposition was offered to the new system may be learned from the Gentleman's Magazine of 1749.
  ‡ Postlethwaite's Dict., Roads.

CHAP.
III.

hibitory tax on many useful articles. Coal in particular was never seen except in the districts where it was produced, or in the districts to which it could be carried by sea, and was indeed always known in the south of England by the name of sea coal.

On byroads, and generally throughout the country north of York and west of Exeter, goods were carried by long trains of packhorses. These strong and patient beasts, the breed of which is now extinct, were attended by a class of men who seem to have borne much resemblance to the Spanish muleteers. A traveller of humble condition often found it convenient to perform a journey mounted on a packsaddle between two baskets, under the care of these hardy guides. The expense of this mode of conveyance was small. But the caravan moved at a foot's pace; and in winter the cold was often insupportable.*

The rich commonly travelled in their own carriages, with at least four horses. Cotton, the facetious poet, attempted to go from London to the Peak with a single pair, but found at Saint Albans that the journey would be insupportably tedious, and altered his plan.† A coach and six is in our time never seen, except as part of some pageant. The frequent mention therefore of such equipages in old books is likely to mislead us. We attribute to magnificence what was really the effect of a very disagreeable necessity. People, in the time of Charles the Second, travelled with six horses, because with a smaller number there was great danger of sticking fast in the mire. Nor were even six horses always sufficient. Vanbrugh, in the succeeding generation, described with great humour the way in which a country gentleman, newly chosen a member of Parliament, went up to London. On that occasion all the exertions of six beasts, two of which had been taken from the plough, could not save the family coach from being imbedded in a quagmire.

CHAP
III.

---

* Loidis and Elmete ; Marshall's Rural Economy of England. In 1739 Roderic Random came from Scotland to Newcastle on a packhorse.

† Cotton's Epistle to J. Bradshaw.

All the various dangers by which the traveller was beset were greatly increased by darkness. He was therefore commonly desirous of having the shelter of a roof during the night; and such shelter it was not difficult to obtain. From a very early period the inns of England had been renowned. Our first great poet had described the excellent accommodation which they afforded to the pilgrims of the fourteenth century. Nine and twenty persons, with their horses, found room in the wide chambers and stables of the Tabard in Southwark. The food was of the best, and the wines such as drew the company on to drink largely. Two hundred years later, under the reign of Elizabeth, William Harrison gave a lively description of the plenty and comfort of the great hostelries. The Continent of Europe, he said, could show nothing like them. There were some in which two or three hundred people, with their horses, could without difficulty be lodged and fed. The bedding, the tapestry, above all, the abundance of clean and fine linen was matter of wonder. Valuable plate was often set on the tables. Nay, there were signs which had cost thirty or forty pounds. In the seventeenth century England abounded with excellent inns of every rank. The traveller sometimes, in a small village, lighted on a public house such as Walton has described, where the brick floor was swept clean, where the walls were stuck round with ballads, where the sheets smelt of lavender, and where a blazing fire, a cup of good ale, and a dish of trouts fresh from the neighbouring brook, were to be procured at small charge. At the larger houses of entertainment were to be found beds hung with silk, choice cookery, and claret equal to the best which was drunk in London.* The innkeepers too, it was said, were not like other innkeepers. On the Continent the landlord was the

* See the prologue to the Canterbury Tales, Harrison's Historical Description of the Island of Great Britain, and Pepys's account of his tour in the summer of 1668. The excellence of the English inns is noticed in the Travels of the Grand Duke Cosmo.

tyrant of those who crossed the threshold. In England he was a servant. Never was an Englishman more at home than when he took his ease in his inn. Even men of fortune, who might in their own mansions have enjoyed every luxury, were often in the habit of passing their evenings in the parlour of some neighbouring house of public entertainment. They seem to have thought that comfort and freedom could in no other place be enjoyed in equal perfection. This feeling continued during many generations to be a national peculiarity. The liberty and jollity of inns long furnished matter to our novelists and dramatists. Johnson declared that a tavern chair was the throne of human felicity; and Shenstone gently complained that no private roof, however friendly, gave the wanderer so warm a welcome as that which was to be found at an inn.

Many conveniences, which were unknown at Hampton Court and Whitehall in the seventeenth century, are in all modern hotels. Yet on the whole it is certain that the improvement of our houses of public entertainment has by no means kept pace with the improvement of our roads and of our conveyances. Nor is this strange; for it is evident that, all other circumstances being supposed equal, the inns will be best where the means of locomotion are worst. The quicker the rate of travelling, the less important is it that there should be numerous agreeable resting places for the traveller. A hundred and sixty years ago a person who came up to the capital from a remote county generally required, by the way, twelve or fifteen meals, and lodging for five or six nights. If he were a great man, he expected the meals and lodging to be comfortable, and even luxurious. At present we fly from York or Exeter to London by the light of a single winter's day. At present, therefore, a traveller seldom interrupts his journey merely for the sake of rest and refreshment. The consequence is that hundreds of excellent inns have fallen into utter decay. In a short time no good houses of that description will be found, except at places where strangers are likely to be detained by business or pleasure.

The mode in which correspondence was carried on between distant places may excite the scorn of the present generation; yet it was such as might have moved the admiration and envy of the polished nations of antiquity, or of the contemporaries of Raleigh and Cecil. A rude and imperfect establishment of posts for the conveyance of letters had been set up by Charles the First, and had been swept away by the civil war. Under the Commonwealth the design was resumed. At the Restoration the proceeds of the Post Office, after all expenses had been paid, were settled on the Duke of York. On most lines of road the mails went out and came in only on the alternate days. In Cornwall, in the fens of Lincolnshire, and among the hills and lakes of Cumberland, letters were received only once a week. During a royal progress a daily post was despatched from the capital to the place where the court sojourned. There was also daily communication between London and the Downs; and the same privilege was sometimes extended to Tunbridge Wells and Bath at the seasons when those places were crowded by the great. The bags were carried on horseback day and night at the rate of about five miles an hour.*

The revenue of this establishment was not derived solely from the charge for the transmission of letters. The Post Office alone was entitled to furnish post horses; and, from the care with which this monopoly was guarded, we may infer that it was found profitable.†

---

* Stat. 12 Car. II. c. 35.; Chamberlayne's State of England, 1684; Angliæ Metropolis, 1690; London Gazette, June 22. 1685, August 15. 1687.

† London Gazette, Sept. 14. 1685.

The general effect of the evidence which has been submitted to the reader seems hardly to admit of doubt. Yet, in spite of evidence, many will still image to themselves the England of the Stuarts as a more pleasant country than the England in which we live. It may at first sight seem strange that society, while constantly moving forward with eager speed, should be constantly looking backward with tender regret. But these two propensities, inconsistent as they may appear, can easily be resolved into the same principle. Both spring from our impatience of the state in which we actually are. That impatience, while it stimulates us to surpass preceding generations, disposes us to overrate their happiness. It is, in some sense, unreasonable and ungrateful in us to be constantly discontented with a condition which is constantly improving. But, in truth, there is constant improvement precisely because there is constant discontent. If we were perfectly satisfied with the present, we should cease to contrive, to labour, and to save with a view to the future. And it is natural that, being dissatisfied with the present, we should form a too favourable estimate of the past.

In truth we are under a deception similar to that which misleads the traveller in the Arabian desert. Beneath the caravan all is dry and bare: but far in advance, and far in the rear, is the semblance of refreshing waters. The pilgrims hasten forward and find nothing but sand where, an hour before, they had seen a lake. They turn their eyes and see a lake where, an hour before, they were toiling through sand. A similar illusion seems to haunt nations through every stage of the long progress from poverty and barbarism to the highest degrees of opulence and civilisation. But, if we resolutely chase the mirage backward, we shall find it recede before us into the regions of fabulous antiquity. It is now the fashion to place the golden age of England in times when noblemen were destitute of comforts the want of which would be intolerable to a

101

modern footman, when farmers and shopkeepers break-
fasted on loaves the very sight of which would raise
a riot in a modern workhouse, when to have a clean
shirt once a week was a privilege reserved for the
higher class of gentry, when men died faster in the
purest country air than they now die in the most pes-
tilential lanes of our towns, and when men died faster
in the lanes of our towns than they now die on the
coast of Guiana. We too shall, in our turn, be out-

stripped, and in our turn be envied. It may well be,
in the twentieth century, that the peasant of Dorset-
shire may think himself miserably paid with twenty
shillings a week; that the carpenter at Greenwich may
receive ten shillings a day; that labouring men may be
as little used to dine without meat as they now are to
eat rye bread; that sanitary police and medical discoveries may have added several more years to the
average length of human life; that numerous comforts and luxuries which are now unknown, or confined
to a few, may be within the reach of every diligent and
thrifty working man. And yet it may then be the
mode to assert that the increase of wealth and the progress of science have benefited the few at the expense
of the many, and to talk of the reign of Queen Victoria
as the time when England was truly merry England,
when all classes were bound together by brotherly sympathy, when the rich did not grind the faces of the
poor, and when the poor did not envy the splendour of
the rich.

Sir Thomas More,   UTOPIA   (Trans. by R. Adams)

1. Do you think More wrote *Utopia* in order to suggest that the customs of the Utopians be adopted by his own society? What other purposes might he have had in writing this book? Does More's attitude toward the Utopians give you any clues about his feeling about his own society?

2. In modern parlance the word "Utopian" has taken on the connotation of ideal, but impractical. Which, if any, of the customs of Utopia seem realistic or workable? Which do not and why?

3. Why is life so happy in Utopia? What is the role of work there? How is it divided? What is the attitude of the Utopians toward wealth? How does it contrast to ours?

4. What does More mean by "living according to nature"? How would you compare More's view of what is natural with Rousseau's and with Darwin's?

5. How is the "pecking order" in Utopia different from that in our own society?

6. What is the relationship between town and country in Utopia? Compare it to that which Macaulay describes in England.

7. What is the religion of the Utopians? How would you compare it to the civil religion discussed by Bellah in the "Faith and Morals" unit?

8. What role does the family play in Utopia? What is the relationship there between men and women?

9. How much room for individual and cultural differences is there in Utopia? Would you say individuals are free there? Would you like to live in Utopia? Why or why not?

More (1478-1535) was an English writer and statesman during the Renaissance. Although Chancellor to Henry VIII, More lost his life at the hands of this monarch. He died a martyr for the Roman Catholicism which Henry had rejected. His *Utopia* (the name means "Nowhere") became the model for a new literary genre - the depiction of an ideal commonwealth; it shows the influence of both humanist social satire and of reports concerning Indian cultures encountered by explorers in the New World during More's time.

THE SECOND BOOK

The Second Book of the Communication of Raphael Hythloday, concerning the best state of a commonwealth, containing the description of Utopia, with a large declaration of the Godly government, and of all the good laws and orders of the same Island.

THE island of Utopia containeth in breadth in the middle part of it (for there it is broadest) two hundred miles. Which breadth continueth through the most part of the land, saving that by little and little it cometh in, and waxeth narrower towards both the ends. Which fetching about a circuit or compass of five hundred miles, do fashion the whole island like to the new moon. Between these two corners the sea runneth in, dividing them asunder by the distance of eleven miles or thereabouts, and there surmounteth into a large and wide sea, which by reason that the land on every side compasseth it about, and sheltereth it from the winds, is not rough, nor mounteth not with great waves, but almost floweth quietly, not much unlike a great standing pool: and maketh almost all the space within the belly of the land in manner of a haven: and to the great commodity of the inhabitants receiveth in ships towards every part of the land. The forefronts or frontiers of the two corners, what with fords and shelves, and what with rocks be very jeopardous and dangerous. In the middle distance between them both standeth up above the water a great rock, which therefore is nothing perilous because it is in sight. Upon the top of this rock is a fair and a strong tower builded, which they hold with a garrison of men. Other rocks there be that lie hid under the water, and therefore be dangerous. The channels be known only to themselves. And therefore it seldom chanceth that any stranger unless he be guided by a Utopian can come into this haven. Insomuch that they themselves could scarcely enter without jeopardy, but that their way is directed and ruled by certain landmarks standing on the shore. By turning, translating, and removing these marks into other places they may destroy their enemies' navies, be they never so many. The outside of the land is also full of havens, but the landing is so surely defenced, what by nature, and what by workmanship of man's hand, that a few defenders may drive back many armies. Howbeit as they say, and as the fashion of the place itself doth partly show, it was not ever compassed about with the sea. But King Utopus, whose name, as conqueror the island beareth (for before that time it was called Abraxa) which also brought the rude and wild people to that excellent perfection in all good fashions, humanity, and civil gentleness, wherein they now go beyond all the people of the world: even at his first arriving and entering upon the land, forthwith obtaining the victory, caused fifteen miles space of uplandish ground, where the sea had no passage, to be cut and digged up.

And so brought the sea round about the land. He set to this work not only the inhabitants of the island (because they should not think it done in contumely and despite) but also all his own soldiers. Thus the work being divided into so great a number of workmen, was with exceeding marvellous speed despatched. Insomuch that the borderers, which at the first began to mock, and to jest at this vain enterprise, then turned their laughter to marvel at the success, and to fear. There be in the island fifty-four large and fair cities, or shire towns, agreeing all together in one tongue, in like manners, institutions and laws. They be all set and situate alike, and in all points fashioned alike, as far forth as the place or plot suffereth.

Of these cities they that be nighest together be twenty-four miles asunder. Again there is none of them distant from the next above one day's journey afoot. There come yearly to Amaurote out of every city three old men wise and well experienced, there to entreat and debate, of the common matters of the land. For this city (because it standeth just in the midst of the island, and is therefore most meet for the ambassadors of all parts of the realm) is taken for the chief and head city. The precincts and bounds of the shires be so commodiously appointed out, and set forth for the cities, that never a one of them all hath of any side less than twenty miles of ground, and of some side also much more, as of that part where the cities be of farther distance asunder. None of the cities desire to enlarge the bounds and limits of their shires. For they count themselves rather the good husbands than the owners of their lands. They have in the country in all parts of the shire houses or farms builded, well appointed and furnished with all sorts of instruments and tools belonging to husbandry. These houses be inhabited of the citizens, which come thither to dwell by course. No household or farm in the country hath fewer than forty persons, men and women, besides two bondmen, which be all under the rule and order of the good man, and the good wife of the house, being both very sage and discreet persons. And every thirty farms or families have one head ruler, which is called a philarch, being as it were a head bailiff. Out of every one of these families or farms cometh every year into the city twenty persons which have continued two years before in the country. In their place so many fresh be sent thither out of the city, which of them that have been there a year already, and be therefore expert and cunning in husbandry, shall be instructed and taught. And they the next year shall teach other. This order is used for fear that either scarceness of victuals, or some other like incommodity should chance, through lack of knowledge, if they should be altogether new, and fresh, and unexpert in husbandry. This manner and fashion of yearly changing and renewing the occupiers of husbandry, though it be solemn and customably used, to the intent that no man shall be constrained against his will to continue long in that hard and sharp kind of life, yet many of them have such a pleasure and delight in husbandry, that they obtain a longer space of years. These husbandmen plough and till the ground, and breed up cattle, and make ready wood, which they carry to the city either by land, or by water, as they may most conveniently. They bring up a great multitude of poultry, and that by a marvellous policy. For the hens do not sit upon the eggs: but by keeping them in a certain equal heat they bring life into them, and hatch them. The chickens, as soon as they be come out of the shell, follow men and women instead of the hens. They bring up very few horses: nor none, but very fierce ones: and for none other use or purpose, but only to exercise their youth in riding and feats of arms. For oxen be put to all the labour of ploughing and drawing. Which they grant to be not so good as horses at a sudden brunt, and (as we say) at a dead lift, but yet they hold opinion that they will abide and suffer much more labour and pain than horses will. And they think that they be not in danger and subject unto so many diseases, and that they be kept and maintained with much less cost and charge: and finally that they be good for meat, when they be past labour. They sow corn only for bread. For their drink is either wine made of grapes, or else of apples, or pears, or else it is clean water. And many times mead made of honey or liquorice sodden in water, for thereof they have great store. And though they know certainly (for they know it perfectly indeed) how much victuals the city with the whole country or shire round about it doth spend: yet they sow much more corn, and breed up much more cattle, than serveth for their own use, and the overplus they part among their borderers. Whatsoever necessary things be lacking in the country, all such stuff they fetch out of the city: where without any exchange they easily obtain it of the magistrates of the city. For every month many of them go into the city on the holy day. When their harvest day draweth near and is at hand, then the philarchs, which be the head officers and bailiffs of husbandry, send word to the magistrates of the city what number of harvest men is needful to be sent to them out of the city. The which company of harvest men being there ready at the day appointed, almost in one fair day despatcheth all the harvest work.

Of the Cities, and namely of Amaurote

As for their cities, he that knoweth one of them, knoweth them all: they be all so like one to another, as farforth as the nature of the place permitteth. I will describe therefore to you one or other of them, for it skilleth not greatly which: but which rather than Amaurote? Of them all this is the worthiest and of most dignity. For the residue acknowledge it for the head city, because there is the council house. Nor to me any of them all is better beloved, as wherein I lived five whole years together. The city of Amaurote standeth upon the side of a low hill in fashion almost four square. For the breadth of it beginneth a little beneath the top of the hill, and still continueth by the space of two miles, until it come to the river of Anyder. The length of it, which lieth by the river's side, is somewhat more. The river of Anyder riseth twenty-four miles above Amaurote out of a little spring. But being increased by other small floods and brooks that run into it, and among other two somewhat big ones, before the city it is half a mile broad, and farther broader. And sixty miles beyond the city it falleth into the Ocean sea. By all that space that lieth between the sea and the city, and a good sort of miles also above the city, the water ebbeth and floweth six hours together with a swift tide. When the sea floweth in, for the length of thirty miles it filleth all the Anyder with salt water, and driveth back the fresh water of the river. And somewhat further it changeth the sweetness of the fresh water with saltness. But a little beyond that the river waxeth sweet, and runneth forby the city fresh and pleasant. And when the sea ebbeth, and goeth back again, the fresh water followeth it almost even to the very fall into the sea. There goeth a bridge over the river made not of piles of timber, but of stonework with gorgeous and substantial arches at that part of the city that is farthest from the sea: to the intent that ships may go along forby all the side of the city without let. They have also another river which indeed is not very great. But it runneth gently and pleasantly. For it riseth even out of the same hill that the city standeth upon, and runneth down a slope through the midst of the city into Anyder. And because it riseth a little without the city, the Amaurotians have inclosed the head spring of it with strong fences and bulwarks, and so have joined it to the city. This is done to the intent that the water should not be stopped nor turned away, or poisoned, if their enemies should chance to come upon them. From thence the water is derived and brought down in canals of brick divers ways into the lower parts of the city. Where that cannot be done, by reason that the place will not suffer it, there they gather the rain water in great cisterns, which doth them as good service. The city is compassed about with a high and thick wall full of turrets and bulwarks. A dry ditch, but deep, and broad, and overgrown with bushes, briers and thorns, goeth about three sides or quarters of the city. To the fourth side the river itself serveth for a ditch. The streets be appointed and set forth very commodious and handsome, both for carriage, and also against the winds. The houses be of fair and gorgeous building, and in the street side they stand joined together in a long row through the whole street without any partition or separation. The streets be twenty feet broad. On the back side of the houses through the whole length of the street, lie large gardens which be closed in round about with the back part of the streets. Every house hath two doors, one into the street, and a postern door on the back side into the garden. These doors be made with two leaves, never locked nor bolted, so easy to be opened, that they will follow the least drawing of a finger, and shut again by themselves. Every man that will, may go in, for there is nothing within the houses that is private, or any man's own. And every tenth year they change their houses by lot. They set great store by their gardens. In them they have vineyards, all manner of fruit, herbs, and flowers, so pleasant, so well furnished and so finely kept, that I never saw thing more fruitful, nor better trimmed in any place. Their study and diligence herein cometh not only of pleasure, but also of a certain strife and contention that is between street and street, concerning the trimming, husbanding, and furnishing of their gardens: every man for his own part. And verily you shall not lightly find in all the city anything, that is more commodious, either for the profit of the citizens, or for pleasure. And therefore it may seem that the first founder of the city minded nothing so much as he did these gardens. For they say that King Utopus himself, even at the first beginning appointed and drew forth the platform of the city into this fashion and figure that it hath now, but the gallant garnishing, and the beautiful setting forth of it, whereunto he saw that one man's age would not suffice: that he left to his posterity. For their chronicles, which they keep written with all diligent circumspection, containing the history of 1760 years, even from the first conquest of the island, record and witness that the houses in the beginning were very low, and like homely cottages or poor shepherd houses, made at all adventures of every rude piece of wood, that came first to hands, with mud walls and ridged roofs, thatched over with straw. But now the houses be curiously builded after a gorgeous and gallant sort, with three stories one over another. The outsides of the walls be made either of hard flint, or of plaster, or else of brick, and the inner sides be well strengthened with timber work.

The roofs be plain and flat, covered with a certain kind of plaster that is of no cost, and yet so tempered that no fire can hurt or perish it, and withstandeth the violence of the weather better than any lead. They keep the wind out of their windows with glass, for it is there much used, and somewhere also with fine linen cloth dipped in oil or amber, and that for two commodities. For by this means more light cometh in, and the wind is better kept out.

Of the Magistrates

Every thirty families or farms, choose them yearly an officer, which in their old language is called the syphogrant, and by a newer name, the philarch. Every ten syphogrants, with all their 300 families be under an officer which was once called the tranibore, now the chief philarch. Moreover as concerning the election of the prince, all the syphogrants, which be in number 200, first be sworn to choose him whom they think most meet and expedient. Then by a secret election, they name prince, one of those four whom the people before named unto them. For out of the four quarters of the city there be four chosen, out of every quarter one, to stand for the election: which be put up to the council. The prince's office continueth all his lifetime, unless he be deposed or put down for suspicion of tyranny. They choose the tranibores yearly, but lightly they change them not. All the other offices be but for one year. The tranibores every third day, and sometimes, if need be, oftener come into the council house with the prince. Their council is concerning the commonwealth. If there be any controversies among the commoners, which be very few, they despatch and end them by-and-by. They take ever two syphogrants to them in counsel, and every day a new couple. And it is provided that nothing touching the commonwealth shall be confirmed and ratified unless it have been reasoned of and debated three days in the council, before it be decreed. It is death to have any consultation for the commonwealth out of the council, or the place of the common election. This statute, they say, was made to the intent that the prince and tranibores might not easily conspire together to oppress the people by tyranny, and to change the state of the weal public. Therefore matters of great weight and importance be brought to the election house of the syphogrants, which open the matter to their families. And afterward, when they have consulted among themselves, they show their device to the council. Sometimes the matter is brought before the council of the whole island. Furthermore this custom also the council useth, to dispute or reason of no matter the same day that it is first proposed or put forth, but to defer it to the next sitting of the council. Because that no man when he hath rashly there spoken that cometh first to his tongue's end, shall then afterward rather study for reasons wherewith to defend and confirm his first foolish sentence, than for the commodity of the commonwealth: as one rather willing the harm or hindrance of the weal public than any loss or diminution of his own existimation. And as one that would not for shame (which is a very foolish shame) be counted anything overseen in the matter at the first. Who at the first ought to have spoken rather wisely, than hastily, or rashly.

Of Sciences, Crafts, and Occupations

Husbandry is a science common to them all in general, both men and women, wherein they be all expert and cunning. In this they be all instruct even from their youth: partly in schools with traditions and precepts, and partly in the country nigh the city, brought up as it were in playing, not only beholding the use of it, but by occasion of exercising their bodies practising it also. Besides husbandry, which (as I said) is common to them all, every one of them learneth one or other several and particular science, as his own proper craft. That is most commonly either clothworking in wool or flax, or masonry, or the smith's craft, or the carpenter's science. For there is none other occupation that any number to speak of doth use there. For their garments, which throughout all the island be of one fashion (saving that there is a difference between the man's garment and the woman's, between the married and the unmarried) and this one continueth for evermore unchanged, seemly and comely to the eye, no let to the moving and wielding of the body, also fit both for winter and summer: as for these garments (I say) every family maketh their own. But of the other foresaid crafts

every man learneth one. And not only the men, but also the women.
But the women, as the weaker sort, be put to the easier crafts: they
work wool and flax. The other more laboursome sciences be committed to the men. For the most part every man is brought up in
his father's craft. For most commonly they be naturally thereto
bent and inclined. But if a man's mind stand to any other, he is by
adoption put into a family of that occupation, which he doth most
fantasy. Whom not only his father, but also the magistrates do diligently look to, that he be put to a discreet and an honest householder. Yea, and if any person, when he hath learned one craft,
be desirous to learn also another, he is likewise suffered and permitted.

When he hath learned both, he occupieth whether he will: unless
the city have more need of the one, than of the other. The chief and
almost the only office of the syphogrants is, to see and take heed that
no man sit idle: but that every one apply his own craft with earnest
diligence. And yet for all that, not to be wearied from early in the
morning, to late in the evening, with continual work, like labouring
and toiling beasts.

For this is worse than the miserable and wretched condition of
bondmen. Which nevertheless is almost everywhere the life of
workmen and artificers, saving in Utopia. For they dividing the
day and the night into twenty-four just hours, appoint and assign
only six of those hours to work; three before noon, upon the which
they go straight to dinner: and after dinner, when they have rested
two hours, then they work three and upon that they go to supper.
About eight of the clock in the evening (counting one of the clock
at the first hour after noon) they go to bed: eight hours they give
to sleep. All the void time, that is between the hours of work, sleep,
and meat, that they be suffered to bestow, every man as he liketh
best himself. Not to the intent that they should misspend this time
in riot or slothfulness: but being then licensed from the labour of
their own occupations, to bestow the time well and thriftly upon
some other good science, as shall please them. For it is a solemn
custom there, to have lectures daily early in the morning, where to
be present they only be constrained that be namely chosen and
appointed to learning. Howbeit a great multitude of every sort of

people, both men and women, go to hear lectures, some one and some another, as every man's nature is inclined. Yet, this notwithstanding, if any man had rather bestow this time upon his own occupation (as it chanceth in many, whose minds rise not in the contemplation of any science liberal) he is not letted, nor prohibited, but is also praised and commended, as profitable to the commonwealth. After supper they bestow one hour in play: in summer in their gardens: in winter in their common halls: where they dine and sup. There they exercise themselves in music, or else in honest and wholesome communication. Diceplay, and such other foolish and pernicious games they know not. But they use two games not much unlike the chess. The one is the battle of numbers, wherein one number stealeth away another. The other is wherein vices fight with virtues, as it were in battle array, or a set field. In the which game is very properly showed, both the strife and discord that vices have among themselves, and again their unity and concord against virtues. And also what vices be repugnant to what virtues: with what power and strength they assail them openly: by what wiles and subtlety they assault them secretly: with what help and aid the virtues resist and overcome the puissance of the vices: by what craft they frustrate their purposes: and finally by what sleight or means the one getteth the victory. But here lest you be deceived, one thing you must look more narrowly upon. For seeing they bestow but six hours in work, perchance you may think that the lack of some necessary things hereof may ensue. But this is nothing so. For that small time is not only enough but also too much for the store and abundance of all things that be requisite, either for the necessity, or commodity of life. The which thing you also shall perceive, if you weigh and consider with yourselves how great a part of the people in other countries liveth idle. First almost all women, which be the half of the whole number: or else if the women be anywhere occupied, there most commonly in their stead the men be idle. Besides this how great, and how idle a company is there of priests, and religious men, as they call them? put thereto all rich men, especially all landed men, which commonly be called gentlemen, and noblemen. Take into this number also their servants: I mean all that flock of stout bragging rush bucklers. Join to them also sturdy and valiant beggars, cloaking their idle life under the colour of some disease or sickness. And truly you shall find them much fewer than you thought, by whose labour all these things be gotten that men use and live by. Now consider with yourself, of these few that do work, how few be occupied, in necessary works. For where money beareth all the swing, there many vain and superfluous occupations must needs be used, to serve only for riotous superfluity and unhonest pleasure. For the same multitude that now is occupied in work, if they were divided into so few occupations as the necessary use of nature requireth; in so great plenty of things as then of necessity would ensue, doubtless the prices would be too little for the artificers to maintain their livings. But if all these, that be now busied about unprofitable occupations, with all the whole flock of them that live idly and slothfully, which consume and waste every one of them more of these things that come by other men's labour, than two of the workmen themselves do: if all these (I say) were set to profitable occupations, you easily perceive how little time would be enough, yea and too much to store us with all things that may be requisite either for necessity, or for commodity, yea or for pleasure, so that the same pleasure be true and natural. And this in Utopia the thing itself maketh manifest and plain. For there in all the city, with the whole country, or shire adjoining to it scarcely 500 persons of all the whole number of men and women, that be neither too old, nor too weak to work, be licensed from labour. Among them be the syphogrants which (though they be by the laws exempt and privileged from labour) yet they exempt not themselves: to the intent they may the rather by their example provoke other to work. The same vacation from labour do they also enjoy, to whom the people persuaded by the commendation of the priests, and secret election of the syphogrants, have given a perpetual license from labour to learning. But if any one of them prove not according to the expectation and hope of him conceived, he is forthwith plucked back to the company of artificers. And contrariwise, often it chanceth that a handicraftsman doth so earnestly bestow his vacant and spare hours in learning, and through diligence so profit therein, that he is taken from his handy occupation, and promoted to the company of the learned. Out of this order of the learned be chosen ambassadors, priests, tranibores, and finally the prince himself. Whom they in their old tongue call Barzanes, and by a newer

115

name, Adamus. The residue of the people being neither idle nor occupied about unprofitable exercises, it may be easily judged in how few hours how much good work by them may be done towards those things that I have spoken of. This commodity they have also above other, that in the most part of necessary occupations they need not so much work, as other nations do. For first of all the building or repairing of houses asketh everywhere so many men's continual labour, because that the unth[r]ifty heir suffereth the houses that his father builded in continuance of time to fall in decay. So that which he might have upholden with little cost, his successor is constrained to build it again anew, to his great charge. Yea many times also the house that stood one man in much money, another is of so nice and so delicate a mind, that he setteth nothing by it. And it being neglected, and therefore shortly falling into ruin, he buildeth up another in another place with no less cost and charge. But among the Utopians, where all things be set in a good order, and the commonwealth in a good stay, it very seldom chanceth, that they choose a new plot to build an house upon. And they do not only find speedy and quick remedies for present faults: but also prevent them that be like to fall. And by this means their houses continue and last very long with little labour and small reparations: insomuch that this kind of workmen sometimes have almost nothing to do. But that they be commanded to hew timber at home, and to square and trim up stones, to the intent that if any work chance, it may the speedier rise. Now, sir, in their apparel, mark (I pray you) how few workmen they need. First of all, whilst they be at work, they be covered homely with leather or skins, that will last seven years. When they go forth abroad they cast upon them a cloak, which hideth the other homely apparel. These cloaks throughout the whole island be all of one colour, and that is the natural colour of the wool. They therefore do not only spend much less woollen cloth than is spent in other countries, but also the same standeth them in much less cost. But linen cloth is made with less labour, and is therefore had more in use. But in linen cloth only whiteness, in woollen only cleanliness is regarded. As for the smallness or fineness of the thread, that is nothing passed for. And this is the cause wherefore in other places four or five cloth gowns of divers colours, and as many silk coats

116

be not enough for one man. Yea and if he be of the delicate and nice sort ten be too few: whereas there one garment will serve a man most commonly two years. For why should he desire more? Seeing if he had them, he should not be the better wrapped or covered from cold, neither in his apparel any whit the comelier. Wherefore, seeing they be all exercised in profitable occupations, and that few artificers in the same crafts be sufficient, this is the cause that plenty of all things being among them, they do sometimes bring forth an innumerable company of people to amend the highways, if any be broken. Many times also, when they have no such work to be occupied about, an open proclamation is made, that they shall bestow fewer hours in work. For the magistrates do not exercise their citizens against their wills in unneedful labours. For why? in the institution of that weal public, this end is only and chiefly pretended and minded, that what time may possibly be spared from the necessary occupations and affairs of the commonwealth, all that the citizens should withdraw from the bodily service to the free liberty of the mind, and garnishing of the same. For herein they suppose the felicity of this life to consist.

Of their living and mutual conversation together

But now will I declare how the citizens use themselves one towards another: what familiar occupying and entertainment there is among the people, and what fashion they use in distributing every thing. First the city consisteth of families, the families most commonly be made of kindreds. For the women, when they be married at a lawful age, they go into their husbands' houses. But the male children with all the whole male offspring continue still in their own family and be governed of the eldest and ancientest father, unless he dote for age: for then the next to him in age is put in his room. But to the intent the prescript number of the citizens should neither decrease, nor above measure increase, it is ordained that no family which in every city be six thousand in the whole, besides them of the country, shall at once have fewer children of the age of fourteen years or thereabout than ten or more than sixteen, for of children under this age no number can be appointed. This measure or num-

117

ber is easily observed and kept, by putting them that in fuller families be above the number into families of smaller increase. But if chance be that in the whole city the store increase above the just number, therewith they fill up the lack of other cities. But if so be that the multitude throughout the whole island pass and exceed the due number, then they choose out of every city certain citizens, and build up a town under their own laws in the next land where the inhabitants have much waste and unoccupied ground, receiving also of the inhabitants to them, if they will join and dwell with them. They thus joining and dwelling together do easily agree in one fashion of living, and that to the great wealth of both the peoples. For they so bring the matter about by their laws, that the ground which before was neither good nor profitable for the one nor for the other, is now sufficient and fruitful enough for them both. But if the inhabitants of that land will not dwell with them to be ordered by their laws, then they drive them out of those bounds which they have limited, and appointed out for themselves. And if they resist and rebel, then they make war against them. For they count this the most just cause of war, when any people holdeth a piece of ground void and vacant, to no good nor profitable use, keeping other from the use and possession of it, which notwithstanding by the law of nature ought thereof to be nourished and relieved. If any chance do so much diminish the number of any of their cities, that it cannot be filled up again, without the diminishing of the just number of the other cities (which they say chanced but twice since the beginning of the land through a great pestilent plague) then they make up the number with citizens fetched out of their own foreign towns, for they had rather suffer their foreign towns to decay and perish, than any city of their own island to be diminished. But now again to the conversation of the citizens among themselves. The eldest (as I said) ruleth the family. The wives be ministers to their husbands, the children to their parents, and to be short the younger to their elders. Every city is divided into four equal parts. In the midst of every quarter there is a market place of all manner of things. Thither the works of every family be brought into certain houses. And every kind of thing is laid up in several barns or storehouses. From hence the father of every family, or every householder fetcheth whatsoever he and his have need of, and carrieth it away with him without money, without exchange, without any gage, or pledge. For why should any thing be denied unto him? Seeing there is abundance of all things, and that it is not to be feared, lest any man will ask more than he needeth. For why should it be thought that that man would ask more than enough, which is sure never to lack? Certainly in all kinds of living creatures either fear of lack doth cause covetousness and ravin, or in man only pride, which counteth it a glorious thing to pass and excel other in the superfluous and vain ostentation of things. The which kind of vice among the Utopians can have no place. Next to the market places that I spake of, stand meat markets: whither be brought not only all sorts of herbs, and the fruits of trees, with bread, but also fish, and all manner of four-footed beasts, and wild fowl that be man's meat. But first the filthiness and ordure thereof is clean washed away in the running river without the city in places appointed meet for the same purpose. From thence the beasts [be] brought in killed, and clean washed by the hands of their bondmen. For they permit not their free citizens to accustom themselves to the killing of beasts, through the use whereof they think that clemency, the gentlest affection of our nature, doth by little and little decay and perish. Neither they suffer any thing that is filthy, loathsome, or uncleanly, to be brought into the city, lest the air by the stench thereof infected and corrupt, should cause pestilent diseases. Moreover every street hath certain great large halls set in equal distance one from another, every one known by a several name. In these halls dwell the syphogrants. And to every one of the same halls be appointed thirty families, on either side fifteen. The stewards of every hall at a certain hour come into the meat markets, where they receive meat according to the number of their halls. But first and chiefly of all, respect is had to the sick, that be cured in the hospitals. For in the circuit of the city, a little without the walls, they have four hospitals, so big, so wide, so ample, and so large, that they may seem four little towns, which were devised of that bigness partly to the intent the sick, be they never so many in number, should not lie too throng or strait, and therefore uneasily and incommodiously: and partly that they which were taken and holden with contagious diseases, such as be wont by infection to creep from one to another, might be laid apart far from the company of the residue. These hospitals be so well appointed, and with all things necessary to health so furnished, and moreover so diligent attendance through the continual presence of cunning physicians is given, that though no man be sent thither against his will, yet notwithstanding there is no sick person in all the city, that had not rather lie there than at home in his own house. When the steward of the sick hath received such meats as the physicians have prescribed, then the best is equally divided among the halls, according to the company of every one, saving that there is had a respect to the prince, the bishop, the tranibores, and to ambassadors and all strangers, if there be any, which be very few and seldom. But they also when they be there, have certain houses appointed and prepared for them. To these halls at the set hours of dinner and supper cometh all the whole syphogranty or ward, warned by the noise of a brazen trumpet: except such as be sick in the hospitals, or else in their own houses. Howbeit no man is prohibited or forbid, after the halls be served, to fetch home meat out of the market to his own house, for they know that no man will do it without a cause reasonable. For though no man be prohibited to dine at home, yet no man doth it willingly: because it is counted a point of small honesty. And also it were a folly to take the pain to dress a bad dinner at home, when they may be welcome to good and fine fare so nigh hand at the hall. In this hall all vile service, all slavery, and drudgery, with all laboursome toil and business, is done by bondmen. But the women of every family by course have the office and charge of cookery for seething and dressing the meat, and ordering all things thereto belonging. They sit at three tables or more, according to the number of their company. The men sit upon the bench next the wall, and the women against them on the other side of the table, that if any sudden evil should chance to them, as many times happeneth to women with child, they may rise without trouble or disturbance of anybody, and go thence into the nursery. The nurses sit several alone with their young sucklings in a certain parlour appointed and deputed to the same purpose, never without fire and clean water, nor yet without cradles, that when they will they may lay down the young infants, and at their pleasure take them out of their swathing clothes, and hold them to the fire, and refresh them with play. Every mother is nurse to her own child, unless either death, or sickness be the let. When that chanceth, the wives of the syphogrants quickly provide a nurse. And that is not hard to be done. For they that can do it, do proffer themselves to no service so gladly as to that. Because that there this kind of pity is much praised: and the child that is nourished, ever after taketh his nurse for his own natural mother. Also among the nurses sit all the children that be under the age of five years. All the other children of both kinds, as well boys as girls, that be under the age of marriage, do either serve at the tables, or else if they be too young thereto, yet they stand by with marvellous silence. That which is given to them from the table they eat, and other several dinner-time they have none. The syphogrant and his wife sit in the midst of the high table, forasmuch as that is counted the honourablest place, and because from thence all the whole company is in their sight. For that table standeth overthwart the over end of the hall. To them be joined two of the ancientest and eldest. For at every table they sit four at a mess. But if there be a church standing in that syphogranty or ward, then the priest and his wife sitteth with the syphogrant, as chief in the company. On both sides of them sit young men, and next unto them again old men. And thus throughout all the house equal of age be set together, and yet be mixed with unequal ages. This, they say, was ordained, to the intent that the sage gravity and reverence of the elders should keep the younger from wanton license of words and behaviour. Forasmuch as nothing can be so secretly spoken or done at the table, but either they that sit on the one side or on the other must needs perceive it. The dishes be not set down in order from the first place, but all the old men (whose places be marked with some special token to be known) be first served of their meat, and then the residue equally. The old men divide their dainties as they think best to the younger that sit on each side of them.

Thus the elders be not defrauded of their due honour, and nevertheless equal commodity cometh to every one. They begin every dinner and supper of reading something that pertaineth to good manners and virtue. But it is short, because no man shall be grieved therewith. Hereof the elders take occasion of honest communica-

121

tion, but neither sad nor unpleasant. Howbeit they do not spend all the whole dinner-time themselves with long and tedious talks: but they gladly hear also the young men: yea, and do purposely provoke them to talk, to the intent that they may have a proof of every man's wit, and towardness, or disposition to virtue, which commonly in the liberty of feasting doth show and utter itself. Their dinners be very short: but their suppers be somewhat longer, because that after dinner followeth labour, after supper sleep and natural rest, which they think to be of more strength and efficacy to wholesome and healthful digestion. No supper is passed without music. Nor their banquets lack no conceits nor junkets. They burn sweet gums and spices for perfumes, and pleasant smells, and sprinkle about sweet ointments and waters, yea, they leave nothing undone that maketh for the cheering of the company. For they be much inclined to this opinion: to think no kind of pleasure forbidden, whereof cometh no harm. Thus therefore and after this sort they live together in the city, but in the country they that dwell alone far from any neighbours, do dine and sup at home in their own houses. For no family there lacketh any kind of victuals, as from whom cometh all that the citizens eat and live by.

Of their journeying or travelling abroad, with divers other matters cunningly reasoned, and wittily discussed

But if any be desirous to visit either their friends that dwell in another city, or to see the place itself: they easily obtain licence of their syphogrants and tranibores, unless there be some profitable let. No man goeth out alone but a company is sent forth together with their prince's letters, which do testify that they have licence to go that journey, and prescribeth also the day of their return. They have a waggon given them, with a common bondman, which driveth the oxen, and taketh charge of them. But unless they have women in their company, they send home the waggon again, as an impediment and a let. And though they carry nothing forth with them, yet in all their journey they lack nothing. For wheresoever they come they be at home. If they tarry in a place longer than one day, then there every one of them falleth to his own occupation, and be very gently entertained of the workmen and companies of the same crafts. If any man of his own head and without leave, walk out of his precinct and bounds, taken without the prince's letters, he is brought again for a fugitive or a runaway with great shame and rebuke, and is sharply punished. If he be taken in that fault again, he is punished with bondage. If any be desirous to walk abroad into the fields, or into the country that belongeth to the same city that he dwelleth in, obtaining the goodwill of his father, and the consent of his wife, he is not prohibited. But into what part of the country soever he cometh he hath no meat given him until he have wrought out his forenoon's task, or else despatched so much work, as there is wont to be wrought before supper. Observing this law and condition, he may go whither he will within the bounds of his own city. For he shall be no less profitable to the city, than if he were within it. Now you see how little liberty they have to loiter: how they can have no cloak or pretence to idleness. There be neither wine taverns, nor ale-houses, nor stews, nor any occasion of vice or wickedness, no lurking corners, no places of wicked counsels or unlawful assemblies. But they be in the present sight, and under the eyes of every man. So that of necessity they must either apply their accustomed labours, or else recreate themselves with honest and laudable pastimes.

This fashion being used among the people, they must of necessity have store and plenty of all things. And seeing they be all thereof partners equally, therefore can no man there be poor or needy. In the council of Amaurote, whither, as I said, every city sendeth three men apiece yearly, as soon as it is perfectly known of what things there is in every place plenty, and again what things be scant in any place: incontinent the lack of the one is performed and filled up with the abundance of the other. And this they do freely without any benefit, taking nothing again of them, to whom the things is given, but those cities that have given of their store to any other city that lacketh, requiring nothing again of the same city, do take such things as they lack of another city, to whom they gave nothing. So the whole island is as it were one family, or household. But when they have made sufficient provision of store for themselves (which they think not done, until they have provided for two years following because of the uncertainty of the next year's proof) then of those things, whereof they have abundance, they carry forth into other countries great plenty: as grain, honey, wool, flax, wood, madder, purple dyed fells, wax, tallow, leather, and living beasts. And the seventh part of all these things they give frankly and freely to the poor of that country. The residue they sell at a reasonable and mean price. By this trade of traffic or merchandise, they bring into their own country, not only great plenty of gold and silver, but also all such things as they lack at home, which is almost nothing but iron. And by reason they have long used this trade, now they have more abundance of these things, than any man will believe. Now therefore they care not whether they sell for ready money, or else upon trust to be paid at a day, and to have the most part in debts. But in so doing they never follow the credence of private men: but the assurance or warrantys of the whole city, by instruments and writings made in that behalf accordingly. When the day of payment is come and expired, the city gathereth up the debt of the private debtors, and putteth it into the common box and so long hath the use and profit of it, until the Utopians their creditors demand it. The most part of it they never ask. For that thing which is to them no profit to take it from other, to whom it is profitable: they think it no right nor conscience. But if the case so stand, that they must lend part of that money to another people, then they require their debt: or when they have war. For the which purpose only they keep at home all the treasure which they have, to be holpen and succoured by it either in extreme jeopardies, or in sudden dangers. But especially and chiefly to hire therewith, and that for unreasonable great wages, strange soldiers. For they had rather put strangers in jeopardy, than their own countrymen: knowing that for money enough, their enemies themselves many times may be bought and sold, or else through treason be set together by the ears among themselves. For this cause they keep an inestimable treasure. But yet not as a treasure: but so they have it, and use it, as in good faith I am ashamed to show: fearing that my words shall not be believed. And this I have more cause to fear, for that I know how difficulty and hardly I myself would have believed another man telling the same, if I had not presently seen it with mine own eyes.

For it must needs be, that how far a thing is dissonant and disagreeing from the guise and trade of the hearers, so far shall it be out of their belief. Howbeit, a wise and indifferent esteemer of things will not greatly marvel perchance, seeing all their other laws and customs do so much differ from ours, if the use also of gold and silver among them be applied, rather to their own fashions than to ours. I mean in that they occupy not money themselves, but keep it for that chance, which as it may happen, so it may be that it shall never come to pass. In the meantime gold and silver, whereof money is made, they do so use, as none of them doth more esteem it, than the very nature of the thing deserveth. And then who doth not plainly see how far it is under iron: as without the which men can no better live than without fire and water. Whereas to gold and silver nature hath given no use, that we may not well lack: if that the folly of men had not set it in higher estimation for the rareness sake. But of the contrary part, nature as a most tender and loving mother, hath placed the best and most necessary things open abroad: as the air, the water and the earth itself. And hath removed and hid farthest from us vain and unprofitable things. Therefore if these metals among them should be fast locked up in some tower, it might be suspected, that the prince and the council (as the people is ever foolishly imagining) intended by some subtilty to deceive the commons, and to take same profit of it to themselves. Furthermore if they should make thereof plate and such other finely and cunningly wrought stuff: if at any time they should have occasion to break it, and melt it again, and therewith to pay their soldiers' wages, they see and perceive very well, that men would be loath to part from those things, that they once began to have pleasure and delight in. To remedy all this they have found out a means, which, as it is agreeable to all their other laws and customs, so it is from ours, where gold is so much set by and so diligently kept, very far discrepant and repugnant: and therefore incredible, but only to them that be wise. For whereas they eat and drink in earthen and glass vessels, which indeed be curiously and properly made, and yet be of very small value: of gold and silver they make commonly chamber pots, and other like vessels, that serve for most vile uses, not only in their common halls, but in every man's private house. Furthermore of the same metals they make great chains, with fetters, and gyves wherein they tie their bondmen. Finally whosoever for any offence be infamed, by their ears hang rings of gold, upon their fingers they wear rings of gold, and about their necks chains of gold, and in conclusion their heads be tied about with gold. Thus by all means that may be they procure to have gold and silver among them in reproach and infamy. And therefore these metals, which other nations do as grievously and sorrowfully forgo, as in a manner from their own lives: if they should altogether at once be taken from the Utopians, no man there would think that he had lost the worth of one farthing. They gather also pearls by the sea-side, and diamonds and carbuncles upon certain rocks, and yet they seek not for them: but by chance finding them, they cut and polish them. And therewith they deck their young infants. Which like as in the first years of their childhood, they make much and be fond and proud of such ornaments, so when they be a little more grown in years and discretion, perceiving that none but children do wear such toys and trifles: they lay them away even of their own shamefacedness, without any bidding of their parents: even as our children, when they wax big, do cast away nuts, brooches, and puppets. Therefore these laws and customs, which be so far different from all other nations, how divers fantasies also and minds they do cause, did I never so plainly perceive, as in the ambassadors of the Anemolians.

These ambassadors came to Amaurote whilest I was there. And because they came to entreat of great and weighty matters, those three citizens apiece out of every city were come thither before them. But all the ambassadors of the next countries, which had been there before, and knew the fashions and manners of the Utopians, among whom they perceived no honour given to sumptuous and costly apparel, silks to be contemned, gold also to be infamed and reproachful, were wont to come thither in very homely and simple apparel. But the Anemolians, because they dwell far thence and had very little acquaintance with them, hearing that they were all apparelled alike, and that very rudely and homely: thinking them not to have the things which they did not wear: being therefore more proud, than wise: determined in the gorgeousness of their apparel to represent very gods, and with the bright shining and glistering of their gay clothing to dazzle the eyes of the silly poor Utopians. So there came in three ambassadors with one hundred servants all apparelled in changeable colours: the most of them in silks: the ambassadors themselves (for at home in their own country they were noblemen) in cloth of gold, with great chains of gold, with gold hanging at their ears, with gold rings upon their fingers, with brooches and aglets of gold upon their caps, which glistered full of pearls and precious stones: to be short, trimmed and adorned with all those things, which among the Utopians were either the punishment of bondmen, or the reproach of infamed persons, or else trifles for young children to play withal. Therefore it would have done a man good at his heart to have seen how proudly they displayed their peacock's feathers, how much they made of their painted sheaths, and how loftily they set forth and advanced themselves, when they compared their gallant apparel with the poor raiment of the Utopians. For all the people were swarmed forth into the streets. And on the other side it was no less pleasure to consider how much they were deceived, and how far they missed of their purpose, being contrariwise taken than they thought they should have been. For to the eyes of all the Utopians, except very few, which had been in other countries for some reasonable cause, all that gorgeousness of apparel seemed shameful and reproachful. Insomuch that they most reverently saluted the vilest and most abject of them for lords: passing over the ambassadors themselves without any honour: judging them by their wearing of golden chains to be bondmen. Yea you should have seen children also, that had cast away their pearls and precious stones, when they saw the like sticking upon the ambassadors' caps, dig and push their mothers under the sides, saying thus to them. Look, mother, how great a lubber doth yet wear pearls and precious stones, as though he were a little child still. But the mother, yea, and that also in good earnest: peace, son, saith she: I think he be some of the ambassadors' fools. Some found fault at their golden chains, as to no use nor purpose, being so small and weak, that a bondman might easily break them, and again so wide and large, that when it pleased him, he might cast them off, and run away at liberty whither he would. But when the ambassadors had been there a day or two and saw so great abun-

127

dance of gold so lightly esteemed, yea in no less reproach, than it was with them in honour: and besides that more gold in the chains and gyves of one fugitive bondman, than all the costly ornaments of them three was worth: they began to abate their courage, and for very shame laid away all that gorgeous array, whereof they were so proud. And specially when they had talked familiarly with the Utopians, and had learned all their fashions and opinions.

For they marvel that any men be so foolish, as to have delight and pleasure in the glistering of a little trifling stone, which may behold any of the stars, or else the sun itself. Or that any man is so mad, as to count himself the nobler for the smaller or finer thread of wool, which selfsame wool (be it now in never so fine a spun thread) did once a sheep wear: and yet was she all that time no other thing than a sheep. They marvel also that gold, which of the own nature is a thing so unprofitable, is now among all people in so high estimation, that man himself, by whom, yea and for the use of whom it is so much set by, is in much less estimation than the gold itself. Insomuch that a lumpish blockheaded churl, and which hath no more wit than an ass, yea and as full of worthlessness and foolishness, shall have nevertheless many wise and good men in subjection and bondage, only for this, because he hath a great heap of gold. Which if it should be taken from him by any fortune, or by some subtle wile of the law (which no less than fortune doth raise up the low and pluck down the high), and be given to the most vile slave and abject drudge of all his household, then shortly after he shall go into the service of his servant, as an augmentation or an overplus beside his money. But they much more marvel at and detest the madness of them which to those rich men, in whose debt and danger they be not, do give almost divine honours, for none other consideration, but because they be rich: and yet knowing them to be such niggardly penny-fathers, that they be sure as long as they live, not the worth of one farthing of that heap of gold shall come to them.

These and such like opinions have they conceived, partly by education, being brought up in that commonwealth, whose laws and customs be far different from these kinds of folly, and partly by good literature and learning. For though there be not many in every city, which be exempt and discharged of all other labours, and appointed only to learning; that is to say, such in whom even from their very childhood they have perceived a singular towardness, a fine wit, and a mind apt to good learning: yet all in their childhood be instruct in learning. And the better part of the people, both men and women throughout all their whole life do bestow in learning those spare hours, which we said they have vacant from bodily labours. They be taught learning in their own native tongue. For it is both copious in words, and also pleasant to the ear, and for the utterance of a man's mind very perfect and sure. The most part of all that side of the world useth the same language, saving that among the Utopians it is finest and purest, and according to the diversity of the countries it is diversely altered. Of all these philosophers, whose names be here famous in this part of the world to us known, before our coming thither not as much as the fame of any of them was come among them. And yet in music, logic, arithmetic, and geometry they have found out in a manner all that our ancient philosophers have taught. But as they in all things be almost equal to our old ancient clerks, so our new logicians in subtle inventions have far passed and gone beyond them. For they have not devised one of all those rules of restrictions, amplifications and suppositions, very wittily invented in the small logicals, which here our children in every place do learn. Furthermore, they were never yet able to find out the second intentions: insomuch that none of them all could ever see man himself in common, as they call him, though he be (as you know) bigger than ever was any giant, yea and pointed to of us even with our finger. But they be in the course of the stars, and the movings of the heavenly spheres very expert and cunning. They have also wittily excogitated and devised instruments of divers fashions: wherein is exactly comprehended and contained the movings and situations of the sun, the moon, and of all the other stars, which appear in their horizon. But as for the amities and dissensions of the planets, and all that deceitful divination by the stars, they never as much as dreamed thereof. Rains, winds, and other courses of tempests they know before by certain tokens, which they have learned by long use and observation. But of the causes of all these things and of the ebbing, flowing and saltness of the sea, and finally of the original beginning and nature of heaven and of the world, they hold partly the same opinions that our old philosophers hold, and partly, as our philosophers vary among themselves, so they also, whiles they bring new reasons of things, do disagree from all them, and yet among themselves in all points they do not accord. In that part of philosophy, which treateth of manners and virtue, their reasons and opinions agree with ours. They dispute of the good qualities of the soul, of the body and of fortune. And whether the name of goodness may be applied to all these, or only to the endowments and gifts of the soul.

They reason of virtue and pleasure. But the chief and principal question is in what thing, be it one or more, the felicity of man consisteth. But in this point they seem almost too much given and inclined to the opinion of them which defend pleasure, wherein they determine either all or the chiefest part of man's felicity to rest. And (which is more to be marvelled at) the defence of this so dainty and delicate an opinion they fetch even from their grave, sharp, bitter, and rigorous religion. For they never dispute of felicity or blessedness, but they join to the reasons of philosophy certain principles taken out of religion: without the which to the investigation of true felicity they think reason of itself weak and imperfect. Those principles be these and such like: That the soul is immortal, and by the bountiful goodness of God ordained to felicity. That to our virtues and good deeds rewards be appointed after this life, and to our evil deeds, punishments. Though these be pertaining to religion, yet they think it meet that they should be believed and granted by proofs of reason. But if these principles were condemned and disannulled, then without any delay they pronounce no man to be so foolish, which would not do all his diligence and endeavour to obtain pleasure by right or wrong, only avoiding this inconvenience, that the less pleasure should not be a let or hindrance to the bigger: or that he laboured not for that pleasure, which would bring after it displeasure, grief, and sorrow. For they judge it extreme madness to follow sharp and painful virtue, and not only to banish the pleasure of life, but also willingly to suffer grief without any hope of profit thereof. For what profit can there be, if a man, when he hath passed over all his life unpleasantly, that is to say, wretchedly, shall have no reward after his death? But now, sir, they think not felicity to rest in all pleasure, but only in that pleasure that is good and honest, and that hereto, as to perfect blessedness our nature is allured and drawn even of virtue, whereto only they that be of the contrary opinion do attribute felicity. For they define virtue to be a life ordered according to nature, and that we be hereunto ordained of God. And that he doth follow the course of nature, which in desiring and refusing things is ruled by reason. Furthermore, that reason doth chiefly and principally kindle in men the love and veneration of the divine majesty. Of whose goodness it is that we be, and that we be in possibility to attain felicity. And that secondly, it moveth and provoketh us to lead our life out of care in joy and mirth, and to help all other in respect of the society of nature to obtain the same. For there was never man so earnest and painful a follower of virtue and hater of pleasure, that would so enjoin you labours, watchings and fastings, but he would also exhort you to ease and lighten, to your power, the lack and misery of others, praising the same as a deed of humanity and pity. Then if it be a point of humanity for man to bring health and comfort to man, and specially (which is a virtue most peculiarly belonging to man) to mitigate and assuage the grief of others, and by taking from them the sorrow and heaviness of life, to restore them to joy, that is to say, to pleasure: why may it not then be said, that nature doth provoke every man to do the same to himself? For a joyful life, that is to say, a pleasant life, is either evil, and if it be so, then thou shouldest not only help no man thereto, but rather, as much as in thee lieth, help all men from it, as noisome and hurtful, or else if thou not only mayst, but also of duty art bound to procure it to others, why not chiefly to thyself, to whom thou art bound to show as much favour as to other? For when nature biddeth thee to be good and gentle to other she commandeth thee not to be cruel and ungentle to thyself. Therefore even very nature (say they) prescribeth to us a joyful life, that is to say, pleasure as the end of all our operations. And they define virtue to be life ordered according to the prescript of nature. But in that, that nature doth allure and provoke men one to help another to live merrily (which surely she doth not without a good cause, for no man is so far above the lot

131

of man's state or condition, that nature doth cark and care for him only, which equally favoureth all that be comprehended under the communion of one shape, form and fashion) verily she commandeth thee to use diligent circumspection, that thou do not so seek for thine own commodities, that thou procure others incommodities. Wherefore their opinion is, that not only covenants and bargains made among private men ought to be well and faithfully fulfilled, observed, and kept, but also common laws, which either a good prince hath justly published, or else the people neither oppressed with tyranny, neither deceived by fraud and guile, hath by their common consent constituted and ratified, concerning the partition of the commodities of life, that is to say, the matter of pleasure. These laws not offended, it is wisdom, that thou look to thine own wealth. And to do the same for the commonwealth is no less than thy duty, if thou bearest any reverent love or any natural zeal and affection to thy native country. But to go about to let another man of his pleasure, whilst thou procurest thine own, that is open wrong. Contrariwise to withdraw something from thyself to give to other, that is a point of humanity and gentleness; which never taketh away so much commodity, as it bringeth again. For it is recompensed with the return of benefits; and the conscience of the good deed, with the remembrance of the thankful love and benevolence of them to whom thou hast done it, doth bring more pleasure to thy mind, than that which thou hast withholden from thyself could have brought to thy body. Finally (which to a godly disposed and a religious mind is easy to be persuaded) God recompenseth the gift of a short and small pleasure with great and everlasting joy. Therefore the matter diligently weighed and considered, thus they think, that all our actions, and in them the virtues themselves, be referred at the last to pleasure, as their end and felicity. Pleasure they call every motion and state of the body or mind wherein man hath naturally delectation. Appetite they join to nature, and that not without a good cause. For like as, not only the senses, but also right reason coveteth whatsoever is naturally pleasant, so that it may be gotten without wrong or injury, not letting or debarring a greater pleasure, nor causing painful labour, even so those things that men by vain imagination do feign against nature to be pleasant (as though it lay in their power to change the things, as they do the names of things) all such pleasures they believe to be of so small help and furtherance to felicity, that they count them great let and hindrance. Because that in whom they have once taken place, all his mind they possess with a false opinion of pleasure. So that there is no place left for true and natural delectations. For there be many things, which of their own nature contain no pleasantness: yea the most part of them much grief and sorrow. And yet through the perverse and malicious flickering enticements of lewd and unhonest desires, be taken not only for special and sovereign pleasures, but also be counted among the chief causes of life. In this counterfeit kind of pleasure they put them that I spake of before; which the better gown they have on, the better men they think themselves. In the which thing they do twice err. For they be no less deceived in that they think their gown the better, than they be, in that they think themselves the better: For if you consider the profitable use of the garment, why should wool of a finer spun thread be thought better, than the wool of a coarse spun thread? Yet they, as though the one did pass the other by nature, and not by their mistaking, advance themselves, and think the price of their own persons thereby greatly increased. And therefore the honour, which in a coarse gown they durst not have looked for, they require, as it were of duty, for their finer gown's sake. And if they be passed by without reverence, they take it angrily and disdainfully. And again is it not a like madness to take a pride in vain and unprofitable honours? For what natural or true pleasure dost thou take of another man's bare head, or bowed knees? Will this ease the pain of thy knees, or remedy the frenzy of thy head? In this image of counterfeit pleasure, they be of a marvellous madness, which for the opinion of nobility, rejoice much in their own conceit. Because it was their fortune to come of such ancestors, whose stock of long time hath been counted rich (for now nobility is nothing else) specially rich in lands. And though their ancestors left them not one foot of land, yet they think themselves not the less noble therefore of one hair. In this number also they count them that take pleasure and delight (as I said) in gems and precious stones, and think themselves almost gods, if they chance to get an excellent one, specially of that kind, which in that time of their own countrymen is had in highest estimation. For one kind of stone keepeth not his price still in all countries and at all times. Nor they buy them not, but taken out of the gold and bare: no, nor so neither, before they have made the seller to swear, that he will warrant and assure it to be a true stone, and no counterfeit gem. Such care they take lest a counterfeit stone should deceive their eyes instead of a right stone. But why shouldst thou not take even as much pleasure in beholding a counterfeit stone, which thine eye cannot discern from a right stone? They should both be of like value to thee, even as to a blind man. What shall I say of them, that keep superfluous riches, to take delectation only in the beholding, and not in the use or occupying thereof? Do they take true pleasure, or else be they deceived with false pleasure? Or of them that be in a contrary vice, hiding the gold which they shall never occupy, nor peradventure never see more; and whiles they take care lest they shall lose it, do lose it indeed? For what is it else, when they hide it in the ground, taking it both from their own use, and perchance from all other men's also? And yet thou, when thou hast hid thy treasure, as one out of all care, hoppest for joy. The which treasure, if it should chance to be stolen, and thou ignorant of the theft shouldst die ten years after: all that ten years' space that thou livedst after thy money was stolen, what matter was it to thee, whether it had been taken away or else safe as thou leftest it? Truly both ways like profit came to thee. To these so foolish pleasures they join dicers, whose madness they know by hearsay and not by use. Hunters also, and hawkers, For what pleasure is there (say they) in casting the dice upon a table; which thou hast done so often, that if there were any pleasure in it, yet the oft use might make thee weary thereof? Or what delight can there be, and not rather displeasure in hearing the barking and howling of dogs? Or what greater pleasure is there to be felt when a dog followeth an hare, than when a dog followeth a dog? for one thing is done in both, that is to say, running, if thou hast pleasure therein. But if the hope of slaughter and the expectation of tearing in pieces the beast doth please thee: thou shouldest rather be moved with pity to see a silly innocent hare murdered of a dog, the weak of the stronger, the fearful of the fierce, the innocent of the cruel and unmerciful. Therefore all this exercise of hunting, as a thing unworthy to be used of free men, the Utopians have rejected to their butchers, to the which craft (as we said before) they appoint their bondmen. For they count hunting the lowest, the vilest, and most abject part of butchery, and the other parts of it more profitable and more honest, as which do bring much more commodity, and do kill beasts only for necessity. Whereas the hunter seeketh nothing but pleasure of the silly and woful beasts' slaughter and murder. The which pleasure, in beholding death, they think doth rise in the very beasts, either of a cruel affection of mind, or else to be changed in continuance of time into cruelty, by long use of so cruel a pleasure. These therefore and all such like, which be innumerable, though the common sort of people doth take them for pleasures, yet they, seeing there is no natural pleasantness in them, do plainly determine them to have no affinity with true and right pleasure. For as touching that they do commonly move the sense with delectation (which seemeth to be a work of pleasure) this doth nothing diminish their opinion. For not the nature of the thing, but their perverse and lewd custom is the cause hereof, which causeth them to accept bitter or sour things for sweet things. Even as women with child in their viciated and corrupt taste, think pitch and tallow sweeter than any honey. Howbeit no man's judgment depraved and corrupt, either by sickness, or by custom, can change the nature of pleasure, more than it can do the nature of other things.

They make divers kinds of true pleasures. For some they attribute to the soul, and some to the body. To the soul they give intelligence and that delectation that cometh of the contemplation of truth. Hereunto is joined the pleasant remembrance of the good life past. The pleasure of the body they divide into two parts. The first is when delectation is sensibly felt and perceived. The second part of bodily pleasure, they say, is that which consisteth and resteth in the quiet and upright state of the body. And that truly is every man's own proper health, intermingled and disturbed with no grief. For this, if it be not let nor assaulted with no grief, is delectable of itself, though it be moved with no external or outward pleasure. For though it be not so plain and manifest to the sense, as the greedy lust of eating and drinking, yet nevertheless many take it for the chiefest pleasure. All the Utopians grant it to be a right great pleasure, and as you would say, the foundation and ground of all pleasures, as which even alone is able to make the state and condition of life delectable and pleasant. And it being once taken away, there is no place left for any pleasure. For to be without grief not having health, that they call insensibility, and not pleasure. The Utopians have long ago rejected and condemned the opinion of them which said that steadfast and quiet health (for this question also hath been diligently debated among them) ought not therefore to be counted a pleasure, because they say it cannot be presently and sensibly perceived and felt by some outward motion. But of the contrary part now they agree almost all in this, that health is a most sovereign pleasure. For seeing that in sickness (say they) is grief, which is a mortal enemy to pleasure, even as sickness is to health, why should not then pleasure be in the quietness of health? For they say it maketh nothing to this matter, whether you say that sickness is a grief, or that in sickness is grief, for all cometh to one purpose. For whether health be a pleasure itself, or a necessary cause of pleasure, as fire is of heat, truly both ways it followeth that they cannot be without pleasure that be in perfect health. Furthermore whilest we eat (say they) then health, which began to be impaired, fighteth by the help of food against hunger. In the which fight, whilest health by little and little getteth the upper hand, that same proceeding, and (as ye would say) that onwardness to the wonted strength, ministreth that pleasure, whereby we be so refreshed. Health therefore, which in the conflict is joyful, shall it not be merry, when it hath gotten the victory? But as soon as it hath recovered the pristinate strength, which thing only in all the fight it coveted, shall it incontinent be astonished? Nor shall it not know nor embrace the own wealth and goodness? For that it is said, health cannot be felt: this, they think, is nothing true. For what man waking, say they, feeleth not himself in health, but he that is not? Is there any man so possessed with stonish insensibility, or with the sleeping sickness, that he will not grant health to be acceptable to him, and delectable? But what other thing is delectation, than that which by another name is called pleasure? They embrace chiefly the pleasures of the mind. For them they count the chiefest and most principal of all. The chief part of them they think doth come of the exercise of virtue, and conscience of good life. Of these pleasures that the body ministreth, they give the pre-eminence to health. For the delight of eating and drinking, and whatsoever hath any like pleasantness, they determine to be pleasures much to be desired, but no other ways than for health's sake. For such things of their own proper nature be not pleasant, but in that they resist sickness privily stealing on. Therefore like as it is a wise man's part, rather to avoid sickness, than to wish for medicines, and rather to drive away and put to flight careful griefs, than to call for comfort: so it is much better not to need this kind of pleasure, than in curing the contrary grief to be eased of the same. The which kind of pleasure, if any man take for his felicity, that man must needs grant, that then he shall be in most felicity, if he live that life, which is led in continual hunger, thirst, itching, eating, drinking, scratching and rubbing. The which life how not only foul it is, but also miserable and wretched who perceiveth not? These doubtless be the basest pleasures of all, as impure and imperfect. For they never come, but accompanied with their contrary griefs. As with the pleasure of eating is joined hunger, and that after no very equal sort. For of these two the grief is both the more vehement, and also of longer continuance. For it riseth before the pleasure, and endeth not until the pleasure die with it. Wherefore such pleasures they think not greatly to be set by, but in that they be necessary. Howbeit they have delight also in these, and thankfully acknowledge the tender love of mother nature, which with most pleasant delectation allureth her children to that, which of necessity they be driven often to use. For how wretched and miserable should our life be, if these daily griefs of hunger and thirst could not be driven away, but with bitter potions and sour medicines, as the other diseases be, wherewith we be seldomer troubled? But beauty, strength, nimbleness, these as peculiar and pleasant gifts of nature they make much of. But those pleasures which be received by the ears, the eyes and the nose, which nature willeth to be proper and peculiar to man (for no other kind of living beasts doth behold the fairness and the beauty of the world, or is moved with any respect of savours, but only for the diversity of meats, neither perceiveth the concordant and discordant distances of sounds and tunes) these pleasures, I say, they accept and allow as certain pleasant rejoicings of life. But in all things this precaution they use, that a less pleasure hinder not a bigger, and that the pleasure be no cause of displeasure, which they think to follow of necessity, if the pleasure be unhonest. But yet to despise the comeliness of beauty, to waste the bodily strength, to turn nimbleness into sluggishness, to consume and make feeble the body with fasting, to do injury to health, and to reject the other pleasant motions of nature unless a man neglect these his commodities, whilest he doth with a fervent zeal procure the wealth of others, or the common profit, for the which pleasure forborn, he is in hope of a greater pleasure at God's hand; else for a vain shadow of virtue, for the wealth and profit of no man, to punish himself, or to the intent he may be able courageously to suffer adversities, which perchance shall never come to him; this to do they think it a point of extreme madness, and a token of a man cruelly minded towards himself, and unkind toward nature, as one so disdaining to be in her danger, that he renounceth and refuseth all her benefits.

This is their sentence and opinion of virtue and pleasure. And they believe that by man's reason none can be found truer than this, unless any godlier be inspired into man from heaven. Wherein whether they believe well or no, neither the time doth suffer us to discuss, neither it is now necessary. For we have taken upon us to show and declare their lores and ordinances, and not to defend them. But this thing I believe verily, howsoever these decrees be, that there is in no place of the world, neither a more excellent people, neither a more flourishing commonwealth. They be light and quick of body, full of activity and nimbleness, and of more strength than a man would judge them by their stature, which for all that is not too low. And though their soil be not very fruitful, nor their air very wholesome, yet against the air they so defend them with temperate diet, and so order and husband their ground with diligent travail, that in no country is greater increase, and plenty of corn and cattle, nor men's bodies of longer life, and subject or apt to fewer diseases. There therefore, a man may see well and diligently exploited and furnished, not only those things which husbandmen do commonly in other countries, as by craft and cunning to remedy the barrenness of the ground; but also a whole wood by the hands of the people plucked up by the roots in one place, and set again in another place. Wherein was had regard and consideration, not of plenty but of commodious carriage, that wood and timber might be nigher to the sea, or the rivers or the cities. For it is less labour and business to carry grain far by land, than wood. The people be gentle, merry, quick, and fine witted, delighting in quietness, and when need requireth, able to abide and suffer much bodily labour. Else they be not greatly desirous and fond of it; but in the exercise and study of the mind they be never weary. When they had heard me speak of the Greek literature or learning (for in Latin there was nothing that I thought they would greatly allow, besides historians and poets) they made wonderful earnest and importunate suit unto me that I would teach and instruct them in that tongue and learning. I began therefore to read unto them, at the first truly more because I would not seem to refuse the labour, than that I hoped that they would anything profit therein. But when I had gone forward a little, and perceived incontinent by their diligence, that my labour should not be bestowed in vain; for they began so easily to fashion their letters, so plainly to pronounce the words, so quickly to learn by heart, and so surely to rehearse the same, that I marvelled at it, saving that the most part of them were fine and chosen wits and of ripe age, picked out of the company of the learned men, which not only of their own free and voluntary will, but also by the commandment of the council, undertook to learn this language. Therefore in less than three years' space there was nothing in the Greek tongue that they lacked. They were able to read good authors without any stay, if the book were not false. This kind of learning, as I suppose, they took so much the sooner, because it is somewhat allied to them. For I think that this nation took their beginning of the Greeks, because their speech, which in all other points is not much unlike the Persian tongue, keepeth divers signs and tokens of the Greek language in the names of their cities and of their magistrates. They have of me (for when I was determined to enter into my fourth voyage, I cast into the ship in the stead of merchandise a pretty fardel of books, because I intended to come again rather never, than shortly) the most part of Plato's works, more of Aristotle's, also Theophrastus of plants, but in divers places (which I am sorry for) imperfect. For whilst we were sailing, a marmoset chanced upon the book, as it was negligently laid by, which wantonly playing therewith plucked out certain leaves, and tore them in pieces. Of them that have written the grammar, they have only Lascaris. For Theodorus I carried not with me, nor never a dictionary but Hesychius, and Dioscorides. They set great store by Plutarch's books. And they be delighted with Lucian's merry conceits and jests. Of the poets they have Aristophanes, Homer, Euripides, and Sophocles in Aldus' small print. Of the historians they have Thucydides, Herodotus, and Herodian. Also my companion, Tricius Apinatus, carried with him physic books, certain small works of Hippocrates and Galen's Microtechne. The which book they have in great estimation. For though there be almost no nation under heaven that hath less need of physic than they, yet this notwithstanding, physic is nowhere in greater honour; because they count the knowledge of it among the goodliest and most profitable parts of philosophy. For whilest they by the help of this philosophy search out the secret mysteries of nature, they think that they not only receive thereby wonderful great pleasure, but also obtain great thanks and favour of the author and maker thereof. Whom they think, according to the fashion of other artificers, to have set forth the marvellous and gorgeous frame of the world for man to behold. Whom only he hath made of wit and capacity to consider and understand the excellence of so great a work. And therefore (say they) doth he bear more goodwill and love to the curious and diligent beholder and viewer of his work and marveller at the same, than he doth to him, which like a very beast without wit and reason, or as one without sense or moving, hath no regard to so great and so wonderful a spectacle. The wits therefore of the Utopians, inured and exercised in learning, be marvellous quick in the invention of feats helping anything to the advantage and wealth of life. Howbeit two feats they may thank us for. That is, the science of imprinting, and the craft of making paper. And yet not only us but chiefly and principally themselves.

For when we showed to them Aldus his print in books of paper, and told them of the stuff whereof paper is made, and of the feat of graving letters, speaking somewhat more, than we could plainly declare (for there was none of us, that knew perfectly either the one or the other) they forthwith very wittily conjectured the thing. And whereas before they wrote only in skins, in barks of trees, and in reeds, now they have attempted to make paper, and to imprint letters. And though at the first it proved not all of the best, yet by often assaying the same they shortly got the feat of both. And have so brought the matter about that if they had copies of Greek authors, they could lack no books. But now they have no more than I rehearsed before, saving that by printing of books they have multiplied and increased the same into many thousands of copies. Whosoever cometh thither to see the land, being excellent in any gift of wit, or through much and long journeying well experienced and seen in the knowledge of many countries (for the which cause we were very welcome to them) him they receive and entertain wonders gently and lovingly. For they have delight to hear what is done in every land, howbeit very few merchantmen come thither, for what should they bring thither, unless it were iron, or else gold and silver, which they had rather carry home again? Also such things as are to be carried out of their land, they think it more wisdom to carry that gear forth themselves, than that others should come thither to fetch it, to the intent they may the better know the outlands on every side of them, and keep in use the feat and knowledge of sailing.

Of Bondmen, Sick Persons, Wedlock, and divers other matters

They neither make bondmen of prisoners taken in battle, unless it be in battle that they fought themselves, nor of bondmen's children, nor to be short, any man whom they can get out of another country, though he were there a bondman. But either such as among themselves for heinous offences be punished with bondage, or else such as in the cities of other lands for great trespasses be condemned to death. And of this sort of bondmen they have most store.

For many of them they bring home sometimes paying very little for them, yea most commonly getting them gratis. These sorts of bondmen they keep not only in continual work and labour, but also in bands. But their own men they handle hardest, whom they judge more desperate, and to have deserved greater punishment, because they being so godly brought up to virtue in so excellent a commonwealth, could not for all that be refrained from misdoing. Another kind of bondmen they have, when a vile drudge being a poor labourer in another country doth choose of his own free will to be a bondman among them. These they handle and order honestly, and entertain almost as gently as their own free citizens, saving that they put them to a little more labour, as thereto accustomed. If any such be disposed to depart thence (which seldom is seen) they neither hold him against his will, neither send him away with empty hands. The sick (as I said) they see to with great affection, and let nothing at all pass concerning either physic or good diet whereby they may be restored again to their health. Them that be sick of incurable diseases they comfort with sitting by them, with talking with them, and to be short, with all manner of helps that may be. But if the disease be not only incurable, but also full of continual pain and anguish; then the priests and the magistrates exhort the man, seeing he is not able to do any duty of life, and by overliving his own death is noisome and irksome to other, and grievous to himself, that he will determine with himself no longer to cherish that pestilent and painful disease. And seeing his life is to him but a torment, that he will not be unwilling to die, but rather take a good hope to him, and either despatch himself out of that painful life, as out of a prison, or a rack of torment, or else suffer himself willingly to be rid out of it by other. And in so doing they tell him he shall do wisely, seeing by his death he shall lose no commodity, but end his pain. And because in that act he shall follow the counsel of the priests, that is to say, of the interpreters of God's will and pleasure, they show him that he shall do like a godly and a virtuous man. They that be thus persuaded, finish their lives willingly, either with hunger, or else die in their sleep without any feeling of death. But they cause none such to die against his will, nor they use no less diligence and attendance about him, believing this to be an honourable death. Else he that killeth himself before that the priests and the council have allowed the cause of his death, him as unworthy both of the earth and of fire, they cast unburied into some stinking marsh. The woman is not married before she be eighteen years old. The man is four years older before he marry.

If either the man or the woman be proved to have bodily offended before their marriage with another, he or she whether it be is sharply punished. And both the offenders be forbidden ever after in all their life to marry: unless the fault be forgiven by the prince's pardon. But both the goodman and the goodwife of the house where that offence was done, as being slack and negligent in looking to their charge, be in danger of great reproach and infamy. That offence is so sharply punished, because they perceive, that unless they be diligently kept from the liberty of this vice, few will join together in the love of marriage, wherein all the life must be led with one, and also all the griefs and displeasures that come therewith must patiently be taken and borne. Furthermore in choosing wives and husbands they observe earnestly and straitly a custom, which seemed to us very fond and foolish. For a sad and an honest matron showeth the woman, be she maid or widow, naked to the wooer. And likewise a sage and discreet man exhibiteth the wooer naked to the woman. At this custom we laughed and disallowed it as foolish. But they on the other part do greatly wonder at the folly of all other nations, which in buying a colt, whereas a little money is in hazard, be so chary and circumspect, that though he be almost all bare, yet they will not buy him, unless the saddle and all the harness be taken off, lest under those coverings be hid some gall or sore. And yet in choosing a wife, which shall be either pleasure, or displeasure to them all their life after, they be so reckless, that all the residue of the woman's body being covered with clothes, they esteem her scarcely by one hand-breadth (for they can see no more but her face), and so do join her to them not without great jeopardy of evil agreeing together, if anything in her body afterward do offend and mislike them.

For all men be not so wise, as to have respect to the virtuous conditions of the party. And the endowments of the body cause the virtues of the mind more to be esteemed and regarded: yea even in the marriages of wise men. Verily so foul deformity may be hid under those coverings, that it may quite alienate and take away the man's mind from his wife, when it shall not be lawful for their bodies to be separate again. If such deformity happen by any chance after the marriage is consummate and finished, well, there is no remedy but patience. Every man must take his fortune, well-a-worth. But it were well done that a law were made whereby all such deceits might be eschewed and avoided beforehand.

And this were they constrained more earnestly to look upon, because they only of the nations in that part of the world be content every man with one wife apiece.

And matrimony is there never broken, but by death; except adultery break the bond, or else the intolerable wayward manners of either party. For if either of them find themselves for any such cause grieved, they may by the licence of the council change and take another. But the other party liveth ever after in infamy and out of wedlock. But for the husband to put way his wife for no fault, but for that some mishap is fallen to her body, this by no means they will suffer. For they judge it a great point of cruelty, that anybody in their most need of help and comfort should be cast off and forsaken, and that old age, which both bringeth sickness with it, and is a sickness itself, should unkindly and unfaithfully be dealt withal. But now and then it chanceth, whereas the man and the woman cannot well agree between themselves, both of them finding other, with whom they hope to live more quietly and merrily, that they by the full consent of them both be divorced asunder and new married to other. But that not without the authority of the council; which agreeth to no divorces, before they and their wives have diligently tried and examined the matter. Yea and then also they be loath to consent to it, because they know this to be the next way to break love between man and wife, to be in easy hope of a new marriage. Breakers of wedlock be punished with most grievous bondage. And if both the offenders were married, then the parties which in that behalf have suffered wrong, be divorced from the adulterers, if they will, and be married together, or else to whom they list. But if either of them both do still continue in love toward so unkind a bedfellow, the use of wedlock is not to them forbidden, if the party be disposed to follow in toiling and drudgery the person which for that offence is condemned to bondage. And very oft it chanceth that the repentance of the one, and the earnest diligence of the other, doth so move the prince with pity and compassion, that he restoreth the bond person from servitude to liberty and freedom again. But if the same party be taken again in that fault there is no other way but death. To other trespassers there is no prescript punishment appointed by any law. But according to the heinousness of the offence, or contrary, so the punishment is moderated by the discretion of the council. The husbands chastise their wives, and the parents their children, unless they have done any so horrible an offence, that the open punishment thereof maketh much for the advancement of honest manners. But most commonly the most heinous faults be punished with the incommodity of bondage. For that they suppose to be to the offenders no less grief, and to the commonwealth more profitable, than if they should hastily put them to death, and make them out of the way. For there cometh more profit of their labour, than of their death, and by their example they fear other the longer from like offences. But if they being thus used, do rebel and kick again, then forsooth they be slain as desperate and wild beasts, whom neither prison nor chain could restrain and keep under. But they which take their bondage patiently be not left all hopeless. For after they have been broken and tamed with long miseries, if then they show such repentance, whereby it may be perceived that they be sorrier for their offence than for their punishment, sometimes by the prince's prerogative, and sometimes by the voice and consent of the people, their bondage either is mitigated, or else clean remitted and forgiven. He that moveth to adultery is in no less danger and jeopardy than if he had committed adultery indeed. For in all offences they count the intent and pretensed purpose as evil as the act or deed itself, for they think that no let ought to excuse him that did his best to have no let. They set great store by fools. And as it is great reproach to do to any of them hurt or injury, so they prohibit not to take pleasure of foolishness. For that, they think, doth much good to the fools. And if any man be so sad and stern, that he cannot laugh neither at their words, nor at their deeds, none of them be committed to his tuition; for fear lest he would not order them gently and favourably enough, to whom they should bring no delectation (for other goodness in them is none) much less any profit should they yield him. To mock a man for his deformity, or for that he lacketh any part or limb of his body, is counted great dishonesty and reproach, not to him that is mocked, but to him that mocketh. Which unwisely doth upbraid any man of that as a vice which was not in his power to eschew. Also as they count and reckon very little wit to be in him, that regardeth not natural beauty and comeliness, so to help the same with paintings, is taken for a vain and a wanton pride, not without great infamy. For they know, even by very experience, that no comeliness of beauty doth so highly commend and advance the wives in the conceit of their husbands, as honest conditions and lowliness. For as love is oftentimes won with beauty, so it is not kept, preserved and continued, but by virtue and obedience. They do not only fear their people from doing evil by punishments, but also allure them to virtue with rewards of honour. Therefore they set up in the market-place the images of notable men, and of such as have been great and bountiful benefactors to the commonwealth, for the perpetual memory of their good acts, and also that the glory and renown of the ancestors may stir and provoke their posterity to virtue. He that inordinately and ambitiously desireth promotions is left all hopeless for ever attaining any promotion as long as he liveth. They live together lovingly. For no magistrate is either haughty or fearful. Fathers they be called, and like fathers they use themselves. The citizens (as it is their duty) do willingly exhibit unto them due honour without any compulsion. Nor the prince himself is not known from the other by his apparel, nor by a crown or diadem, or cap of maintenance, but by a little sheaf of corn carried before him. And so a taper of wax is borne before the bishop, whereby only he is known. They have but few laws. For to people so instruct and institute very few do suffice. Yea this thing they chiefly reprove among other nations, that innumerable books of laws and expositions upon the same be not sufficient. But they think it against all right and justice that men should be bound to those laws, which either be in number more than be able to be read, or else blinder and darker, than that any man can well understand them. Furthermore they utterly exclude and banish all proctors, and sergeants at the law; which craftily handle matters, and subtly dispute of the laws. For they think it most meet, that every man should plead his own matter, and tell the same tale before the judge that he would tell to his man of law. So shall there be less circumstance of words, and the truth shall sooner come to light, whiles the judge with a discreet judgment doth weigh the words of him whom no lawyer hath instruct with deceit, and whiles he helpeth and beareth out simple wits against the false and malicious circumventions of crafty children. This is hard to be observed in other countries, in so infinite a number of blind and intricate laws. But in Utopia every man is a cunning lawyer. For (as I said) they have very few laws; and the plainer and grosser that any interpretation is, that they allow as most just. For all laws (say they) be made and published only to the intent that by them every man should be put in remembrance of his duty. But the crafty and subtle interpretation of them can put very few in that remembrance (for they be but few that do perceive them), whereas the simple, the plain and gross meaning of the laws is open to every man.

Else as touching the vulgar sort of the people, which be both most in number, and have most need to know their duties, were it not as good for them, that no law were made at all, as when it is made, to bring so blind an interpretation upon it, that without great wit and long arguing no man can discuss it? To the finding out whereof neither the gross judgment of the people can attain, neither the whole life of them that be occupied in working for their livings can suffice thereto. These virtues of the Utopians have caused their next neighbours and borderers, which live free and under no subjection (for the Utopians long ago, have delivered many of them from tyranny) to take magistrates of them, some for a year, and some for five years' space. Which when the time of their office is expired, they bring home again with honour and praise, and take new ones again with them into their country. These nations have undoubtedly very well and wholesomely provided for their commonwealths. For seeing that both the making and the marring of the weal public doth depend and hang upon the manners of the rulers and magistrates, what officers could they more wisely have chosen, than those which cannot be led from honesty by bribes (for to them that shortly after shall depart thence into their own country money should be unprofitable) nor yet be moved either with favour, or malice towards any man, as being strangers, and unacquainted with the people? The which two vices of affection and avarice, where they take place in judgments, incontinent they break justice, the strongest and surest bond of a commonwealth. These peoples which fetch their officers and rulers from them, the Utopians call their fellows. And other to whom they have been beneficial, they call their friends. As touching leagues, which in other places beween country and country be so oft concluded, broken and made again, they never make none with any nation. For to what purpose serve leagues? say they. As though nature had not set sufficient love between man and man. And who so regardeth not nature, think you that he will pass for words? They be brought into this opinion chiefly, because that in those parts of the world, leagues between princes be wont to be kept and observed very slenderly. For here in Europe, and especially in these parts where the faith and religion of Christ reigneth, the majesty of leagues is everywhere esteemed holy and inviolable, partly through the justice and goodness of princes, and partly through the reverence of great bishops. Which like as they make no promise themselves but they do very religiously perform the same, so they exhort all princes in any wise to abide by their promises, and them that refuse or deny so to do, by their pontifical power and authority they compel thereto. And surely they think well that it might seam a very reproachful thing, if in the leagues of them which by a peculiar name be called faithful, faith should have no place. But in that new found part of the world, which is scarcely so far from us beyond the line equinoctial as our life and manners be dissident from theirs, no trust nor confidence is in leagues. But the more and holier ceremonies the league is knit up with, the sooner it is broken by some cavillation found in the words, which many times of purpose be so craftily put in and placed, that the bands can never be so sure nor so strong, but they will find some hole open to creep out at, and to break both league and truth. The which crafty dealing, yea the which fraud and deceit, if they should know it to be practised among private men in their bargains and contracts, they would incontinent cry out at it with a sour countenance, as an offence most detestable, and worthy to be punished with a shameful death: yea even very they that advance themselves authors of like council given to princes. Wherefore it may well be thought, either that all justice is but a base and a low virtue, and which abaseth itself far under the high dignity of kings; or at the least-

wise, that there be two justices, the one meet for the inferior sort of
the people, going afoot and creeping below on the ground, and
bound down on every side with many bands because it shall not run
at rovers; the other a princely virtue, which like as it is of much
higher majesty than the other poor justice, so also it is of much more
liberty, as to the which nothing is unlawful that it lusteth after.
These manners of princes (as I said) which be there so evil keepers
of leagues, cause the Utopians, as I suppose, to make no leagues at
all, which perchance would change their mind if they lived here.
Howbeit they think that though leagues be never so faithfully
observed and kept, yet the custom of making leagues was very evil
begun. For this causeth men (as though nations which be separate
asunder, by the space of a little hill or a river, were coupled together
by no society or bond of nature) to think themselves born adversaries
and enemies one to another, and that it is lawful for the one to seek
the death and destruction of the other, if leagues were not: yea, and
that after the leagues be accorded, friendship doth not grow and
increase; but the licence of robbing and stealing doth still remain, as
farforth as for lack of foresight and advisement in writing the
words of the league, any sentence or clause to the contrary is not
therein sufficiently comprehended. But they be of a contrary opinion.
That is, that no man ought to be counted an enemy, which hath
done no injury. And that the fellowship of nature is a strong league;
and that men be better and more surely knit together by love and
benevolence, than by covenants of leagues; by hearty affection of
mind, than by words.

Of Warfare

War or battle as a thing very beastly, and yet to no kind of beasts
in so much use as it is to man, they do detest and abhor. And contrary to the custom almost of all other nations, they count nothing
so much against glory, as glory gotten in war. And therefore
though they do daily practise and exercise themselves in the discipline of war, and that not only the men, but also the women upon
certain appointed days, lest they should be to seek in the feat of
arms, if need should require, yet they never [to] go to battle, but

either in the defence of their own country, or to drive out of their friends' land the enemies that have invaded it, or by their power to deliver from the yoke and bondage of tyranny some people, that be oppressed with tyranny. Which thing they do of mere pity and compassion. Howbeit they send help to their friends; not ever in their defence, but sometimes also to requite and revenge injuries before to them done. But this they do not unless their counsel and advice in the matter be asked, whilest it is yet new and fresh. For if they find the cause probable, and if the contrary part will not restore again such things as be of them justly demanded, then they be the chief authors and makers of the war. Which they do not only as oft as by inroads and invasions of soldiers, preys and booties be driven away, but then also much more mortally, when their friends' merchants in any land, either under the pretence of unjust laws, or else by the wresting and wrong understanding of good laws, do sustain an unjust accusation under the colour of justice. Neither the battle which the Utopians fought for the Nephelogetes against the Alaopolitanes a little before our time was made for any other cause, but that the Nephelogete merchantmen, as the Utopians thought, suffered wrong of the Alaopolitanes, under the pretence of right. But whether it were right or wrong, it was with so cruel and mortal war revenged, the countries round about joining their help and power to the puissance and malice of both parties, that most flourishing and wealthy peoples, being some of them shrewdly shaken, and some of them sharply beaten, the mischiefs were not finished nor ended, until the Alaopolitanes at the last were yielded up as bondmen into the jurisdiction of the Nephelogetes. For the Utopians fought not this war for themselves. And yet the Nephelogetes before the war, when the Alaopolitanes flourished in wealth, were nothing to be compared with them. So eagerly the Utopians prosecute the injuries done to their friends, yea, in money matters; and not their own likewise. For if they by cunning or guile be defrauded of their goods, so that no violence be done to their bodies, they wreak their anger by abstaining from occupying with that nation, until they have made satisfaction. Not for because they set less store by their own citizens, than by their friends; but that they take the loss of their friends' money more heavily than the loss of their own. Because that their friends' merchantmen, forasmuch as that they lose is their own private goods, sustain great damage by the loss. But their own citizens lose nothing but of the common goods, and of that which was at home plentiful and almost superfluous, else had it not been sent forth. Therefore no man feeleth the loss. And for this cause they think it too cruel an act, to revenge that loss with the death of many, the incommodity of the which loss no man feeleth neither in his life, neither in his living. But if it chance that any of their men in any other country be maimed or killed, whether it be done by a common or a private counsel, knowing and trying out the truth of the matter by their ambassadors, unless the offenders be rendered unto them in recompense of the injury, they will not be appeased; but incontinent they proclaim war against them. The offenders yielded, they punish either with death or with bondage. They be not only sorry, but also ashamed to achieve the victory with much bloodshed, counting it great folly to buy precious wares too dear. They rejoice and avaunt themselves, if they vanquish and oppress their enemies by craft and deceit. And for that act they make a general triumph, and as if the matter were manfully handled, they set up a pillar of stone in the place where they so vanquished their enemies, in token of the victory. For then they glory, then they boast and crack that they have played the men indeed, when they have so overcome, as no other living creature but only man could; that is to say, by the might and puissance of wit. For with bodily strength (say they) bears, lions, boars, wolves, dogs and other wild beasts do fight. And as the most part of them do pass us in strength and fierce courage, so in wit and reason we be much stronger than they all. Their chief and principal purpose in war, is to obtain that thing, which if they had before obtained, they would not have moved battle. But if that be not possible, they take so cruel vengeance of them, which be in the fault, that ever after they be afraid to do the like. This is their chief and principal intent, which they immediately and first of all prosecute, and set forward. But yet so, that they be more circumspect in avoiding and eschewing jeopardies, than they be desirous of praise and renown. Therefore immediately after that war is once solemnly denounced, they procure many proclamations signed with their own common seal to be set up privily at one time in their enemies' land, in places most frequented. In these proclamations they promise **great** rewards to him that will kill their enemies' prince, and somewhat less gifts, but them very great also, for every head of them, whose names be in the said proclamations contained. They be those whom they count their chief adversaries, next unto the prince. Whatsoever is prescribed unto him that killeth any of the proclaimed persons, that is doubled to him that bringeth any of the same to them alive; yea, and to the proclaimed persons themselves, if they will change their minds and come into them, taking their parts, they proffer the same great rewards with pardon and surety of their lives. Therefore it quickly cometh to pass that they have all other men in suspicion, and be unfaithful and mistrusting among themselves one to another, living in great fear, and in no less jeopardy. For it is well known, that divers times the most part of them (and specially the prince himself) hath been betrayed of them, in whom they put their most hope and trust. So that there is no manner of act nor deed that gifts and rewards do not enforce men unto. And in rewards they keep no measure. But remembering and considering into how great hazard and jeopardy they call them, endeavour themselves to recompense the greatness of the danger with like great benefits. And therefore they promise not only wonderful great abundance of gold, but also lands of great revenues lying in most safe places among their friends. And their promises they perform faithfully without any fraud or deceit. This custom of buying and selling adversaries among other people is disallowed, as a cruel act of a base and a cowardish mind. But they in this behalf think themselves much praiseworthy, as who like wise men by this means despatch great wars without any battle or skirmish. Yea they count it also a deed of pity and mercy, because that by the death of a few offenders the lives of a great number of innocents, as well of their own men as also of their enemies, be ransomed and saved, which in fighting should have been slain. For they do no less pity the base and common sort of their enemies' people, than they do their own; knowing that they be driven to war against their wills by the furious madness of their princes and heads. If by none of these means the matter go forward as they would have it, then they procure occasions of debate and dissension to be spread among their enemies. As by bringing the prince's brother, or some of the noblemen, in hope to obtain the kingdom. If this way prevail not, then they raise up the people that be next neighbours and borderers to their enemies, and them they set in their necks under the colour of some old title of right, such as kings do never lack. To them they promise their help and aid in their war. And as for money they give them abundance. But of their own citizens they send to them few or none. Whom they make so much of and love so entirely, that they would not be willing to change any of them for their adversary's prince. But their gold and silver, because they keep it all for this only purpose, they lay it out frankly and freely; as who should live even as wealthily, if they had bestowed it every penny. Yea, and besides their riches, which they keep at home, they have also an infinite treasure abroad, by reason that (as I said before) many nations be in their debt. Therefore they hire soldiers out of all countries and send them to battle, but chiefly of the Zapoletes. This people is five hundred miles from Utopia eastward. They be hideous, savage and fierce, dwelling in wild woods and high mountains, where they were bred and brought up. They be of an hard nature, able to abide and sustain heat, cold and labour, abhorring from all delicate dainties, occupying no husbandry nor tillage of the ground, homely and rude both in the building of their houses and in their apparel, given unto no goodness, but only to the breeding and bringing up of cattle. The most part of their living is by hunting and stealing. They be born only to war, which they diligently and earnestly seek for. And when they have gotten it, they be wonders glad thereof. They go forth of their country in great companies together, and whosoever lacketh soldiers, there they proffer their service for small wages. This is only the craft that they have to get their living by. They maintain their life by seeking their death. For them with whom they be in wages they fight hardily, fiercely, and faithfully. But they bind themselves for no certain time. But upon this condition they enter into bonds, that the next day they will take part with the other side for greater wages, and the next day after that, they will be ready to come back again for a little more money. There be few wars thereaway, wherein is not a great number of them in both parties. Therefore it daily chanceth that nigh kinsfolk, which were hired together on one part, and there very friendly and familiarly used themselves one with another, shortly after being separate into contrary parts, run one against another enviously and fiercely, and forgetting both kindred and friendship, thrust their swords one in another. And that for none other cause, but that they be hired of contrary princes for a little money. Which they do so highly regard and esteem, that they will easily be provoked to change parts for a halfpenny more wages by the day. So quickly they have taken a smack in covetousness. Which for all that is to them no profit. For that they get by fighting, immediately they spend unthriftily and wretchedly in riot. This people fight for the Utopians against all nations, because they give them greater wages than any other nation will. For the Utopians like as they seek good men to use well, so they seek these evil and vicious men to abuse. Whom, when need requireth, with promises of great rewards they put forth into great jeopardies. From whence the most part of them never cometh again to ask their rewards. But to them that remain alive they pay that which they promised faithfully, that they may be the more willing to put themselves in like dangers another time. Nor the Utopians pass not how many of them they bring to destruction. For they believe that they should do a very good deed for all mankind, if they could rid out of the world all that foul stinking den of that most wicked and cursed people. Next unto these they use the soldiers of them whom they fight for. And then the help of their other friends. And last of all, they join to their own citizens. Among whom they give to one of tried virtue and prowess the rule, governance, and conduction of the whole army. Under him they appoint two other, which, whilest he is safe, be both private and out of office. But if he be taken or slain, the one of the other two succeedeth him, as it were by inheritance. And if the second miscarry, then the third taketh his room, lest that (as the chance of battle is uncertain and doubtful) the jeopardy or death of the captain should bring the whole army in hazard. They choose soldiers, out of every city, those which put forth themselves willingly. For they thrust no man forth into war against his will. Because they believe, if any man be fearful and faint-hearted of nature, he will not only do no manful and hardy

154

act himself, but also be occasion of cowardice to his fellows. But if any battle be made against their own country, then they put these cowards (so that they be strong-bodied) in ships among other bold-hearted men. Or else they dispose them upon the walls, from whence they may not fly. Thus what for shame that their enemies be at hand, and what for because they be without hope of running away, they forget all fear. And many times extreme necessity turneth cowardice into prowess and manliness. But as none of them is thrust forth of his country into war against his will, so women that be willing to accompany their husbands in times of war be not prohibited or stopped. Yet they provoke and exhort them to it with praises. And in set field the wives do stand every one by her own husband's side. Also every man is compassed next about with his own children, kinsfolks, and alliance; that they, whom nature chiefly moveth to mutual succour, thus standing together, may help one another. It is a great reproach and dishonesty for the husband to come home without his wife, or the wife without her husband, or the son without his father. And therefore if the other part stick so hard by it that the battle come to their hands, it is fought with great slaughter and bloodshed, even to the utter destruction of both parts. For as they make all the means and shifts that may be to keep themselves from the necessity of fighting, so that they may despatch the battle by their hired soldiers; so when there is no remedy, but that they must needs fight themselves, then they do as courageously fall to it, as before, whiles they might, they did wisely avoid it. Nor they be not most fierce at the first brunt. But in continuance by little and little their fierce courage increaseth, with so stubborn and obstinate minds, that they will rather die than give back an inch. For that surety of living, which every man hath at home being joined with no careful anxiety or remembrance how their posterity shall live after them (for this pensiveness oftentimes breaketh and abateth courageous stomachs) maketh them stout and hardy, and disdainful to be conquered. Moreover their knowledge in chivalry and feats of arms putteth them in a good hope. Finally the wholesome and virtuous opinions, wherein they were brought up even from their childhood, partly through learning, and partly through the good ordinances and laws of their weal public, augment and increase their

manful courage. By reason whereof they neither set so little store by
their lives, that they will rashly and unadvisedly cast them away:
nor they be not so far in lewd and fond love therewith, that they
will shamefully covet to keep them, when honesty biddeth leave
them. When the battle is hottest and in all places most fierce and
fervent, a band of chosen and picked young men, which be sworn
to live and die together, take upon them to destroy their adversary's
captain. Him they invade, now with privy wiles, now by open
strength. At him they strike both near and far off. He is assailed
with a long and a continual assault, fresh men still coming in the
wearied men's places. And seldom it chanceth (unless he save himself by flying) that he is not either slain, or else taken prisoner and
yielded to his enemies alive. If they win the field, they persecute
not their enemies with the violent rage of slaughter. For they had
rather take them alive than kill them. Neither they do so follow
the chase and pursuit of their enemies, but they leave behind them
one part of their host in battle array under their standards. Insomuch that if all their whole army be discomfited and overcome saving the rearward, and that they therewith achieve the victory, then
they had rather let all their enemies 'scape, than to follow them out
of array. For they remember, it hath chanced unto themselves more
than once; the whole power and strength of their host being vanquished and put to flight, whilest their enemies rejoicing in the victory have persecuted them flying some one way and some another;
a few of their men lying in an ambush, there ready at all occasions,
have suddenly risen upon them thus dispersed and scattered out of
array, and through presumption of safety unadvisedly pursuing the
chase, and have incontinent changed the fortune of the whole battle,
and spite of their teeth wresting out of their hands the sure and
undoubted victory, being a little before conquered, have for their
part conquered the conquerors. It is hard to say whether they be
craftier in laying an ambush, or wittier in avoiding the same. You
would think they intend to fly, when they mean nothing less. And
contrariwise when they go about that purpose, you would believe it
were the least part of their thought. For if they perceive themselves
either overmatched in number, or closed in too narrow a place, then
they remove their camp either in the night season with silence, or

by some policy they deceive their enemies, or in the daytime they retire back so softly, that it is no less jeopardy to meddle with them when they give back, than when they press on. They fence and fortify their camp surely with a deep and a broad trench. The earth thereof is cast inward. Nor they do not set drudges and slaves awork about it. It is done by the hands of the soldiers themselves. All the whole army worketh upon it, except them that watch in harness before the trench for sudden adventures. Therefore by the labour of so many a large trench closing in a great compass of ground is made in less time than any man would believe. Their armour or harness, which they wear, is sure and strong to receive strokes, and handsome for all movings and gestures of the body, insomuch that it is not unwieldy to swim in. For in the discipline of their warfare among other feats they learn to swim in harness. Their weapons be arrows afar off, which they shoot both strongly and surely, not only footmen, but also horsemen. At hand strokes they use not swords but pollaxes, which be mortal, as well in sharpness, as in weight, both for foins and down strokes. Engines for war they devise and invent wonders wittily. Which when they be made they keep very secret, lest if they should be known before need require, they should be but laughed at and serve to no purpose. But in making them, hereunto they have chief respect, that they be both easy to be carried, and handsome to be moved and turned about. Truce taken with their enemies for a short time they do so firmly and faithfully keep, that they will not break it; no, not though they be thereunto provoked. They do not waste nor destroy their enemies' land with foragings, nor they burn not up their corn. Yea, they save it as much as may be from being overrun and trodden down either with men or horses, thinking that it groweth for their own use and profit. They hurt no man that is unarmed, unless he be an espial. All cities that be yielded unto them they defend. And such as they win by force of assault, they neither despoil nor sack, but them that withstood and dissuaded the yielding up of the same, they put to death; the other soldiers they punish with bondage. All the weak multitude they leave untouched. If they know that any citizens counselled to yield and render up the city, to them they give part of the condemned men's goods. The residue they distribute and give freely among them, whose help they had in the same war. For none of themselves taketh any portion of the prey. But when the battle is finished and ended, they put their friends to never a penny cost of all the charges that they were at, but lay it upon their necks that be conquered. Them they burden with the whole charge of their expenses, which they demand of them partly in money to be kept for like use of battle, and partly in lands of great revenues to be paid unto them yearly for ever. Such revenues they have now in many countries. Which by little and little rising of divers and sundry causes be increased above seven hundred thousand ducats by the year. Thither they send forth some of their citizens as lieutenants, to live there sumptuously like men of honour and renown. And yet, this notwithstanding, much money is saved, which cometh to the common treasury; unless it so chance that they had rather trust the country with the money. Which many times they do so long, until they have need to occupy it. And it seldom happeneth that they demand all. Of these lands they assign part unto them which, at their request and exhortation, put themselves in such jeopardies as I spake of before. If any prince stir up war against them, intending to invade their land, they meet him incontinent out of their own borders with great power and strength. For they never lightly make war in their own countries. Nor they be never brought into so extreme necessity as to take help out of foreign lands into their own island.

Of the Religions in Utopia

There be divers kinds of religion not only in sundry parts of the island, but also in divers places of every city. Some worship for God, the sun; some, the moon; some, some other of the planets. There be that give worship to a man that was once of excellent virtue or of famous glory, not only as God, but also as the chiefest and highest God. But the most and the wisest part (rejecting all these) believe that there is a certain godly power unknown, everlasting, incomprehensible, inexplicable, far above the capacity and reach of man's wit, dispersed throughout all the world, not in bigness, but in virtue and power. Him they call the father of all. To him alone they attribute the beginnings, the increasings, the proceedings, the

changes and the ends of all things. Neither they give divine honours
to any other than to him. Yea all the other also, though they be in
divers opinions, yet in this point they agree all together with the
wisest sort, in believing that there is one chief and principal God,
the maker and ruler of the whole world: whom they all commonly
in their country language call Mithra. But in this they disagree,
that among some he is counted one, and among some another. For
every one of them, whatsoever that is which he taketh for the chief
God, thinketh it to be the very same nature, to whose only divine
might and majesty the sum and sovereignty of all things by the consent of all people is attributed and given. Howbeit they all begin by
little and little to forsake and fall from this variety of superstitions,
and to agree together in that religion which seemeth by reason to
pass and excel the residue. And it is not to be doubted, but all the
other would long ago have been abolished, but that whatsoever un-
prosperous thing happened to any of them, as he was minded to
change his religion, the fearfulness of people did take it, not as a
thing coming by chance, but as sent from God out of heaven. As
though the God whose honour he was forsaking would revenge that
wicked purpose against him. But after they heard us speak of the
name of Christ, of his doctrine, laws, miracles, and of the no less
wonderful constancy of so many martyrs, whose blood willingly
shed brought a great number of nations throughout all parts of the
world into their sect; you will not believe with how glad minds,
they agreed unto the same: whether it were by the secret inspiration
of God, or else for that they thought it next unto that opinion, which
among them is counted the chiefest. Howbeit I think this was no
small help and furtherance in the matter, that they heard us say,
that Christ instituted among his, all things common; and that the
same community doth yet remain amongst the rightest Christian
companies. Verily howsoever, it came to pass, many of them consented together in our religion, and were washed in the holy water
of baptism. But because among us four (for no more of us was
left alive, two of our company being dead) there was no priest;
which I am right sorry for; they being entered and instructed in
all other points of our religion, lack only those sacraments, which
here none but priests do minister. Howbeit they understand and

perceive them and be very desirous of the same. Yea, they reason and dispute the matter earnestly among themselves, whether without the sending of a Christian bishop, one chosen out of their own people may receive the order of priesthood. And truly they were minded to choose one. But at my departure from them they had chosen none. They also which do not agree to Christ's religion, fear no man from it, nor speak against any man that hath received it. Saving that one of our company in my presence was sharply punished. He as soon as he was baptised began against our wills, with more earnest affection than wisdom, to reason of Christ's religion; and began to wax so hot in his matter, that he did not only prefer our religion before all other, but also did utterly despise and condemn all other, calling them profane, and the followers of them wicked and devilish and the children of everlasting damnation. When he had thus long reasoned the matter, they laid hold on him, accused him and condemned him into exile, not as a despiser of religion, but as a seditious person and a raiser up of dissension among the people. For this is one of the ancientest laws among them; that no man shall be blamed for reasoning in the maintenance of his own religion. For King Utopus, even at the first beginning, hearing that the inhabitants of the land were, before his coming thither, at continual dissension and strife among themselves for their religions; perceiving also that this common dissension (whilest every several sect took several parts in fighting for their country) was the only occasion of his conquest over them all: as soon as he had gotten the victory, first of all he made a decree, that it should be lawful for every man to favour and follow what religion he would, and that he might do the best he could to bring other to his opinion, so that he did it peaceably, gently, quietly, and soberly, without haste and contentious rebuking and inveighing against other. If he could not by fair and gentle speech induce them unto his opinion yet he should use no kind of violence, and refrain from displeasant and seditious words. To him that would vehemently and fervently in this cause strive and contend was decreed banishment or bondage. This law did King Utopus make not only for the maintenance of peace, which he saw through continual contention and mortal hatred utterly extinguished; but also because he thought this decree should make for the furtherance of religion. Whereof he durst define and determine nothing unadvisedly, as doubting whether God desiring manifold and divers sorts of honour, would inspire sundry men with sundry kinds of religion. And this surely he thought a very unmeet and foolish thing, and a point of arrogant presumption, to compel all other by violence and threatenings to agree to the same that thou believest to be true. Furthermore though there be one religion which alone is true, and all other vain and superstitious, yet did he well foresee (so that the matter were handled with reason, and sober modesty) that the truth of its own power would at the last issue out and come to light. But if contention and debate in that behalf should continually be used, as the worst men be most obstinate and stubborn, and in their evil opinion most constant; he perceived that then the best and holiest religion would be trodden underfoot and destroyed by most vain superstitions, even as good corn is by thorns and weeds overgrown and choked. Therefore all this matter he left undiscussed, and gave to every man free liberty and choice to believe what he would. Saving that he earnestly and straightly charged them, that no man should conceive so vile and base an opinion of the dignity of man's nature, as to think that the souls do die and perish with the body; or that the world runneth at all adventures governed by no divine providence. And therefore they believe that after this life vices be extremely punished and virtues bountifully rewarded. Him that is of a contrary opinion they count not in the number of men, as one that hath abased the high nature of his soul to the vileness of brute beasts' bodies, much less in the number of their citizens, whose laws and ordinances, if it were not for fear, he would nothing at all esteem. For you may be sure that he will study either with craft privily to mock, or else violently to break the common laws of his country, in whom remaineth no further fear than of the laws, nor no further hope than of the body. Wherefore he that is thus minded is deprived of all honours, excluded from all offices and rejected from all common administrations in the weal public. And thus he is of all sort despised, as of an unprofitable and of a base and vile nature. Howbeit they put him to no punishment, because they be persuaded that it is in no man's power to believe what he list. No, nor they constrain him not with threatenings to dissemble his

mind and show countenance contrary to his thought. For deceit
and falsehood and all manner of lies, as next unto fraud, they do
marvellously detest and abhor. But they suffer him not to dispute in
his opinion, and that only among the common people. For else
apart among the priests and men of gravity they do not only suffer,
but also exhort him to dispute and argue, hoping that at the last,
that madness will give place to reason. There be also other, and of
them no small number, which be not forbidden to speak their minds,
as grounding their opinion upon some reason, being in their living
neither evil nor vicious. Their heresy is much contrary to the other.
For they believe that the souls of brute beasts be immortal and everlasting. But nothing to be compared with ours in dignity, neither
ordained and predestinate to like felicity. For all they believe certainly and surely that man's bliss shall be so great, that they do
mourn and lament every man's sickness, but no man's death, unless
it be one whom they see depart from his life carefully and against
his will. For this they take for a very evil token, as though the soul
being in despair and vexed in conscience, through some privy and
secret forefeeling of the punishment now at hand, were afraid to
depart. And they think he shall not be welcome to God, which,
when he is called, runneth not to him gladly, but is drawn by force
and sore against his will. They therefore that see this kind of death
do abhor it, and them that so die they bury with sorrow and silence.
And when they have prayed God to be merciful to the soul and mer-
cifully to pardon the infirmities thereof, they cover the dead corse
with earth. Contrariwise all that depart merrily and full of good
hope, for them no man mourneth, but followeth the hearse with
joyful singing, commending the souls to God with great affection.
And at the last, not with mourning sorrow, but with a great reverence they burn the bodies. And in the same place they set up a
pillar of stone, with the dead man's titles therein graved. When
they be come home they rehearse his virtuous manners and his good
deeds. But no part of his life is so oft or gladly talked of as his
merry death. They think that this remembrance of their virtue and
goodness doth vehemently provoke and enforce the quick to virtue.
And that nothing can be more pleasant and acceptable to the dead.
Whom they suppose to be present among them, when they talk of

them, though to the dull and feeble eyesight of mortal men they be invisible. For it were an inconvenient thing that the blessed should not be at liberty to go whither they would. And it were a point of great unkindness in them to have utterly cast away the desire of visiting and seeing their friends, to whom they were in their lifetime joined by mutual love and charity. Which in good men after their death they count to be rather increased than diminished. They believe therefore that the dead be presently conversant among the quick, as beholders and witnesses of all their words and deeds. Therefore, they go more courageously to their business as having a trust and affiance in such overseers. And this same belief of the present conversation of their forefathers and ancestors among them feareth them from all secret dishonesty. They utterly despise and mock soothsayings and divinations of things to come by the flight or voices of birds, and all other divinations of vain superstition, which in other countries be in great observation. But they highly esteem and worship miracles that come by no help of nature, as works and witnesses of the present power of God. And such they say do chance there very often. And sometimes in great and doubtful matters, by common intercession and prayers, they procure and obtain them with a sure hope and confidence, and a steadfast belief.

They think that the contemplation of nature and the praise thereof coming, is to God a very acceptable honour. Yet there be many so earnestly bent and affectioned to religion, that they pass nothing for learning, nor give their minds to no knowledge of things. But idleness they utterly forsake and eschew, thinking felicity after this life to be gotten and obtained by busy labours and good exercises. Some therefore of them attend upon the sick, some amend highways, cleanse ditches, repair bridges, dig turfs, gravel and stones, fell and cleave wood, bring wood, corn, and other things into the cities in carts, and serve not only in common works, but also in private labours as servants, yea, more than bondmen. For whatsoever unpleasant, hard and vile work is anywhere, from the which labour, loathsomeness and desperation doth frighten other, all that they take upon them willingly and gladly, procuring quiet and rest to other, remaining in continual work and labour themselves, not upbraiding others therewith.

Now I have declared and described unto you, as truly as I could the form and order of that commonwealth, which verily in my judgment is not only the best, but also that which alone of good right may claim and take upon it the name of a commonwealth or public weal. For in other places they speak still of the commonwealth, but every man procureth his own private wealth. Here where nothing is private, the common affairs be earnestly looked upon. And truly on both parts they have good cause so to do as they do. For in other countries who knoweth not that he shall starve for hunger, unless he make some several provision for himself, though the commonwealth flourish never so much in riches? And therefore he is compelled even of very necessity to have regard to himself, rather than to the people, that is to say, to other. Contrariwise, there where all things be common to every man, it is not to be doubted that any man shall lack anything necessary for his private uses, so that the common storehouses and barns be sufficiently stored. For there nothing is distributed after a niggish sort, neither there is any poor man or beggar. And though no man have anything, yet every man is rich. For what can be more rich, than to live joyfully and merrily, without all grief and pensiveness; not caring for his own living, nor vexed or troubled with his wife's importunate complaints, not dreading poverty to his son, nor sorrowing for his daughter's dowry? Yea they take no care at all for the living and wealth of themselves and all theirs, of their wives, their children, their nephews, their children's children, and all the succession that ever shall follow in their posterity. And yet besides this there is no less provision for them that were once labourers and be now weak and impotent, than for them that do now labour and take pain. Here now would I see, if any man dare be so bold as to compare with this equity, the justice of other nations; among whom, I forsake God, if I can find any sign or token of equity and justice. For what justice is this, that a

164

rich goldsmith, or an usurer, or to be short, any of them which either do nothing at all, or else that which they do is such that it is not very necessary to the commonwealth, should have a pleasant and a wealthy living, either by idleness, or by unnecessary business; when in the meantime poor labourers, carters, ironsmiths, carpenters and ploughmen, by so great and continual toil, as drawing and bearing beasts be scant able to sustain, and again so necessary toil, that without it no commonwealth were able to continue and endure one year, do yet get so hard and poor a living, and live so wretched and miserable a life, that the state and condition of the labouring beasts may seem much better and wealthier? For they be not put to so continual labour, nor their living is not much worse, yea to them much pleasanter, taking no thought in the mean season for the time to come. But these silly poor wretches be presently tormented with barren and unfruitful labour. And the remembrance of their poor indigent and beggarly old age killeth them up. For their daily wages is so little, that it will not suffice for the same day, much less it yieldeth any overplus, that may daily be laid up for the relief of old age. Is not this an unjust and an unkind public weal, which giveth great fees and rewards to gentlemen, as they call them, and to goldsmiths, and to such other, which be either idle persons, or else only flatterers, and devisers of vain pleasures; and of the contrary part maketh no gentle provision for poor ploughmen, colliers, labourers, carters, ironsmiths, and carpenters: without whom no commonwealth can continue. But when it hath abused the labours of their lusty and flowering age, at the last when they be oppressed with old age and sickness, being needy, poor, and indigent of all things, then forgetting their so many painful watchings, not remembering their so many and so great benefits, recompenseth and acquitteth them most unkindly with miserable death. And yet besides this the rich men not only by private fraud, but also by common laws, do every day pluck and snatch away from the poor some part of their daily living. So whereas it seemed before unjust to recompense with unkindness their pains that have been beneficial to the public weal, now they have to this their wrong and unjust dealing (which is yet a much worse point) given the name of justice, yea and that by force of a law. Therefore, when I consider and weigh in my mind all these commonwealths, which nowadays anywhere do flourish, so God help me, I can perceive nothing but a certain conspiracy of rich men procuring their own commodities under the name and title of the commonwealth. They invent and devise all means and crafts, first how to keep safely, without fear of losing, that they have unjustly gathered together, and next how to hire and abuse the work and labour of the poor for as little money as may be. These devices, when the rich men have decreed to be kept and observed for the commonwealth's sake, that is to say for the wealth also of the poor people, then they be made laws. But these most wicked and vicious men, when they have by their insatiable covetousness divided among themselves all those things, which would have sufficed all men, yet how far be they from the wealth and felicity of the Utopian commonwealth? Out of the which, in that all the desire of money with the use thereof is utterly secluded and banished, how great a heap of cares is cut away! How great an occasion of wickedness and mischief is plucked up by the roots! For who knoweth not, that fraud, theft, ravine, brawling, quarreling, brabling, strife, chiding, contention, murder, treason, poisoning, which by daily punishments are rather revenged than refrained, do die when money dieth? And also that fear, grief, care, labours and watchings do perish even the very same moment that money perisheth? Yea poverty itself, which only seemed to lack money, if money were gone, it also would decrease and vanish away. And that you may perceive this more plainly, consider with yourselves some barren and unfruitful year, wherein many thousands of people have starved for hunger. I dare be bold to say, that in the end of that penury so much corn or grain might have been found in the rich men's barns, if they had been searched, as being divided among them whom famine and pestilence have killed, no man at all should have felt that plague and penury. So easily might men get their living, if that same worthy princess, lady money, did not alone stop up the way between us and our living, which a God's name was very excellently devised and invented, that by her the way thereto should be opened. I am sure the rich men perceive this, nor they be not ignorant how much better it were to lack no necessary thing, than to abound with overmuch superfluity; to be rid out of innumerable cares and troubles, than to be besieged with great riches. And I doubt not that either the respect of every man's private commodity, or else the authority of our saviour Christ (which for his great wisdom could not but know what were best, and for his inestimable goodness could not but counsel to that which he knew to be best) would have brought all the world long ago into the laws of this weal public, if it were not that one only beast, the princess and mother of all mischief, pride, doth withstand and let it. She measureth not wealth and prosperity by her own commodities, but by the miseries and incommodities of other: she would not by her good will be made a goddess, if there were no wretches left, whom she might be lady over to mock and scorn; over whose miseries her felicity might shine, whose poverty she might vex, torment and increase by gorgeously setting forth her riches. This hell-hound creepeth into men's hearts, and plucketh them back from entering the right path of life, and is so deeply rooted in men's breasts, that she cannot be plucked out. This form and fashion of a weal public, which I would gladly wish unto all nations, I am glad yet that it hath chanced to the Utopians, which have followed those institutions of life, whereby they have laid such foundations of their commonwealth, as shall continue and last not only wealthily, but also, as far as man's wit may judge and conjecture, shall endure for ever. For seeing the chief causes of ambition and sedition with other vices be plucked up by the roots and abandoned at home, there can be no jeopardy of domestical dissension, which alone hath cast under foot and brought to nought the well fortified and strongly-defenced wealth and riches of many cities. But forasmuch as perfect concord remaineth, and wholesome laws be executed at home the envy of all foreign princes be not able to shake or move the empire, though they have many times long ago gone about to do it, being evermore driven back.

Thus when Raphael had made an end of his tale, though many things came to my mind, which in the manners and laws of that people seemed to be instituted and founded of no good reason, not only in the fashion of their chivalry, and in their sacrifices and religions, and in other of their laws, but also, yea and chiefly, in that which is the principal foundation of all their ordinances, that is to say, in the community of their life and living, without any occupying of money, by the which thing only all nobility, magnificence, worship, honour and majesty, the true ornaments and honours, as the common opinion is, of a commonwealth, utterly be overthrown and destroyed; yet because I knew that he was weary of talking, and was not sure whether he could abide that anything should be said against his mind; specially because I remembered that he had reprehended this fault in other, which be afraid lest they should seem not to be wise enough, unless they could find some fault in other men's inventions; therefore I praising both their institutions and his communication, took him by the hand, and led him in to supper; saying that we would choose another time to weigh and examine the same matters, and to talk with him more at large therein. Which would to God it might once come to pass. In the meantime, as I cannot agree and consent to all things that he said, being else without doubt a man singularly well learned, and also in all worldly matters exactly and profoundly experienced, so must I needs confess and grant that many things be in the Utopian weal public, which in our cities I may rather wish for, than hope after.

Thus endeth the afternoon's talk of Raphael Hythloday concerning the laws and institutions of the Island of Utopia.

IMPRINTED AT LONDON BY ABRAHAM VELE,
DWELLING IN PAUL'S CHURCH YARD
AT THE SIGN OF THE LAMB.
ANNO 1551.

4

Aristotle, POLITICS   (Trans. by B. Jowett)

1. In what ways can you see Aristotle's influence on Thomas More?

2. How does Aristotle arrive at his conclusions? Why does he begin his discussion of society with an analysis of the family?

3. According to Aristotle, are all human beings essentially the same or are there fundamentally different types of people? How does Aristotle attempt to justify slavery? What are the inconsistencies in his argument? Were the Romans following Aristotle's ideas in their treatment of slaves as described by Gibbon?

4. What is the difference between men and women, according to Aristotle? How may Aristotle's views have contributed to sex discrimination in Western culture?

5. What are Aristotle's opinions concerning the various occupations or ways of gaining wealth? What is his view of money? If each occupation received the status which Aristotle assigned it, what would the resulting society be like?

6. One dominating feature of all of Aristotle's philosophy is his assumption that everything has a fixed nature which corresponds to the goal or purpose of that thing. What is the nature and purpose of society according to Aristotle? Would Aristotle see any possibility for the advancement or progress of society? What is the relationship of the society to the individual members of it?

Aristotle (384-322 B.C.) has been encountered several times already in this course. His philosophical studies encompassed virtually every area of human knowledge and were based on wide-ranging collections of empirical data gathered for him by students.

POLITICA

BOOK I

EVERY STATE is a community of some kind, and every community is established with a view to some good; for mankind always act in order to obtain that which they think good. But, if all communities aim at some good, the state or political community, which is the highest of all, and which embraces all the rest, aims at good in a greater degree than any other, and at the highest good.

Some people think that the qualifications of a statesman, king, householder, and master are the same, and that they differ, not in kind, but only in the number of their subjects. For example, the ruler over a few is called a master; over more, the manager of a household; over a still larger number, a statesman or king, as if there were no difference between a great household and a small state. The distinction which is made between the king and the statesman is as follows: When the government is personal, the ruler is a king; when, according to the rules of the political science, the citizens rule and are ruled in turn, then he is called a statesman.

But all this is a mistake; for governments differ in kind, as will be evident to any one who considers the matter according to the method which has hitherto guided us. As in other departments of science, so in politics, the compound should always be resolved into the simple elements or least parts of the whole. We must therefore look at the elements of which the state is composed, in order that we may see in what the different kinds of rule differ from one another, and whether any scientific result can be attained about each one of them.

He who thus considers things in their first growth and origin, whether a state or anything else, will obtain the clearest view of them. In the first place there must be a union of those who cannot exist without each other; namely, of male and female, that the race may continue (and this is a union which is formed, not of deliberate purpose, but because, in common with other animals and plants, mankind have a natural desire to leave behind them an image of themselves), and of natural ruler and subject, that both may be preserved. For that which can foresee by the exercise of mind is by nature intended to be lord and master, and that which can with its body give effect to such foresight is a subject, and by nature a slave; hence master and slave have the same interest. Now nature has distinguished between the female and the slave. For she is not niggardly, like the smith who fashions the Delphian knife for many uses; she makes each thing for a single use, and every instrument is best made when intended for one and not for many uses. But among barbarians no distinction is made between women and slaves, because there is no natural ruler among them: they are a community of slaves, male and female. Wherefore the poets say,—

'It is meet that Hellenes should rule over barbarians';
as if they thought that the barbarian and the slave were by nature one.

Out of these two relationships between man and woman, master and slave, the first thing to arise is the family, and Hesiod is right when he says,—

'First house and wife and an ox for the plough,'
for the ox is the poor man's slave. The family is the association established by nature for the supply of men's everyday wants, and the members of it are called by Charondas 'companions of the cupboard,' and by Epimenides the Cretan, 'companions of the manger.' But when several families are united, and the association aims at something more than the supply of daily needs, the first society to be formed is the village. And the most natural form of the village appears to be that of a colony from the family,

composed of the children and grandchildren, who are said to be 'suckled with the same milk.' And this is the reason why Hellenic states were originally governed by kings; because the Hellenes were under royal rule before they came together, as the barbarians still are. Every family is ruled by the eldest, and therefore in the colonies of the family the kingly form of government prevailed because they were of the same blood. As Homer says:

'Each one gives law to his children and to his wives.'

For they lived dispersedly, as was the manner in ancient times. Wherefore men say that the Gods have a king, because they themselves either are or were in ancient times under the rule of a king. For they imagine, not only the forms of the Gods, but their ways of life to be like their own.

When several villages are united in a single complete community, large enough to be nearly or quite self-sufficing, the state comes into existence, originating in the bare needs of life, and continuing in existece for the sake of a good life. And therefore, if the earlier forms of society are natural, so is the state, for it is the end of them, and the nature of a thing is its end. For what each thing is when fully developed, we call its nature, whether we are speaking of a man, a horse, or a family. Besides, the final cause and end of a thing is the best, and to be self-sufficing is the end and the best.

Hence it is evident that the state is a creation of nature, and that man is by nature a political animal. And he who by nature and not by mere accident is without a state, is either a bad man or above humanity; he is like the

'Tribeless, lawless, heartless one,'

whom Homer denounces—the natural outcast is forthwith a lover of war; he may be compared to an isolated piece at draughts.

Now, that man is more of a political animal than bees or any other gregarious animals is evident. Nature, as we often say, makes nothing in vain, and man is the only animal whom she has endowed with the gift of speech. And whereas mere voice is but an indication of pleasure or pain, and is therefore found in other animals (for their nature attains to the perception of pleasure and pain and the intimation of them to one another, and no further), the power of speech is intended to set forth the expedient and inexpedient, and therefore likewise the just and the unjust. And it is a characteristic of man that he alone has any sense of good and evil, of just and unjust, and the like, and the association of living beings who have this sense makes a family and a state.

Further, the state is by nature clearly prior to the family and to the individual, since the whole is of necessity prior to the part; for example, if the whole body be destroyed, there will be no foot or hand, except in an equivocal sense, as we might speak of a stone hand; for when destroyed the hand will be no better than that. But things are defined by their working and power; and we ought not to say that they are the same when they no longer have their proper quality, but only that they have the same name. The proof that the state is a creation of nature and prior to the individual is that the individual, when isolated, is not self-sufficing; and therefore he is like a part in relation to the whole. But he who is unable to live in society, or who has no need because he is sufficient for himself, must be either a beast or a god: he is no part of a state. A social instinct is implanted in all men by nature, and yet he who first founded the state was the greatest of benefactors. For man, when perfected, is the best of animals, but, when separated from law and justice, he is the worst of all; since armed injustice is the more dangerous, and he is equipped at birth with arms, meant to be used by intelligence and virtue, which he may use for the worst ends. Wherefore, if he have not virtue, he is the most unholy and the most savage of animals, and the most full of lust and gluttony. But justice is the bond of men in states, for the administration of justice, which is the determination of what is just, is the principle of order in political society.

Seeing then that the state is made up of households, before speaking of the state we must speak of the management of the household. The parts of household management correspond to the persons who compose the household, and a complete household consists of slaves and freemen. Now we should begin by examining everything in its fewest possible elements; and the first and fewest possible parts of a family are master and slave, husband and wife, father and children. We have therefore to consider what each of these three relations is and ought to be:—I mean the relation of master and servant, the marriage relation (the conjunction of man and wife has no name of its own), and thirdly, the procreative relation (this also has no proper name). And there is another element of a household, the so-called art of getting wealth, which, according to some, is identical with household management, according to others, a principal part of it; the nature of this art will also have to be considered by us.

Let us first speak of master and slave, looking to the needs of practical life and also seeking to attain some better theory of their relation than exists at present. For some are of opinion that the rule of a master is a science, and that the management of a household, and the mastership of slaves, and the political and royal rule, as I was saying at the outset; are all the same. Others affirm that the rule of a master over slaves is contrary to nature, and that the distinction between slave and freeman exists by law only, and not by nature; and being an interference with nature is therefore unjust.

Property is a part of the household, and the art of acquiring property is a part of the art of managing the household; for no man can live well, or indeed live at all,

unless he be provided with necessaries. And as in the arts which have a definite sphere the workers must have their own proper instruments for the accomplishment of their work, so it is in the management of a household. Now instruments are of various sorts; some are living, others lifeless; in the rudder, the pilot of a ship has a lifeless, in the look-out man a living instrument; for in the arts the servant is a kind of instrument. Thus, too, a possession is an instrument for maintaining life. And so, in the arrangement of the family, a slave is a living possession, and property a number of such instruments; and the servant is himself an instrument which takes precedence of all other instruments. For if every instrument could accomplish its own work, obeying or anticipating the will of others, like the statues of Daedalus, or the tripods of Hephaestus, which, says the poet,
'of their own accord entered the assembly of the Gods';
if, in like manner, the shuttle would weave and the plectrum touch the lyre without a hand to guide them, chief workmen would not want servants, nor masters slaves. Here, however, another distinction must be drawn; the instruments commonly so called are instruments of production, whilst a possession is an instrument of action. The shuttle, for example, is not only of use; but something else is made by it, whereas of a garment or of a bed there is only the use. Further, as production and action are different in kind, and both require instruments, the instruments which they employ must likewise differ in kind. But life is action and not production, and therefore the slave is the minister of action. Again, a possession is spoken of as a part is spoken of; for the part is not only a part of something else, but wholly belongs to it; and this is also true of a possession. The master is only the master of the slave; he does not belong to him, whereas the slave is not only the slave of his master, but wholly belongs to him. Hence we see what is the nature and office of a slave; he who is

by nature not his own but another's man, is by nature a slave; and he may be said to be another's man who, being a human being, is also a possession. And a possession may be defined as an instrument of action, separable from the possessor.

But is there any one thus intended by nature to be a slave, and for whom such a condition is expedient and right, or rather is not all slavery a violation of nature?

There is no difficulty in answering this question, on grounds both of reason and of fact. For that some should rule and others be ruled is a thing not only necessary, but expedient; from the hour of their birth, some are marked out for subjection, others for rule.

And there are many kinds both of rulers and subjects (and that rule is better which is exercised over better subjects—for example, to rule over men is better than to rule over wild beasts; for the work is better which is executed by better workmen, and where one man rules and another is ruled, they may be said to have a work); for in all things which form a composite whole and which are made up of parts, whether continuous or discrete, a distinction between the ruling and the subject element comes to light. Such a duality exists in living creatures, but not in them only; it originates in the constitution of the universe; even in things which have no life there is a ruling principle, as in a musical mode. But we are wandering from the subject. We will therefore restrict ourselves to the living creature, which, in the first place, consists of soul and body: and of these two, the one is by nature the ruler, and the other the subject. But then we must look for the intentions of nature in things which retain their nature, and not in things which are corrupted. And therefore we must study the man who is in the most perfect state both of body and soul, for in him we shall see the true relation of the two; although in bad or corrupted natures the body will often appear to rule over the soul, because they are in an evil and unnatural condition. At all events we may firstly observe in living creatures both a despotical and a constitutional rule; for the soul rules the body with a despotical rule, whereas the intellect rules the appetites with a constitutional and royal rule. And it is clear that the rule of the soul over the body, and of the mind and the rational element over the passionate, is natural and expedient; whereas the equality of the two or the rule of the inferior is always hurtful. The same holds good of animals in relation to men; for tame animals have a better nature than wild, and all tame animals are better off when they are ruled by man; for then they are preserved. Again, the male is by nature superior, and the female inferior; and the one rules, and the other is ruled; this principle, of necessity, extends to all mankind. Where then there is such a difference as that between soul and body, or between men and animals (as in the case of those whose business is to use their body, and who can do nothing bettter), the lower sort are by nature slaves, and it is better for them as for all inferiors that they should be under the rule of a master. For he who can be, and therefore is, another's, and he who participates in rational principle enough to apprehend, but not to have, such a principle, is a slave by nature. Whereas the lower animals cannot even apprehend a principle; they obey their instincts. And indeed the use made of slaves and of tame animals is not very different; for both with their bodies minister to the needs of life. Nature would like to distinguish between the bodies of freemen and slaves, making the one strong for servile labour, the other upright, and although useless for such services, useful for political life in the arts both of war and peace. But the opposite often happens—that some have the souls and others have the bodies of freemen. And doubtless if men differed from one another in the mere forms of their bodies as much as the statutes of the Gods do from men, all would acknowledge that the inferior class should be slaves of the superior. And if this is true of the body, how much more just that a similar distinction should exist in the soul? But the beauty of the body is seen, whereas the beauty of the soul is not seen. It is clear, then, that some men are by nature free, and others slaves, and that for these latter slavery is both expedient and right.

But that those who take the opposite view have in a certain way right on their side, may be easily seen. For the words slavery and slave are used in two senses. There is a slave or slavery by law as well as by nature. The law of which I speak is a sort of convention—the law by which whatever is taken in war is supposed to belong to the victors. But this right many jurists impeach, as they would an orator who brought forward an unconstitional measure: they detest the notion that, because one man has the power of doing violence and is superior in brute strength, another shall be his slave and subject. Even among philosophers there is a difference of opinion. The origin of the dispute, and what makes the views invade each other's territory, is as follows: in some sense virtue, when furnished with means, has actually the greatest power of exercising force: and as superior power is only found where there is superior excellence of some kind, power seems to imply virtue, and the dispute to be simply one about justice (for it is due to one party identifying justice with goodwill, while the other identifies it with the mere rule of the stronger). If these views are thus set out separately, the other views have no force or plausibility against the view that the superior in virtue ought to rule, or be master. Others, clinging, as they think, simply to a principle of justice (for law and custom are a sort of justice), assume that slavery in accordance with the custom of war is justified by law, but at the same moment they deny this. For what if the cause of the war be unjust? And again, no one would ever say that he is a slave who is unworthy to be a slave. Were this the case, men of the highest rank would be slaves and the children of slaves if they or their parents chance to have been taken captive and sold. Wherefore Hellenes do not like to call Hellenes slaves, but confine the term to barbarians. Yet, in using this language, they really mean the natural slave of whom we spoke at first; for it must be admitted that some are slaves everywhere, others nowhere. The same principle applies to nobility. Hellenes regard themselves as noble everywhere, and not only in their own country, but they deem the barbarians noble only when at home, thereby implying that there are two sorts of nobility and freedom, the one absolute, the other relative. The Helen of Theodectes says:

'Who would presume to call me servant who am on both sides sprung from the stem of the Gods?'

What does this mean but that they distinguish freedom and slavery, noble and humble birth, by the two principles of good and evil? They think that as men and animals beget men and animals, so from good men a good man springs. But this is what nature, though she may intend it, cannot always accomplish.

We see then that there is some foundation for this difference of opinion, and that all are not either slaves by nature or freemen by nature, and also that there is in some cases a marked distinction between the two classes, rendering it expedient and right for the one to be slaves and the others to be masters: the one practising obedience, the others exercising the authority and lordship which nature intended them to have. The abuse of this authority is injurious to both; for the interests of part and whole, of body and soul, are the same, and the slave is a part of the master, a living but separated part of his bodily frame. Hence, where the relation of master and slave between them is natural they are friends and have a common interest, but where it rests merely on law and force the reverse is true.

The previous remarks are quite enough to show that the
rule of a master is not a constitutional rule, and that all
the different kinds of rule are not, as some affirm, the
same with each other. For there is one rule exercised over
subjects who are by nature free, another over subjects
who are by nature slaves. The rule of a household is a
monarchy, for every house is under one head: whereas
constitutional rule is a government of freemen and equals.
The master is not called a master because he has science,
but because he is of a certain character, and the same
remark applies to the slave and the freeman. Still there
may be a science for the master and a science for the
slave. The science of the slave would be such as the man
of Syracuse taught, who made money by instructing slaves
in their ordinary duties. And such a knowledge may be
carried further, so as to include cookery and similar menial
arts. For some duties are of the more necessary, others of
the more honourable sort; as the proverb says, 'slave before slave, master before master.' But all such branches of
knowledge are servile. There is likewise a science of the
master, which teaches the use of slaves; for the master as
such is concerned, not with the acquisition, but with the
use of them. Yet this so-called science is not anything
great or wonderful; for the master need only know how
to order that which the slave must know how to execute.
Hence those who are in a position which places them
above toil have stewards who attend to their households
while they occupy themselves with philosophy or with
politics. But the art of acquiring slaves, I mean of justly
acquiring them, differs both from the art of the master
and the art of the slave, being a species of hunting or war.
Enough of the distinction between master and slave.

Let us now inquire into property generally, and into
the art of getting wealth, in accordance with our usual
method, for a slave has been shown to be a part of property. The first question is whether the art of getting wealth

is the same with the art of managing a household or a part of it, or instrumental to it; and if the last, whether in the way that the art of making shuttles is instrumental to the art of weaving, or in the way that the casting of bronze is instrumental to the art of the statuary, for they are not instrumental in the same way, but the one provides tools and the other material; and by material I mean the substratum out of which any work is made; thus wool is the material of the weaver, bronze of the statuary. Now it is easy to see that the art of household management is not identical with the art of getting wealth, for the one uses the material which the other provides. For the art which uses household stores can be no other than the art of household management. There is, however, a doubt whether the art of getting wealth is a part of household management or a distinct art. If the getter of wealth has to consider whence wealth and property can be procured, but there are many sorts of property and riches, then are husbandry, and the care and provision of food in general, parts of the wealth-getting art or distinct arts? Again, there are many sorts of food, and therefore there are many kinds of lives both of animals and men; they must all have food, and the differences in their food have made differences in their ways of life. For of beasts, some are gregarious, others are solitary; they live in the way which is best adapted to sustain them, accordingly as they are carnivorous or herbivorous or omnivorous: and their habits are determined for them by nature in such a manner that they may obtain with greater facility the food of their choice. But, as different species have different tastes, the same things are not naturally pleasant to all of them; and therefore the lives of carnivorous or herbivorous animals further differ among themselves. In the lives of men too there is a great difference. The laziest are shepherds, who lead an idle life, and get their subsistence without trouble from tame animals; their flocks having to wander

181

from place to place in search of pasture, they are compelled to follow them, cultivating a sort of living farm. Others support themselves by hunting, which is of different kinds. Some, for example, are brigands, others, who dwell near lakes or marshes or rivers or a sea in which there are fish, are fishermen, and others live by the pursuit of birds or wild beasts. The greater number obtain a living from the cultivated fruits of the soil. Such are the modes of subsistence which prevail among those whose industry springs up of itself, and whose food is not acquired by exchange and retail trade—there is the shepherd, the husbandman, the brigand, the fisherman, the hunter. Some gain a comfortable maintenance out of two employments, eking out the deficiencies of one of them by another: thus the life of a shepherd may be combined with that of a brigand, the life of a farmer with that of a hunter. Other modes of life are similarly combined in any way which the needs of men may require. Property, in the sense of a bare livelihood, seems to be given by nature herself to all, both when they are first born, and when they are grown up. For some animals bring forth, together with their offspring, so much food as will last until they are able to supply themselves; of this the vermiparous or oviparous animals are an instance; and the viviparous animals have up to a certain time a supply of food for their young in themselves, which is called milk. In like manner we may infer that, after the birth of animals, plants exist for their sake, and that the other animals exist for the sake of man, the tame for use and food, the wild, if not all, at least the greater part of them, for food, and for the provision of clothing and various instruments. Now if nature makes nothing incomplete, and nothing in vain, the inference must be that she has made all animals for the sake of man. And so, in one point of view, the art of war is a natural art of acquisition, for the art of acquisition includes hunting, an art which we ought to practise against wild beasts, and against men who, though intended by nature to be governed, will not submit; for war of such a kind is naturally just.

Of the art of acquisition then there is one kind which by nature is a part of the management of a household, in so far as the art of household management must either find ready to hand, or itself provide, such things necessary to life, and useful for the community of the family or state, as can be stored. They are the elements of true riches; for the amount of property which is needed for a good life is not unlimited, although Solon in one of his poems says that

'No bound to riches has been fixed for man.'

But there is a boundary fixed, just as there is in the other arts; for the instruments of any art are never unlimited, either in number or size, and riches may be defined as a number of instruments to be used in a household or in a state. And so we see that there is a natural art of acquisition which is practised by managers of households and by statesmen, and what is the reason of this.

There is another variety of the art of acquisition which is commonly and rightly called an art of wealth-getting, and has in fact suggested the notion that riches and property have no limit. Being nearly connected with the preceding, it is often identified with it. But though they are not very different, neither are they the same. The kind already described is given by nature, the other is gained by experience and art.

Let us begin our discussion of the question with the following considerations:

Of everything which we possess there are two uses: both belong to the thing as such, but not in the same manner, for one is the proper, and the other the improper or secondary use of it. For example, a shoe is used for wear, and is used for exchange; both are uses of the shoe. He who gives a shoe in exchange for money or food to him who wants one, does indeed use the shoe as a shoe, but this is not its proper or primary purpose, for a shoe is not made to be an object of barter. The same may be said of all possessions, for the art of exchange extends to all of them, and it arises at first from what is natural, from the circumstance that some have too little, others too much. Hence we may infer that retail trade is not a natural part of the art of getting wealth; had it been so, men would have ceased to exchange when they had enough. In the first community, indeed, which is the family, this art is obviously of no use, but it begins to be useful when the society increases. For the members of the family originally had all things in common; later, when the family divided into parts, the parts shared in many things, and different parts in different things, which they had to give in exchange for what they wanted, a kind of barter which is still practised among barbarous nations who exchange with one another the necessaries of life and nothing more; giving and receiving wine, for example, in exchange for corn, and the like. This sort of barter is not part of the wealth-getting art and is not contrary to nature, but is needed for the satisfaction of men's natural wants. The other or more complex form of exchange grew, as might have been inferred, out of the simpler. When the inhabitants of one country became more dependent on those of another, and they imported what they needed, and exported what they had too much of, money necessarily came into use. For the various necessaries of life are not easily carried about, and hence men agreed to employ in their dealings with each other something which was intrinsically useful and easily applicable to the purposes of life, for example, iron, silver, and the like. Of this the value was at first measured simply by size and weight, but in process of time they put a stamp upon it, to save the trouble of weighing and to mark the value.

When the use of coin had once been discovered, out of

the barter of necessary articles arose the other art of wealth-getting, namely, retail trade; which was at first probably a simple matter, but became more complicated as soon as men learned by experience whence and by what exchanges the greatest profit might be made. Originating in the use of coin, the art of getting wealth is generally thought to be chiefly concerned with it, and to the art which produces riches and wealth; having to consider how they may be accumulated. Indeed, riches is assumed by many to be only a quantity of coin, because the arts of getting wealth and retail trade are concerned with coin. Others maintain that coined money is a mere sham, a thing not natural, but conventional only, because, if the users substitute another commodity for it, it is worthless, and because it is not useful as a means to any of the necessities of life, and, indeed, he who is rich in coin may often be in want of necessary food. But how can that be wealth of which a man may have a great abundance and yet perish with hunger, like Midas in the fable, whose insatiable prayer turned everything that was set before him into gold?

Hence men seek after a better notion of riches and of the art of getting wealth than the mere acquisition of coin, and they are right. For natural riches and the natural art of wealth-getting are a different thing; in their true form they are part of the management of a household; whereas retail trade is the art of producing wealth, not in every way, but by exchange. And it is thought to be concerned with coin; for coin is the unit of exchange and the measure or limit of it. And there is no bound to the riches which spring from this art of wealth-getting. As in the art of medicine there is no limit to the pursuit of health, and as in the other arts there is no limit to the pursuit of their several ends, for they aim at accomplishing their ends to the uttermost (but of the means there is a limit, for the end is always the limit), so, too, in this art of wealth-getting there is no limit of the end, which is riches of the spurious kind, and the acquisition of wealth. But the art of wealth-getting which consists in household management, on the other hand, has a limit; the unlimited acquisition of wealth is not its business. And, therefore, in one point of view, all riches must have a limit; nevertheless, as a matter of fact, we find the opposite to be the case; for all getters of wealth increase their hoard of coin without limit. The source of the confusion is the near connexion between the two kinds of wealth-getting; in either, the instrument is the same, although the use is different, and so they pass into one another; for each is a use of the same property, but with a difference: accumulation is the end in the one case, but there is a further end in the other. Hence some persons are led to believe that getting wealth is the object of household management, and the whole idea of their lives is that they ought either to increase their money without limit, or at any rate not to lose it. The origin of this disposition in men is that they are intent upon living only, and not upon living well; and, as their desires are unlimited, they also desire that the means of gratifying them should be without limit. Those who do aim at a good life seek the means of obtaining bodily pleasures; and, since the enjoyment of these appears to depend on property, they are absorbed in getting wealth: and so there arises the second species of wealth-getting. For, as their enjoyment is in excess, they seek an art which produces the excess of enjoyment; and, if they are not able to supply their pleasures by the art of getting wealth, they try other arts, using in turn every faculty in a manner contrary to nature. The quality of courage, for example, is not intended to make wealth, but to inspire confidence; neither is this the aim of the general's or of the physician's art; but the one aims at victory and the other at health. Nevertheless, some men turn every quality or art into a means of getting wealth;

this they conceive to be the end, and to the promotion of the end they think all things must contribute.

Thus, then, we have considered the art of wealth-getting which is unnecessary, and why men want it; and also the necessary art of wealth-getting, which we have seen to be different from the other, and to be a natural part of the art of managing a household, concerned with the provision of food, not, however, like the former kind, unlimited, but having a limit.

And we have found the answer to our original question, Whether the art of getting wealth is the business of the manager of a household and of the statesman or not their business?—viz. that wealth is presupposed by them. For as political science does not make men, but takes them from nature and uses them, so too nature provides them with earth or sea or the like as a source of food. At this stage begins the duty of the manager of a household, who has to order the things which nature supplies;—he may be compared to the weaver who has not to make but to use wool, and to know, too, what sort of wool is good and serviceable or bad and unserviceable. Were this otherwise, it would be difficult to see why the art of getting wealth is a part of the management of a household and the art of medicine not; for surely the members of a household must have health just as they must have life or any other necessary. The answer is that as from one point of view the master of the house and the ruler of the state have to consider about health, from another point of view not they but the physician; so in one way the art of household management, in another way the subordinate art, has to consider about wealth. But, strictly speaking, as I have already said, the means of life must be provided beforehand by nature; for the business of nature is to furnish food to that which is born, and the food of the offspring is always what remains over of that from which it is produced. Wherefore the art of getting wealth out of fruits and animals is always natural.

There are two sorts of wealth-getting, as I have said; one is a part of household management, the other is retail trade: the former necessary and honourable, while that which consists in exchange is justly censured; for it is unnatural, and a mode by which men gain from one another. The most hated sort, and with the greatest reason, is usury, which makes a gain out of money itself, and not from the natural object of it. For money was intended to be used in exchange, but not to increase at interest. And this term interest, which means the birth of money from money, is applied to the breeding of money because the offspring resembles the parent. Wherefore of all modes of getting wealth this is the most unnatural.

Enough has been said about the theory of wealth-getting; we will now proceed to the practical part. The discussion of such matters is not unworthy of philosophy, but to be engaged in them practically is illiberal and irksome. The useful parts of wealth-getting are, first, the knowledge of live-stock,—which are most profitable, and where, and how,—as, for example, what sort of horses or sheep or oxen or any other animals are most likely to give a return. A man ought to know which of these pay better than others, and which pay best in particular places, for some do better in one place and some in another. Secondly, husbandry, which may be either tillage or planting, and the keeping of bees and of fish, or fowl, or of any animals which may be useful to man. These are the divisions of the true or proper art of wealth-getting and come first. Of the other, which consists in exchange, the first and most important division is commerce (of which there are three kinds—the provision of a ship, the conveyance of goods, exposure for sale—these again differing as they are safer or more profitable), the second is usury, the third, service for hire—of this, one kind is employed in the mechanical arts, the other in unskilled and bodily labour. There is still a third sort of wealth-getting intermediate between this and the first or natural mode which is partly natural, but is also concerned with exchange, viz. the industries that make their profit from the earth, and from things growing from the earth which, although they bear no fruit, are nevertheless profitable; for example, the cutting of timber and all mining. The art of mining, by which minerals are obtained, itself has many branches, for there are various kinds of things dug out of the earth. Of the several divisions of wealth-getting I now speak generally; a minute consideration of them might be useful in practice, but it would be tiresome to dwell upon them at greater length now.

Those occupations are most truly arts in which there is the least element of chance; they are the meanest in which the body is most deteriorated, the most servile in which there is the greatest use of the body, and the most illiberal in which there is the least need of excellence.

Works have been written upon these subjects by various persons; for example, by Chares the Parian, and Apollodorus the Lemnian, who have treated of Tillage and Planting, while others have treated of other branches; any one who cares for such matters may refer to their writings. It would be well also to collect the scattered stories of the ways in which individuals have succeeded in amassing a fortune; for all this is useful to persons who value the art of getting wealth. There is the anecdote of Thales the Milesian and his financial device, which involves a principle of universal application, but is attributed to him on account of his reputation for wisdom. He was reproached for his poverty, which was supposed to show that philosophy was of no use. According to the story, he knew by his skill in the stars while it was yet winter that there would be a great harvest of olives in the coming

189

year; so, having a little money, he gave deposits for the use of all the olive-presses in Chios and Miletus, which he hired at a low price because no one bid against him. When the harvest-time came, and many were wanted all at once and of a sudden, he let them out at any rate which he pleased, and made a quantity of money. Thus he showed the world that philosophers can easily be rich if they like, but that their ambition is of another sort. He is supposed to have given a striking proof of his wisdom, but, as I was saying, his device for getting wealth is of universal application, and is nothing but the creation of a monopoly. It is an art often practised by cities when they are in want of money; they make a monopoly of provisions.

There was a man of Sicily, who, having money deposited with him, bought up all the iron from the iron mines; afterwards, when the merchants from their various markets came to buy, he was the only seller, and without much increasing the price he gained 200 per cent. Which when Dionysius heard, he told him that he might take away his money, but that he must not remain at Syracuse, for he thought that the man had discovered a way of making money which was injurious to his own interests. He made the same discovery as Thales; they both contrived to create a monopoly for themselves. And statesmen as well ought to know these things; for a state is often as much in want of money and of such devices for obtaining it as a household, or even more so; hence some public men devote themselves entirely to finance.

Of household management we have seen that there are three parts—one is the rule of a master over slaves, which has been discussed already, another of a father, and the third of a husband. A husband and father, we saw, rules over wife and children, both free, but the rule differs, the rule over his children being a royal, over his wife a constitutional rule. For although there may be exceptions to the order of nature, the male is by nature fitter for command than the female, just as the elder and full-grown is superior to the younger and more immature. But in most constitutional states the citizens rule and are ruled by turns, for the idea of a constitutional state implies that the natures of the citizens are equal, and do not differ at all. Nevertheless, when one rules and the other is ruled we endeavour to create a difference of outward forms and names and titles of respect, which may be illustrated by the saying of Amasis about his foot-pan. The relation of the male to the female is of this kind, but there the inequality is permanent. The rule of a father over his children is royal, for he rules by virtue both of love and of the respect due to age, exercising a kind of royal power. And therefore Homer has appropriately called Zeus 'father of Gods and men,' because he is the king of them all. For a king is the natural superior of his subjects, but he should be of the same kin or kind with them, and such is the relation of elder and younger, of father and son.

Thus it is clear that household management attends more to men than to the acquisition of inanimate things, and to human excellence more than to the excellence of property which we call wealth, and to the virtue of freemen more than to the virtue of slaves. A question may indeed be raised, whether there is any excellence at all in a slave beyond and higher than merely instrumental and ministerial qualities—whether he can have the virtues of temperance, courage, justice, and the like; or whether slaves possess only bodily and ministerial qualities. And, whichever way we answer the question, a difficulty arises; for, if they have virtue, in what will they differ from freemen? On the other hand, since they are men and share in rational principle, it seems absurd to say that they have no virtue. A similar question may be raised about women and children, whether they too have virtues: ought a

191

woman to be temperate and brave and just, and is a child
to be called temperate, and intemperate, or not? So in
general we may ask about the natural ruler, and the natural subject, whether they have the same or different
virtues. For if a noble nature is equally required in both,
why should one of them always rule, and the other always
be ruled? Nor can we say that this is a question of degree,
for the difference between ruler and subject is a difference
of kind, which the difference of more and less never is.
Yet how strange is the supposition that the one ought, and
that the other ought not, to have virtue! For if the ruler
is intemperate and unjust, how can he rule well? if the
subject, how can he obey well? If he be licentious and
cowardly, he will certainly not do his duty. It is evident,
therefore, that both of them must have a share of virtue,
but varying as natural subjects also vary among themselves. Here the very constitution of the soul has shown
us the way; in it one part naturally rules, and the other
is subject, and the virtue of the ruler we maintain to be
different from that of the subject;—the one being the
virtue of the rational, and the other of the irrational part.
Now, it is obvious that the same principle applies generally, and therefore almost all things rule and are ruled
according to nature. But the kind of rule differs;—the
freeman rules over the slave after another manner from
that in which the male rules over the female, or the man
over the child; although the parts of the soul are present
in all of them, they are present in different degrees. For
the slave has no deliberative faculty at all; the woman
has, but it is without authority, and the child has, but it
is immature. So it must necessarily be supposed to be with
the moral virtues also; all should partake of them, but
only in such manner and degree as is required by each
for the fulfilment of his duty. Hence the ruler ought to
have moral virtue in perfection, for his function, taken
absolutely, demands a master artificer, and rational prin-

ARISTOTLE

ciple is such an artificer; the subjects, on the other hand, require only that measure of virtue which is proper to each of them. Clearly, then, moral virtue belongs to all of them; but the temperance of a man and of a woman, or the courage and justice of a man and of a woman, are not, as Socrates maintained, the same; the courage of a man is shown in commanding, of a woman in obeying. And this holds of all other virtues, as will be more clearly seen if we look at them in detail, for those who say generally that virtue consists in a good disposition of the soul, or in doing rightly, or the like, only deceive themselves. Far better than such definitions is their mode of speaking, who, like Gorgias, enumerate the virtues. All classes must be deemed to have their special attributes; as the poet says of women,

'Silence is a woman's glory,'

but this is not equally the glory of man. The child is imperfect, and therefore obviously his virtue is not relative to himself alone, but to the perfect man and to his teacher, and in like manner the virtue of the salve is relative to a master. Now we determined that a slave is useful for the wants of life, and therefore he will obviously require only so much virtue as will prevent him from failing in his duty through cowardice or lack of self-control. Some one will ask whether, if what we are saying is true, virtue will not be required also in the artisans, for they often fail in their work through the lack of self-control? But is there not a great difference in the two cases? For the slave shares in his master's life; the artisan is less closely connected with him, and only attains excellence in proportion as he becomes a slave. The meaner sort of mechanic has a special and separate slavery; and whereas the slave exists by nature, not so the shoemaker or other artisan. It is manifest, then, that the master ought to be the source of such excellence in the slave, and not a mere possessor of the art of mastership which trains the slave in his duties. Wherefore they are mistaken who forbid us to converse with slaves and say that we should employ command only, for slaves stand even more in need of admonition than children.

So much for this subject; the relations of husband and wife, parent and child, their several virtues, what in their intercourse with one another is good, and what is evil, and how we may pursue the good and escape the evil, will have to be discussed when we speak of the different forms of government. For, inasmuch as every family is a part of a state, and these relationships are the parts of a family, and the virtue of the part must have regard to the virtue of the whole, women and children must be trained by education with an eye to the constitution, if the virtues of either of them are supposed to make any difference in the virtues of the state. And they must make a difference: for the children grow up to be citizens, and half the free persons in a state are women.

Of these matters, enough has been said; of what remains, let us speak at another time. Regarding, then, our present inquiry as complete, we will make a new beginning. And, first, let us examine the various theories of a perfect state.

5

Auguste Comte, THE POSITIVE PHILOSOPHY

Max Weber,   THE PROTESTANT ETHIC AND THE SPIRIT
           OF CAPITALISM   (Trans. by Talcott Parsons)

1. Explain the three states, or conditions, which com-
    prise the "great fundamental law" which Comte be-
    lieved governed the evolution of the mind.

2. Does Comte view the three conditions as integrated,
    progressive, or equally separate phenomena in the
    development of human intelligence? Justify your
    answer.

3. How is the positive explanation derived?

4. What is positive philosophy?

5. How does Weber define the term "rationalism"?

6. What does Weber say is the most fateful force in
    our modern life? Why? Do you agree or disagree?
    Explain.

7. Does Weber equate unlimited greed for gain with
    capitalism? Explain.

8. According to Weber, what are the peculiarities of
    Western capitalism? How does his view of modern
    Western civilization contrast with Comte's view?

9. What is the meaning and significance of the "Prot-
    estant work ethic"?

10. Explain Weber's theory concerning the development
    of capitalism. Do you agree or disagree? Justify
    your answer.

11. Does Weber consider wealth evil? Explain.

August Comte (1798-1857), a French social thinker and philosopher, used science as a means of studying society. He founded the philosophy called positivism, and originated a concept of social science which he called sociology. Comte's ideas have influenced students of historical and social theory and such authors as Herbert Spencer and John Stuart Mill.

THE POSITIVE PHILOSOPHY

AUGUSTE COMTE

A general statement of any system of philosophy may be either a sketch of a doctrine to be established, or a summary of a doctrine already established. If greater value belongs to the last, the first is still important, as characterizing from its origin the subject to be treated. In a case like the present, where the proposed study is vast and hitherto indeterminate, it is especially important that the field of research should be marked out with all possible accuracy. For this purpose, I will glance at the considerations which have originated this work, and which will be fully elaborated in the course of it.

In order to understand the true value and character of the Positive Philosophy, we must take a brief general view of the progressive course of the human mind, regarded as a whole; for no conception can be understood otherwise than through its history.

From the study of the development of human intelligence, in all directions, and through all times, the discovery arises of a great fundamental law, to which it is necessarily subject, and which has a solid foundation of proof, both in the facts of our organization and in our historical experience. The law is this:—that each of our leading conceptions,—each branch of our knowledge,—passes successively through three different theoretical conditions: the Theological, or fictitious; the Metaphysical, or abstract; and the Scientific, or positive. In other words, the human mind, by its nature, employs in its progress three methods of philosophizing, the character of which is

197

essentially different, and even radically opposed: viz., the theological method, the metaphysical, and the positive. Hence arise three philosophies, or general systems of conceptions on the aggregate of phenomena, each of which excludes the others. The first is the necessary point of departure of the human understanding; and the third is its fixed and definitive state. The second is merely a state of transition.

In the theological state, the human mind, seeking the essential nature of beings, the first and final causes (the origin and purpose) of all effects,—in short, Absolute knowledge,—supposes all phenomena to be produced by the immediate action of supernatural beings.

In the metaphysical state, which is only a modification of the first, the mind supposes, instead of supernatural beings, abstract forces, veritable entities (that is, personified abstractions) inherent in all beings, and capable of producing all phenomena. What is called the explanation of phenomena is, in this stage, a mere reference of each to its proper entity.

In the final, the positive state, the mind has given over the vain search after Absolute notions, the origin and destination of the universe, and the causes of phenomena, and applies itself to the study of their laws,—that is, their invariable relations of succession and resemblance. Reasoning and observation, duly combined, are the means of this knowledge. What is now understood when we speak of an explanation of facts is simply the establishment of a connection between single phenomena and some general facts, the number of which continually diminishes with the progress of science.

The Theological system arrived at the highest perfection of which it is capable when it substituted the providential action of a single Being for the varied operations of the numerous divinities which had been before imagined. In the same way, in the last stage of the Metaphysical system, men substitute one great entity (Nature) as the cause of all phenomena, instead of the multitude of entities at first supposed. In the same way, again, the ultimate perfection of the Positive system would be (if such perfection could be hoped for) to represent all phenomena as particular aspects of a single general fact;—such as Gravitation, for instance.

The importance of the working of this general law will be established hereafter. At present, it must suffice to point out some of the grounds of it.

There is no science which, having attained the positive stage, does not bear marks of having passed through the others. Some time since it was (whatever it might be) composed, as we can now perceive, of metaphysical abstractions; and, further back in the course of time, it took its form from theological conceptions. We shall have only too much occasion to see, as we proceed, that our most advanced sciences still bear very evident marks of the two earlier periods through which they have passed.

The progress of the individual mind is not only an illustration, but an indirect evidence of that of the general mind. The point of departure of the individual and of the race being the same, the phases of the mind of a man correspond to the epochs of the mind of the race. Now, each of us is aware, if he looks back upon his own history, that he was a theologian in his childhood, a metaphysician in his youth, and a natural philosopher in his manhood. All men who are up to their age can verify this for themselves.

Besides the observation of facts, we have theoretical reasons in support of this law.

The most important of these reasons arises from the necessity that always exists for some theory to which to refer our facts, combined with the clear impossibility that, at the outset of human knowledge, men could have formed theories out of the observation of facts. All good intellects have repeated, since Bacon's time, that there can be no real knowledge but that which is based on observed facts. This is incontestable, in our present advanced stage; but, if we look back to the primitive stage of human knowledge, we shall see that it must have been otherwise then. If it is true that every theory must be based upon observed facts, it is equally true that facts cannot be observed without the guidance of some theory. Without such guidance, our facts would be desultory and fruitless; we could not retain them: for the most part we could not even perceive them.

Thus, between the necessity of observing facts in order to form a theory, and having a theory in order to observe facts, the human mind would have been entangled in a vicious circle, but for the natural opening afforded by Theological conceptions. This is the fundamental reason for the theological character of the primitive philosophy. This necessity is confirmed by the perfect suitability of the theological philosophy to the earliest researches of the human mind. It is remarkable that the most inaccessible questions,—those of the nature of beings, and the origin and purpose of phenomena,—should be the first to occur in a primitive state, while those which are really within our reach are regarded as almost unworthy of serious study. The reason is evident enough:—that experience alone can teach us the measure of our powers; and if men had not begun by an exaggerated estimate of what they can do, they would never have done all that they are capable of. Our organization requires this. At such a period there could have been no reception of a positive philosophy, whose function is to discover the laws of phenomena, and whose leading characteristic it is to regard as interdicted to human reason those sublime mysteries which theology explains, even to their minutest details, with the most attractive facility. It is just so under a practical view of the nature of the researches with which men first occupied themselves. Such inquiries offered the powerful charm of unlimited empire over the external world,—a world destined wholly for our use, and involved in every way with our existence. The theological philosophy, presenting this view, administered exactly the stimulus necessary to incite the human mind to the irksome labour without which it could make no progress. We can now scarcely conceive of such a state of things, our reason having become sufficiently mature to enter upon laborious scientific researches, without needing any such stimulus as wrought upon the imaginations of astrologers an alchemists. We have motive enough in the hope of discovering the laws of phenomena, with a view to the con-

200

firmation or rejection of a theory. But it could not be so in the earliest days; and it is to the chimeras of astrology and alchemy that we owe the long series of observations and experiments on which our positive science is based. Kepler felt this on behalf of astronomy, and Berthollet on behalf of chemistry. Thus was a spontaneous philosophy, the theological, the only possible beginning, method, and provisional system, out of which the Positive philosophy could grow. It is easy, after this, to perceive how Metaphysical methods and doctrines must have afforded the means of transition from the one to the other.

The human understanding, slow in its advance, could not step at once from the theological into the positive philosophy. The two are so radically opposed, that an intermediate system of conceptions has been necessary to render the transition possible. It is only in doing this, that Metaphysical conceptions have any utility whatever. In contemplating phenomena, men substitute for supernatural direction a corresponding entity. This entity may have been supposed to be derived from the supernatural action: but it is more easily lost sight of, leaving attention free for the facts themselves, till, at length, metaphysical agents have ceased to be anything more than the abstract names of phenomena. It is not easy to say by what other process than this our minds could have passed from supernatural considerations to natural; from the theological system to the positive.

The Law of human development being thus established, let us consider what is the proper nature of the Positive Philosophy.

As we have seen, the first characteristic of the Positive Philosophy is that it regards all phenomena as subjected to invariable natural *Laws.* Our business is,—seeing how vain is any research into what are called *Causes,* whether first or final,—to pursue an accurate discovery of these Laws, with a view to reducing them to the smallest possible number. By speculating upon causes, we could solve no difficulty about origin and purpose. Our real business is to analyse accurately the circumstances of phenomena, and to connect them by the natural relations of succession and resemblance. The best illustration of this is in the case of the doctrine of Gravitation. We say that the general phenomena of the universe are *explained* by it, because it connects under one head the whole immense variety of astronomical facts; exhibiting the constant tendency of atoms towards each other in direct proportion to their masses, and in inverse proportion to the squares of their distances; whilst the general fact itself is a mere extension of one which is perfectly familiar to us, and which we therefore say that we know;—the weight of bodies on the surface of the earth. As to what weight and attraction are, we have nothing to do with that, for it is not a matter of knowledge at all. Theologians and metaphysicians may imagine and refine about such questions; but positive philosophy rejects them. When any attempt has been made to explain them, it has ended only in saying that attraction is universal weight, and that weight is terrestrial attraction: that is, that the two orders of phenomena are identical; which is the point from which the question set out. Again, M. Fourier, in his fine series of researches on Heat, has given us all the most important and precise laws of the phenomena of heat, and many large and new truths, without once inquiring into its nature, as his predecessors had done when they disputed about calorific matter and the action of an universal ether. In treating his subject in the Positive method, he finds inexhaustible material for all his activity of research, without betaking himself to insoluble questions.

Before ascertaining the stage which the Positive Philosophy has reached, we must bear in mind that the different kinds of our knowledge have passed through the three stages of progress at different rates, and have not therefore arrived at the same time. The rate of advance depends on the nature of the knowledge in question, so distinctly that, as we shall see hereafter, this consideration constitutes an accessory to the fundamental law of progress. Any kind of knowledge reaches the positive stage early in proportion to its generality, simplicity, and independence of other departments. Astronomical science, which is above all made up of facts that are general, simple, and independent of other sciences, arrived first; then terrestrial Physics; then Chemistry; and, at length, Physiology.

It is difficult to assign any precise date to this revolution in science. It may be said, like everything else, to have been always going on; and especially since the labours of Aristotle and the school of Alexandria; and then from the introduction of natural science into the West of Europe by the Arabs. But, if we must fix upon some marked period, to serve as a rallying point, it must be that,—about two centuries ago,—when the human mind was astir under the precepts of Bacon, the conceptions of Descartes, and the discoveries of Galileo. Then it was that the spirit of the Positive philosophy rose up in opposition to that of the superstitious and scholastic systems which had hitherto obscured the true character of all science. Since that date, the progress of the Positive philosophy, and the decline of the other two, have been so marked that no rational mind now doubts that the revolution is destined to go on to its completion,—every branch of knowledge being, sooner or later, brought within the operation of Positive philosophy. This is not yet the case. Some are still lying outside: and not till they are brought in will the Positive philosophy possess that character of universality which is necessary to its definitive constitution.

In mentioning just now the four principal categories of phenomena,—astronomical, physical, chemical, and physiological,—there was an omission which will have been noticed. Nothing was said of Social phenomena. Though involved with the physiological, Social phenomena demand a distinct classification, both on account of their importance and of their difficulty. They are the most individual, the most complicated, the most dependent on all others; and therefore they must be the latest,—even if they had no special obstacle to encounter. This branch of science has not hitherto entered into the domain of Positive philosophy. Theological and metaphysical methods, exploded in other departments, are as yet exclusively applied, both in the way of inquiry and discussion, in all treatment of Social subjects, though the best minds are heartily weary of eternal disputes about divine right and the sovereignty of the people. This is the great, while it is evidently the only gap which has to be filled, to constitute, solid and entire, the Positive Philosophy. Now that the human mind has grasped celestial and terrestrial physics,—mechanical and chemical; organic physics, both vegetable and animal,—there remains one science, to fill up the series of sciences of observation,—Social physics. This is what men have now most need of: and this it is the principal aim of the present work to establish.

It would be absurd to pretend to offer this new science at once in a complete state. Others, less new, are in very unequal conditions of forwardness. But the same character of positivity which is impressed on all the others will be shown to belong to this. This once done, the philosophical system of the moderns will be in fact complete, as there will then be no phenomenon which does not naturally enter into some one of the five great categories. All our fundamental conceptions having become homogeneous, the Positive state will be fully established. It can never again change its character, though it will be for ever in course of development by additions of new knowledge. Having acquired the character of universality which has hitherto been the only advantage resting with the two preceding systems, it will supersede them by its natural superiority, and leave to them only an historical existence.

We have stated the special aim of this work. Its secondary and general aim is this:—to review what has been effected in the Sciences, in order to show that they are not radically separate, but all branches from the same trunk. If we had confined ourselves to the first and special object of the work, we should have produced merely a study of Social physics: whereas, in introducing the second and general we offer a study of Positive philosophy, passing in review all the positive sciences already formed.

The purpose of this work is not to give an account of the Natural Sciences. Besides that it would be endless, and that it would require a scientific preparation such as no one man possesses, it would be apart from our object, which is to go

204

through a course of not Positive Science, but Positive Philosophy. We have only to consider each fundamental science in its relation to the whole positive system, and to the spirit which characterizes it; that is, with regard to its methods and its chief results.

The two aims, though distinct, are inseparable; for, on the one hand, there can be no positive philosophy without a basis of social science, without which it could not be all-comprehensive; and, on the other hand, we could not pursue Social science without having been prepared by the study of phenomena less complicated than those of society, and furnished with a knowledge of laws and anterior facts which have a bearing upon social science. Though the fundamental sciences are not all equally interesting to ordinary minds, there is no one of them that can be neglected in an inquiry like the present; and in the eye of philosophy, all are of equal value to human welfare. Even those which appear the least interesting have their own value, either on account of the perfection of their methods, or as being the necessary basis of all the others.

Lest it should be supposed that our course will lead us into a wilderness of such special studies as are at present the bane of a true positive philosophy, we will briefly advert to the existing prevalence of such special pursuit. In the primitive state of human knowledge there is no regular division of intellectual labour. Every student cultivates all the sciences. As knowledge accrues, the sciences part off; and students devote themselves each to some one branch. It is owing to this division of employment, and concentration of whole minds upon a single department, that science has made so prodigious an advance in modern times; and the perfection of this division is one of the most important characteristics of the Positive philosophy. But, while admitting all the merits of this change, we cannot be blind to the eminent disadvantages which arise from the limitation of minds to a particular study. It is inevitable that each should be possessed with exclusive notions, and be therefore incapable of the general superiority of ancient students, who actually owed that general superiority to the inferiority of their knowledge. We must consider whether the evil can be avoided without losing the good of the modern arrangement; for the evil is becoming urgent. We all acknowledge that the divisions established for the convenience of scientific pursuit are radically artificial; and yet there are very few who can embrace in idea the whole of any one science: each science moreover being itself only a part of a great whole. Almost every one is busy about his own particular section, without much thought about its relation to the general system of positive knowledge. We must not be blind to the evil, nor slow in seeking a remedy. We must not forget that this is the weak side of the positive philosophy, by which it may yet be attacked, with some hope of success, by the adherents of the theological and metaphysical systems. As to the remedy, it certainly does not lie in a return to the ancient confusion of pursuits, which would be mere retrogression, if it were possible, which it is not. It lies in perfecting the division of employments itself,—in carrying it one degree higher,—in constituting one more specialty from the study of scientific generalities. Let us have a new class of students, suitably prepared, whose business it shall be to take the respective sciences as they are, determine the spirit of each, ascertain their relations and mutual connection, and reduce their respective principles to the smallest number of general principles, in conformity with the fundamental rules of the Positive Method. At the same time, let other students be prepared for their special pursuit by an education which recognizes the whole scope of positive science, so as to profit by the labours of the students of generalities, and so as to correct reciprocally, under that guidance, the results obtained by each. We see some approach already to this arrangement. Once established, there would be nothing to apprehend from any extent of division of employments. When we once have a class of learned men, at the disposal of all others, whose business it shall be to connect each new discovery with the general system, we may dismiss all fear of the great whole being lost sight of in the pursuit of the details of knowledge. The organization of scientific research will then be complete; and it will henceforth have occasion only

206

to extend its development, and not to change its character. After all, the formation of such a new class as is proposed would be merely an extension of the principle which has created all the classes we have. While science was narrow, there was only one class: as it expanded, more were instituted. With a further advance a fresh need arises, and this new class will be the result.

The general spirit of a course of Positive Philosophy having been thus set forth, we must now glance at the chief advantages which may be derived, on behalf of human progression, from the study of it. Of these advantages, four may be especially pointed out.

◄ I. The study of the Positive Philosophy affords the only rational means of exhibiting the logical laws of the human mind, which have hitherto been sought by unfit methods. To explain what is meant by this, we may refer to a saying of M. de Blainville, in his work on Comparative Anatomy, that every active, and especially every living being, may be regarded under two relations—the Statical and the Dynamical; that is, under conditions or in action. It is clear that all considerations range themselves under the one or the other of these heads. Let us apply this classification to the intellectual functions.

If we regard these functions under their Statical aspect— that is, if we consider the conditions under which they exist— we must determine the organic circumstances of the case, which inquiry involves it with anatomy and physiology. If we look at the Dynamic aspect, we have to study simply the exercise and results of the intellectual powers of the human race, which is neither more nor less than the general object of the Positive Philosophy. In short, looking at all scientific theories as so many great logical facts, it is only by the thorough observation of these facts that we can arrive at the knowledge of logical laws. These being the only means of knowledge of intellectual phenomena, the illusory psychology, which is the last phase of theology, is excluded. It pretends to accomplish the discovery of the laws of the human mind by contemplating it in itself; that is, by separating it from causes and effects. Such an attempt, made in defiance of the physiological study of our intellectual organs, and of the observation of rational methods of procedure, cannot succeed at this time of day.

The Positive Philosophy, which has been rising since the time of Bacon, has now secured such a preponderance, that the metaphysicians themselves profess to ground their pretended science on an observation of facts. They talk of external and internal facts, and say that their business is with the latter. This is much like saying that vision is explained by luminous objects painting their images upon the retina. To this the physiologists reply that another eye would be needed to see the image. In the same manner, the mind may observe all phenomena but its own. It may be said that a man's intellect may observe his passions, the seat of the reason being somewhat apart from that of the emotions in the brain; but there can be nothing like scientific observation of the passions, except from without, as the stir of the emotions disturbs the observing faculties more or less. It is yet more out of the question to make an intellectual observation of intellectual processes. The observing and observed organs are here the same, and its action cannot be pure and natural. In order to observe, your intellect must pause from activity; yet it is this very activity that you want to observe. If you cannot effect the pause, you cannot observe: if you do effect it, there is nothing to observe. The results of such a method are in proportion to its absurdity. After two thousand years of psychological pursuit, no one proposition is established to the satisfaction of its followers. They are divided, to this day, into a multitude of schools, still disputing about the very elements of their doctrine. This interior observation gives birth to almost as many theories as there are observers. We ask in vain for any one discovery, great or small, which has been made under this method. The psychologists have done some good in keeping up the activity of our understandings, when

208

there was no better work for our faculties to do; and they may have added something to our stock of knowledge. If they have done so, it is by practising the Positive method—by observing the progress of the human mind in the light of science; that is, by ceasing, for the moment, to be psychologists.

The view just given in relation to logical Science becomes yet more striking when we consider the logical Art.

The Positive Method can be judged of only in action. It cannot be looked at by itself, apart from the work on which it is employed. At all events, such a contemplation would be only a dead study, which could produce nothing in the mind which loses time upon it. We may talk for ever about the method, and state it in terms very wisely, without knowing half so much about it as the man who has once put it in practice upon a single particular of actual research, even without any philosophical intention. Thus it is that psychologists, by dint of reading the precepts of Bacon and the discourses of Descartes, have mistaken their own dreams for science.

Without saying whether it will ever be possible to establish *à priori* a true method of investigation, independent of a philosophical study of the sciences, it is clear that the thing has never been done yet, and that we are not capable of doing it now. We cannot as yet explain the great logical procedures, apart from their applications. If we ever do, it will remain as necessary then as now to form good intellectual habits by studying the regular application of the scientific methods which we shall have attained.

This, then, is the first great result of the Positive Philosophy —the manifestation by experiment of the laws which rule the Intellect in the investigation of truth; and, as a consequence the knowledge of the general rules suitable for that object.

II. The second effect of the Positive Philosophy, an effect not less important and far more urgently wanted, will be to regenerate Education. The best minds are agreed that our

European education, still essentially theological, metaphysical, and literary, must be superseded by a Positive training, conformable to our time and needs. Even the governments of our day have shared, where they have not originated, the attempts to establish positive instruction; and this is a striking indication of the prevalent sense of what is wanted. While encouraging such endeavours to the utmost, we must not however conceal from ourselves that everything yet done is inadequate to the object. The present exclusive specialty of our pursuits, and the consequent isolation of the sciences, spoil our teaching. If any student desires to form an idea of natural philosophy as a whole, he is compelled to go through each department as it is now taught, as if he were to be only an astronomer, or only a chemist; so that, be his intellect what it may, his training must remain very imperfect. And yet his object requires that he should obtain general positive conceptions of all the classes of natural phenomena. It is such an aggregate of conceptions, whether on a great or on a small scale, which must henceforth be the permanent basis of all human combinations. It will constitute the mind of future generations. In order to this regeneration of our intellectual system, it is necessary that the sciences, considered as branches from one trunk, should yield us, as a whole, their chief methods and their most important results. The specialties of science can be pursued by those whose vocation lies in that direction. They are indispensable; and they are not likely to be neglected; but they can never of themselves renovate our system of Education; and, to be of their full use, they must rest upon the basis of that general instruction which is a direct result of the Positive Philosophy.

◄¶ III. The same special study of scientific generalities must also aid the progress of the respective positive sciences: and this constitutes our third head of advantages.

The divisions which we establish between the sciences are, though not arbitrary, essentially artificial. The subject of our

210

researches is one: we divide it for our convenience, in order to deal the more easily with its difficulties. But it sometimes happens—and especially with the most important doctrines of each science—that we need what we cannot obtain under the present isolation of the sciences,—a combination of several special points of view; and for want of this, very important problems wait for their solution much longer than they otherwise need do. To go back into the past for an example: Descartes' grand conception with regard to analytical geometry is a discovery which has changed the whole aspect of mathematical science, and yielded the germ of all future progress; and it issued from the union of two sciences which had always before been separately regarded and pursued. The case of pending questions is yet more impressive; as, for instance, in Chemistry, the doctrine of Definite Proportions. Without entering upon the discussion of the fundamental principle of this theory, we may say with assurance that, in order to determine it—in order to determine whether it is a law of nature that atoms should necessarily combine in fixed numbers,—it will be indispensable that the chemical point of view should be united with the physiological. The failure of the theory with regard to organic bodies indicates that the cause of this immense exception must be investigated; and such an inquiry belongs as much to physiology as to chemistry. Again, it is as yet undecided whether azote is a simple or a compound body. It was concluded by almost all chemists that azote is a simple body; the illustrious Berzelius hesitated, on purely chemical considerations; but he was also influenced by the physiological observations that animals which receive no azote in their food have as much of it in their tissues as carnivorous animals. From this we see how physiology must unite with chemistry to inform us whether azote is simple or compound, and to institute a new series of researches upon the relation between the composition of living bodies and their mode of alimentation.

Such is the advantage which, in the third place, we shall owe to Positive philosophy—the elucidation of the respective sciences by their combination.

211

►◄[IV. The Positive Philosophy offers the only solid basis for that Social Reorganization which must succeed the critical condition in which the most civilized nations are now living.

It cannot be necessary to prove to anybody who reads this work that Ideas govern the world, or throw it into chaos; in other words, that all social mechanism rests upon Opinions. The great political and moral crisis that societies are now undergoing is shown by a rigid analysis to arise out of intellectual anarchy. While stability in fundamental maxims is the first condition of genuine social order, we are suffering under an utter disagreement which may be called universal. Till a certain number of general ideas can be acknowledged as a rallying-point of social doctrine, the nations will remain in a revolutionary state; whatever palliatives may be devised; and their institutions can be only provisional. But whenever the necessary agreement on first principles can be obtained, appropriate institutions will issue from them, without shock or resistance; for the causes of disorder will have been arrested by the mere fact of the agreement. It is in this direction that those must look who desire a natural and regular, a normal state of society.

Now, the existing disorder is abundantly accounted for by the existence, all at once, of three incompatible philosophies, —the theological, the metaphysical, and the positive. Any one of these might alone secure some sort of social order; but while the three co-exist, it is impossible for us to understand one another upon any essential point whatever. If this is true, we have only to ascertain which of the philosophies must, in the nature of things, prevail; and, this ascertained, every man, whatever may have been his former views, cannot but concur in its triumph. The problem once recognized cannot remain long unsolved; for all considerations whatever point to the Positive Philosophy as the one destined to prevail. It alone has been advancing during a course of centuries, throughout which the others have been declining. The fact is incontestable. Some may deplore it, but none can destroy it, nor therefore neglect it but under penalty of being betrayed by illusory speculations. This general revolution of the human

212

mind is nearly accomplished. We have only to complete the Positive Philosophy by bringing Social phenomena within its comprehension, and afterwards consolidating the whole into one body of homogeneous doctrine. The marked preference which almost all minds, from the highest to the commonest, accord to positive knowledge over vague and mystical conceptions, is a pledge of what the reception of this philosophy will be when it has acquired the only quality that it now wants—a character of due generality. When it has become complete, its supremacy will take place spontaneously, and will re-establish order throughout society. There is, at present, no conflict but between the theological and the metaphysical philosophies. They are contending for the task of reorganizing society; but it is a work too mighty for either of them. The positive philosophy has hitherto intervened only to examine both, and both are abundantly discredited by the process. It is time now to be doing something more effective, without wasting our forces in needless controversy. It is time to complete the vast intellectual operation begun by Bacon, Descartes, and Galileo, by constructing the system of general ideas which must henceforth prevail among the human race. This is the way to put an end to the revolutionary crisis which is tormenting the civilized nations of the world.

Leaving these four points of advantage, we must attend to one precautionary reflection.

Because it is proposed to consolidate the whole of our acquired knowledge into one body of homogeneous doctrine, it must not be supposed that we are going to study this vast variety as proceeding from a single principle, and as subjected to a single law. There is something so chimerical in attempts at universal explanation by a single law, that it may be as well to secure this Work at once from any imputation of the kind, though its development will show how undeserved such an imputation would be. Our intellectual resources are too narrow, and the universe is too complex, to leave any hope that it will ever be within our power to carry scientific perfection to its last degree of simplicity. Moreover, it appears as if the value of such an attainment, supposing it

213

possible, were greatly overrated. The only way, for instance, in which we could achieve the business, would be by connecting all natural phenomena with the most general law we know,—which is that of Gravitation, by which astronomical phenomena are already connected with a portion of terrestrial physics. Laplace has indicated that chemical phenomena may be regarded as simple atomic effects of the Newtonian attraction, modified by the form and mutual position of the atoms. But supposing this view provable (which it cannot be while we are without data about the constitution of bodies), the difficulty of its application would doubtless be found so great that we must still maintain the existing division between astronomy and chemistry, with the difference that we now regard as natural that division which we should then call artificial. Laplace himself presented his idea only as a philosophic device, incapable of exercising any useful influence over the progress of chemical science. Moreover, supposing this insuperable difficulty overcome, we should be no nearer to scientific unity, since we then should still have to connect the whole of physiological phenomena with the same law, which certainly would not be the least difficult part of the enterprise. Yet, all things considered, the hypothesis we have glanced at would be the most favourable to the desired unity.

The consideration of all phenomena as referable to a single origin is by no means necessary to the systematic formation of science, any more than to the realization of the great and happy consequences that we anticipate from the positive philosophy. The only necessary unity is that of Method, which is already in great part established. As for the doctrine, it need not be *one;* it is enough that it should be *homogeneous.* It is, then, under the double aspect of unity of method and homogeneousness of doctrine that we shall consider the different classes of positive theories in this work. While pursuing the philosophical aim of all science, the lessening of the number of general laws requisite for the explanation of natural phenomena, we shall regard as presumptuous every attempt, in all future time, to reduce them rigorously to one.

Having thus endeavoured to determine the spirit and in-

214

fluence of the Positive Philosophy, and to mark the goal of our labours, we have now to proceed to the exposition of the system; that is, to the determination of the universal, or encyclopædic order, which must regulate the different classes of natural phenomena, and consequently the corresponding positive sciences.

Max Weber (1864-1920), trained in sociology and law, became one of the leading German sociologists. His provocative analyses did not fit entirely within any of the major schools of sociology of his day, but they have influenced all subsequent sociological thought. The publication in 1906 of his essay, *The Protestant Ethic and the Spirit of Capitalism*, set off a scholarly controversy which continues to this day. Weber attempted to develop a theory concerning the psychological conditions which made possible the development of capitalist civilization.

A PRODUCT of modern European civilization, studying any problem of universal history, is bound to ask himself to what combination of circumstances the fact should be attributed that in Western civilization, and in Western civilization only, cultural phenomena have appeared which (as we like to think) lie in a line of development having *universal* significance and value.

Only in the West does science exist at a stage of development which we recognize to-day as valid. Empirical knowledge, reflection. on problems of the cosmos and of life, philosophical and theological wisdom of the most profound sort, are not confined to it, though in the case of the last the full development of a systematic theology must be credited to Christianity under the influence of Hellenism, since there were only fragments in Islam and in a few Indian sects. In short, knowledge and observation of great refinement have existed elsewhere, above all in India, China, Babylonia, Egypt. But in Babylonia and elsewhere astronomy lacked—which makes its development all the more astounding—the mathematical foundation which it first received from the Greeks. The Indian geometry had no rational proof; that was another product of the Greek intellect, also the creator of mechanics and physics. The Indian natural sciences, though well developed in observation, lacked the method of experiment, which was, apart from beginnings in antiquity, essentially a product of the Renaissance, as was the modern laboratory.

217

Max Weber, *The Protestant Ethic and The Spirit of Capitalism*. Trans. by Talcott Parsons. c. 1958 by Charles Scribner's Sons. Reproduced by permission of Charles Scribner's Sons.

The capitalism of promoters, large-scale speculators, concession hunters, and much modern financial capitalism even in peace time, but, above all, the capitalism especially concerned with exploiting wars, bears this stamp even in modern Western countries, and some, but only some, parts of large-scale international trade are closely related to it, to-day as always.

But in modern times the Occident has developed, in addition to this, a very different form of capitalism which has appeared nowhere else: the rational capitalistic organization of (formally) free labour. Only suggestions of it are found elsewhere. Even the organization of unfree labour reached a considerable degree of rationality only on plantations and to a very limited extent in the *Ergasteria* of antiquity. In the manors, manorial workshops, and domestic industries on estates with serf labour it was probably somewhat less developed. Even real domestic industries with free labour have definitely been proved to have existed in only a few isolated cases outside the Occident. The frequent use of day labourers led in a very few cases—especially State monopolies, which are, however, very different from modern industrial organization—to manufacturing organizations, but never to a rational organization of apprenticeship in the handicrafts like that of our Middle Ages.

Rational industrial organization, attuned to a regular market, and neither to political nor irrationally speculative opportunities for profit, is not, however, the only peculiarity of Western capitalism. The modern rational organization of the capitalistic enterprise would not have been possible without two other important factors in its development: the separation of business from the household, which completely dominates modern economic life, and closely connected with it rational book-keeping. A spatial separation of places of work from those of residence exists elsewhere, as in the Oriental bazaar and in the *ergasteria* of other cultures. The development of capitalistic associations with their own accounts is also found in the Far East, the Near East, and in antiquity. But compared to the modern independence of business enterprises, those are only small beginnings. The reason for this was particularly that the indispensable requisites for this independence, our rational business book-keeping and our legal separation of corporate from personal property, were entirely lacking, or had only begun to develop. The tendency everywhere else was for acquisitive enterprises to arise as parts of a royal or manorial *household* (of the *oikos*), which is, as Rodbertus has perceived, with all its superficial similarity, a fundamentally different, even opposite, development.

However, all these peculiarities of Western capitalism have derived their significance in the last analysis only from their association with the capitalistic organization of labour. Even what is generally called commercialization, the development of negotiable securities and the rationalization of speculation, the exchanges, etc., is connected with it. For without the rational capitalistic organization of labour, all this, so far as it was possible at all, would have nothing like the same significance, above all for the social structure and all the specific problems of the modern Occident connected with it. Exact calculation—the basis of everything else—is only possible on a basis of free labour.

One of the fundamental elements of the spirit of modern capitalism, and not only of that but of all modern culture: rational conduct on the basis of the idea of the calling, was born—that is what this discussion has sought to demonstrate—from the spirit of Christian asceticism. One has only to re-read the passage from Franklin, quoted at the beginning of this essay, in order to see that the essential elements of the attitude which was there called the spirit of capitalism are the same as what we have just shown to be the content of the Puritan worldly asceticism, only without the religious basis, which by Franklin's time had died away. The idea that modern labour has an ascetic character is of course not new. Limitation to specialized work, with a renunciation of the Faustian universality of man which it involves, is a condition of any valuable work in the modern world; hence deeds and renunciation inevitably condition each other to-day. This fundamentally ascetic trait of middle-class life, if it attempts to be a way of life at all, and not simply the absence of any, was what Goethe wanted to teach, at the height of his wisdom, in the *Wander-jahren*, and in the end which he gave to the life of his *Faust.* For him the realization meant a renunciation, a departure from an age of full and beautiful humanity, which can no more be repeated in the course of our cultural development than can the flower of the Athenian culture of antiquity.

The Puritan wanted to work in a calling; we are forced to do so. For when asceticism was carried out of monastic cells into everyday life, and began to dominate worldly morality, it did its part in building the tremendous cosmos of the modern economic order. This order is now bound to the technical and economic conditions of machine production which to-day determine the lives of all the individuals who are born into this mechanism, not only those directly concerned with economic acquisition, with irresistible force. Perhaps it will so determine them until the last ton of fossilized coal is burnt. In Baxter's view the care for external goods should only lie on the shoulders of the "saint like a light cloak, which can be thrown aside at any moment". But fate decreed that the cloak should become an iron cage.

Since asceticism undertook to remodel the world and to work out its ideals in the world, material goods have gained an increasing and finally an inexorable power over the lives of men as at no previous period in history. To-day the spirit of religious asceticism—whether finally, who knows?—has escaped from the cage. But victorious capitalism, since it rests on mechanical foundations, needs its support no longer. The rosy blush of its laughing heir, the Enlightenment, seems also to be irretrievably fading, and the idea of duty in one's calling prowls about in our lives like the ghost of dead religious beliefs. Where the fulfilment of the calling cannot directly be related to the highest spiritual and cultural values, or when, on the other hand, it need not be felt simply as economic compulsion, the individual generally abandons the attempt to justify it at all. In the field of its highest development, in the United States, the pursuit of wealth, stripped of its religious and ethical meaning, tends to become associated with purely mundane passions, which often actually give it the character of sport.

No one knows who will live in this cage in the future, or whether at the end of this tremendous development entirely new prophets will arise, or there will be a great rebirth of old ideas and ideals, or, if neither, mechanized petrification, embellished with a sort of

221

convulsive self-importance. For of the last stage of this cultural development, it might well be truly said: "Specialists without spirit, sensualists without heart; this nullity imagines that it has attained a level of civilization never before achieved."

But this brings us to the world of judgments of value and of faith, with which this purely historical discussion need not be burdened. The next task would be rather to show the significance of ascetic rationalism, which has only been touched in the foregoing sketch, for the content of practical social ethics, thus for the types of organization and the functions of social groups from the conventicle to the State.

6

John Stuart Mill,   ON THE SUBJECTION OF WOMEN

1. How does Mill answer Aristotle's arguments, especially the argument that the subjection of women is natural?

2. What two faults does Mill find in the existing social relations between the sexes? Why have these faults not been corrected by reason?

3. How did the inequality of the sexes arise? How was it continued? Why has it not disappeared in a more liberal age?

4. What indications did Mill see in his own time which suggest that change in the relation between the sexes might be imminent?

5. Why does Mill think it absurd to fear that freedom will force women into occupations for which they are unsuited?

6. What good is to be expected from Mill's proposed changes in laws, education, and public opinion? According to Mill, how would society benefit by the equality of the sexes?

7. How has the status of women changed since Mill's writing? Do you feel Mill's arguments are still relevant to current issues.

John Stuart Mill (1806-1873) was born in London. The essay, "On the Subjection of Women," was Mill's last published work. He had often treated the subject in his earlier political writings. "On the Subjection of Women" was written with the cooperation of his stepdaughter, Helen Taylor, and was also partly the product of conversations with his wife, Harriet Taylor.

THE SUBJECTION OF WOMEN

THE object of this Essay is to explain, as clearly as I am able, the grounds of an opinion which I have held from the very earliest period when I had formed any opinions at all on social or political matters, and which, instead of being weakened or modified, has been constantly growing stronger by the progress of reflection and the experience of life: That the principle which regulates the existing social relations between the two sexes—the legal subordination of one sex to the other—is wrong in itself, and now one of the chief hindrances to human improvement; and that it ought to be replaced by a principle of perfect equality, admitting no power or privilege on the one side, nor disability on the other.

The very words necessary to express the task I have undertaken, show how arduous it is. But it would be a mistake to suppose that the difficulty of the case must lie in the insufficiency or obscurity of the grounds of reason on which my conviction rests. The difficulty is that which exists in all cases in which there is a mass of feeling to be contended against. So long as an opinion is strongly rooted in the feelings, it gains rather than loses in stability by having a preponderating weight of argument against it. For if it were accepted as a result of argument, the refutation of the argument might shake the solidity of the conviction; but when it rests solely on feeling, the worse it fares in argumentative contest, the more persuaded its adherents are that their feeling must have some deeper ground, which the arguments do not reach; and while the feeling remains, it is always throwing up fresh entrenchments of argument to repair any breach made in the old. And there are so many causes tending to make the feelings connected with this subject the

most intense and most deeply-rooted of all those which
gather round and protect old institutions and customs,
that we need not wonder to find them as yet less
undermined and loosened than any of the rest by the
progress of the great modern spiritual and social transition ; nor suppose that the barbarisms to which men
cling longest must be less barbarisms than those which
they earlier shake off.

In every respect the burthen is hard on those who
attack an almost universal opinion. They must be
very fortunate as well as unusually capable if they
obtain a hearing at all. They have more difficulty in
obtaining a trial, than any other litigants have in
getting a verdict. If they do extort a hearing, they
are subjected to a set of logical requirements totally
different from those exacted from other people. In
all other cases, the burthen of proof is supposed to
lie with the affirmative. If a person is charged with
a murder, it rests with those who accuse him to give
proof of his guilt, not with himself to prove his inno-
cence. If there is a difference of opinion about the
reality of any alleged historical event, in which the
feelings of men in general are not much interested, as
the Siege of Troy for example, those who maintain
that the event took place are expected to produce their
proofs, before those who take the other side can be
required to say anything ; and at no time are these
required to do more than show that the evidence produced by the others is of no value. Again, in practical
matters, the burthen of proof is supposed to be with
those who are against liberty ; who contend for any
restriction or prohibition ; either any limitation of
the general freedom of human action, or any disqualification or disparity of privilege affecting one person
or kind of persons, as compared with others. The
a priori presumption is in favour of freedom and
impartiality. It is held that there should be no restraint not required by the general good, and that the
law should be no respecter of persons, but should treat
all alike, save where dissimilarity of treatment is

required by positive reasons, either of justice or of policy. But of none of these rules of evidence will the benefit be allowed to those who maintain the opinion I profess. It is useless for me to say that those who maintain the doctrine that men have a right to command and women are under an obligation to obey, or that men are fit for government and women unfit, are on the affirmative side of the question, and that they are bound to show positive evidence for the assertions, or submit to their rejection. It is equally unavailing for me to say that those who deny to women any freedom or privilege rightly allowed to men, having the double presumption against them that they are opposing freedom and recommending partiality, must be held to the strictest proof of their case, and unless their success be such as to exclude all doubt, the judgement ought to go against them. These would be thought good pleas in any common case: but they will not be thought so in this instance. Before I could hope to make any impression, I should be expected not only to answer all that has ever been said by those who take the other side of the question, but to imagine all that could be said by them—to find them in reasons, as well as answer all I find: and besides refuting all arguments for the affirmative, I shall be called upon for invincible positive arguments to prove a negative. And even if I could do all this, and leave the opposite party with a host of unanswered arguments against them, and not a single unrefuted one on their side, I should be thought to have done little; for a cause supported on the one hand by universal usage, and on the other by so great a preponderance of popular sentiment, is supposed to have a presumption in its favour, superior to any conviction which an appeal to reason has power to produce in any intellects but those of a high class.

I do not mention these difficulties to complain of them; first, because it would be useless; they are inseparable from having to contend through people's understandings against the hostility of their feelings

P

and practical tendencies: and truly the understandings of the majority of mankind would need to be much better cultivated than has ever yet been the case, before they can be asked to place such reliance in their own power of estimating arguments, as to give up practical principles in which they have been born and bred, and which are the basis of much of the existing order of the world, at the first argumentative attack which they are not capable of logically resisting. I do not therefore quarrel with them for having too little faith in argument, but for having too much faith in custom and the general feeling. It is one of the characteristic prejudices of the reaction of the nineteenth century against the eighteenth, to accord to the unreasoning elements in human nature the infallibility which the eighteenth century is supposed to have ascribed to the reasoning elements. For the apotheosis of Reason we have substituted that of Instinct; and we call everything instinct which we find in ourselves and for which we cannot trace any rational foundation. This idolatry, infinitely more degrading than the other, and the most pernicious of the false worships of the present day, of all of which it is now the main support, will probably hold its ground until it gives way before a sound psychology, laying bare the real root of much that is bowed down to as the intention of Nature and the ordinance of God. As regards the present question, I am willing to accept the unfavourable conditions which the prejudice assigns to me. I consent that established custom, and the general feeling, should be deemed conclusive against me, unless that custom and feeling from age to age can be shown to have owed their existence to other causes than their soundness, and to have derived their power from the worse rather than the better parts of human nature. I am willing that judgement should go against me, unless I can show that my judge has been tampered with. The concession is not so great as it might appear; for to prove this, is by far the easiest portion of my task.

THE SUBJECTION OF WOMEN

The generality of a practice is in some cases a strong presumption that it is, or at all events once was, conducive to laudable ends. This is the case, when the practice was first adopted, or afterwards kept up, as a means to such ends, and was grounded on experience of the mode in which they could be most effectually attained. If the authority of men over women, when first established, had been the result of a conscientious comparison between different modes of constituting the government of society; if, after trying various other modes of social organization—the government of women over men, equality between the two, and such mixed and divided modes of government as might be invented—it had been decided, on the testimony of experience, that the mode in which women are wholly under the rule of men, having no share at all in public concerns, and each in private being under the legal obligation of obedience to the man with whom she has associated her destiny, was the arrangement most conducive to the happiness and well-being of both; its general adoption might then be fairly thought to be some evidence that, at the time when it was adopted, it was the best: though even then the considerations which recommended it may, like so many other primeval social facts of the greatest importance, have subsequently, in the course of ages, ceased to exist. But the state of the case is in every respect the reverse of this. In the first place, the opinion in favour of the present system, which entirely subordinates the weaker sex to the stronger, rests upon theory only; for there never has been trial made of any other: so that experience, in the sense in which it is vulgarly opposed to theory, cannot be pretended to have pronounced any verdict. And in the second place, the adoption of this system of inequality never was the result of deliberation, or forethought, or any social ideas, or any notion whatever of what conduced to the benefit of humanity or the good order of society. It arose simply from the fact that from the very earliest twilight of human society, every woman (owing

228

to the value attached to her by men, combined with her inferiority in muscular strength) was found in a state of bondage to some man. Laws and systems of polity always begin by recognizing the relations they find already existing between individuals. They convert what was a mere physical fact into a legal right, give it the sanction of society, and principally aim at the substitution of public and organized means of asserting and protecting these rights, instead of the irregular and lawless conflict of physical strength. Those who had already been compelled to obedience became in this manner legally bound to it. Slavery, from being a mere affair of force between the master and the slave, became regularized and a matter of compact among the masters, who, binding themselves to one another for common protection, guaranteed by their collective strength the private possessions of each, including his slaves. In early times, the great majority of the male sex were slaves, as well as the whole of the female. And many ages elapsed, some of them ages of high cultivation, before any thinker was bold enough to question the rightfulness, and the absolute social necessity, either of the one slavery or of the other. By degrees such thinkers did arise: and (the general progress of society assisting) the slavery of the male sex has, in all the countries of Christian Europe at least (though, in one of them, only within the last few years) been at length abolished, and that of the female sex has been gradually changed into a milder form of dependence. But this dependence, as it exists at present, is not an original institution, taking a fresh start from considerations of justice and social expediency—it is the primitive state of slavery lasting on, through successive mitigations and modifications occasioned by the same causes which have softened the general manners, and brought all human relations more under the control of justice and the influence of humanity. It has not lost the taint of its brutal origin. No presumption in its favour, therefore, can be drawn from the fact of its existence. The only such presumption which it could be supposed to have, must be grounded on its having lasted till now, when so many other things which came down from the same odious source have been done away with. And this, indeed, is what makes it strange to ordinary ears, to hear it asserted that the inequality of rights between men and women has no other source than the law of the strongest.

That this statement should have the effect of a paradox, is in some respects creditable to the progress of civilization, and the improvement of the moral sentiments of mankind. We now live—that is to say, one or two of the most advanced nations of the world now live—in a state in which the law of the strongest seems to be entirely abandoned as the regulating principle of the world's affairs : nobody professes it, and, as regards most of the relations between human beings, nobody is permitted to practise it. When any one succeeds in doing so, it is under cover of some pretext which gives him the semblance of having some general social interest on his side. This being the ostensible state of things, people flatter themselves that the rule of mere force is ended ; that the law of the strongest cannot be the reason of existence of anything which has remained in full operation down to the present time. However any of our present institutions may have begun, it can only, they think, have been preserved to this period of advanced civilization by a well-grounded feeling of its adaptation to human nature, and conduciveness to the general good. They do not understand the great vitality and durability of institutions which place right on the side of might ; how intensely they are clung to ; how the good as well as the bad propensities and sentiments of those who have power in their hands, become identified with retaining it ; how slowly these bad institutions give way, one at a time, the weakest first, beginning with those which are least interwoven with the daily habits of life ; and how very rarely those who have obtained legal power because they first had physical, have ever lost their hold of it until the physical power had passed over to the other side. Such shifting of the physical force not having taken place in the case of women; this fact, combined with all the peculiar and characteristic features of the particular case, made it certain from the first that this branch of the system of right founded on might, though softened in its most atrocious features at an earlier period than several of the others, would be the very last to disappear. It was inevitable that this one case of a social relation grounded on force would survive through generations of institutions grounded on equal justice, an almost solitary exception to the general character of their laws and customs; but which, so long as it does not proclaim its own origin, and as discussion has not brought out its true character, is not felt to jar with modern civilization, any more than domestic slavery among the Greeks jarred with their notion of themselves as a free people.

The truth is, that people of the present and the last two or three generations have lost all practical sense of the primitive condition of humanity; and only the few who have studied history accurately, or have much frequented the parts of the world occupied by the living representatives of ages long past, are able to form any mental picture of what society then was. People are not aware how entirely, in former ages, the law of superior strength was the rule of life; how publicly and openly it was avowed, I do not say cynically or shamelessly—for these words imply a feeling that there was something in it to be ashamed of, and no such notion could find a place in the faculties of any person in those ages, except a philosopher or a saint. History gives a cruel experience of human nature, in showing how exactly the regard due to the life, possessions, and entire earthly happiness of any class of persons, was measured by what they had the power of enforcing; how all who made any resistance to authorities that had arms in their hands, however dreadful might be the provocation, had not only the law of force but all other laws, and all the notions of social obligation against them; and, in the eyes of those whom they resisted, were not only guilty of crime, but of the worst of all crimes, deserving the most cruel chastisement which human beings could inflict. The first small vestige of a feeling of obligation in a superior to acknowledge any right in inferiors, began when he had been induced, for convenience, to make some promise to them. Though these promises, even when sanctioned by the most solemn oaths, were for many ages revoked or violated on the most trifling provocation or temptation, it is probable that this, except by persons of still worse than the average morality, was seldom done without some twinges of conscience. The ancient republics, being mostly grounded from the first upon some kind of mutual compact, or at any rate formed by an union of persons not very unequal in strength, afforded, in consequence, the first instance of a portion of human relations fenced round, and placed under the dominion of another law than that of force. And though the original law of force remained in full operation between them and their slaves, and also (except so far as limited by express compact) between a commonwealth and its subjects, or other independent commonwealths; the banishment of that primitive law, even from so narrow a field, commenced the regeneration of human nature, by giving birth to sentiments of which experience soon demonstrated the immense value even for material interests, and which thenceforward only required to be enlarged, not created. Though slaves were no part of the commonwealth, it was in the free states that slaves were first felt to have rights as human beings. The Stoics were, I believe, the first (except so far as the Jewish law constitutes an exception) who taught as a part of morality that men were bound by moral obligations to their slaves. No one, after Christianity became ascendant, could ever again have been a stranger to this belief, in theory; nor, after the rise of the Catholic Church, was it ever without persons to stand up for it. Yet to enforce it was the most arduous task which Christianity ever had to perform. For more than a thousand years the Church kept up the contest, with hardly any perceptible success. It was not for want of power over men's minds. Its power was prodigious. It could make kings and nobles resign their most valued possessions to enrich the Church. It could make thousands, in the prime of life and the height of worldly advantages, shut themselves up in convents to work out their salvation by poverty, fasting, and prayer. It could send hundreds of thousands across land and sea, Europe and Asia, to give their lives for the deliverance of the Holy Sepulchre. It would make kings relinquish wives who were the objects of their passionate attachment, because the Church declared that they were within the seventh (by our calculation the fourteenth) degree of relationship. All this it did; but it could not make men fight less with one another, nor tyrannize less cruelly over the serfs, and, when they were able, over burgesses. It could not make them renounce either of the applications of force; force militant, or force triumphant. This they could never be induced to do until they were themselves in their turn compelled by superior force. Only by the growing power of kings was an end put to fighting except between kings, or competitors for kingship; only by the growth of a wealthy and warlike bourgeoisie in the fortified towns, and of a plebeian infantry which proved more powerful in the field than the undisciplined chivalry, was the insolent tyranny of the nobles over the bourgeoisie and peasantry brought within some bounds. It was persisted in not only until, but long after, the oppressed had obtained a power enabling them often to take conspicuous vengeance; and on the Continent much of it continued to the time of the French Revolution, though in England the earlier and better organization of the democratic classes put an end to it sooner, by establishing equal laws and free national institutions.

Some will object, that a comparison cannot fairly be made between the government of the male sex and the forms of unjust power which I have adduced in illustration of it, since these are arbitrary, and the effect of mere usurpation, while it on the contrary is natural. But was there ever any domination which did not appear natural to those who possessed it? There was a time when the division of mankind into two classes, a small one of masters and a numerous one of slaves, appeared, even to the most cultivated minds, to be a natural, and the only natural, condition of the human race. No less an intellect, and one which contributed no less to the progress of human thought, than Aristotle, held this opinion without doubt or misgiving; and rested it on the same premisses on which the same assertion in regard to the dominion of men over women is usually based, namely that there are different natures among mankind, free natures, and slave natures; that the Greeks were of a free nature, the barbarian races of Thracians and Asiatics of a slave nature. But why need I go back to Aristotle? Did not the slave-owners of the Southern United States maintain the same doctrine, with all the fanaticism with which men cling to the theories that justify their passions and legitimate their personal interests? Did they not call heaven and earth to witness that the dominion of the white man over the black is natural, that the black race is by nature incapable of freedom, and marked out for slavery?—some even going so far as to say that the freedom of manual labourers is an unnatural order of things anywhere. Again, the theorists of absolute monarchy have always affirmed it to be the only natural form of government; issuing from the patriarchal, which was the primitive and spontaneous form of society, framed on the model of the paternal, which is anterior to society itself, and, as they contend, the most natural authority of all. Nay, for that matter, the law of force itself, to those who could not plead any other, has always seemed the most natural of all grounds for the exercise of authority. Conquering races hold it to be Nature's own dictate that the conquered should obey the conquerors, or, as they euphoniously paraphrase it, that the feebler and more unwarlike races should submit to the braver and manlier. The smallest acquaintance with human life in the Middle Ages shows how supremely natural the dominion of the feudal nobility over men of low condition appeared to the nobility themselves, and how unnatural the conception seemed, of a person of the inferior class claiming equality with them, or exercising authority over them. It hardly seemed less so to the class held in subjection. The emancipated serfs and burgesses, even in their most vigorous struggles, never made any pretension to a share of authority; they only demanded more or less of limitation to the power of tyrannizing over them. So true is it that unnatural generally means only uncustomary, and that everything which is usual appears natural. The subjection of women to men being a universal custom, any departure from it quite naturally appears unnatural. But how entirely, even in this case, the feeling is dependent on custom, appears by ample experience. Nothing so much astonishes the people of distant parts of the world, when they first learn anything about England, as to be told that it is under a queen: the thing seems to them so unnatural as to be almost incredible. To Englishmen this does not seem in the least degree unnatural, because they are used to it; but they do feel it unnatural that women should be soldiers or members of Parliament. In the feudal ages, on the contrary, war and politics were not thought unnatural to women, because not unusual; it seemed natural that women of the privileged classes should be of manly character, inferior in nothing but bodily strength to their husbands and fathers. The independence of women seemed rather less unnatural to the Greeks than to other ancients, on account of the fabulous Amazons (whom they believed to be historical), and the partial example afforded by the Spartan women; who, though no less subordinate by law than in other Greek states, were more free in fact, and being trained to bodily exercises in the same manner with men, gave ample proof that they were not naturally disqualified for them. There can be little doubt that Spartan experience suggested to Plato, among many other of his doctrines, that of the social and political equality of the two sexes.

But, it will be said, the rule of men over women differs from all these others in not being a rule of force : it is accepted voluntarily ; women make no complaint, and are consenting parties to it. In the first place, a great number of women do not accept it. Ever since there have been women able to make their sentiments known by their writings (the only mode of publicity which society permits to them), an increasing number of them have recorded protests against their present social condition : and recently many thousands of them, headed by the most eminent women known to the public, have petitioned Parliament for their admission to the Parliamentary Suffrage. The claim of women to be educated as solidly, and in the same branches of knowledge, as men, is urged with growing intensity, and with a great prospect of success ; while the demand for their admission into professions and occupations hitherto closed against them, becomes every year more urgent. Though there are not in this country, as there are in the United States, periodical Conventions and an organized party to agitate for the Rights of Women, there is a numerous and active Society organized and managed by women, for the more limited object of obtaining the political franchise. Nor is it only in our own country and in America that women are beginning to protest, more or less collectively, against the disabilities under which they labour. France, and Italy, and Switzerland, and Russia now afford examples of the same thing. How many more women there are who silently cherish similar aspirations, no one can possibly know ; but there are abundant tokens how many *would* cherish them, were they not so strenuously taught to repress them as contrary to the proprieties of their sex. It must be remembered, also, that no enslaved class ever asked for complete liberty at once. When Simon de Montfort called the deputies of the commons to sit for the first time in Parliament, did any of them dream of demanding that an assembly, elected by their constituents, should make and destroy ministries, and dictate to the king in affairs of State ? No such thought entered into the imagination of the most ambitious of them. The nobility had already these pretensions ; the commons pretended to nothing but to be exempt from arbitrary taxation, and from the gross individual oppression of the king's officers. It is a political law of nature that those who are under any power of ancient origin never begin by complaining of the power itself, but only of its oppressive exercise. There is never any want of women who complain of ill usage by their husbands. There would be infinitely more, if complaint were not the greatest of all provocatives to a repetition and increase of the ill usage. It is this which frustrates all attempts to maintain the power but protect the woman against its abuses. In no other case (except that of a child) is the person who has been proved judicially to have suffered an injury, replaced under the physical power of the culprit who inflicted it. Accordingly wives, even in the most extreme and protracted cases of bodily ill usage, hardly ever dare avail themselves of the laws made for their protection : and if, in a moment of irrepressible indignation, or by the interference of neighbours, they are induced to do so, their whole effort afterwards is to disclose as little as they can, and to beg off their tyrant from his merited chastisement.

All causes, social and natural, combine to make it unlikely that women should be collectively rebellious to the power of men. They are so far in a position different from all other subject classes, that their masters require something more from them than actual service. Men do not want solely the obedience of women, they want their sentiments. All men, except the most brutish, desire to have, in the woman most nearly connected with them, not a forced slave but a willing one ; not a slave merely, but a favourite.

They have therefore put everything in practice to enslave their minds. The masters of all other slaves rely, for maintaining obedience, on fear; either fear of themselves, or religious fears. The masters of women wanted more than simple obedience, and they turned the whole force of education to effect their purpose. All women are brought up from the very earliest years in the belief that their ideal of character is the very opposite to that of men; not self-will, and government by self-control, but submission, and yielding to the control of others. All the moralities tell them that it is the duty of women, and all the current sentimentalities that it is their nature, to live for others; to make complete abnegation of themselves, and to have no life but in their affections. And by their affections are meant the only ones they are allowed to have—those to the men with whom they are connected, or to the children who constitute an additional and indefeasible tie between them and a man. When we put together three things—first, the natural attraction between opposite sexes; secondly, the wife's entire dependence on the husband, every privilege or pleasure she has being either his gift, or depending entirely on his will; and lastly, that the principal object of human pursuit, consideration, and all objects of social ambition, can in general be sought or obtained by her only through him—it would be a miracle if the object of being attractive to men had not become the polar star of feminine education and formation of character. And, this great means of influence over the minds of women having been acquired, an instinct of selfishness made men avail themselves of it to the utmost as a means of holding women in subjection, by representing to them meekness, submissiveness, and resignation of all individual will into the hands of a man, as an essential part of sexual attractiveness. Can it be doubted that any of the other yokes which mankind have succeeded in breaking, would have subsisted till now if the same means had existed, and had been as sedulously used, to bow down their minds to it? If it had been made the object of the life of every young plebeian to find personal favour in the eyes of some patrician, of every young serf with some seigneur; if domestication with him, and a share of his personal affections, had been held out as the prize which they all should look out for, the most gifted and aspiring being able to reckon on the most desirable prizes; and if, when this prize had been obtained, they had been shut out by a wall of brass from all interests not centring in him, all feelings and desires but those which he shared or inculcated; would not serfs and seigneurs, plebeians and patricians, have been as broadly distinguished at this day as men and women are? and would not all but a thinker here and there have believed the distinction to be a fundamental and unalterable fact in human nature?

The preceding considerations are amply sufficient to show that custom, however universal it may be, affords in this case no presumption, and ought not to create any prejudice, in favour of the arrangements which place women in social and political subjection to men. But I may go farther, and maintain that the course of history, and the tendencies of progressive human society, afford not only no presumption in favour of this system of inequality of rights, but a strong one against it; and that, so far as the whole course of human improvement up to this time, the whole stream of modern tendencies, warrants any inference on the subject, it is, that this relic of the past is discordant with the future, and must necessarily disappear.

For what is the peculiar character of the modern world—the difference which chiefly distinguishes modern institutions, modern social ideas, modern life itself, from those of times long past? It is, that human beings are no longer born to their place in life, and chained down by an inexorable bond to the place they are born to, but are free to employ their faculties, and such favourable chances as offer, to achieve the lot which may appear to them most desirable. Human

239

society of old was constituted on a very different principle. All were born to a fixed social position, and were mostly kept in it by law, or interdicted from any means by which they could emerge from it. As some men are born white and others black, so some were born slaves and others freemen and citizens; some were born patricians, others plebeians; some were born feudal nobles, others commoners and *roturiers*. A slave or serf could never make himself free, nor, except by the will of his master, become so. In most European countries it was not till towards the close of the Middle Ages, and as a consequence of the growth of regal power, that commoners could be ennobled. Even among nobles, the eldest son was born the exclusive heir to the paternal possessions, and a long time elapsed before it was fully established that the father could disinherit him. Among the industrious classes, only those who were born members of a guild, or were admitted into it by its members, could lawfully practise their calling within its local limits; and nobody could practise any calling deemed important, in any but the legal manner—by processes authoritatively prescribed. Manufacturers have stood in the pillory for presuming to carry on their business by new and improved methods. In modern Europe, and most in those parts of it which have participated most largely in all other modern improvements, diametrically opposite doctrines now prevail. Law and government do not undertake to prescribe by whom any social or industrial operation shall or shall not be conducted, or what modes of conducting them shall be lawful. These things are left to the unfettered choice of individuals. Even the laws which required that workmen should serve an apprenticeship, have in this country been repealed: there being ample assurance that in all cases in which an apprenticeship is necessary, its necessity will suffice to enforce it. The old theory was, that the least possible should be left to the choice of the individual agent; that all he had to do should, as far as practicable, be laid down for him by superior wisdom. Left to himself he was sure to go wrong. The modern conviction, the fruit of a thousand years of experience, is, that things in which the individual is the person directly interested, never go right but as they are left to his own discretion ; and that any regulation of them by authority, except to protect the rights of others, is sure to be mischievous. This conclusion, slowly arrived at, and not adopted until almost every possible application of the contrary theory had been made with disastrous result, now (in the industrial department) prevails universally in the most advanced countries, almost universally in all that have pretensions to any sort of advancement. It is not that all processes are supposed to be equally good, or all persons to be equally qualified for everything ; but that freedom of individual choice is now known to be the only thing which procures the adoption of the best processes, and throws each operation into the hands of those who are best qualified for it. Nobody thinks it necessary to make a law that only a strong-armed man shall be a blacksmith. Freedom and competition suffice to make blacksmiths strong armed men, because the weak-armed can earn more by engaging in occupations for which they are more fit. In consonance with this doctrine, it is felt to be an overstepping of the proper bounds of authority to fix beforehand, on some general presumption, that certain persons are not fit to do certain things. It is now thoroughly known and admitted that if some such presumptions exist, no such presumption is infallible. Even if it be well grounded in a majority of cases, which it is very likely not to be, there will be a minority of exceptional cases in which it does not hold : and in those it is both an injustice to the individuals, and a detriment to society, to place barriers in the way of their using their faculties for their own benefit and for that of others. In the cases, on the other hand, in which the unfitness is real, the ordinary motives of human conduct will on the whole suffice to prevent the incompetent person from making, or from persisting in, the attempt.

If this general principle of social and economical science is not true; if individuals, with such help as they can derive from the opinion of those who know them, are not better judges than the law and the government, of their own capacities and vocation; the world cannot too soon abandon this principle, and return to the old system of regulations and disabilities. But if the principle is true, we ought to act as if we believed it, and not to ordain that to be born a girl instead of a boy, any more than to be born black instead of white, or a commoner instead of a nobleman, shall decide the person's position through all life—shall interdict people from all the more elevated social positions, and from all, except a few, respectable occupations. Even were we to admit the utmost that is ever pretended as to the superior fitness of men for all the functions now reserved to them, the same argument applies which forbids a legal qualification for members of Parliament. If only once in a dozen years the conditions of eligibility exclude a fit person, there is a real loss, while the exclusion of thousands of unfit persons is no gain; for if the constitution of the electoral body disposes them to choose unfit persons, there are always plenty of such persons to choose from. In all things of any difficulty and importance, those who can do them well are fewer than the need, even with the most unrestricted latitude of choice: and any limitation of the field of selection deprives society of some chances of being served by the competent, without ever saving it from the incompetent.

At present, in the more improved countries, the disabilities of women are the only case, save one, in which laws and institutions take persons at their birth, and ordain that they shall never in all their lives be allowed to compete for certain things. The one exception is that of royalty. Persons still are born to the throne; no one, not of the reigning family, can ever occupy it, and no one even of that family can, by any means but the course of hereditary succession, attain it. All other dignities and social advantages are open to the whole male sex: many indeed are only attainable by wealth, but wealth may be striven for by any one, and is actually obtained by many men of the very humblest origin. The difficulties, to the majority, are indeed insuperable without the aid of fortunate accidents; but no male human being is under any legal ban: neither law nor opinion superadd artificial obstacles to the natural ones. Royalty, as I have said, is excepted: but in this case every one feels it to be an exception—an anomaly in the modern world, in marked opposition to its customs and principles, and to be justified only by extraordinary special expediencies, which, though individuals and nations differ in estimating their weight, unquestionably do in fact exist. But in this exceptional case, in which a high social function is, for important reasons, bestowed on birth instead of being put up to competition, all free nations contrive to adhere in substance to the principle from which they nominally derogate; for they circumscribe this high function by conditions avowedly intended to prevent the person to whom it ostensibly belongs from really performing it; while the person by whom it is performed, the responsible minister, does obtain the post by a competition from which no full-grown citizen of the male sex is legally excluded. The disabilities, therefore, to which women are subject from the mere fact of their birth, are the solitary examples of the kind in modern legislation. In no instance except this, which comprehends half the human race, are the higher social functions closed against any one by a fatality of birth which no exertions, and no change of circumstances, can overcome; for even religious disabilities (besides that in England and in Europe they have practically almost ceased to exist) do not close any career to the disqualified person in case of conversion.

The social subordination of women thus stands out an isolated fact in modern social institutions; a solitary breach of what has become their fundamental law; a single relic of an old world of thought and practice exploded in everything else, but retained in the one thing of most universal interest; as if a gigantic dolmen, or a vast temple of Jupiter Olympius, occupied the site of St. Paul's and received daily worship, while the surrounding Christian churches were only resorted to on fasts and festivals. This entire discrepancy between one social fact and all those which accompany it, and the radical opposition between its nature and the progressive movement which is the boast of the modern world, and which has successively swept away everything else of an analogous character, surely affords, to a conscientious observer of human tendencies, serious matter for reflection. It raises a prima facie presumption on the unfavourable side, far outweighing any which custom and usage could in such circumstances create on the favourable; and should at least suffice to make this, like the choice between republicanism and royalty, a balanced question.

The least that can be demanded is, that the question should not be considered as prejudged by existing fact and existing opinion, but open to discussion on its merits, as a question of justice and expediency: the decision on this, as on any of the other social arrangements of mankind, depending on what an enlightened estimate of tendencies and consequences may show to be most advantageous to humanity in general, without distinction of sex. And the discussion must be a real discussion, descending to foundations, and not resting satisfied with vague and general assertions. It will not do, for instance, to assert in general terms, that the experience of mankind has pronounced in favour of the existing system. Experience cannot possibly have decided between two courses, so long as there has only been experience of one. If it be said that the doctrine of the equality of the sexes rests only on theory, it must be remembered that the contrary doctrine also has only theory to rest upon. All that is proved in its favour by direct experience, is that mankind have been able to exist under it, and to attain the degree of improvement and prosperity which we now see; but whether that prosperity has been attained sooner, or is now greater, than it would have been under the other system, experience does not say. On the other hand, experience does say, that every step in improvement has been so invariably accompanied by a step made in raising the social position of women, that historians and philosophers have been led to adopt their elevation or debasement as on the whole the surest test and most correct measure of the civilization of a people or an age. Through all the progressive period of human history, the condition of women has been approaching nearer to equality with men. This does not of itself prove that the assimilation must go on to complete equality ; but it assuredly affords some presumption that such is the case.

Neither does it avail anything to say that the *nature* of the two sexes adapts them to their present functions and position, and renders these appropriate to them. Standing on the ground of common sense and the constitution of the human mind, I deny that any one knows, or can know, the nature of the two sexes, as long as they have only been seen in their present relation to one another. If men had ever been found in society without women, or women without men, or if there had been a society of men and women in which the women were not under the control of the men, something might have been positively known about the mental and moral differences which may be inherent in the nature of each. What is now called the nature of women is an eminently artificial thing— the result of forced repression in some directions, unnatural stimulation in others. It may be asserted without scruple, that no other class of dependents have had their character so entirely distorted from its natural proportions by their relation with their masters ; for, if conquered and slave races have been, in some respects, more forcibly repressed, whatever in them has not been crushed down by an iron heel has generally been let alone, and if left with any liberty of development, it has developed itself according to its own laws ; but in the case of women, a hot-house and stove cultivation has always been carried on of some of the capabilities of their nature, for the benefit and pleasure of their masters. Then, because certain products of the general vital force sprout luxuriantly and reach a great development in this heated atmosphere and under this active nurture and watering, while other shoots from the same root, which are left outside in the wintry air, with ice purposely heaped all round them, have a stunted growth, and some are burnt off with fire and disappear ; men, with that inability to recognize their own work which distinguishes the unanalytic mind, indolently believe that the tree grows of itself in the way they have made it grow, and that it would die if one half of it were not kept in a vapour bath and the other half in the snow.

Of all difficulties which impede the progress of thought, and the formation of well-grounded opinions on life and social arrangements, the greatest is now the unspeakable ignorance and inattention of mankind in respect to the influences which form human character. Whatever any portion of the human species now are, or seem to be, such, it is supposed, they have a natural tendency to be : even when the most elementary knowledge of the circumstances in which they have been placed, clearly points out the causes that made them what they are. Because a cottier deeply in arrears to his landlord is not industrious, there are people who think that the Irish are naturally idle. Because constitutions can be overthrown when the authorities appointed to execute them turn their arms against them, there are people who think the French incapable of free government. Because the Greeks cheated the Turks, and the Turks only plundered the Greeks, there are persons who think that the Turks are naturally more sincere : and because women, as is often said, care nothing about politics except their personalities, it is supposed that the general good is naturally less interesting to women than to men. History, which is now so much better understood than formerly, teaches another lesson : if only by showing the extraordinary susceptibility of human nature to external influences, and the extreme variableness of those of its manifestations which are supposed to be most universal and uniform. But in history, as in travelling, men usually see only what they already had in their own minds; and few learn much from history, who do not bring much with them to its study.

Hence, in regard to that most difficult question, what are the natural differences between the two sexes—a subject on which it is impossible in the present state of society to obtain complete and correct knowledge—while almost everybody dogmatizes upon it, almost all neglect and make light of the only means by which any partial insight can be obtained into it. This is, an analytic study of the most important department of psychology, the laws of the influence of circumstances on character. For, however great and apparently ineradicable the moral and intellectual differences between men and women might be, the evidence of their being natural differences could only be negative. Those only could be inferred to be natural which could not possibly be artificial—the residuum, after deducting every characteristic of either sex which can admit of being explained from education or external circumstances. The profoundest knowledge of the laws of the formation of character is indispensable to entitle any one to affirm even that there is any difference, much more what the difference is, between the two sexes considered as moral and rational beings; and since no one, as yet, has that knowledge (for there is hardly any subject which, in proportion to its importance, has been so little studied), no one is thus far entitled to any positive opinion on the subject. Conjectures are all that can at present be made; conjectures more or less probable, according as more or less authorized by such knowledge as we yet have of the laws of psychology, as applied to the formation of character.

247

One thing we may be certain of—that what is contrary to women's nature to do, they never will be made to do by simply giving their nature free play. The anxiety of mankind to interfere in behalf of nature, for fear lest nature should not succeed in effecting its purpose, is an altogether unnecessary solicitude. What women by nature cannot do, it is quite superfluous to forbid them from doing. What they can do, but not so well as the men who are their competitors, competition suffices to exclude them from ; since nobody asks for protective duties and bounties in favour of women ; it is only asked that the present bounties and protective duties in favour of men should be recalled. If women have a greater natural inclination for some things than for others, there is no need of laws or social inculcation to make the majority of them do the former in preference to the latter. Whatever women's services are most wanted for, the free play of competition will hold out the strongest inducements to them to undertake. And, as the words imply, they are most wanted for the things for which they are most fit ; by the apportionment of which to them, the collective faculties of the two sexes can be applied on the whole with the greatest sum of valuable result.

The general opinion of men is supposed to be, that the natural vocation of a woman is that of a wife and mother. I say, is supposed to be, because, judging from acts—from the whole of the present constitution of society—one might infer that their opinion was the direct contrary. They might be supposed to think that the alleged natural vocation of women was of all things the most repugnant to their nature ; insomuch that if they are free to do anything else—if any other means of living, or occupation of their time and faculties, is open, which has any chance of appearing desirable to them—there will not be enough of them who will be willing to accept the condition said to be natural to them.

THE SUBJECTION OF WOMEN

THERE remains a question, not of less importance than those already discussed, and which will be asked the most importunately by those opponents whose conviction is somewhat shaken on the main point. What good are we to expect from the changes proposed in our customs and institutions ? Would mankind be at all better off if women were free ? If not, why disturb their minds, and attempt to make a social revolution in the name of an abstract right ?

It is hardly to be expected that this question will be asked in respect to the change proposed in the condition of women in marriage. The sufferings, immoralities, evils of all sorts, produced in innumerable cases by the subjection of individual women to individual men, are far too terrible to be overlooked. Unthinking or uncandid persons, counting those cases alone which are extreme, or which attain publicity, may say that the evils are exceptional ; but no one can be blind to their existence, nor, in many cases, to their intensity. And it is perfectly obvious that the abuse of the power cannot be very much checked while the power remains. It is a power given, or offered, not to good men, or to decently respectable men, but to all men ; the most brutal, and the most criminal. There is no check but that of opinion, and such men are in general within the reach of no opinion but that of men like themselves. If such men did not brutally tyrannize over the one human being whom the law compels to bear everything from them, society must already have reached a paradisaical state. There could be no need any longer of laws to curb men's vicious propensities. Astraea must not only have returned to earth, but the heart of the worst man must have become her temple. The law of servitude in marriage is a monstrous contradiction to all the principles of the modern world, and to all the experience through which those principles have been slowly and painfully worked out. It is the sole case, now that negro slavery has been abolished, in which a human being in the plenitude of every faculty is delivered up to the tender mercies of another human being, in the hope forsooth that this other will use the power solely for the good of the person subjected to it. Marriage is the only actual bondage known to our law. There remain no legal slaves, except the mistress of every house.

It is not, therefore, on this part of the subject, that the question is likely to be asked, *Cui bono?* We may be told that the evil would outweigh the good, but the reality of the good admits of no dispute. In regard, however, to the larger question, the removal of women's disabilities—their recognition as the equals of men in all that belongs to citizenship—the opening to them of all honourable employments, and of the training and education which qualifies for those employments— there are many persons for whom it is not enough that the inequality has no just or legitimate defence ; they require to be told what express advantage would be obtained by abolishing it.

To which let me first answer, the advantage of having the most universal and pervading of all human relations regulated by justice instead of injustice. The vast amount of this gain to human nature, it is hardly possible, by any explanation or illustration, to place in a stronger light than it is placed by the bare statement, to any one who attaches a moral meaning to words. All the selfish propensities, the self-worship, the unjust self-preference, which exist among mankind, have their source and root in, and derive their principal nourishment from, the present constitution of the relation between men and women. Think what it is to a boy, to grow up to manhood in the belief that without any merit or any exertion of his own, though he may be the most frivolous and empty or the most ignorant and stolid of mankind, by the mere fact of being born a male he is by right the superior of all

and every one of an entire half of the human race:
including probably some whose real superiority to himself he has daily or hourly occasion to feel; but even
if in his whole conduct he habitually follows a woman's
guidance, still, if he is a fool, she thinks that of course
she is not, and cannot be, equal in ability and judgement to himself; and if he is not a fool, he does
worse—he sees that she is superior to him, and believes
that, notwithstanding her superiority, he is entitled to
command and she is bound to obey. What must be
the effect on his character, of this lesson? And men
of the cultivated classes are often not aware how deeply
it sinks into the immense majority of male minds.
For, among right-feeling and well-bred people, the
inequality is kept as much as possible out of sight;
above all, out of sight of the children. As much
obedience is required from boys to their mother as to
their father: they are not permitted to domineer over
their sisters, nor are they accustomed to see these
postponed to them, but the contrary; the compensa-
tions of the chivalrous feeling being made prominent,
while the servitude which requires them is kept in the
background. Well brought-up youths in the higher
classes thus often escape the bad influences of the
situation in their early years, and only experience them
when, arrived at manhood, they fall under the dominion
of facts as they really exist. Such people are little
aware, when a boy is differently brought up, how early
the notion of his inherent superiority to a girl arises
in his mind; how it grows with his growth and
strengthens with his strength; how it is inoculated
by one schoolboy upon another; how early the youth
thinks himself superior to his mother, owing her perhaps forbearance, but no real respect; and how sublime
and sultan-like a sense of superiority he feels, above
all, over the woman whom he honours by admitting
her to a partnership of his life. Is it imagined that
all this does not pervert the whole manner of existence
of the man, both as an individual and as a social
being? It is an exact parallel to the feeling of a heredi-

tary king that he is excellent above others by being born a king, or a noble by being born a noble. The relation between husband and wife is very like that between lord and vassal, except that the wife is held to more unlimited obedience than the vassal was. However the vassal's character may have been affected, for better and for worse, by his subordination, who can help seeing that the lord's was affected greatly for the worse ? whether he was led to believe that his vassals were really superior to himself, or to feel that he was placed in command over people as good as himself, for no merits or labours of his own, but merely for having, as Figaro says, taken the trouble to be born. The self-worship of the monarch, or of the feudal superior, is matched by the self-worship of the male. Human beings do not grow up from childhood in the possession of unearned distinctions, without pluming themselves upon them. Those whom privileges not acquired by their merit, and which they feel to be disproportioned to it, inspire with additional humility, are always the few, and the best few. The rest are only inspired with pride, and the worst sort of pride, that which values itself upon accidental advantages, not of its own achieving. Above all, when the feeling of being raised above the whole of the other sex is combined with personal authority over one individual among them ; the situation, if a school of conscientious and affectionate forbearance to those whose strongest points of character are conscience and affection, is to men of another quality a regularly constituted Academy or Gymnasium for training them in arrogance and over-bearingness ; which vices, if curbed by the certainty of resistance in their intercourse with other men, their equals, break out towards all who are in a position to be obliged to tolerate them, and often revenge themselves upon the unfortunate wife for the involuntary restraint which they are obliged to submit to elsewhere.

The example afforded, and the education given to the sentiments, by laying the foundation of domestic existence upon a relation contradictory to the first

principles of social justice, must, from the very nature
of man, have a perverting influence of such magnitude,
that it is hardly possible with our present experience
to raise our imaginations to the conception of so great
a change for the better as would be made by its
removal. All that education and civilization are doing
to efface the influences on character of the law of
force, and replace them by those of justice, remains
merely on the surface, as long as the citadel of the
enemy is not attacked. The principle of the modern
movement in morals and politics, is that conduct, and
conduct alone, entitles to respect : that not what men
are, but what they do, constitutes their claim to
deference ; that, above all, merit, and not birth, is
the only rightful claim to power and authority. If no
authority, not in its nature temporary, were allowed
to one human being over another, society would not
be employed in building up propensities with one hand
which it has to curb with the other. The child would
really, for the first time in man's existence on earth,
be trained in the way he should go, and when he was
old there would be a chance that he would not depart
from it. But so long as the right of the strong to
power over the weak rules in the very heart of society,
the attempt to make the equal right of the weak the
principle of its outward actions will always be an uphill
struggle ; for the law of justice, which is also that of
Christianity, will never get possession of men's inmost
sentiments ; they will be working against it, even when
bending to it.

The second benefit to be expected from giving to
women the free use of their faculties, by leaving them
the free choice of their employments, and opening to
them the same field of occupation and the same prizes
and encouragements as to other human beings, would
be that of doubling the mass of mental faculties available for the higher service of humanity. Where there
is now one person qualified to benefit mankind and
promote the general improvement, as a public teacher,
or an administrator of some branch of public or social

s

affairs, there would then be a chance of two. Mental superiority of any kind is at present everywhere so much below the demand; there is such a deficiency of persons competent to do excellently anything which it requires any considerable amount of ability to do; that the loss to the world, by refusing to make use of one-half of the whole quantity of talent it possesses, is extremely serious. It is true that this amount of mental power is not totally lost. Much of it is employed, and would in any case be employed, in domestic management, and in the few other occupations open to women; and from the remainder indirect benefit is in many individual cases obtained, through the personal influence of individual women over individual men. But these benefits are partial; their range is extremely circumscribed; and if they must be admitted, on the one hand, as a deduction from the amount of fresh social power that would be acquired by giving freedom to one-half of the whole sum of human intellect, there must be added, on the other, the benefit of the stimulus that would be given to the intellect of men by the competition; or (to use a more true expression) by the necessity that would be imposed on them of deserving precedency before they could expect to obtain it.

This great accession to the intellectual power of the species, and to the amount of intellect available for the good management of its affairs, would be obtained, partly, through the better and more complete intellectual education of women, which would then improve *pari passu* with that of men. Women in general would be brought up equally capable of understanding business, public affairs, and the higher matters of speculation, with men in the same class of society; and the select few of the one as well as of the other sex, who were qualified not only to comprehend what is done or thought by others, but to think or do something considerable themselves, would meet with the same facilities for improving and training their capacities in the one sex as in the other. In this way, the widening of the sphere of action for women would operate for good, by raising their education to the level of that of men, and making the one participate in all improvements made in the other. But independently of this, the mere breaking down of the barrier would of itself have an educational virtue of the highest worth. The mere getting rid of the idea that all the wider subjects of thought and action, all the things which are of general and not solely of private interest, are men's business, from which women are to be warned off—positively interdicted from most of it, coldly tolerated in the little which is allowed them—the mere consciousness a woman would then have of being a human being like any other, entitled to choose her pursuits, urged or invited by the same inducements as any one else to interest herself in whatever is interesting to human beings, entitled to exert the share of influence on all human concerns which belongs to an individual opinion, whether she attempted actual participation in them or not—this alone would effect an immense expansion of the faculties of women, as well as enlargement of the range of their moral sentiments.

Besides the addition to the amount of individual talent available for the conduct of human affairs, which certainly are not at present so abundantly provided in that respect that they can afford to dispense with one-half of what nature proffers ; the opinion of women would then possess a more beneficial, rather than a greater, influence upon the general mass of human belief and sentiment. I say a more beneficial, rather than a greater influence ; for the influence of women over the general tone of opinion has always, or at least from the earliest known period, been very considerable. The influence of mothers on the early character of their sons, and the desire of young men to recommend themselves to young women, have in all recorded times been important agencies in the formation of character, and have determined some of the chief steps in the progress of civilization. Even in the Homeric age, αἰδώς towards the Τρωάδας ἑλκεσι-

πέπλους is an acknowledged and powerful motive of
action in the great Hector. The moral influence of
women has had two modes of operation. First, it has
been a softening influence. Those who were most
liable to be the victims of violence, have naturally
tended as much as they could towards limiting its
sphere and mitigating its excesses. Those who were
not taught to fight, have naturally inclined in favour of
any other mode of settling differences rather than that
of fighting. In general, those who have been the greatest
sufferers by the indulgence of selfish passion, have been
the most earnest supporters of any moral law which
offered a means of bridling passion. Women were powerfully instrumental in inducing the northern conquerors
to adopt the creed of Christianity, a creed so much more
favourable to women than any that preceded it. The
conversion of the Anglo-Saxons and of the Franks may
be said to have been begun by the wives of Ethelbert
and Clovis. The other mode in which the effect of
women's opinion has been conspicuous, is by giving
a powerful stimulus to those qualities in men, which,
not being themselves trained in, it was necessary for
them that they should find in their protectors. Courage, and the military virtues generally, have at all
times been greatly indebted to the desire which men
felt of being admired by women: and the stimulus
reaches far beyond this one class of eminent qualities,
since, by a very natural effect of their position, the
best passport to the admiration and favour of women
has always been to be thought highly of by men.
From the combination of the two kinds of moral influence thus exercised by women, arose the spirit of
chivalry: the peculiarity of which is, to aim at com-
bining the highest standard of the warlike qualities with
the cultivation of a totally different class of virtues—
those of gentleness, generosity, and self-abnegation,
towards the non-military and defenceless classes generally, and a special submission and worship directed
towards women; who were distinguished from the
other defenceless classes by the high rewards which

they had it in their power voluntarily to bestow on those who endeavoured to earn their favour, instead of extorting their subjection. Though the practice of chivalry fell even more sadly short of its theoretic standard than practice generally falls below theory, it remains one of the most precious monuments of the moral history of our race; as a remarkable instance of a concerted and organized attempt by a most disorganized and distracted society, to raise up and carry into practice a moral ideal greatly in advance of its social condition and institutions; so much so as to have been completely frustrated in the main object, yet never entirely inefficacious, and which has left a most sensible, and for the most part a highly valuable impress on the ideas and feelings of all subsequent times.

The chivalrous ideal is the acme of the influence of women's sentiments on the moral cultivation of mankind: and if women are to remain in their subordinate situation, it were greatly to be lamented that the chivalrous standard should have passed away, for it is the only one at all capable of mitigating the demoralizing influences of that position. But the changes in the general state of the species rendered inevitable the substitution of a totally different ideal of morality for the chivalrous one. Chivalry was the attempt to infuse moral elements into a state of society in which everything depended for good or evil on individual prowess, under the softening influences of individual delicacy and generosity. In modern societies, all things, even in the military department of affairs, are decided, not by individual effort, but by the combined operations of numbers; while the main occupation of society has changed from fighting to business, from military to industrial life. The exigencies of the new life are no more exclusive of the virtues of generosity than those of the old, but it no longer entirely depends on them. The main foundations of the moral life of modern times must be justice and prudence; the respect of each for the rights of every other, and the

257

ability of each to take care of himself. Chivalry left without legal check all forms of wrong which reigned unpunished throughout society; it only encouraged a few to do right in preference to wrong, by the direction it gave to the instruments of praise and admiration. But the real dependence of morality must always be upon its penal sanctions—its power to deter from evil. The security of society cannot rest on merely rendering honour to right, a motive so comparatively weak in all but a few, and which on very many does not operate at all. Modern society is able to repress wrong through all departments of life, by a fit exertion of the superior strength which civilization has given it, and thus to render the existence of the weaker members of society (no longer defenceless but protected by law) tolerable to them, without reliance on the chivalrous feelings of those who are in a position to tyrannize. The beauties and graces of the chivalrous character are still what they were, but the rights of the weak, and the general comfort of human life, now rest on a far surer and steadier support; or rather, they do so in every relation of life except the conjugal.

At present the moral influence of women is no less real, but it is no longer of so marked and definite a character: it has more nearly merged in the general influence of public opinion. Both through the contagion of sympathy, and through the desire of men to shine in the eyes of women, their feelings have great effect in keeping alive what remains of the chivalrous ideal—in fostering the sentiments and continuing the traditions of spirit and generosity. In these points of character, their standard is higher than that of men; in the quality of justice, somewhat lower. As regards the relations of private life it may be said generally, that their influence is, on the whole, encouraging to the softer virtues, discouraging to the sterner: though the statement must be taken with all the modifications dependent on individual character. In the chief of the greater trials to which virtue is subject in the concerns of life—the conflict between interest and principle—the tendency of women's influence is of a very mixed character. When the principle involved happens to be one of the very few which the course of their religious or moral education has strongly impressed upon themselves, they are potent auxiliaries to virtue: and their husbands and sons are often prompted by them to acts of abnegation which they never would have been capable of without that stimulus. But, with the present education and position of women, the moral principles which have been impressed on them cover but a comparatively small part of the field of virtue, and are, moreover, principally negative; forbidding particular acts, but having little to do with the general direction of the thoughts and purposes. I am afraid it must be said, that disinterestedness in the general conduct of life— the devotion of the energies to purposes which hold out no promise of private advantages to the family— is very seldom encouraged or supported by women's influence. It is small blame to them that they discourage objects of which they have not learnt to see the advantage, and which withdraw their men from them, and from the interests of the family. But the consequence is that women's influence is often anything but favourable to public virtue.

Women have, however, some share of influence in giving the tone to public moralities since their sphere of action has been a little widened, and since a considerable number of them have occupied themselves practically in the promotion of objects reaching beyond their own family and household. The influence of women counts for a great deal in two of the most marked features of modern European life—its aversion to war, and its addiction to philanthropy. Excellent characteristics both; but unhappily, if the influence of women is valuable in the encouragement it gives to these feelings in general, in the particular applications the direction it gives to them is at least as often mischievous as useful. In the philanthropic department more particularly, the two provinces chiefly cultivated by women are religious proselytism and charity. Religious proselytism at home, is but another word for embittering of religious animosities : abroad, it is usually a blind running at an object, without either knowing or heeding the fatal mischiefs—fatal to the religious object itself as well as to all other desirable objects—which may be produced by the means employed. As for charity, it is a matter in which the immediate effect on the persons directly concerned, and the ultimate consequence to the general good, are apt to be at complete war with one another : while the education given to women—an education of the sentiments rather than of the understanding—and the habit inculcated by their whole life, of looking to immediate effects on persons, and not to remote effects on classes of persons—make them both unable to see, and unwilling to admit, the ultimate evil tendency of any form of charity or philanthropy which commends itself to their sympathetic feelings. The great and continually increasing mass of unenlightened and short-sighted benevolence, which, taking the care of people's lives out of their own hands, and relieving them from the disagreeable consequences of their own acts, saps the very foundations of the self-respect, self-help, and self-control which are the essential conditions both of individual prosperity and of social virtue—this waste of resources and of benevolent feelings in doing harm instead of good, is immensely swelled by women's contributions, and stimulated by their influence. Not that this is a mistake likely to be made by women, where they have actually the practical management of schemes of beneficence. It sometimes happens that women who administer public charities—with that insight into present fact, and especially into the minds and feelings of those with whom they are in immediate contact, in which women generally excel men—recognize in the clearest manner the demoralizing influence of the alms given or the help afforded, and could give lessons on the subject to many a male political economist. But women who only give their money, and are not brought face to face with the effects it produces, how can they be expected to foresee them? A woman born to the present lot of women, and content with it, how should she appreciate the value of self-dependence? She is not self-dependent; she is not taught self-dependence; her destiny is to receive everything from others, and why should what is good enough for her be bad for the poor? Her familiar notions of good are of blessings descending from a superior. She forgets that she is not free, and that the poor are; that if what they need is given to them unearned, they cannot be compelled to earn it: that everybody cannot be taken care of by everybody, but there must be some motive to induce people to take care of themselves; and that to be helped to help themselves, if they are physically capable of it, is the only charity which proves to be charity in the end.

These considerations show how usefully the part which women take in the formation of general opinion, would be modified for the better by that more enlarged instruction, and practical conversancy with the things which their opinions influence, that would necessarily arise from their social and political emancipation. But the improvement it would work through the influence they exercise, each in her own family, would be still more remarkable.

It is often said that in the classes most exposed to temptation, a man's wife and children tend to keep him honest and respectable, both by the wife's direct influence, and by the concern he feels for their future welfare. This may be so, and no doubt often is so, with those who are more weak than wicked; and this beneficial influence would be preserved and strengthened under equal laws; it does not depend on the woman's servitude, but is, on the contrary, diminished by the disrespect which the inferior class of men always at heart feel towards those who are subject to their power. But when we ascend higher in the scale, we come among a totally different set of moving forces. The wife's influence tends, as far as it goes, to prevent the husband from falling below the common standard of approbation of the country. It tends quite as strongly to hinder him from rising above it. The wife is the auxiliary of the common public opinion. A man who is married to a woman his inferior in intelligence, finds her a perpetual dead weight, or, worse than a dead weight, a drag, upon every aspiration of his to be better than public opinion requires him to be. It is hardly possible for one who is in these bonds, to attain exalted virtue. If he differs in his opinion from the mass—if he sees truths which have not yet dawned upon them, or if, feeling in his heart truths which they nominally recognize, he would like to act up to those truths more conscientiously than the generality of mankind—to all such thoughts and desires, marriage is the heaviest of drawbacks, unless he be so fortunate as to have a wife as much above the common level as he himself is.

For, in the first place, there is always some sacrifice of personal interest required ; either of social consequence, or of pecuniary means ; perhaps the risk of even the means of subsistence. These sacrifices and risks he may be willing to encounter for himself ; but he will pause before he imposes them on his family. And his family in this case means his wife and daughters ; for he always hopes that his sons will feel as he feels himself, and that what he can do without, they will do without, willingly, in the same cause. But his daughters—their marriage may depend upon it : and his wife, who is unable to enter into or understand the objects for which these sacrifices are made—who, if she thought them worth any sacrifice, would think so on trust, and solely for his sake—who can participate in none of the enthusiasm or the self-approbation he himself may feel, while the things which he is disposed to sacrifice are all in all to her ; will not the best and most unselfish man hesitate the longest before bringing on her this consequence ? If it be not the comforts of life, but only social consideration, that is at stake, the burthen upon his conscience and feelings

is still very severe. Whoever has a wife and children
has given hostages to Mrs. Grundy. The approbation
of that potentate may be a matter of indifference to
him, but it is of great importance to his wife. The
man himself may be above opinion, or may find sufficient compensation in the opinion of those of his own
way of thinking. But to the women connected with
him, he can offer no compensation. The almost invariable tendency of the wife to place her influence in
the same scale with social consideration, is sometimes
made a reproach to women, and represented as a
peculiar trait of feebleness and childishness of character
in them: surely with great injustice. Society makes
the whole life of a woman, in the easy classes, a continued self-sacrifice; it exacts from her an unremitting
restraint of the whole of her natural inclinations, and
the sole return it makes to her for what often deserves
the name of a martyrdom, is consideration. Her consideration is inseparably connected with that of her
husband, and after paying the full price for it, she
finds that she is to lose it, for no reason of which she
can feel the cogency. She has sacrificed her whole life
to it, and her husband will not sacrifice to it a whim,
a freak, an eccentricity; something not recognized or
allowed for by the world, and which the world will
agree with her in thinking a folly, if it thinks no
worse! The dilemma is hardest upon that very meri-
torious class of men, who, without possessing talents
which qualify them to make a figure among those with
whom they agree in opinion, hold their opinion from
conviction, and feel bound in honour and conscience
to serve it, by making profession of their belief, and
giving their time, labour, and means, to anything
undertaken in its behalf. The worst case of all is
when such men happen to be of a rank and position
which of itself neither gives them, nor excludes them
from, what is considered the best society; when their
admission to it depends mainly on what is thought of
them personally—and however unexceptionable their
breeding and habits, their being identified with opinions

and public conduct unacceptable to those who give the tone to society would operate as an effectual exclusion. Many a woman flatters herself (nine times out of ten quite erroneously) that nothing prevents her and her husband from moving in the highest society of her neighbourhood—society in which others well known to her, and in the same class of life, mix freely—except that her husband is unfortunately a Dissenter, or has the reputation of mingling in low radical politics. That it is, she thinks, which hinders George from getting a commission or a place, Caroline from making an advantageous match, and prevents her and her husband from obtaining invitations, perhaps honours, which, for aught she sees, they are as well entitled to as some folks. With such an influence in every house, either exerted actively, or operating all the more powerfully for not being asserted, is it any wonder that people in general are kept down in that mediocrity of respectability which is becoming a marked characteristic of modern times ?

There is another very injurious aspect in which the effect, not of women's disabilities directly, but of the broad line of difference which those disabilities create between the education and character of a woman and that of a man, requires to be considered. Nothing can be more unfavourable to that union of thoughts and inclinations which is the ideal of married life. Intimate society between people radically dissimilar to one another, is an idle dream. Unlikeness may attract, but it is likeness which retains ; and in proportion to the likeness is the suitability of the individuals to give each other a happy life. While women are so unlike men, it is not wonderful that selfish men should feel the need of arbitrary power in their own hands, to arrest *in limine* the lifelong conflict of inclinations, by deciding every question on the side of their own preference. When people are extremely unlike, there can be no real identity of interest. Very often there is conscientious difference of opinion between married people, on the highest points of duty. Is there any

264

reality in the marriage union where this takes place ?
Yet it is not uncommon anywhere, when the woman
has any earnestness of character ; and it is a very
general case indeed in Catholic countries, when she is
supported in her dissent by the only other authority
to which she is taught to bow, the priest. With the
usual barefacedness of power not accustomed to find
itself disputed, the influence of priests over women is
attacked by Protestant and Liberal writers, less for
being bad in itself, than because it is a rival authority
to the husband, and raises up a revolt against his
infallibility. In England, similar differences occasionally exist when an Evangelical wife has allied herself
with a husband of a different quality ; but in general
this source at least of dissension is got rid of, by
reducing the minds of women to such a nullity, that
they have no opinions but those of Mrs. Grundy, or
those which the husband tells them to have. When
there is no difference of opinion, differences merely of
taste may be sufficient to detract greatly from the
happiness of married life. And though it may stimulate the amatory propensities of men, it does not con-
duce to married happiness, to exaggerate by differences
of education whatever may be the native differences of
the sexes. If the married pair are well-bred and well-
behaved people, they tolerate each other's tastes ; but
is mutual toleration what people look forward to, when
they enter into marriage ? These differences of inclination will naturally make their wishes different, if not
restrained by affection or duty, as to almost all domestic
questions which arise. What a difference there must
be in the society which the two persons will wish to
frequent, or be frequented by ! Each will desire asso-
ciates who share their own tastes : the persons agreeable to one, will be indifferent or positively disagreeable
to the other ; yet there can be none who are not
common to both, for married people do not now live
in different parts of the house and have totally different
visiting lists, as in the reign of Louis XV. They cannot
help having different wishes as to the bringing up of

the children : each will wish to see reproduced in them their own tastes and sentiments : and there is either a compromise, and only a half-satisfaction to either, or the wife has to yield—often with bitter suffering ; and, with or without intention, her occult influence continues to counterwork the husband's purposes.

It would of course be extreme folly to suppose that these differences of feeling and inclination only exist because women are brought up differently from men, and that there would not be differences of taste under any imaginable circumstances. But there is nothing beyond the mark in saying that the distinction in bringing-up immensely aggravates those differences, and renders them wholly inevitable. While women are brought up as they are, a man and a woman will but rarely find in one another real agreement of tastes and wishes as to daily life. They will generally have to give it up as hopeless, and renounce the attempt to have, in the intimate associate of their daily life, that *idem velle, idem nolle*, which is the recognized bond of any society that is really such : or if the man succeeds in obtaining it, he does so by choosing a woman who is so complete a nullity that she has no *velle* or *nolle* at all, and is as ready to comply with one thing as another if anybody tells her to do so. Even this calculation is apt to fail ; dullness and want of spirit are not always a guarantee of the submission which is so confidently expected from them. But if they were, is this the ideal of marriage ? What, in this case, does the man obtain by it, except an upper servant, a nurse, or a mistress ? On the contrary, when each of two persons, instead of being a nothing, is a something ; when they are attached to one another, and are not too much unlike to begin with ; the constant partaking in the same things, assisted by their sympathy, draws out the latent capacities of each for being interested in the things which were at first interesting only to the other ; and works a gradual assimilation of the tastes and characters to one another, partly by the insensible modification of each, but more by a real enriching of the two natures, each acquiring the tastes and capacities of the other in addition to its own. This often happens between two friends of the same sex, who are much associated in their daily life : and it would be a common, if not the commonest, case in marriage, did not the totally different bringing-up of the two sexes make it next to an impossibility to form a really well-assorted union. Were this remedied, whatever differences there might still be in individual tastes, there would at least be, as a general rule, complete unity and unanimity as to the great objects of life. When the two persons both care for great objects, and are a help and encouragement to each other in whatever regards these, the minor matters on which their tastes may differ are not all-important to them ; and there is a foundation for solid friendship, of an enduring character, more likely than anything else to make it, through the whole of life, a greater pleasure to each to give pleasure to the other, than to receive it.

I have considered, thus far, the effects on the pleasures and benefits of the marriage union which depend on the mere unlikeness between the wife and the husband : but the evil tendency is prodigiously aggravated when the unlikeness is inferiority. Mere unlikeness, when it only means difference of good qualities, may be more a benefit in the way of mutual improvement, than a drawback from comfort. When each emulates, and desires and endeavours to acquire, the other's peculiar qualities, the difference does not produce diversity of interest, but increased identity of it, and makes each still more valuable to the other. But when one is much the inferior of the two in mental ability and cultivation, and is not actively attempting by the other's aid to rise to the other's level, the whole influence of the connexion upon the development of the superior of the two is deteriorating : and still more so in a tolerably happy marriage than in an unhappy one. It is not with impunity that the superior in intellect shuts himself up with an inferior, and elects that inferior for his chosen, and sole completely inti-

267

mate, associate. Any society which is not improving, is deteriorating : and the more so, the closer and more familiar it is. Even a really superior man almost always begins to deteriorate when he is habitually (as the phrase is) king of his company : and in his most habitual company the husband who has a wife inferior to him is always so. While his self-satisfaction is incessantly ministered to on the one hand, on the other he insensibly imbibes the modes of feeling, and of looking at things, which belong to a more vulgar or a more limited mind than his own. This evil differs from many of those which have hitherto been dwelt on, by being an increasing one. The association of men with women in daily life is much closer and more complete than it ever was before. Men's life is more domestic. Formerly, their pleasures and chosen occupations were among men, and in men's company : their wives had but a fragment of their lives. At the present time, the progress of civilization, and the turn of opinion against the rough amusements and convivial excesses which formerly occupied most men in their hours of relaxation—together with (it must be said) the improved tone of modern feeling as to the reciprocity of duty which binds the husband towards the wife—have thrown the man very much more upon home and its inmates, for his personal and social pleasures : while the kind and degree of improvement which has been made in women's education, has made them in some degree capable of being his companions in ideas and mental tastes, while leaving them, in most cases, still hopelessly inferior to him. His desire of mental communion is thus in general satisfied by a communion from which he learns nothing. An unimproving and unstimulating companionship is substituted for (what he might otherwise have been obliged to seek) the society of his equals in powers and his fellows in the higher pursuits. We see, accordingly, that young men of the greatest promise generally cease to improve as soon as they marry, and, not improving, inevitably degenerate. If the wife does not push the husband forward, she always holds him back. He ceases to care for what she does not care for ; he no longer desires, and ends by disliking and shunning, society congenial to his former aspirations, and which would now shame his falling-off from them ; his higher faculties both of mind and heart cease to be called into activity. And this change coinciding with the new and selfish interests which are created by the family, after a few years he differs in no material respect from those who have never had wishes for anything but the common vanities and the common pecuniary objects.

What marriage may be in the case of two persons of cultivated faculties, identical in opinions and purposes, between whom there exists that best kind of equality, similarity of powers and capacities with reciprocal superiority in them—so that each can enjoy the luxury of looking up to the other, and can have alternately the pleasure of leading and of being led in the path of development—I will not attempt to describe. To those who can conceive it, there is no need ; to those who cannot, it would appear the dream of an enthusiast. But I maintain, with the profoundest conviction, that this, and this only, is the ideal of marriage; and that all opinions, customs, and institutions which favour any other notion of it, or turn the conceptions and aspirations connected with it into any other direction, by whatever pretences they may be coloured, are relics of primitive barbarism. The moral regeneration of mankind will only really commence, when the most fundamental of the social relations is placed under the rule of equal justice, and when human beings learn to cultivate their strongest sympathy with an equal in rights and in cultivation.

Thus far, the benefits which it has appeared that the world would gain by ceasing to make sex a disqualification for privileges and a badge of subjection, are social rather than individual ; consisting in an increase of the general fund of thinking and acting power, and an improvement in the general conditions

269

of the association of men with women. But it would be a grievous understatement of the case to omit the most direct benefit of all, the unspeakable gain in private happiness to the liberated half of the species ; the difference to them between a life of subjection to the will of others, and a life of rational freedom. After the primary necessities of food and raiment, freedom is the first and strongest want of human nature. While mankind are lawless, their desire is for lawless freedom. When they have learnt to understand the meaning of duty and the value of reason, they incline more and more to be guided and restrained by these in the exercise of their freedom ; but they do not therefore desire freedom less ; they do not become disposed to accept the will of other people as the representative and interpreter of those guiding principles. On the contrary, the communities in which the reason has been most cultivated, and in which the idea of social duty has been most powerful, are those which have most strongly asserted the freedom of action of the individual—the liberty of each to govern his conduct by his own feelings of duty, and by such laws and social restraints as his own conscience can subscribe to.

He who would rightly appreciate the worth of personal independence as an element of happiness, should consider the value he himself puts upon it as an ingredient of his own. There is no subject on which there is a greater habitual difference of judgement between a man judging for himself, and the same man judging for other people. When he hears others complaining that they are not allowed freedom of action— that their own will has not sufficient influence in the regulation of their affairs—his inclination is, to ask, what are their grievances ? what positive damage they sustain ? and in what respect they consider their affairs to be mismanaged ? and if they fail to make out, in answer to these questions, what appears to him a sufficient case, he turns a deaf ear, and regards their complaint as the fanciful querulousness of people whom nothing reasonable will satisfy. But he has a quite

different standard of judgement when he is deciding
for himself. Then, the most unexceptionable administration of his interests by a tutor set over him, does
not satisfy his feelings: his personal exclusion from
the deciding authority appears itself the greatest grievance of all, rendering it superfluous even to enter into
the question of mismanagement. It is the same with
nations. What citizen of a free country would listen
to any offers of good and skilful administration, in
return for the abdication of freedom? Even if he
could believe that good and skilful administration can
exist among a people ruled by a will not their own,
would not the consciousness of working out their own
destiny under their own moral responsibility be a compensation to his feelings for great rudeness and imperfection in the details of public affairs? Let him rest
assured that whatever he feels on this point, women
feel in a fully equal degree. Whatever has been said
or written, from the time of Herodotus to the present,
of the ennobling influence of free government—the
nerve and spring which it gives to all the faculties,
the larger and higher objects which it presents to the
intellect and feelings, the more unselfish public spirit,
and calmer and broader views of duty, that it engenders, and the generally loftier platform on which
it elevates the individual as a moral, spiritual, and
social being—is every particle as true of women as of
men. Are these things no important part of individual
happiness? Let any man call to mind what he himself felt on emerging from boyhood—from the tutelage
and control of even loved and affectionate elders—and
entering upon the responsibilities of manhood. Was
it not like the physical effect of taking off a heavy
weight, or releasing him from obstructive, even if not
otherwise painful, bonds? Did he not feel twice as
much alive, twice as much a human being, as before?
And does he imagine that women have none of these
feelings? But it is a striking fact, that the satisfactions and mortifications of personal pride, though all
in all to most men when the case is their own, have

less allowance made for them in the case of other people, and are less listened to as a ground or a justification of conduct, than any other natural human feelings ; perhaps because men compliment them in their own case with the names of so many other qualities, that they are seldom conscious how mighty an influence these feelings exercise in their own lives. No less large and powerful is their part, we may assure ourselves, in the lives and feelings of women. Women are schooled into suppressing them in their most natural and most healthy direction, but the internal principle remains, in a different outward form. An active and energetic mind, if denied liberty, will seek for power : refused the command of itself, it will assert its personality by attempting to control others. To allow to any human beings no existence of their own but what depends on others, is giving far too high a premium on bending others to their purposes. Where liberty cannot be hoped for, and power can, power becomes the grand object of human desire ; those to whom others will not leave the undisturbed management of their own affairs, will compensate themselves, if they can, by meddling for their own purposes with the affairs of others. Hence also women's passion for personal beauty, and dress and display ; and all the evils that flow from it, in the way of mischievous luxury and social immorality. The love of power and the love of liberty are in eternal antagonism. Where there is least liberty, the passion for power is the most ardent and unscrupulous. The desire of power over others can only cease to be a depraving agency among mankind, when each of them individually is able to do without it : which can only be where respect for liberty in the personal concerns of each is an established principle.

But it is not only through the sentiment of personal dignity, that the free direction and disposal of their own faculties is a source of individual happiness, and to be fettered and restricted in it, a source of unhappiness, to human beings, and not least to women. There is nothing, after disease, indigence, and guilt, so fatal to the pleasurable enjoyment of life as the want of a worthy outlet for the active faculties. Women who have the cares of a family, and while they have the cares of a family, have this outlet, and it generally suffices for them : but what of the greatly increasing number of women, who have had no opportunity of exercising the vocation which they are mocked by telling them is their proper one ? What of the women whose children have been lost to them by death or distance, or have grown up, married, and formed homes of their own ? There are abundant examples of men who, after a life engrossed by business, retire with a competency to the enjoyment, as they hope, of rest, but to whom, as they are unable to acquire new interests and excitements that can replace the old, the change to a life of inactivity brings ennui, melancholy, and premature death. Yet no one thinks of the parallel case of so many worthy and devoted women, who, having paid what they are told is their debt to society —having brought up a family blamelessly to manhood and womanhood—having kept a house as long as they had a house needing to be kept—are deserted by the sole occupation for which they have fitted themselves ; and remain with undiminished activity but with no employment for it, unless perhaps a daughter or daughter-in-law is willing to abdicate in their favour the discharge of the same functions in her younger household. Surely a hard lot for the old age of those who have worthily discharged, as long as it was given to them to discharge, what the world accounts their only social duty. Of such women, and of those others to whom this duty has not been committed at all— many of whom pine through life with the consciousness of thwarted vocations, and activities which are not suffered to expand—the only resources, speaking generally, are religion and charity. But their religion, though it may be one of feeling, and of ceremonial observance, cannot be a religion of action, unless in the form of charity. For charity many of them are by nature admirably fitted; but to practise it use-

fully, or even without doing mischief, requires the
education, the manifold preparation, the knowledge
and the thinking powers, of a skilful administrator.
There are few of the administrative functions of government for which a person would not be fit, who is fit
to bestow charity usefully. In this as in other cases
(pre-eminently in that of the education of children),
the duties permitted to women cannot be performed
properly, without their being trained for duties which,
to the great loss of society, are not permitted to them.
And here let me notice the singular way in which the
question of women's disabilities is frequently presented
to view, by those who find it easier to draw a ludicrous
picture of what they do not like, than to answer the
arguments for it. When it is suggested that women's
executive capacities and prudent counsels might sometimes be found valuable in affairs of state, these lovers
of fun hold up to the ridicule of the world, as sitting
in parliament or in the cabinet, girls in their teens, or
young wives of two or three and twenty, transported
bodily, exactly as they are, from the drawing-room to
the House of Commons. They forget that males are
not usually selected at this early age for a seat in
Parliament, or for responsible political functions.
Common sense would tell them that if such trusts
were confided to women, it would be to such as having
no special vocation for married life, or preferring
another employment of their faculties (as many women
even now prefer to marriage some of the few honourable
occupations within their reach), have spent the best
years of their youth in attempting to qualify themselves for the pursuits in which they desire to engage;
or still more frequently perhaps, widows or wives of
forty or fifty, by whom the knowledge of life and
faculty of government which they have acquired in
their families, could by the aid of appropriate studies
be made available on a less contracted scale. There
is no country of Europe in which the ablest men have
not frequently experienced, and keenly appreciated,
the value of the advice and help of clever and ex-

perienced women of the world, in the attainment both
of private and of public objects; and there are important matters of public administration to which few
men are equally competent with such women; among
others, the detailed control of expenditure. But what
we are now discussing is not the need which society
has of the services of women in public business, but
the dull and hopeless life to which it so often condemns
them, by forbidding them to exercise the practical
abilities which many of them are conscious of, in any
wider field than one which to some of them never was,
and to others is no longer, open. If there is anything
vitally important to the happiness of human beings,
it is that they should relish their habitual pursuit.
This requisite of an enjoyable life is very imperfectly
granted, or altogether denied, to a large part of mankind; and by its absence many a life is a failure,
which is provided, in appearance, with every requisite
of success. But if circumstances which society is not
yet skilful enough to overcome, render such failures
often for the present inevitable, society need not itself
inflict them. The injudiciousness of parents, a youth's
own inexperience, or the absence of external opportunities for the congenial vocation, and their presence
for an uncongenial, condemn numbers of men to pass
their lives in doing one thing reluctantly and ill, when
there are other things which they could have done
well and happily. But on women this sentence is
imposed by actual law, and by customs equivalent to
law. What, in unenlightened societies, colour, race,
religion, or in the case of a conquered country, nation-
ality, are to some men, sex is to all women; a peremptory exclusion from almost all honourable occupations,
but either such as cannot be fulfilled by others, or such
as those others do not think worthy of their acceptance.
Sufferings arising from causes of this nature usually
meet with so little sympathy, that few persons are
aware of the great amount of unhappiness even now
produced by the feeling of a wasted life. The case
will be even more frequent, as increased cultivation

creates a greater and greater disproportion between the ideas and faculties of women, and the scope which society allows to their activity.

When we consider the positive evil caused to the disqualified half of the human race by their disqualification—first in the loss of the most inspiriting and elevating kind of personal enjoyment, and next in the weariness, disappointment, and profound dissatisfaction with life, which are so often the substitute for it ; one feels that among all the lessons which men require for carrying on the struggle against the inevitable imperfections of their lot on earth, there is no lesson which they more need, than not to add to the evils which nature inflicts, by their jealous and prejudiced restrictions on one another. Their vain fears only substitute other and worse evils for those which they are idly apprehensive of : while every restraint on the freedom of conduct of any of their human fellow creatures (otherwise than by making them responsible for any evil actually caused by it), dries up *pro tanto* the principal fountain of human happiness, and leaves the species less rich, to an inappreciable degree, in all that makes life valuable to the individual human being.

THE END

7

Herbert Spencer,   PRINCIPLES OF SOCIOLOGY

Thorstein Veblen,   THEORY OF THE LEISURE CLASS

1. Spencer feels that the principles of evolutionary
    development which apply to other species of ani-
    mals also govern the human species. How does this
    view shape his analysis of human society?

2. What is Spencer's concept of progress in human
    society? What does he offer as evidence of this
    progress? Where does he think it will lead?

3. What is Spencer's attitude toward non-Western cul-
    tures? What is the value of studying other cul-
    tures for Spencer? How does Spencer use the an-
    thropological evidence he has gathered?

4. How does Spencer compare the relation between man
    and society with that between the individual and
    the species in other types of animals?

5. What are Spencer's criteria for evaluating a social
    institution like the family? What makes some fami-
    ly arrangements better than others? What is the
    relationship between ethics and evolutionary devel-
    opment, according to Spencer? What dangers do you
    see in applying scientific theories of evolution
    to human society?

6. What does Veblen say are the underlying motivations
    for the ways people dress?

7. How are people led to believe that it is desirable
    to be stylishly dressed?

8. Why do men of the leisure class desire that the
    clothing of their women reflect a great amount of
    leisure? Why do the men not make this display for
    themselves?

9. What characteristics do the garments of liveried
    servants, women, and priests have in common? What
    do they reflect about the people who wear them?

10. As the wealthy class grows larger, what happens to former symbols of pecuniary standing?

11. How true are Veblen's observations as applied to styles of dress today?

Herbert Spencer (1820-1903) was an English philosopher and one of the first true sociologists. He applied evolutionary theory to human society even before the publication of Darwin's *Origin of Species* and is generally cited as an exponent of social Darwinism, a now discredited nineteenth-century position which argued that the elimination of "unfit" members of society through natural selection would bring about social improvement. Our excerpt is drawn from the *Synthetic Philosophy* (or Principles of Sociology) a three-volume work published between 1862 and 1896.

THE MAINTENANCE OF SPECIES.

§ 272. As full understanding of the social relations cannot be gained without studying their genesis, so neither can full understanding of the domestic relations; and fully to understand the genesis of the domestic relations, we must go further back than the history of man carries us.

Of every species it is undeniable that individuals which die must be replaced by new individuals, or the species as a whole must die. No less obvious is it that if the death-rate in a species is high, the rate of multiplication must be high, and conversely. This proportioning of reproduction to mortality is requisite for mankind as for every other kind. Hence the facts exhibited by living beings at large must be considered that the facts exhibited by human beings may be clearly comprehended.

§ 273. Regarding the continued life of the species as in every case the end to which all other ends are secondary (for if the species disappears all other ends disappear), let us look at the several modes there are of achieving this end. The requirement that a due number of adults shall arise in successive generations, may be fulfilled in variously-modified ways, which subordinate the existing and next-succeeding members of the species in various degrees.

Low creatures having small powers of meeting the life-destroying activities around, and still smaller powers of protecting progeny, can maintain their kinds only if the mature individual produces the germs of new individuals in immense numbers; so that, unprotected and defenceless though the germs are, one or two may escape destruction. And manifestly, the larger the part of the parental substance transformed into germs (and often most of it is so transformed), the smaller the part that can be devoted to individual life.

With each germ is usually laid up some nutritive matter, available for growth before it commences its own struggle for existence. From a given quantity of matter devoted by the parent to reproduction, there may be formed either a larger number of germs with a smaller quantity of nutritive matter each, or a smaller number with a larger quantity each. Hence result differences in the rates of juvenile mortality. Here of a million minute ova left uncared for, the majority are destroyed before they are hatched; multitudes of the remainder, with the feeblest powers of getting food and evading enemies, die or are devoured soon after they are hatched; so that very few have considerable lengths of individual life. Conversely, when the conditions to be met by the species make it advantageous that there should be fewer ova and more nutriment bequeathed to each, the young individuals, beginning life at more advanced stages of development, survive longer. The species is maintained without the sacrifice of so many before arrival at maturity.

All varieties in the proportions of these factors occur. An adult individual, the single survivor from hundreds of thousands of germs, may itself be almost wholly sacrificed individually in the production of germs equally numerous; in which case the species is maintained at enormous cost, both to adults and to young. Or the adult, devoting but a moderate portion of its substance to the production of multitudinous germs, may enjoy a considerable amount of life; in which case the cost of maintaining the species is shown in a great mortality of the young. Or the adult, sacrificing its substance almost entirely, may produce a moderate number of ova severally well provided with nutriment and well protected, among which the mortality is not so great; and in this case the cost of maintaining the species falls more on the adult and less on the young.

§ 274. Thus while, in one sense, the welfare of a species depends on the welfare of its individuals, in another sense, the welfare of the species is at variance with the welfare of its individuals; and further, the sacrifice of individuals may tell in different proportions on the undeveloped and on the mature.

Already in the *Principles of Biology*, §§ 319–51, the antagonism between Individuation and Genesis under its general aspects has been set forth. Here certain of its special aspects concern us. To comprehend them clearly, which we shall find it important to do, we must look at them more closely.

§ 343. If, disregarding conduct that is entirely private, we consider only that species of conduct which involves direct relations with other persons ; and if under the name government we include all control of such conduct, however arising ; then we must say that the earliest kind of government, the most general kind of government, and the government which is ever spontaneously recommencing, is the government of ceremonial observance. More may be said. This kind of government, besides preceding other kinds, and besides having in all places and times approached nearer to universality of influence, has ever had, and continues to have, the largest share in regulating men's lives.

Proof that the modifications of conduct called " manners " and " behaviour," arise before those which political and religious restraints cause, is yielded by the fact that, besides preceding social evolution, they precede human evolution: they are traceable among the higher animals. The dog afraid of being beaten, comes crawling up to his master; clearly manifesting the desire to show submission. Nor is it solely to human beings that dogs use such propitiatory actions. They do the like one to another. All have occasionally seen how, on the approach of some formidable Newfoundland or mastiff, a small spaniel, in the extremity of its terror, throws itself on its back with legs in the air. Instead of threatening resistance by growls and showing of teeth, as it might have done had not resistance been hopeless, it spontaneously assumes the attitude that would result from defeat in battle; tacitly saying—" I am conquered, and at your mercy." Clearly then, besides certain modes of behaviour expressing affection, which are established still earlier in creatures lower than man, there are established certain modes of behaviour expressing subjection.

After recognizing this fact, we shall be prepared to recognize the fact that daily intercourse among the lowest savages, whose small loose groups, scarcely to be called social, are without political or religious regulation, is under a considerable amount of ceremonial regulation. No ruling agency beyond that arising from personal superiority, characterizes a horde of Australians ; but every such horde has imperative observances. Strangers meeting must remain some time silent; a mile from an encampment approach has to be heralded by loud *cooeys*; a green bough is used as an emblem of peace; and brotherly feeling is indicated by exchange of names. Similarly the Tasmanians, equally devoid of government save that implied by predominance of a leader during war, had settled ways of indicating peace and defiance. The Esquimaux, too, though without social ranks or anything like chieftainship, have understood usages for the treatment of guests. Kindred evidence may be joined with this. Ceremonial control is highly developed in many places where other forms of control are but rudimentary. The wild Comanche " exacts the observance of his rules of etiquette from strangers," and " is greatly offended " by any breach of them. When Araucanians meet, the inquiries, felicitations, and condolences which custom demands, are so elaborate that " the formality occupies ten or fifteen minutes." Of the ungoverned Bedouins we read that " their manners are sometimes dashed with a strange ceremoniousness; " and the salutations of Arabs are such that the " compliments in a well-bred man never last less than ten minutes." " We were particularly struck," says Livingstone, " with the punctiliousness of manners shown by the Balonda." " The Malagasy have many different forms of salutation, of which they make liberal use. . . . Hence in their general intercourse there is much that is stiff, formal, and precise." A Samoan orator, when speaking in Parliament, " is not contented with a mere word of salutation, such as ' gentlemen,' but he must, with great minuteness, go over the names and titles, and a host of ancestral references, of which they are proud."

That ceremonial restraint, preceding other forms of restraint, continues ever to be the most widely-diffused form of restraint, we are shown by such facts as that in all intercourse between members of each society, the decisively governmental actions are usually prefaced by this government of observances. The embassy may fail, negotiation may be brought to a close by war, coercion of one society by another may set up wider political rule with its peremptory commands; but there is habitually this more general and vague regulation of conduct preceding the more special and definite. So within a community, acts of relatively stringent control coming from ruling agencies, civil and religious, begin with and are qualified by, this ceremonial control; which not only initiates but, in a sense, envelops all other. Functionaries, ecclesiastical and political, coercive as their proceedings may be, conform them in large measure to the requirements of courtesy. The priest, however, arrogant his assumption, makes a civil salute; and the officer of the law performs his duty subject to certain propitiatory words and movements.

Yet another indication of primordialism may be named. This species of control establishes itself anew with every fresh relation among individuals. Even between intimates greetings signifying continuance of respect, begin each renewal of intercourse. And in presence of a stranger, say in a railway-carriage, a certain self-restraint, joined with some small act like the offer of a newspaper, shows the spon-

59

taneous rise of a propitiatory behaviour such as even **the** rudest of mankind are not without.

So that the modified forms of action caused in men by the presence of their fellows, constitute that comparatively vague control out of which other more definite controls are evolved—the primitive undifferentiated kind of government from which the political and religious governments are differentiated, and in which they ever continue immersed.

§ 344. This proposition looks strange mainly because, when studying less-advanced societies, we carry with us our developed conceptions of law and religion. Swayed by them, we fail to perceive that what we think the essential parts of sacred and secular regulations were originally subordinate parts, and that the essential parts consisted of ceremonial observances.

It is clear, *à priori*, that this must be so if social phenomena are evolved. A political system or a settled cult, cannot suddenly come into existence, but implies pre-established subordination. Before there are laws, there must be submission to some potentate enacting and enforcing them. Before religious obligations are recognized, there must be acknowledged one or more supernatural powers. Evidently, then, the behaviour expressing obedience to a ruler, visible or invisible, must precede in time the civil or religious restraints he imposes. And this inferable precedence of ceremonial government is a precedence we everywhere find.

How, in the political sphere, fulfilment of forms implying subordination is the primary thing, early European history shows us. During times when the question, who should be master, was in course of settlement, now in small areas and now in larger areas uniting them, there was scarcely any of the regulation which developed civil government brings; but there was insistance on allegiance humbly expressed. While each man was left to guard himself, and blood-feuds between families were unchecked by the central power—while the right of private vengeance was so well recognized that the Salic law made it penal to carry off enemies' heads from the stakes on which they were exhibited near the dwellings of those who had killed them; there was a rigorous demanding of oaths of fidelity to political superiors and periodic manifestations of loyalty. Simple homage, growing presently into liege homage, was paid by smaller rulers to greater; and the vassal who, kneeling ungirt and swordless before his suzerain, professed his subjection and then entered on possession of his lands, was little interfered with so long as he continued to display his vassalage in court and in camp. Refusal to go through the required observances was tantamount to rebellion; as at the present time in China, where disregard of the forms of behaviour prescribed towards each grade of officers, " is considered to be nearly equivalent to a rejection of their authority." Among peoples in lower stages this connexion of social traits is still better shown. The extreme ceremoniousness of the Tahitians, " appears to have accompanied them to the temples, to have distinguished the homage and the service they rendered to their gods, to have marked their affairs of state, and the carriage of the people toward their rulers, to have pervaded the whole of their social intercourse." Meanwhile, they were destitute " of even oral laws and institutes: " there was no public administration of justice. Again, if any one in Tonga neglected the proper salute in presence of a superior noble, some calamity from the gods was expected as a punishment for the omission; and Mariner's list of Tongan virtues commences with " paying respect to the gods, nobles, and aged persons." When to this we add his statement that many actions reprobated by the Tongans are not thought intrinsically wrong, but are wrong merely if done against gods or nobles, we get proof that along with high development of ceremonial control, the sentiments and ideas out of which civil government comes were but feebly developed. Similarly in the ancient American States. The laws of the Mexican king, Montezuma I., mostly related to the intercourse of, and the distinctions between, classes. In Peru, " the most common punishment was death, for they said that a culprit was not punished for the delinquencies he had committed, but for having broken the commandment of the Ynca." There had not been reached the stage in which the transgressions of man against man are the wrongs to be redressed, and in which there is consequently a proportioning of penalties to injuries; but the real crime was insubordination: implying that insistance on marks of subordination constituted the essential part of government. In Japan, so elaborately ceremonious in its life, the same theory led to the same result. And here we are reminded that even in societies so advanced as our own, there survive traces of a kindred early condition. " Indictment for felony," says Wharton, " is [for a transgression] against the peace of our lord the King, his crown and dignity in general: " the injured individual being ignored. Evidently obedience was the primary requirement, and behaviour expressing it the first modification of conduct insisted on.

Religious control, still better, perhaps, than political control, shows this general truth. When we find that rites performed at graves, becoming afterwards religious rites performed at altars in temples, were at first acts done for the benefit of the ghost, either as originally conceived or as ideally expanded into a deity—when we find that the sacrifices and libations, the immolations and blood-offerings and mutilations, all begun to profit or to please the double of the dead man, were continued on larger scales where the double of the dead man was especially feared—when we find that fasting as a funeral rite gave origin to religious fasting, that praises of the deceased and prayers to him grew into religious praises and prayers; we are shown why primitive

287

religion consisted almost wholly of propitiatory observances. Though in certain rude societies now existing, one of the propitiations is the repetition of injunctions given by the departed father or chief, joined in some cases with expressions of penitence for breach of them; and though we are shown by this that from the outset there exists the germ out of which grow the sanctified precepts eventually constituting important adjuncts to religion; yet, since the supposed supernatural beings are at first conceived as retaining after death the desires and passions that distinguished them during life, this rudiment of a moral code is originally but an insignificant part of the cult: due rendering of those offerings and praises and marks of subordination by which the goodwill of the ghost or god is to be obtained, forming the chief part. Everywhere proofs occur. We read of the Tahitians that " religious rites were connected with almost every act of their lives; " and it is so with the uncivilized and semi-civilized in general. The Sandwich Islanders, along with little of that ethical element which the conception of religion includes among ourselves, had a rigorous and elaborate ceremonial. Noting that *tabu* means literally, " sacred to the gods," I quote from Ellis the following account of its observance in Hawaii:—

" During the season of strict tabu, every fire or light in the island or district must be extinguished; no canoe must be launched on the water, no person must bathe; and except those whose attendance was required at the temple, no individual must be seen out of doors; no dog must bark, no pig must grunt, no cock must crow. . . . On these occasions they tied up the mouths of the dogs and pigs, and put the fowls under a calabash, or fastened a piece of cloth over their eyes."

And how completely the idea of transgression was associated in the mind of the Sandwich Islander with breach of ceremonial observance, is shown in the fact that " if any one made a noise on a *tabu* day . . . he must die." Through stages considerably advanced, religion continues to be thus constituted. When questioning the Nicaraguans concerning their creed, Oviedo, eliciting the fact that they confessed their sins to an appointed old man, asks what sort of sins they confessed; and the first clause of the answer is—" we tell him when we have broken our festivals and not kept them." Similarly among the Peruvians, " the most notable sin was neglect in the service of the huacas " [spirits, &c.]; and a large part of life was spent by them in propitiating the apotheosized dead. How elaborate the observances, how frequent the festivals, how lavish the expenditure, by which the ancient Egyptians sought the goodwill of supernatural beings, the records everywhere prove; and that with them religious duty consisted in thus ministering to the desires of ancestral ghosts, deified in various degrees, is shown by the before-quoted prayer of Rameses to his father Ammon, in which he claims his help in battle because of the many bulls he has sacrificed to him. With the Hebrews in pre-Mosaic times it was the same. As Kuenen remarks, the " great work and enduring merit " of Moses, was that he gave dominance to the moral element in religion. In his reformed creed, " Jahveh is distinguished from the rest of the gods in this, that he will be served, not merely by sacrifices and feasts, but also, nay, in the first place, by the observance of the moral commandments." That the piety of the Greeks included diligent performance of rites at tombs, and that the Greek god was especially angered by non-observance of propitiatory ceremonies, are familiar facts; and credit with a god was claimed by the Trojan, as by the Egyptian, not on account of rectitude, but on account of oblations made; as is shown by Chryses' prayer to Apollo. So too, Christianity, originally a renewed development of the ethical element at the expense of the ceremonial element, losing as it spread those early traits which distinguished it from lower creeds, displayed in mediæval Europe, a relatively large amount of ceremony and a relatively small amount of morality. In the Rule of St. Benedict, nine chapters concern the moral and general duties of the brothers, while thirteen concern the religious ordinances. And how criminality was ascribed to disregard of such ordinances, the following passage from the Rule of St. Columbanus shows:—

"A year's penance for him who loses a consecrated wafer; six months for him who suffers it to be eaten by mites; twenty days for him who lets it turn red; forty days for him who contemptuously flings it into water; twenty days for him who brings it up through weakness of stomach; but, if through illness, ten days. He who neglects his Amen to the Benedicite, who speaks when eating, who forgets to make the sign of the cross on his spoon, or on a lantern lighted by a younger brother, is to receive six or twelve stripes."

That from the times when men condoned crimes by building chapels or going on pilgrimages, down to present times when barons no longer invade one another's territories or torture Jews, there has been a decrease of ceremony along with an increase of morality, is clear; though if we look at unadvanced parts of Europe, such as Naples or Sicily, we see that even now observance of rites is in them a much larger component of religion than obedience to moral rules. And when we remember how modern is Protestantism, which, less elaborate and imperative in its forms, does not habitually compound for transgression by acts expressing subordination, and how recent is the spread of dissenting Protestantism, in which this change is carried further, we are shown that postponement of ceremony to morality characterizes religion only in its later stages.

Mark, then, what follows. If the two kinds of control which eventually grow into civil and religious governments, originally include scarcely anything beyond observance of ceremonies, the precedence of ceremonial control over other controls is a corollary.

§ 345. Divergent products of evolution betray their kinship by severally retaining certain traits which belonged to that from which they were evolved; and the implication is that whatever traits they have in common, arose earlier in time than did the traits which distinguish them from one another. If fish, reptiles, birds, and mammals, all possess vertebral columns, it follows, on the evolution-hypothesis, that the vertebral column became part of the organization at an earlier period than did the teeth in sockets and the mammæ which distinguish one of these groups, or than did the toothless beak and the feathers which distinguish another of these groups; and so on. Applying this principle in the present case, it is inferable that if the controls classed as civil, religious, and social, have certain common characters, such characters, older than are these now differentiated controls, must have belonged to the primitive control out of which they developed. Ceremonies, then, have the highest antiquity; for these differentiated controls all exhibit them.

There is the making of presents: this is one of the acts showing subordination to a ruler in early stages; it is a religious rite, performed originally at the grave and later on at the altar; and from the beginning it has been a means of vertebral columns, it follows, on the evolution-hypothesis, propitiation in social intercourse. There are the obeisances: these, of their several kinds, serve to express reverence in its various degrees, to gods, to rulers, and to private persons: here the prostration is habitually seen, now in the temple, now before the monarch, now to a powerful man: here there is genuflexion in presence of idols, rulers, and fellow-subjects; here the salaam is more or less common to the three cases; here uncovering of the head is a sign alike of worship, of loyalty, and of respect; and here the bow serves the same three purposes. Similarly with titles: father is a name of honour applied to a god, to a king, and to an honoured individual; so too is lord; so are sundry other names. The same thing holds of humble speeches: professions of inferiority and obedience on the part of the speaker, are used to secure divine favour, the favour of a ruler, and the favour of a private person. Once more, it is thus with words of praise: telling a deity of his greatness constitutes a large element of worship; despotic monarchs are addressed in terms of exaggerated eulogy; and where ceremony is dominant in social intercourse, extravagant compliments are addressed to private persons.

In many of the less advanced societies, and also in the more advanced that have retained early types of organization, we find other examples of observances expressing subjection, which are common to the three kinds of control— political, religious, and social. Among Malayo-Polynesians the offering of the first fish and of first fruits, is a mark of respect alike to gods and to chiefs; and the Fijians make the same gifts to their gods as they do to their chiefs— food, turtles, whale's-teeth. In Tonga, " if a great chief takes an oath, he swears by the god; if an inferior chief takes an oath, he swears by his superior relation, who, of course, is a greater chief." In Fiji, " all are careful not to tread on the threshold of a place set apart for the gods: persons of rank stride over; others pass over on their hands and knees. The same form is observed in crossing the threshold of a chief's house." In Siam, " at the full moon of the fifth month the Talapoins [priests] wash the idol with perfumed water. . . . The people also wash the Sancrats and other Talapoins; and then in the families children wash their parents." China affords good instances. " At his accession, the Emperor kneels thrice and bows nine times before the altar of his father, and goes through the same ceremony before the throne on which is seated the Empress Dowager. On his then ascending his throne, the great officers, marshalled according to their ranks, kneel and bow nine times." And the equally ceremonious Japanese furnish kindred evidence. " From the Emperor to the lowest subject in the realm there is a constant succession of prostrations. The former, in want of a human being superior to himself in rank, bows humbly to some pagan idol; and every one of his subjects, from prince to peasant, has some person before whom he is bound to cringe and crouch

in the dirt:" religious, political, and social subordination
are expressed by the same form of behaviour.

These indications of a general truth which will be abundantly exemplified when discussing each kind of ceremonial
observance, I here give in brief, as further showing that the
control of ceremony precedes in order of evolution the civil
and religious controls, and must therefore be first dealt with.

§ 431. Before stating definitely the conclusions, already
foreshadowed, that are to be drawn respecting the future
of ceremony, we have to note that its restraints not only
form a part of the coercive *régime* proper to those lower social types characterized by predominant militancy, but also
that they form part of a discipline by which men are adapted to a higher social life.

While the antagonistic or anti-social emotions in men,
have that predominance which is inevitable while war is
habitual, there must be tendencies, great and frequent, to
words and acts generating enmity and endangering social
coherence. Hence the need for prescribed forms of behaviour which, duly observed, diminish the risk of quarrels.
Hence the need for a ceremonial rule rigorous in proportion
as the nature is selfish and explosive.

Not *à priori* only, but *à posteriori*, it is inferable that
established observances have the function of educating, in
respect of its minor actions, the anti-social nature into a
form fitted for social life. Of the Japanese, living for these
many centuries under an unmitigated despotism, castes severely restricted, sanguinary laws, and a ceremonial system
rigorous and elaborate, there has arisen a character which,
while described by Mr. Rundell as " haughty, vindictive,

and licentious," yet prompts a behaviour admirable in its suavity. Mr. Cornwallis asserts that amiability and an un-ruffled temper are the universal properties of the women in Japan; and by Mr. Drummond they are credited with a natural grace which it is impossible to describe. Among the men, too, the sentiment of honour, based upon that re-gard for reputation to which ceremonial observance largely appeals, carries them to great extremes of consideration. Another verifying fact is furnished by another despotical-ly-governed and highly ceremonious society, Russia. Cus-tine says—" If fear renders the men serious, it also renders them extremely polite. I have never elsewhere seen so many men of all classes treating each other with such re-spect." Kindred, if less pronounced, examples of this con-nexion are to be found in Western countries. The Italian, long subject to tyrannical rule, and in danger of his life if he excites the vengeful feelings of a fellow-citizen, is distin-guished by his conciliatory manner. In Spain, where gov-ernmental dictation is unlimited, where women are harshly treated, and where " no labourer ever walks outside his door without his knife," there is extreme politeness. Contrari-wise our own people, long living under institutions which guard them against serious consequences from giving offence, greatly lack suavity, and show a comparative in-attention to minor civilities.

Both deductively and inductively, then, we see that ceremonial government is one of the agencies by which so-cial co-operation is facilitated among those whose natures are in large measure anti-social.

§ 432. And this brings us to the general truth that within each embodied set of restraining agencies—the cere-monial as well as the political and ecclesiastical which grow out of it—there gradually evolves, a special kind of disem-bodied control, which eventually becomes independent.

Political government, having for its original end subordination; and inflicting penalties on men who injure others not because of the intrinsic badness of their acts but because their acts break the ruler's commands; has ever been habituating men to obey regulations conducive to social order; until there has grown up a consciousness that these regulations have not simply an extrinsic authority derived from a ruler's will, but have an intrinsic authority derived from their utility. The once arbitrary, fitful, and often irrational, dictates of a king, grow into an established system of laws, which formulate the needful limitations to men's actions arising from one another's claims. And these limitations men more and more recognize and conform to, not only without thinking of the monarch's injunctions, but without thinking of the injunctions set forth in Acts of Parliament. Simultaneously, out of the supposed wishes of the ancestral ghost, which now and again developing into the traditional commands of some expanded ghost of a great man, become divine injunctions, arises the set of requirements classed as religious. Within these, at first almost exclusively concerning acts expressing submission to the celestial king, there evolve the rules we distinguish as moral. As society advances, these moral rules become of a kind formulating the conduct requisite for personal, domestic, and social wellbeing. For a long time imperfectly differentiated from the essential political rules, and to the last enforcing their authority, these moral rules, originally regarded as sacred only because of their supposed divine origin, eventually acquire a sacredness derived from their observed utility in controlling certain parts of human conduct—parts not controlled, or little controlled, by civil law. Ideas of moral duty develop and consolidate into a moral code, which eventually becomes independent of its theological root. In the meantime, from within that part of ceremonial rule which has evolved into a system of regulations for social intercourse, there grows a third class of restraints: and these, in like manner, become at length independent. From observances which, in their primitive forms, express partly subordination to a superior and partly attachment to him, and which, spreading downwards, become general forms of behaviour, there finally come observances expressing a proper regard for the individualities of other persons, and a true sympathy in their welfare. Ceremonies which originally have no other end than to propitiate a dominant person, pass, some of them, into rules of politeness; and these gather an authority distinct from that which they originally had. Apt evidence is furnished by the " Ritual Remembrancer " of the Chinese, which gives directions for all the actions of life. Its regulations " are interspersed with truly excellent observations regarding mutual forbearance and kindness in society, which is regarded as the true principle of etiquette." The higher the social evolution, the more does this inner element of ceremonial rule grow, while the outer formal element dwindles. As fast as the principles of natural politeness, seen to originate in sympathy, distinguish themselves from the code of ceremonial within which they originate, they replace its authority by a higher authority, and go on dropping its non-essentials while developing further its essentials.

So that as law differentiates from personal commands, and as morality differentiates from religious injunctions, so politeness differentiates from ceremonial observance. To which I may add, so does rational usage differentiate from fashion.

§ 433. Thus guided by retrospect we cannot doubt about the prospect. With further development of the social type based on voluntary co-operation, will come a still greater disuse of obeisances, of complimentary forms of address, of titles, of badges, &c., &c. The feelings alike of those by whom, and those to whom, acts expressing subordination are performed, will become more and more averse to them.

Of course the change will be, and should be, gradual. Just as, if political freedom is gained faster than men become adequately self-controlled, there results social disorder—just as abolition of religious restraints while yet moral restraints have not grown strong enough, entails increase of misconduct; so, if the observances regulating social intercourse lose their sway faster than the feelings which prompt true politeness develop, there inevitably follows more or less rudeness in behaviour and consequent liability to discord. It needs but to name certain of our lower classes, such as colliers and brickmakers, whose relations to masters and others are such as to leave them scarcely at all restrained, to see that considerable evils arise from a premature decay of ceremonial rule.

The normal advance toward that highest state in which the minor acts of men towards one another, like their major acts, are so controlled by internal restraints as to make external restraints needless, implies increasing fulfilment of two conditions. Both higher emotions and higher intelligence are required. There must be a stronger fellow feeling with all around, and there must be an intelligence developed to the extent needful for instantly seeing how all words and acts will tell upon their states of mind—an intelligence which, by each expression of face and cadence of speech, is informed what is the passing state of emotion, and how emotion has been affected by actions just committed.

297

§ 722. No group of institutions illustrates with greater clearness the process of social evolution; and none shows more undeniably how social evolution conforms to the law of evolution at large. The germs out of which the professional agencies arise, forming at first a part of the regulative agency, differentiate from it at the same time that they differentiate from one another; and, while severally being rendered more multiform by the rise of subdivisions, severally become more coherent within themselves and more definitely marked off. The process parallels completely that by which the parts of an individual organism pass from their initial state of simplicity to their ultimate state of complexity.

Originally one who was believed by himself and others to have power over demons—the mystery-man or medicine-man—using coercive methods to expel disease-producing spirits, stood in the place of doctor; and when his appliances, at first supposed to act supernaturally, came to be understood as acting naturally, his office eventually lost its priestly character altogether: the resulting physician class, originally uniform, eventually dividing into distinguishable sub-classes while acquiring a definite embodiment.

Less early, because implying more developed groups, arose those who as exhibitors of joy, now in the presence of the living ruler and now in the supposed presence of the de-

ceased ruler, were at first simultaneously singers and danc-
ers, and, becoming specialized from the people at large,
presently became distinct from one another: whence, in
course of time, two groups of professionals, whose official
laudations, political or religious, extended in their range
and multiplied in their kinds. And then by like steps were
separated from one another vocal and instrumental mu-
sicians, and eventually composers; within which classes
also there arose subdivisions.

Ovations, now to the living king and now to the dead
king, while taking saltatory and musical forms, took also
verbal forms, originally spontaneous and irregular, but
presently studied and measured: whence, first, the unrhyth-
mical speech of the orator, which under higher emotional
excitement grew into the rhythmical speech of the priest-
poet, chanting verses—verses that finally became established
hymns of praise. Meanwhile from accompanying rude imi-
tations of the hero's acts, performed now by one and now by
several, grew dramatic representations, which little by little
elaborated, fell under the regulation of a chief actor, who
prefigured the playwright. And out of these germs, all pertaining to worship, came eventually the various professions
of poets, actors, dramatists, and the subdivisions of these.

The great deeds of the hero-god, recited, chanted or sung,
and mimetically rendered, naturally came to be supplemented by details, so growing into accounts of his life; and
thus the priest-poet gave origin to the biographer, whose
narratives, being extended to less sacred personages, became
secularized. Stories of the apotheosized chief or king, joined
with stories of his companions and amplified by narratives
of accompanying transactions, formed the first histories.
And from these accounts of the doings of particular men and
groups of men, partly true but passing by exaggeration into
the mythical, came the wholly mythical, or fiction; which
then and always preserved the biographico-historical character. Add to which that out of the criticisms and reflections

299

scattered through this personal literature an impersonal literature slowly emerged: the whole group of these products having as their deepest root the eulogies of the priest-poet.

Prompted as were the medicine-men of savages and the priests of early civilized peoples to increase their influence, they were ever stimulated to acquire knowledge of natural actions and the properties of things; and, being in alleged communication with supernatural beings, they were supposed to acquire such knowledge from them. Hence, by implication, the priest became the primitive man of science; and, led by his special experiences to speculate about the causes of things, thus entered the sphere of philosophy: both his science and his philosophy being pursued in the service of his religion.

Not only his higher culture but his alleged intercourse with the gods, whose mouthpiece he was, made him the authority in cases of dispute; and being also, as historian, the authority concerning past transactions and traditional usages, or laws, he acquired in both capacities the character of judge. Moreover, when the growth of legal administration brought the advocate, he, though usually of lay origin, was sometimes clerical.

Distinguished in early stages as the learned man of the tribe or society, and especially distinguished as the possessor of that knowledge which was thought of most value—knowledge of unseen things—the priest of necessity became the first teacher. Transmitting traditional statements concerning ghosts and gods, at first to neophytes of his class only but afterwards to the cultured classes, he presently, beyond instruction in supernatural things, gave instruction in natural things; and having been the first secular teacher has retained a large share in secular teaching even down to our own days.

As making a sacrifice was the original priestly act, and as the building of an altar for the sacrifice was by implication a priestly act, it results that the making of a shelter over the altar, which in its developed form became the temple, was also a priestly act. When the priest, ceasing to be himself the executant, directed the artificers, he continued to be the designer; and when he ceased to be the actual designer, the master-builder or architect thereafter continued to fulfil his general directions. And then the temple and the palace in sundry early societies, being at once the residence of the apotheosized ruler and the living ruler (even now a palace usually contains a small temple) and being the first kinds of developed architecture, eventually gave origin to secular architecture.

A rude carved or modelled image of a man placed on his grave, gave origin to the sculptured representation of a god inclosed in his temple. A product of priestly skill at the outset, it continued in some cases to be such among early civilized peoples; and always thereafter, when executed by an artisan, conformed to priestly direction. Extending presently to the representation of other than divine and semi-divine personages, it eventually thus passed into its secularized form.

So was it with painting. At first used to complete the carved representation of the revered or worshiped personage, and being otherwise in some tribes used by the priest and his aids for exhibiting the tribal hero's deeds, it long remained subservient to religion, either for the colouring of statues (as it does still in Roman Catholic images of saints, &c.), or for the decoration of temples, or for the portraiture of deceased persons on sarcophagi and stelæ; and when it gained independence it was long employed almost wholly for the rendering of sacred scenes: its eventual secularization being accompanied by its subdivision into a variety of kinds and of the executant artists into correlative groups.

Thus the process of professional evolution betrays throughout the same traits. In stages like that described by Huc as still existing among the Tibetans, where " the Lama is not merely a priest; he is the painter, poet, sculptor, architect, physician," there are joined in the same individual, or group of individuals, the potentialities out of which gradually arise the specialized groups we know as professions. While out of the one primitive class there come by progressive divergences many classes, each of these classes itself undergoes a kindred change: there are formed in it subdivisions and even sub-subdivisions, which become gradually more marked; so that, throughout, the advance is from an indefinite homogeneity to a definite heterogeneity.

§ 723. In presence of the fact that the immense majority of mankind adhere pertinaciously to the creeds, political and religious, in which they were brought up; and in presence of the further fact that on behalf of their creeds, however acquired, there are soon enlisted prejudices which practically shut out adverse evidence; it is not to be expected that the foregoing illustrations, even joined with kindred illustrations previously given, will make them see that society is a growth and not a manufacture, and has its laws of evolution.

From prime ministers down to plough-boys there is either ignorance or disregard of the truth that nations acquire their vital structures by natural processes and not by artificial devices. If the belief is not that social arrangements have been divinely ordered thus or thus, then it is that they have been made thus or thus by kings, or if not by kings then by parliaments. That they have come about by small accumulated changes not contemplated by rulers, is an open secret which only of late has been recognized by a few and is still unperceived by the many—educated as well as uneducated. Though the turning of the land into a food-producing surface, cleared, fenced, drained, and covered with farming appliances, has been achieved by men working for individual profit not by legislative direction—though villages, towns, cities, have insensibly grown up under the desires of men to satisfy their wants—though by spontaneous co-operation of citizens have been formed canals, railways, telegraphs, and other means of communication and distribution; the natural forces which have done all this are ignored as of no account in political thinking. Our immense manufacturing system with its multitudinous inventions, supplying both home and foreign consumers, and the immense mercantile marine by which its products are taken all over the globe and other products brought back, have naturally and not artificially originated. That transformation by which, in thousands of years, men's occupations have been so specialized that each, aiding to satisfy some small division of his fellow citizen's needs has his own needs satisfied by the work of hundreds of others, has taken place without design and unobserved. Knowledge developing into science, which has become so vast in mass that no one can grasp a tithe of it, and which now guides productive activities at large, has resulted from the workings of individuals prompted not by the ruling agency but by their own inclinations. So, too, has been created the still vaster mass distinguished as literature, yielding the gratifications filling so large a space in our lives. Nor is it otherwise with the literature of the hour. That ubiquitous journalism which provides satisfactions for men's more urgent mental wants, has resulted from the activities of citizens severally pursuing private benefits. And supplementing these come the innumerable companies, associations, unions, societies, clubs, subserving enterprise, philanthropy, culture, art, amusement; as well as the multitudinous institutions annually receiving millions by endowments and subscriptions: all of them arising from the unforced co-operations of citizens. And yet so hypnotized are nearly all by fixedly contemplating the doings of ministers and parliaments, that they have no eyes for this marvellous organization which has been growing for thousands of years without governmental help—nay, indeed, in spite of governmental hindrances. For in agriculture, manufactures, commerce, banking, journalism, immense injuries have been done by laws—injuries afterwards healed by social forces which have thereupon set up afresh the normal courses of growth. So unconscious are men of the life of the social organism that though the spontaneous actions of its units, each seeking livelihood, generate streams of food which touch at their doors every hour—though the water for the morning bath, the lights for their rooms, the fires in their grates, the bus or tram which takes them to the City, the business they carry on (made possible by the distributing system they share in), the evening " Special " they glance at, the theatre or concert to which they presently go, and the cab home, all result from the unprompted workings of this organized humanity, they remain blind. Though by its vital activities capital is drafted to places where it is most wanted, supplies of commodities balanced in every locality and prices universally adjusted—all without official supervision; yet, being oblivious of the truth that these processes are socially originated without design of any one, they cannot believe that society will be bettered by natural agencies. And hence when they see an evil to be cured or a good to be achieved, they ask for legal coercion as the only possible means.

More than this is true. If, as every parliamentary debate and every political meeting shows, the demands for legislation pay no attention to that beneficent social development which has done so much and may be expected to increase in efficiency, still more do they ignore the *laws* of that development—still less do they recognize a natural order in the changes by which society passes from its lower to its higher stages. Though, as we have seen, the process of evolution exemplified in the genesis of the professions is similar in character to the process exemplified in the genesis of political and ecclesiastical institutions and everywhere else; and though the first inquiry rationally to be made respecting any proposed measure should be whether or not it falls within the lines of this evolution, and what must be the effects of running counter to the normal course of things; yet not only is no such question ever entertained, but one who raised it would be laughed down in any popular assemblage and smiled at as a dreamer in the House of Commons: the only course thought wise in either the cultured or the uncultured gathering being that of trying to estimate immediate benefits and evils.

Nor will any argument or any accumulation of evidence suffice to change this attitude until there has arisen a different type of mind and a different quality of culture. The politician will still spend his energies in rectifying some evils and making more—in forming, reforming, and again reforming—in passing acts to amend acts that were before amended; while social schemers will continue to think that they have only to cut up society and re-arrange it after their ideal pattern and its parts will join together again and work as intended!

INDUSTRIAL INSTITUTIONS.

§ 734. We have contemplated the topical division of labour and the local division of labour. There remains the detailed division of labour—that which arises within each producing or distributing establishment. This it is which we commonly think of when the phrase is used.

Specializations thus distinguished make their appearance in comparatively early stages. Says Burton in his *Abeokuta* :—

" Africans, like Asiatics, are great at division of labour," in building a house, for instance. "Some hoed a deep hole . . . Another gang was working the clay . . .; whilst a third party was engaged in preparing grass thatch and palm leaves for the roof. When the actual building begins there will be one gang to carry clay balls to the scene of action, a second of labourers who fling the same balls into wall shape and pat them down, a third, boys and girls, who hand other balls from the ground or the scaffolding to the masons above, a trimmer to plumb and set things square with his wooden shovel, and finally thatchers to finish off."

The growth of that division of labour which ends in producing a commodity, our own early history sufficiently illustrates. In the middle of the 16th century—

"Several distinct classes of workmen were employed in the making of cloth. There were weavers, walkers, fullers, fulling-mill men, shearmen, dyers, forcers of wool, carders, and sorters of wool, and spinners, carders and spullars of yarn."

And how these subdivisions gradually multiply is shown in the fact that even fifty years ago the classes of operatives engaged in the woollen manufacture had increased from the twelve above named to double that number.

But no adequate conception of this detailed division of labour can be formed so long as we contemplate only the manual labourers, and leave out of sight the mental labourers who direct them. In an undeveloped industry the maker of a commodity is at once brain-worker and hand-worker; but in a developed industry brain-work and hand-work have separated, and while hand-work has become greatly sub-divided, brain-work also has become greatly sub-divided. Here, as given to me by a friend who is partner in a manufacturing establishment at Birmingham, is a sketch of its organization. In the regulative division the first class includes only the heads of the firm, of whom one is chief. In the next class stand the engineering superior, works manager, head of estimate department, head of cash department, head of finished warehouse. Then comes the third class of brain-workers, who are women—invoice clerk, storekeeper, and assistant in cash department. Next are two intermediaries between head and hands—foreman of casting department and foreman-fitter or engineering mechanic, who both have subordinates aiding in their functions. From these regulative classes we descend to the operative classes; and of these there are eleven kinds in the first grade, nine kinds in the second grade, and seven kinds in the third grade. Thus there are eight kinds of brain-workers, four kinds of half-brain and half hand-workers, and twenty-seven kinds of hand-workers.

Limiting our further attention to the operative parts of industrial establishments, we may fitly distinguish between two leading forms of the division of labour exhibited in them—the simultaneous and the successive. There are cases in which the different parts of some ultimate product are being at the same time formed by different groups of artisans, to be afterwards joined together by yet other artisans; and there are cases in which the ultimate product passes from hand to hand through a series of operatives, each of whom works upon it his or her particular modification. Let us look at an example of each kind.

The superintendent of the Midland Railway works at Derby, has furnished me with an account of the different classes of men engaged in producing the component parts of locomotive engines. It is needless to give their names and special functions. The fact which here concerns us is that the classes number nearly forty, and, if the different kinds of fitting be counted, about fifty: all their various products being finally put together by the erector and his aids.

Of the serial division of labour a good instance comes from a large establishment for the manufacture of biscuits. To begin with there is a department for the reception and storage of raw materials. Weighing out the proportions of ingredients for any particular kind of biscuit, is the first process. Next comes the mixing mill, into which attendants pour these ingredients. From this emerges the prepared dough, which, passing into the rolling-presses, comes out in sheets of the proper thickness. Out of these the stamping machines cut out biscuits of the desired sizes and shapes, and deliver them on to trays. These trays, placed in the mouths of vast ovens and slowly carried through them on horizontal revolving bands, are delivered at the other side duly baked. Carried then by a mechanical apparatus to the sorting-room the classed biscuits are thence transferred to those who pack. Finally comes labeling and stamping the boxes.

Again we are shown how close are the analogies between the sociological division of labour and the physiological division of labour. Beyond the fact that, as in the social organism so in the individual organism, there are regulative parts and operative parts—the nervous organs and the various other organs—we have the fact that among these organs there is both a simultaneous and a serial division of labour. While we see bones, muscles, heart, lungs, liver, kidneys, &c., carrying on their respective functions at the same time, we see the parts of the alimentary canal performing their functions one after another. There come in succession mastication, insalivation, deglutition, trituration, chymification, chylification, and eventually absorption by the lacteals.

And here indeed it is curious to remark a unique case in which two sets of sociological divisions of labour of the serial kind, are joined to this physiological series of divisions of labour. We have first the ploughing, harrowing, sowing, reaping, carting, threshing, hauling to market, transfer to corn-factor's stores, removal thence to be ground, and final carriage of the flour to the bakers; where, also, certain serial processes are gone through in making loaves, or, if we follow that part of the flour from which biscuits are made, we see that there are linked together the processes above described. Finally, in one who eats of the loaves or the biscuits, there occurs the physiological series of divisions of labour. So that from the ploughing to the absorption of nutriment, three series of divisions of labour become, in a sense, parts of a united series.

§ 735. One more section must be added. Conformity to the general law of evolution has been noted in several places. Here, going behind that redistribution of matter and motion which universally constitutes Evolution, let us observe how, in the industrial world, there is everywhere exemplified the law that motion is along the line of least resistance or the line of greatest traction or the resultant of the two.

The growth of a society as a whole takes place most over regions where the obstacles to be overcome are least. Along one frontier hostile tribes exist, while in another direction there are no enemies; hence population spreads there. On this side lies a fertile tract while on that a barren tract lies; and the resistances to living being in these directions relatively great or relatively small, the social mass increases where it is relatively small. Again, one part of the habitat is malarious while another is salubrious, and the lower rate of mortality in the last determines multiplication of the inhabitants there.

The topical division of labour presents us with kindred causes and results. Sea-side people, close to a store of food, find it easier to subsist by getting this out of the water than by going inland to compete with those who plough; and if fish are plentiful and the inland demand great, the fishing population grows. So with wheat-growing and sheep-farming: the nature of each district renders it easier for its inhabitants to subsist by one of these than by the other, and their efforts follow the lines of least resistance. When, in any region, there has taken place that adaptation of nature which the appropriate occupation produces, there is resistance to alteration of function; as, for example, there would be if the body of Lancashire weavers had to become coal-miners. Even a change in the topical division of labour, such as migration of most of the woollen manufacture from Gloucestershire to Yorkshire, illustrates the same influence; since, by the proximity to a wool-importing place, and by the presence of abundant coal, serving as a better source of power than water, the resistance to the production of cloth as measured in cost of freight, labour, and fuel (severally representing so much human effort) is less than it was in the original seat of the industry.

In the local division of labour, analogous causes operate and work analogous effects. As political economists have pointed out, each choice of a business is determined by the totality of incentives and deterrents, and the business chosen is that which offers the least resistance to the gratification of the totality of desires. So, too, is it on passing from producer to consumer. If in a village the labourer's wife buys bread from a baker, it is because the difficulties to be overcome in the home-production of bread, render the resistance to that course greater that those resistances to the course chosen which are represented by extra cost; and if the farmer, ceasing to make his own beer, buys of a local brewer, it is again because in the average of cases the expenditure of effort has by modern conditions been rendered smaller in the last way than in the first.

Nor is it only in such elaborations of the division of labour, and developments of correlative social structures, that we see movement along lines of least resistance. We see it also in the activities of these structures. The law of supply and demand, implying streams of commodities from places where they are abundant to places where they are deficient, and a consequent balancing, is a corollary of this same law. For since money everywhere represents labour, buying in the cheapest market is satisfying a want with the least expenditure of labour; and selling in the dearest market and so getting the largest amount of this representative of labour, diminishes the labour afterwards required.

§ 853. How long this phase of social life to which we are approaching will last, and in what way it will come to an end, are of course questions not to be answered. Probably the issue will be here of one kind and there of another. A sudden bursting of bonds which have become intolerable may in some cases happen: bringing on a military despotism. In other cases practical extinction may follow a gradual decay, arising from abolition of the normal relation between merit and benefit, by which alone the vigour of a race can be maintained. And in yet further cases may come conquest by peoples who have not been emasculated by fostering their feebles—peoples before whom the socialistic organization will go down like a house of cards, as did that of the ancient Peruvians before a handful of Spaniards.

But if the process of evolution which, unceasing throughout past time, has brought life to its present height, continues throughout the future, as we cannot but anticipate, then, amid all the rhythmical changes in each society, amid all the lives and deaths of nations, amid all the supplantings of race by race, there will go on that adaptation of human nature to the social state which began when savages first gathered together into hordes for mutual defence—an adaptation finally complete. Many will think this a wild imagination. Though everywhere around them are creatures with structures and instincts which have been gradually so moulded as to subserve their own welfares and the welfares of their species, yet the immense majority ignore the implication that human beings, too, have been undergoing in the past, and will undergo in the future, progressive adjustments to the lives imposed on them by circumstances. But there are a few who think it rational to conclude that what has happened with all lower forms must happen with the highest form—a few who infer that among types of men those most fitted for making a well-working society will, hereafter as heretofore, from time to time emerge and spread at the expense of types less fitted, until a fully fitted type has arisen.

The view thus suggested must be accepted with qualifications. If we carry our thoughts as far forward as palæolithic implements carry them back, we are introduced, not to an absolute optimism but to a relative optimism. The cosmic process brings about retrogression as well as progression, where the conditions favour it. Only amid an infinity of modifications, adjusted to an infinity of changes of circumstances, do there now and then occur some which constitute an advance: other changes meanwhile caused in other organisms, usually not constituting forward steps in organization, and often constituting steps backwards. Evolution does not imply a latent tendency to improve, everywhere in operation. There is no uniform ascent from lower to higher, but only an occasional production of a form which, in virtue of greater fitness for more complex conditions, becomes capable of a longer life of a more varied kind. And while such higher type begins to dominate over lower types and to spread at their expense, the lower types survive in habitats or modes of life that are not usurped, or are thrust into inferior habitats or modes of life in which they retrogress.

What thus holds with organic types must hold also with types of societies. Social evolution throughout the future, like social evolution throughout the past, must, while producing step after step higher societies, leave outstanding many lower. Varieties of men adapted here to inclement regions, there to regions that are barren, and elsewhere to regions unfitted, by ruggedness of surface or insalubrity, for supporting large populations, will, in all probability, continue to form small communities of simple structures. Moreover, during future competitions among the higher races there will probably be left, in the less desirable regions, minor nations formed of men inferior to the highest; at the same time that the highest overspread all the great areas which are desirable in climate and fertility. But while the entire assemblage of societies thus fulfils the law of evolution by increase of heterogeneity,—while within each of them contrasts of structure, caused by differences of environments and entailed occupations, cause unlikenesses implying further heterogeneity; we may infer that the primary process of evolution—integration—which up to the present time has been displayed in the formation of larger and larger nations, will eventually reach a still higher stage and bring yet greater benefits. As, when small tribes were welded into great tribes, the head chief stopped inter-tribal warfare; as, when small feudal governments became subject to a king, feudal wars were prevented by him; so, in time to come, a federation of the highest nations, exercising supreme authority (already foreshadowed by occasional agreements among " the Powers "), may, by forbidding wars between any of its constituent nations, put an end to the re-barbarization which is continually undoing civilization.

When this peace-maintaining federation has been formed, there may be effectual progress towards that equilibrium between constitution and conditions—between inner faculties and outer requirements—implied by the final stage of human evolution. Adaptation to the social state, now perpetually hindered by anti-social conflicts, may then go on unhindered; and all the great societies, in other respects differing, may become similar in those cardinal traits which

313

result from complete self-ownership of the unit and exercise over him of nothing more than passive influence by the aggregate. On the one hand, by continual repression of aggressive instincts and exercise of feelings which prompt ministration to public welfare, and on the other hand by the lapse of restraints, gradually becoming less necessary, there must be produced a kind of man so constituted that while fulfilling his own desires he fulfils also the social needs. Already, small groups of men, shielded by circumstances from external antagonisms, have been moulded into forms of moral nature so superior to our own, that, as said of the Let-htas, the account of their goodness " almost savours of romance "; and it is reasonable to infer that what has even now happened on a small scale, may, under kindred conditions, eventually happen on a large scale. Long studies, showing among other things the need for certain qualifications above indicated, but also revealing facts like that just named, have not caused me to recede from the belief expressed nearly fifty years ago that—" The ultimate man will be one whose private requirements coincide with public ones. He will be that manner of man who, in spontaneously fulfilling his own nature, incidentally performs the functions of a social unit; and yet is only enabled so to fulfil his own nature by all others doing the like."

THE END.

314

Thorstein Veblen (1857-1929) was born in Wisconsin of Norwegian parents. *The Theory of the Leisure Class* was his first published book, appearing when he was forty-two, and it gave him immediate prominence after a painfully unpromising early career. His critical analysis of many of the accepted values of the leisure class may have contributed to the initial hostile reception of his work.

THE THEORY OF THE LEISURE CLASS

Dress as an Expression of the Pecuniary Culture

IT WILL BE in place, by way of illustration, to show in some detail how the economic principles so far set forth apply to everyday facts in some one direction of the life process. For this purpose no line of consumption affords a more apt illustration than expenditure on dress. It is especially the rule of the conspicuous waste of goods that finds expression in dress, although the other, related principles of pecuniary repute are also exemplified in the same contrivances. Other methods of putting one's pecuniary standing in evidence serve their end effectually, and other methods are in vogue always and everywhere; but expenditure on dress has this advantage over most other methods, that our apparel is always in evidence and affords an indication of our pecuniary standing to all observers at the first glance. It is also true that admitted expenditure for display is more obviously present, and is, perhaps, more universally practiced in the matter of dress than in any other line of consumption. No one finds difficulty in assenting to the commonplace that the greater part of the expenditure incurred by all classes for apparel is incurred for the sake of a respectable appearance rather than for the protection of the person. And probably at no other point is the sense of shabbiness so keenly felt as it is if we fall short of the standard set by social usage in this matter of dress. It is true of dress in even a higher degree than of most other items of consumption, that people will undergo a very considerable degree of privation in the comforts or the necessaries of life in order to afford what is considered a decent amount of wasteful consumption; so that it is by no means an uncommon occurrence, in an inclement climate, for people to go ill clad in order to appear well dressed. And the commercial value of the goods used for clothing in any modern community is made up to a much larger extent of the fashionableness, the reputability of the goods than of the mechanical service which they render in clothing the person of the wearer. The need of dress is eminently a "higher" or spiritual need.

This spiritual need of dress is not wholly, nor even chiefly, a naïve propensity for display of expenditure. The law of conspicuous waste guides consumption in apparel, as in other things, chiefly at the second remove, by shaping the canons of taste and decency. In the common run of cases the conscious motive of the wearer or purchaser of conspicuously wasteful apparel is the need of conforming to. established usage, and of living up to the accredited standard of taste and reputability. It is not only that one must be guided by the code of proprieties in dress in order to avoid the mortification that comes of unfavorable notice and comment, though that motive in itself counts for a great deal; but besides that, the requirement of expensiveness is so ingrained into our habits of thought in matters of dress that any other than expensive apparel is instinctively odious to us. Without reflection or analysis, we feel that what is inexpensive is unworthy. "A cheap coat makes a cheap man." "Cheap and nasty" is recognized to hold true in dress with even less mitigation than in other lines of consumption. On the ground both of taste and of serviceability, an inexpensive article of apparel is held to be inferior, under the maxim "cheap and nasty." We find

317

things beautiful, as well as serviceable, somewhat in proportion as they are costly. With few and inconsequential exceptions, we all find a costly hand-wrought article of apparel much preferable, in point of beauty and of serviceability, to a less expensive imitation of it, however cleverly the spurious article may imitate the costly original; and what offends our sensibilities in the spurious article is not that it falls short in form or color, or, indeed, in visual effect in any way. The offensive object may be so close an imitation as to defy any but the closest scrutiny; and yet so soon as the counterfeit is detected, its æsthetic value, and its commercial value as well, declines precipitately. Not only that, but it may be asserted with but small risk of contradiction that the æsthetic value of a detected counterfeit in dress declines somewhat in the same proportion as the counterfeit is cheaper than its original. It loses caste æsthetically because it falls to a lower pecuniary grade.

But the function of dress as an evidence of ability to pay does not end with simply showing that the wearer consumes valuable goods in excess of what is required for physical comfort. Simple conspicuous waste of goods is effective and gratifying as far as it goes; it is good *prima facie* evidence of pecuniary success, and consequently *prima facie* evidence of social worth. But dress has subtler and more far-reaching possibilities than this crude, first-hand evidence of wasteful consumption only. If, in addition to showing that the wearer can afford to consume freely and uneconomically, it can also be shown in the same stroke that he or she is not under the necessity of earning a livelihood, the evidence of social worth is enhanced in a very considerable degree. Our dress, therefore, in order to serve its purpose effectually, should not only be expensive, but it should also make plain to all observers that the wearer is not engaged in any kind of productive labor. In the evolutionary process by which our system of dress has been elaborated into its present admirably perfect adaptation to its purpose, this subsidiary line of evidence has received due attention. A detailed examination of what passes in popular apprehension for elegant apparel will show that it is contrived at every point to convey the impression that the wearer does not habitually put forth any useful effort. It goes without saying that no apparel can be considered elegant, or even decent, if it shows the effect of manual labor on the part of the wearer, in the way of soil or wear. The pleasing effect of neat and spotless garments is chiefly, if not altogether, due to their carrying the suggestion of leisure—exemption from personal contact with industrial processes of any kind. Much of the charm that invests the patent-leather shoe, the stainless linen, the lustrous cylindrical hat, and the walking-stick, which so greatly enhance the native dignity of a gentleman, comes of their pointedly suggesting that the wearer cannot when so attired bear a hand in any employment that is directly and immediately of any human use. Elegant dress serves its purpose of elegance not only in that it is expensive, but also because it is the insignia of leisure. It not only shows that the wearer is able to consume a relatively large value, but it argues at the same time that he consumes without producing.

The dress of women goes even farther than that of men in the way of demonstrating the wearer's abstinence from productive employment. It needs no argument to enforce the generalization that the more elegant styles of feminine bonnets go even farther towards making work impossible than does the man's high hat. The woman's shoe adds the so-called French heel to the evidence of enforced leisure afforded by its polish; because this high heel obviously makes any, even the simplest and most necessary manual work extremely difficult. The like is true even in a higher degree of the skirt and the rest of the drapery which characterizes woman's dress. The substantial reason for our tenacious attachment to the skirt is just this: it is expensive and it hampers the wearer at every turn and incapacitates her for all useful exertion. The like is true of the feminine custom of wearing the hair excessively long.

But the woman's apparel not only goes beyond that of the modern man in the degree in which it argues exemption from labor; it also adds a peculiar and highly characteristic feature which differs in kind from anything habitually practiced by the men. This feature is the class of contrivances of which the corset is the typical example. The corset is, in economic theory, substantially a mutilation, undergone for the purpose of lowering the subject's vitality and rendering her permanently and obviously unfit for work. It is true, the corset impairs the personal attractions of the wearer, but the loss suffered on that score is offset by the gain in reputability which comes of her visibly increased expensiveness and infirmity. It may broadly be set down that the womanliness of woman's apparel resolves itself, in point of substantial fact, into the more effective hindrance to useful exertion offered by the garments peculiar to women. This difference between masculine and feminine apparel is here simply pointed out as a characteristic feature. The ground of its occurrence will be discussed presently.

So far, then, we have, as the great and dominant norm of dress, the broad principle of conspicuous waste. Subsidiary

319

to this principle, and as a corollary under it, we get as a second norm the principle of conspicuous leisure. In dress construction this norm works out in the shape of divers contrivances going to show that the wearer does not and, as far as it may conveniently be shown, can not engage in productive labor. Beyond these two principles there is a third of scarcely less constraining force, which will occur to any one who reflects at all on the subject. Dress must not only be conspicuously expensive and inconvenient, it must at the same time be up to date. No explanation at all satisfactory has hitherto been offered of the phenomenon of changing fashions. The imperative requirement of dressing in the latest accredited manner, as well as the fact that this accredited fashion constantly changes from season to season, is sufficiently familiar to every one, but the theory of this flux and change has not been worked out. We may of course say, with perfect consistency and truthfulness, that this principle of novelty is another corollary under the law of conspicuous waste. Obviously, if each garment is permitted to serve for but a brief term, and if none of last season's apparel is carried over and made further use of during the present season, the wasteful expenditure on dress is greatly increased. This is good as far as it goes, but it is negative only. Pretty much all that this consideration warrants us in saying is that the norm of conspicuous waste exercises a controlling surveillance in all matters of dress, so that any change in the fashions must conform to the requirement of wastefulness; it leaves unanswered the question as to the motive for making and accepting a change in the prevailing styles, and it also fails to explain why conformity to a given style at a given time is so imperatively necessary as we know it to be.

For a creative principle, capable of serving as motive to invention and innovation in fashions, we shall have to go back to the primitive, non-economic motive with which apparel originated—the motive of adornment. Without going into an extended discussion of how and why this motive asserts itself under the guidance of the law of expensiveness, it may be stated broadly that each successive innovation in the fashions is an effort to reach some form of display which shall be more acceptable to our sense of form and color or of effectiveness, than that which it displaces. The changing styles are the expression of a restless search for something which shall commend itself to our æsthetic sense; but as each innovation is subject to the selective action of the norm of conspicuous waste, the range within which innovation can take place is somewhat restricted. The innovation must not only be more beautiful, or perhaps oftener less offensive, than that which it displaces, but it must also come up to the accepted standard of expensiveness.

It would seem at first sight that the result of such an unremitting struggle to attain the beautiful in dress should be a gradual approach to artistic perfection. We might naturally expect that the fashions should show a well-marked trend in the direction of some one or more types of apparel eminently becoming to the human form; and we might even feel that we have substantial ground for the hope that today, after all the ingenuity and effort which have been spent on dress these many years, the fashions should have achieved a relative perfection and a relative stability, closely approximating to a permanently tenable artistic ideal. But such is not the case. It would be very hazardous indeed to assert that the styles of today are intrinsically more becoming than those of ten years ago, or than those of twenty, or fifty, or one hundred years ago. On the other hand, the assertion freely goes uncontradicted that styles in vogue two thousand years ago are more becoming than the most elaborate and painstaking constructions of today.

The explanation of the fashions just offered, then, does not fully explain, and we shall have to look farther. It is well known that certain relatively stable styles and types of costume have been worked out in various parts of the world; as, for instance, among the Japanese, Chinese, and other Oriental nations; likewise among the Greeks, Romans, and other Eastern peoples of antiquity; so also, in later times, among the peasants of nearly every country of Europe. These national or popular costumes are in most cases adjudged by competent critics to be more becoming, more artistic, than the fluctuating styles of modern civilized apparel. At the same time they are also, at least usually, less obviously wasteful; that is to say, other elements than that of a display of expense are more readily detected in their structure.

These relatively stable costumes are, commonly, pretty strictly and narrowly localized, and they vary by slight and systematic gradations from place to place. They have in every case been worked out by peoples or classes which are poorer than we, and especially they belong in countries and localities and times where the population, or at least the class to which the costume in question belongs, is relatively homogeneous, stable, and immobile. That is to say, stable costumes which will bear the test of time and perspective are worked out under circumstances where the norm of conspicuous waste asserts itself less imperatively than it does in the large modern civilized cities, whose relatively mobile wealthy population today sets the pace in matters of fashion. The countries and classes which have in this way worked out stable and artistic costumes have been so placed that the pecuniary emulation among them has taken the direction of a competition in conspicuous leisure rather than in conspicuous consumption of goods. So that it will hold true in a general way that fashions are least stable and least becoming in those communities where the principle of a conspicuous waste of goods asserts itself most imperatively, as among ourselves. All this points to an antagonism between expensiveness and artistic apparel. In point of practical fact, the norm of conspicuous waste is incompatible with the requirement that dress should be beautiful or becoming. And this antagonism offers an explanation of that restless change in fashion which neither the canon of expensiveness nor that of beauty alone can account for.

The standard of reputability requires that dress should show wasteful expenditure; but all wastefulness is offensive to native taste. The psychological law has already been pointed out that all men—and women perhaps even in a higher degree—abhor futility, whether of effort or of expenditure—much as Nature was once said to abhor a vacuum. But the principle of conspicuous waste requires an obviously futile expenditure; and the resulting conspicuous expensiveness of dress is therefore intrinsically ugly. Hence we find that in all innovations in dress, each added or altered detail strives to avoid condemnation by showing some ostensible purpose, at the same time that the requirement of conspicuous waste prevents the purposefulness of these innovations from becoming anything more than a somewhat transparent pretense. Even in its freest flights, fashion rarely if ever gets away from a simulation of some ostensible use. The ostensible usefulness of the fashionable details of dress, however, is always so transparent a make-believe, and their substantial futility presently forces itself so baldly upon our attention as to become unbearable, and then we take refuge in a new style. But the new style must conform to the requirement of reputable wastefulness and futility. Its futility presently becomes as odious as that of its predecessor; and the only remedy which the law of waste allows us is to seek relief in some new construction, equally futile and equally untenable. Hence the essential ugliness and the unceasing change of fashionable attire.

Having so explained the phenomenon of shifting fashions, the next thing is to make the explanation tally with everyday facts. Among these everyday facts is the well-known liking which all men have for the styles that are in vogue at any given time. A new style comes into vogue and remains in favor for a season, and, at least so long as it is a novelty, people very generally find the new style attractive. The prevailing fashion is felt to be beautiful. This is due partly to the relief it affords in being different from what went before it, partly to its being reputable. As indicated in the last chapter, the canon of reputability to some extent shapes our tastes, so that under its guidance anything will be accepted as becoming until its novelty wears off, or until the warrant of reputability is transferred to a new and novel structure serving the same general purpose. That the alleged beauty, or "loveliness," of the styles in vogue at any given time is transient and spurious only is attested by the fact that none of the many shifting fashions will bear the test of time. When seen in the perspective of half-a-dozen years or more, the best of our fashions strike us as grotesque, if not unsightly. Our transient attachment to whatever happens to be the latest rests on other than æsthetic grounds, and lasts only until our abiding æsthetic sense has had time to assert itself and reject this latest indigestible contrivance.

The process of developing an æsthetic nausea takes more or less time; the length of time required in any given case being inversely as the degree of intrinsic odiousness of the style in question. This time relation between odiousness and instability in fashions affords ground for the inference that the more rapidly the styles succeed and displace one another, the more offensive they are to sound taste. The presumption, therefore, is that the farther the community, especially the wealthy classes of the community, develop in wealth and mobility and in the range of their human contact, the more imperatively will the law of conspicuous waste assert itself in matters of dress, the more will the sense of beauty tend to fall into abeyance or be overborne by the canon of pecuniary reputability, the more rapidly will fashions shift and change, and the more grotesque and intolerable will be the varying styles that successively come into vogue.

There remains at least one point in this theory of dress yet to be discussed. Most of what has been said applies to men's attire as well as to that of women; although in modern times it applies at nearly all points with greater force to that of women. But at one point the dress of women differs substantially from that of men. In woman's dress there is obviously greater insistence on such features as testify to the wearer's exemption from or incapacity for all vulgarly productive employment. This characteristic of woman's apparel is of interest, not only as completing the theory of dress, but also as confirming what has already been said of the economic status of women, both in the past and in the present.

As has been seen in the discussion of woman's status under the heads of Vicarious Leisure and Vicarious Consumption, it has in the course of economic development become the office of the woman to consume vicariously for the head of the household; and her apparel is contrived with this object in view. It has come about that obviously productive labor is in a peculiar degree derogatory to respectable women, and therefore special pains should be taken in the construction of women's dress, to impress upon the beholder the fact (often indeed a fiction) that the wearer does not and can not habitually engage in useful work. Propriety requires respectable women to abstain more consistently from useful effort and to make more of a show of leisure than the men of the same social classes. It grates painfully on our nerves to contemplate the necessity of any well-bred woman's earning a livelihood by useful work. It is not "woman's sphere." Her sphere is within the household, which she should "beautify," and of which she should be the "chief ornament." The male head of the household is not currently spoken of as its ornament. This feature taken in conjunction with the other fact that propriety requires more unremitting attention to expensive display in the dress and other paraphernalia of women, goes to enforce the view already implied in what has gone before. By virtue of its descent from a patriarchal past, our social system makes it the woman's function in an especial degree to put in evidence her household's ability to pay. According to the modern civilized scheme of life, the good name of the household to which she belongs should be the special care of the woman; and the system of honorific expenditure and conspicuous leisure by which this good name is chiefly sustained is therefore the woman's sphere. In the ideal scheme, as it tends to realize itself in the life of the higher pecuniary classes, this attention to conspicuous waste of substance and effort should normally be the sole economic function of the woman.

At the stage of economic development at which the women were still in the full sense the property of the men, the performance of conspicuous leisure and consumption came to be part of the services required of them. The women being not their own masters, obvious expenditure and leisure on their part would redound to the credit of their master rather than to their own credit; and therefore the more expensive and the more obviously unproductive the women of the household are, the more creditable and more effective for the purpose of reputability of the household or its head will their life be. So much so that the women have been required not only to afford evidence of a life of leisure, but even to disable themselves for useful activity.

It is at this point that the dress of men falls short of that of women, and for sufficient reason. Conspicuous waste and conspicuous leisure are reputable because they are evidence of pecuniary strength; pecuniary strength is reputable or honorific because, in the last analysis, it argues success and superior force; therefore the evidence of waste and leisure put forth by any individual in his own behalf cannot consistently take such a form or be carried to such a pitch as to argue incapacity or marked discomfort on his part; as the exhibition would in that case show not superior force, but inferiority, and so defeat its own purpose. So, then, wherever wasteful expenditure and the show of abstention from effort is normally, or on an average, carried to the extent of showing obvious discomfort or voluntarily induced physical disability, there the immediate inference is that the individual in question does not perform this wasteful expenditure and undergo this disability for her own personal gain in pecuniary repute, but in behalf of some one else to whom she stands in a relation of economic dependence; a relation which in the last analysis must, in economic theory, reduce itself to a relation of servitude.

To apply this generalization to women's dress, and put the matter in concrete terms: the high heel, the skirt, the impracticable bonnet, the corset, and the general disregard of the wearer's comfort which is an obvious feature of all civilized women's apparel, are so many items of evidence to the effect that in the modern civilized scheme of life the woman is still, in theory, the economic dependent of the man—that, perhaps in a highly idealized sense, she still is the man's chattel. The homely reason for all this conspicuous leisure and attire on the part of women lies in the fact that they are servants to whom, in the differentiation of economic functions, has been delegated the office of putting in evidence their master's ability to pay.

There is a marked similarity in these respects between the apparel of women and that of domestic servants, especially liveried servants. In both there is a very elaborate show of unnecessary expensiveness, and in both cases there is also a notable disregard of the physical comfort of the wearer. But the attire of the lady goes farther in its elaborate insistence on the idleness, if not on the physical infirmity of the wearer, than does that of the domestic. And this is as it should be;

for in theory, according to the ideal scheme of the pecuniary culture, the lady of the house is the chief menial of the household.

Besides servants, currently recognized as such, there is at least one other class of persons whose garb assimilates them to the class of servants and shows many of the features that go to make up the womanliness of woman's dress. This is the priestly class. Priestly vestments show, in accentuated form, all the features that have been shown to be evidence of a servile status and a vicarious life. Even more strikingly than the everyday habit of the priest, the vestments, properly so called, are ornate, grotesque, inconvenient, and, at least ostensibly, comfortless to the point of distress. The priest is at the same time expected to refrain from useful effort and, when before the public eye, to present an impassively disconsolate countenance, very much after the manner of a well-trained domestic servant. The shaven face of the priest is a further item to the same effect. This assimilation of the priestly class to the class of body servants, in demeanor and apparel, is due to the similarity of the two classes as regards economic function. In economic theory, the priest is a body servant, constructively in attendance upon the person of the divinity whose livery he wears. His livery is of a very expensive character, as it should be in order to set forth in a beseeming manner the dignity of his exalted master; but it is contrived to show that the wearing of it contributes little or nothing to the physical comfort of the wearer, for it is an item of vicarious consumption, and the repute which accrues from its consumption is to be imputed to the absent master, not to the servant.

The line of demarcation between the dress of women, priests, and servants, on the one hand, and of men, on the other hand, is not always consistently observed in practice, but it will scarcely be disputed that it is always present in a more or less definite way in the popular habits of thought. There are of course also free men, and not a few of them, who, in their blind zeal for faultless reputable attire, transgress the theoretical line between man's and woman's dress, to the extent of arraying themselves in apparel that is obviously designed to vex the mortal frame; but everyone recognizes without hesitation that such apparel for men is a departure from the normal. We are in the habit of saying that such dress is "effeminate"; and one sometimes hears the remark that such or such an exquisitely attired gentleman is as well dressed as a footman.

Certain apparent discrepancies under this theory of dress merit a more detailed examination, especially as they mark a more or less evident trend in the later and maturer development of dress. The vogue of the corset offers an apparent exception from the rule of which it has here been cited as an illustration. A closer examination, however, will show that this apparent exception is really a verification of the rule that the vogue of any given element or feature in dress rests on its utility as an evidence of pecuniary standing. It is well known that in the industrially more advanced communities the corset is employed only within certain fairly well defined social strata. The women of the poorer classes, especially of the rural population, do not habitually use it, except as a holiday luxury. Among these classes the women have to work hard, and it avails them little in the way of a pretense of leisure to so crucify the flesh in everyday life. The holiday use of the contrivance is due to imitation of a higher-class canon of decency. Upwards from this low level of indigence and manual labor, the corset was until within a generation or two nearly indispensable to a socially blameless standing for all women, including the wealthiest and most reputable. This rule held so long as there still was no large class of people wealthy enough to be above the imputation of any necessity for manual labor and at the same time large enough to form a self-sufficient, isolated social body whose mass would afford a foundation for special rules of conduct within the class, enforced by the current opinion of the class alone. But now there has grown up a large enough leisure class possessed of such wealth that any aspersion on the score of enforced manual employment would be idle and harmless calumny; and the corset has therefore in large measure fallen into disuse within this class.

The exceptions under this rule of exemption from the corset are more apparent than real. They are the wealthy classes of countries with a lower industrial structure—nearer the archaic, quasi-industrial type—together with the later accessions of the wealthy classes in the more advanced industrial communities. The latter have not yet had time to divest themselves of the plebeian canons of taste and of reputability carried over from their former, lower pecuniary grade. Such survival of the corset is not infrequent among the higher social classes of those American cities, for instance, which have recently and rapidly risen into opulence. If the word be used as a technical term, without any odious implication, it may be said that the corset persists in great measure through the period of snobbery—the interval of uncertainty and of transition from a lower to the upper levels of pecuniary culture. That is to say, in all countries which have inherited the cor-

327

set it continues in use wherever and so long as it serves its purpose as an evidence of honorific leisure by arguing physical disability in the wearer. The same rule of course applies to other mutilations and contrivances for decreasing the visible efficiency of the individual.

Something similar should hold true with respect to divers items of conspicuous consumption, and indeed something of the kind does seem to hold to a slight degree of sundry features of dress, especially if such features involve a marked discomfort or appearance of discomfort to the wearer. During the past one hundred years there is a tendency perceptible, in the development of men's dress especially, to discontinue methods of expenditure and the use of symbols of leisure which must have been irksome, which may have served a good purpose in their time, but the continuation of which among the upper classes today would be a work of supererogation; as, for instance, the use of powdered wigs and of gold lace, and the practice of constantly shaving the face. There has of late years been some slight recrudescence of the shaven face in polite society, but this is probably a transient and unadvised mimicry of the fashion imposed upon body servants, and it may fairly be expected to go the way of the powdered wig of our grandfathers.

These indices, and others which resemble them in point of the boldness with which they point out to all observers the habitual uselessness of those persons who employ them, have been replaced by other, more delicate methods of expressing the same fact; methods which are no less evident to the trained eyes of that smaller, select circle whose good opinion is chiefly sought. The earlier and cruder method of advertisement held its ground so long as the public to which the exhibitor had to appeal comprised large portions of the community who were not trained to detect delicate variations in the evidences of wealth and leisure. The method of advertisement undergoes a refinement when a sufficiently large wealthy class has developed, who have the leisure for acquiring skill in interpreting the subtler signs of expenditure. "Loud" dress becomes offensive to people of taste, as evincing an undue desire to reach and impress the untrained sensibilities of the vulgar. To the individual of high breeding, it is only the more honorific esteem accorded by the cultivated sense of the members of his own high class that is of material consequence. Since the wealthy leisure class has grown so large, or the contact of the leisure-class individual with members of his own class has grown so wide, as to constitute a human environment sufficient for the honorific purpose, there arises a tendency to exclude the baser elements of the population from the scheme even as spectators whose applause or mortification should be sought. The result of all this is a refinement of methods, a resort to subtler contrivances, and a spiritualization of the scheme of symbolism in dress. And as this upper leisure class sets the pace in all matters of decency, the result for the rest of society also is a gradual amelioration of the scheme of dress. As the community advances in wealth and culture, the ability to pay is put in evidence by means which require a progressively nicer discrimination in the beholder. This nicer discrimination between advertising media is in fact a very large element of the higher pecuniary culture.

8

Lester Ward, DYNAMIC SOCIOLOGY

Ruth Benedict, PATTERNS OF CULTURE

1. What is Ward's concept of social progress? How
    does social progress differ from the evolutionary
    progress of living things in general? Contrast
    Ward's views with Spencer's on this point.

2. What does Ward mean by the arts? How do the arts
    to which he refers differ from the fine arts, and
    why is Ward's view of the latter so negative? Do
    you see any inconsistency in his views here? What
    are the greatest advancements which the arts have
    made possible?

3. How does Ward's artificial view of society con-
    flict with Aristotle's natural view? Was Ward's
    view perhaps made possible by the downfall of
    Aristotle which had occurred earlier in the scien-
    tific revolution of the seventeenth century? (Con-
    sult selection from Butterfield in "Man and the
    Universe.)

4. What does Ward mean when he calls his sociology
    dynamic? Is his book an impartial analysis of
    society or did he write it in order to bring about
    change in society? How does his approach contrast
    with that of Benedict on this point?

5. What does Benedict mean by a pattern of culture?
    What is cultural integration? In what way does
    each culture have its own unique personality like
    the personality of an individual?

6. What are Benedict's criticisms of the earlier an-
    thropologists? How do they apply to Spencer? How
    does Benedict feel that a cultural institution
    should be understood?

7. How is Benedict's approach to primitive cultures
    very different from both Spencer's and Ward's?
    What is the value of studying primitive cultures?

Do you see any similarities between Benedict's approach to primitive cultures and More's approach to the Utopians?

8. What is the relationship between society and history, according to Benedict? Why are both history and psychology necessary for understanding a culture? Why are biological and racial factors not to be considered?

9. Can Benedict's approach be applied to our own culture? How are Benedict's statements concerning our culture similar to Veblen's and even Weber's?

Lester Frank Ward (1841-1913) was one of the most important early American sociologists. The son of poor parents, he was a self-made man. Employed for forty years as a civil servant, Ward attended night school and eventually received a degree in geology. His real interest, however, was in education and sociology; in 1883 he published *Dynamic Sociology*, from which this excerpt is taken. His vision of society was a democratic one and challenged the emphasis of the Social Darwinists on natural selection.

DYNAMIC SOCIOLOGY

DYNAMIC SOCIOLOGY aims at the organization of happiness. In this it differs from moral science, which also aims at the production of the greatest happiness, but which seeks this end by the aid of rules for the control of individual conduct. Such rules are *moral* in their character, *i. e.*, they are based on the feelings. They are in the nature of appeals. They may be appeals to the reason, but in behalf of the feelings. Usually, however, they are appeals to the sympathies. They are suggested to the framer directly by experience and observation. Feeling, either egoistic or altruistic, originates them. They are not in the nature of inventions. They may be thought out, but they are not *devised*. They rest upon the most obvious, not upon the most recondite, truths of human nature. They do not recognize any natural forces as at work in the domain of human action. They rather assume the non-conformity of human action with law. But for such assumption they would possess no justification. For, as well appeal to the winds or the tides as to the equally fixed forces of society. It is this which has rendered all regulative systems so unsuccessful. It is only as these appeals have been accompanied by corresponding active measures that they have succeeded at all. Without knowing it, moral systematists have, to a certain extent, recognized the laws of conduct, and have adopted real physical means for controlling action. These, of course, have produced effects, though, from ignorance of the true character of those laws, the effects have often been quite different from, sometimes precisely the reverse of, those desired and expected. But this is only to say that ignorance and error respecting natural laws have operated in the same manner in the department of social, as of physical, phenomena.

Moral science—even that which discards teleology and professes to be rational—is essentially empirical. As a science, as Mr. Spencer admits,* it belongs to the department of pathology. It is little more than a system of therapeutics. Not only so, but it is a system whose method, like the prevailing methods in medicine, is curative rather than preventive.

Now, as previously shown (vol. i, pp. 57, 104, 149), the distinguishing mark of every practical science is the manner in which the forces within its domain admit of being controlled by artificial devices. Until a field of phenomena has been subjected to this test, it can not be said to have been fairly secured to science. Of the two means of controlling natural forces, the direct and the indirect, the former has accomplished comparatively very little. As was early pointed out (vol. i, p. 40), the direct method is that of the brute. The savage employs it extensively and makes no progress. All stagnant peoples depend chiefly upon it. The acts which lie behind it are impulsive acts; they spring from feeling, not from intellect. Every thing that emanates from feeling is conservative and non-progressive. All progress is due to intellectual activity.

Of the two great classes of means which men employ for the attainment of the ultimate end toward which all actions are directed, viz., direct means and indirect means, the phenomena usually classed under the head of moral science belong to the former. They bear the same relation to mind that brute-force bears to muscle. As the race rose in mental capacity, both the primary co-ordinate departments of mind—feeling and intellect—rose together, and for the primordial method of gratifying desire—muscular effort—the two substitutes—appeal to sympathy and rational strat-

* " Data of Ethics," p. 276 (§ 105).

egy—developed simultaneously. Out of the former have grown the existing codes of morals; out of the latter, the arts and sciences. But the direct method could no more prove progressive when founded on mind than when founded on muscle, and the code of morals has remained nearly the same throughout all ages. The progress attained by the indirect method is the progress of the arts and sciences. But, for reasons existing in the nature of things, the indirect method has only been applied to the department of physical phenomena, not to those of moral and of social phenomena. Hence, these departments have languished or remained stationary under the influence of the direct method alone.

Dynamic sociology consists in applying the indirect method to the control of the social forces.

Defining social progress now more specially as *whatever increases the sum total of human happiness*, since this simply follows from our general definition (*supra*, p. 108), this may be regarded as the proximate end, whose attainment is equivalent to the attainment of the ultimate end. This latter being impossible, except by the application of the direct method, which, as we have seen, promises no advance, it becomes important to strive toward some practical means to which the indirect method may be applied. Social progress is such a means, and it may be attained through intellectual effort.

Adhering strictly to the definition here given of social progress, as whatever increases the sum total of human happiness, the problem presented becomes that of ascertaining in what such progress must specifically consist. What modifications must be effected in the social state to secure the required consummation?

To solve this problem it will be necessary to enter somewhat into an examination of the existing structure of society. The question must be considered whether society, as at present constituted, contains any of the elements requisite to rendering it progressive in this sense, and, if so, what these elements are; or whether, in order to secure this end, elements wholly new and foreign to society must be introduced, and, if so, what they are required to be.

In the latter case, the task might well be regarded as hopeless. If history and experience furnished no suggestion, either positive or negative, no example which clearly points to any utilitarian progress, and none which warns against stagnation or degeneracy, that would indeed be a bold mind which should venture to recommend a novel and untried scheme conceived to be adapted to securing that object. But such happily is not the case. There has certainly, upon the whole, been social progress, although brought about in the same cosmical way in which physiological progress has been achieved, viz., through the operation of the blind forces of nature.

It has already been shown (*supra*, pp. 119, 120) that development in biology is scarcely more than a corollary from the fact of continued existence. Absolute stagnation for any length of time can not be conceived of. It is negatived by the law of the instability of the homogeneous. Therefore, all organized life must either progress or retrogress. Assuming the tendency toward retrogression equal to that toward progression, the state of things which biology reveals would ensue. For retrograde forms would succumb at their inception, and forms at first progressive and afterward, owing to whatever changes in the environment, become retrogressive, would, as surely as this continued long enough, disappear, while only progressive forms could persist. We should therefore behold just such a world as we in fact behold. Development, therefore, or progress in organization, necessarily follows from persistence in life.

It has also been shown (*supra*, p. 124) that in biology progress in organization is attended by increase in the capacity for feeling. This fact points strongly to the quality of progress required by our definition. For increase of feeling implies increase of enjoyment. The only means

335

of defeating this would be to render the increased pains more than great enough to balance the increased pleasures. But this assumes a degree of inadaptation so great as necessarily to render the organism thus affected retrogressive and ultimately to extinguish it.* Increase of feeling must, therefore, in all organisms that persist under it, be attended with a corresponding increase of enjoyment.

The application of these principles to man and to society is very simple and perfectly legitimate. A state of absolute stagnation can not exist in any race or society. All must either be advancing or receding, however slowly or rhythmically. Moreover, social advancement which is able to persist must be of the kind that secures increase of enjoyment upon the whole and in the long run; although, in so complex a field as that of human society, the apparent exceptions to this law may be many, and the law itself difficult to prove *a posteriori*.

States of social organization, apparently the highest, often result in the most complete subjection of the masses, and certainly diminish the sum of happiness except of a few. Ill-founded schemes of government, religion, public economy, finance, art, or even literature, may proceed so much in disregard of the real welfare of the people as in fact, though apparently highly developed and progressive, to reduce the tone of existence and greatly to lessen the normal degree of enjoyment. But such a state is, in fact, retrogressive. It marks the decline in the life of a society, stamps it as in process of becoming *effete*, and ushers in a period of obvious degeneracy which, if not arrested, must end in social extinction.

Existing society consists of a variety of distinct elements. The state in which we observe it has been brought about by the influence of numerous causal factors. It is not enough to state generally that social progress is due to this great cosmical tendency which we have traced through-

* Spencer, "Data of Ethics," pp. 14, 26 (§§ 4, 9).

out the lower departments of life. It is certainly true that this tendency exists, and that it is the remote cause of social as well as of biological progress. But even the biologist looks closer and analyzes the various more immediate elements which combine to constitute this tendency. Much more, then, is it the duty of the sociologist to analyze the progressive tendency in society and to determine the nature of its elements.

Just as in biology there are found, upon close investigation, two general classes of elements, favorable and adverse, so in society there are found to exist both progressive and anti-progressive elements. The field of social phenomena differs, however, from that of life in general in one very important respect—the existence of an intellectual force. This force has been developed in the same cosmical manner as the other social forces—the desires; but it nevertheless differs so fundamentally from these as to mark a step in the general progress of nature analogous to that which the development of the former marked when they separated the sentient from the insentient world. This great step finds its fullest expression in the broad antithesis which we have denoted by the terms direct and indirect method, as applied to the efforts of sentient beings to attain their ends. In the world of feeling below man, these efforts have been made according to the direct method alone, and have succeeded only in accomplishing the maintenance and perpetuation of life. Progress has here been due to other causes, chiefly to the various kinds of adaptation or selection; but in man the indirect method was early applied, and while in certain cases, in consequence of error and ignorance, it had a reactive effect, and brought about gradual degeneration or speedy destruction, in others it proved progressive, and with greater or less rapidity elevated the condition of the race.

The immediate result of the application of the indirect, or intellectual, method was the introduction of a large number of purely human institutions, or devices for attaining desired ends, which in their most general sense we may denominate *arts*.

While considering the various "modes of acquisition" in Chapter VII (vol. i, p. 524), it was shown that intellectual operations rest fundamentally upon a quality which, when directed toward objects capable of feeling, takes the name of *deception*. Such recondite truths are sometimes exemplified in an interesting manner by the natural history of words.

The word *art* furnishes a case in point. Applied to inanimate objects it sounds harmless enough, but observe the difference when applied to animals or men. In its derivative, "artful," we have the same general conception as in "artificial," except that acts to which the former may be applied refer to things which can suffer, while those to which the latter is applied are feelingless.

We may perceive from such illustrations that the idea underlying the word *art*, and present in all its applications and derivatives, is the essential, distinguishing principle of purely intellectual action. Therefore, all the productions of purely intellectual effort may in this general sense be denominated arts. And now the additional truth must be formally set down that, while certain arts are devised in ignorance and error, and result in the subversion of progress, the greater part of them are conceived in a sufficiently true appreciation of the nature of the force which they seek to control to succeed in their purpose, and result in securing a greater or less degree of material and social advantage, rendering them progressive. This may be illustrated by the history of human invention, which is simply a branch of human art, and constitutes the department of it which most perfectly elucidates the true character of all forms of artificial operation. For even here a great many devices fail to accomplish the objects expected by their designers, and some prove productive of harmful effects.

When we come to animals, the progressive principle is clearly discernible. The relative perfection of animals is no longer confined to their respective powers of endurance or security of perpetuation, but lies also in immediate connection with their peculiar characteristic as sentient beings, capable of enjoying their own organisms. Therefore, that organism is, in general, most perfect which possesses the greatest variety of parts, on the principle that every normal movement yields pleasure, and that pleasure is increased as the facilities for activity are rendered more extensive and varied.

Therefore, it is fairly established that on the whole there has been progress in the animal kingdom throughout the geological ages of the earth, because each successive age has produced some beings of a more varied and elaborate organization than those of the age preceding it.

While, therefore, in the animal as well as in the vegetable kingdom, there still exist forms and species as low perhaps as any that ever existed even at the beginning, still there has been progress, because, while these lower forms continue to exist the same as then, yet the highest forms now in existence are infinitely superior to the highest forms in those remote ages, and in some respect superior to the highest of any preceding age.

But, as we look over this subject, we can not fail to be struck with the·fact that this progress has not been so much due to the individual efforts of species as to external circumstances, viz., physical changes taking place in the earth, occasioning differences in the shape of the surface, in the temperature, and in the quality of the atmosphere and of the water. It is not so much a development of species as the evolution of new species under the operation of what we may call the law of *favorable conditions*, according to which new and superior species have successively made their appearance as fast as the terrestrial transformations would permit. For instance, no land animals could of course appear until there was land on which to dwell, and that did not exist to any extent till two great geological ages had gone by. Nor could these then exist (since all land animals must be air-breathing animals) until a long and luxuriant vegetation had extracted the superabundant quantities of carbonic acid from the air and buried its carbon in the earth, liberating its oxygen to purify the atmosphere (vol. i, p. 272). These conditions must first be fulfilled before the higher types could be brought forth.

Thus we see that this progress in the animal world is due in the main to a corresponding progress in the physical conditions of the earth. And this enables us to make the first grand division of the subject into that progress which is due to external causes, or objective progress, and that which is due to special efforts of individuals, or subjective progress.

The former of these divisions belongs properly to astronomy, geology, and botany. The latter belongs in the main to zoölogy, and in so far neither has more than a collateral bearing upon the question before us. But, if we scan closely this latter branch—namely, that part of the progress of animal life which has been produced by the special efforts of individuals—we may observe that it is capable of a further subdivision into two branches. One of these leads to the consideration of the development of species by "natural selection," whereby, through the unremitting and almost desperate efforts of every individual of every species to overcome the obstacles to its existence, great and radical changes have been wrought in the habits, character, and morphology of species.

The other branch of this inquiry, which it is impossible wholly to separate from the first, takes cognizance of the immaterial part, and shows what influence mind exerts upon the animal world in promoting its advancement.

The remark may here be made that the influences of external circumstances and of physical effort are not always such as to advance the species. On the whole, there has doubtless been progress from both these influences, but there have been periods of retrogression from unfavorable conditions, and perhaps degeneration of species by periods of superabundant supply and exemption from necessary exertion.

When we reach the plane which man occupies in the animal world, these laws of adaptation, selection, and survival, while they are not altogether superseded, and perhaps operate as powerfully as on the lower creatures, nevertheless become of comparatively small importance in consequence of the vastly more potent influences due to the development of the intellectual faculty which operates according to the indirect method. The progress which man has made, though from any absolute standard it may appear slow and even secular, is nevertheless, as compared to that which is brought about either by cosmical alterations in the environment or by the law of adaptation, or direct and indirect equilibration,* extremely rapid; as much more rapid than that which results from the biological laws just named as this is more rapid than that which results from the cosmical laws (vol. i. p. 477). This progress, too, is effected in spite of the frequent disastrous conflagrations which ignorance and error occasion by a perverse use of the Promethean fire (*infra*, p. 287).

PROGRESSIVE AGENCIES.

In all the departments of life, the faculties are perpetually crowding the opportunities. All organisms, by their inherent tendency to develop, are constantly pressing upon the environment. The organ is always in excess of the function. Gratification is never equal to desire. There is a permanent residuum ever striving after more complete satisfaction. In the animals below man, a great degree of correspondence is generally established, but never so great but that the least giving way of the wall of circumstances by which a species is surrounded results in an immediate advance of the species to occupy the ground yielded. This truth is forcibly exemplified by all the phenomena which the domestication of animals and plants presents. In nature they are in a state of equilibrium, each aiding the inorganic conditions to keep all others in their existing state. Human interference disturbs this equilibrium, selects one, and protects it from the influence of the rest, improves the inorganic conditions, and gives free scope to the forces in excess which reside in every species; whereupon development becomes rapid, and is only arrested when brought again into conflict with adverse elements upon a new and higher plane of life. This power to advance in structure as fast as opportunities are offered is due to the original and universal *nisus* of the life-principle itself, and rests fundamentally upon the peculiar characteristics of the primordial life-substance—that remarkably unstable, restless, and, as it were, dissatisfied form of matter—protoplasm. The never wholly satisfied desires of sentient beings are but the modes of manifestation of this fundamental tendency in the higher forms of life. With the progress of cephalization, the manifestations of uneasiness and dissatisfaction become more pronounced, and the attempts to break through environing barriers more successful. But not until it has advanced so far as to admit of the substitution, to however small a degree, of the indirect for

342

the direct method, does this success become complete, and the emancipation of the creature take place. This stage is reached only in man, and the progressive tendency can thenceforward only be traced in him. But even in him no degree of development is ever reached in which there does not still perpetually remain an excess of desires over gratifications, a multitude of wants unsatisfied. The faculties still continue to crowd the opportunities, organic vitality presses upon functional exercise, reproduction encroaches upon nutrition, population trenches upon the means of subsistence.

Social contact occasions mutual dependence, and renders a means of communication a paramount necessity.

Taking into consideration all the varied wants which must have existed at the inception of human society, we may conveniently arrange them under two great groups, which will then be denoted in the most general manner by the two words respectively—

1. Communication.
2. Subsistence.

Not but that the race had enjoyed some degree of ability to communicate together prior to the stage of development mentioned, but only that it was at this stage that there arose the necessity for greatly increased faculties in this direction. And, as regards subsistence, it was then, too, that it became essential to augment the supply far beyond that which unaltered nature yields to the ordinary methods by which animals secure it.

By following the history of the human race from that stage to the latest and highest yet reached, it will be perceived that it has been along these two particular lines that progress has always moved, nearly every recognized step having consisted either in increasing the facilities for the intercommunication of ideas among men or in augmenting their power to extract from nature additional supplies of the necessaries of life.

343

We have next to consider the manner in which the desires, whose satisfaction is attained through a better supply of the means of subsistence, have influenced the progress of the human race. In a previous chapter (vol. i, p. 485), this general subject was treated somewhat in detail, but from an entirely distinct point of view. The nature of the Social Forces was then under consideration, and, although what were there denominated the "preservative forces" were shown to be identical with the desires above mentioned, still, the object was then simply to establish the existence of such forces and to prove their identity, in point of uniformity, reliableness, and susceptibility to scientific study and intelligent control, with all other acknowledged natural forces; while we have here to do only with the actual product of these forces after they have been subjected to the guidance of the intellect. In the former case, the total product, both progressive and non-progressive, was considered; in the present case, only a small portion of that product, the portion to which the indirect method has been applied, is taken into account. We were then studying these propelling influences themselves; we are now studying the directive influence which in various times and manners has enabled them to succeed where otherwise they must have failed. It is in this that progress really consists. The forces themselves are blind. Intelligence alone can light their path. Without it, however intense may be their degree, they must perpetually dash against immovable barriers which restrict their march. Multiplication must be constantly checked by premature destruction. Migration must be arrested by the annihilation of the emigrant or the infant colony. Subsistence, as provided by unaided nature, is limited, and life must be limited to correspond. The forces can not be extinguished; the desires must continue to press for satisfaction; but, in the absence of any *artificial* source of supply, equilibration must be speedily reached and progress must cease.

The means through which this statical condition has been disturbed, and a dynamic state preserved by the human race, is the agency which is generally known as *practical*, or *useful. art*. In order to distinguish it from that which is somewhat inappropriately recognized as art *par excellence*, or "fine art," let us call it *inventive art*, and the other *imaginative*, or *creative*, *art*.

It is somewhat unfortunate, perhaps, that two departments of mental activity, so remotely connected psychologically and sociologically, should have received the same name. Although we are here really little concerned with the latter, yet, in order to add somewhat to the symmetry of the general treatment of the subject, as well as to point out, once for all, the chief distinctions between them, for which a more appropriate place may not be found, a few words with regard to the true position of the fine arts may be justified.

It is obvious that inventive art rests primarily upon the preservative forces of society. It is directed almost exclusively to the satisfaction of the ordinary wants of mankind, which, as we saw, are all more or less completely reducible to the demands of nature for the three prime necessities—food, clothing, and shelter.

It is less obvious, but by no means purely fanciful, or maintained for the love of theory and system, that imaginative art rests primarily upon the other principal co-ordinate branch of the social forces, viz., the reproductive forces. When we consider to how large a degree all ideas of beauty are associated with the sentiment of love, and how closely all forms of love are related to sexual love, and this in turn to the sexual instinct, this at first perhaps somewhat startling proposition may meet with a qualified acceptance. Fully to appreciate whatever degree of truth it may possess, however, the present highly derivative and etherealized character of these sentiments as exhibited by the *élite* of mankind must be temporarily put out of the mind, and a mental image formed of the true character of those sentiments in undeveloped races, and also in the lower animals. Here we see the parental instinct disappearing more or less in the male and confining itself to the mother, in whom it is an ac-

knowledged adjunct of the sexual system. Filial and fraternal affection also disappears, and the only form of love
remaining is that of sex. The universal preference for the
nude in art is undoubtedly in great part due to the vague
but still influential charm which notions of sex add to the
product. Nor is it to lower our estimate of art frankly to
admit this, and to maintain that all classes of innocent emotion are equally pure.

Sculpture, the oldest of the arts, illustrates this truth
most forcibly, and is closely followed by painting, which
was originally confined principally to the delineation of the
human form. Architecture, which unites the inventive
with the imaginative, forms an exception, and, in its earliest
as well as in its highest application, is more intimately connected with the religious sentiment. Music, however, though
a late development, bears a clear relation to the romantic in
human nature. Of poetry, it may be said that it has much
closer affinities with the department of art that has the means
of intercommunication for its object and literature for one
of its boldest achievements, than it has with the practical arts
proper, which we are now considering. Poetry is to language what the remaining fine arts are to the useful arts; yet
its fundamental attachment to the sentiments derived from
the development of the reproductive system is plainly shown
in the almost universal connection of poetry with romance.

There is nothing dynamical in the influence of the fine
arts. Enjoyable in themselves, and therefore sources of happiness, their influence is confined to the immediate present,
and is incapable of contributing any permanent aid to social
progress. Their study belongs entirely to the department of
social statics, and this brief notice of them is merely intended
to fix their true position and exhibit their negative character.

As was remarked at the outset, human art has advanced
on two general lines—the one in the direction of securing better means of intercommunication, the other in the direction

of securing better means of subsistence. The first of these divisions must be regarded as embracing the response of the developing intellect to the demands of the mind ; the second, as its response to the demands of the body. In seeking a convenient subdivision of this latter branch of human art, it appears that, while its progress has presented a somewhat uniform movement without the several abrupt steps which are so conspicuous in the other branch, still there has been, in the history of those races which now occupy the most advanced position, an enormous acceleration within the last three centuries as compared with the same period at any previous time—far greater even than that which took place in the progress of letters under the stimulus of the epoch-making art of printing. This sudden swelling out of the stream, which had previously undergone only the normal increase due to its numerous tributaries coming in at irregular intervals and with varying volumes, has been so rapid and so vast as to constitute an historical if not a logical subdivision of the entire subject. Its cause, it is true, is not far to seek, and is found almost wholly in the application, since the middle of the seventeenth century, of what is known as the Scientific Method to the development of inventive art.

This fact confronts us on the threshold with the much-discussed and ill-settled question of the relation of science to art. It is this fact, too, that has lent the chief support to the view, which may be said latterly to prevail, that art precedes science ; and in a certain sense this is unquestionably true. But the prevalence of this idea is unavoidably accompanied by a train of erroneous and, we may add, pernicious implications. It serves to keep alive the originally false conception of the meaning of the word *empirical*. If empiricism means—and this is what is maintained—the method by trial, depending on failure to detect error and on repeated trials to discover truth, then is inductive science, and especially all successful experimentation, purely empirical. For this is the special characteristic of the latter—that it depends upon successive trials of one hypothesis after another until the true solution is at last reached. Let us hear on this subject the views of one of the ablest and most successful experimenters that science has produced, whose right to speak *ex cathedra* upon it no one will question. Only a short time previous to his death (November 24, 1877), Professor Joseph Henry, in his annual address as president of the Philosophical Society of Washington,* thus described the true method of experimental research:

"The first step in the investigation is to reproduce the phenomenon; the next, is to form in the mind a provisional hypothesis as to its cause, and in the choice of this we are governed by analogy. For example, if it appears to resemble some of the phenomena of electricity, we *assume* that it is produced by electricity; we next endeavor to ascertain by what known action of electricity such an effect could possibly be produced; for this purpose we invent an hypothesis, or *imagine* some peculiar action of electricity sufficient to produce the effect in question; we then say to ourselves, If this be true, it will logically follow that a specific result will follow if we make a certain experiment. The experiment is devised and tried, but no positive result is obtained. In order to this negative result, the logical deductions must have been in error, or the experiment must have been defective, or the hypothesis itself erroneous.

"We examine each of the two former steps, and finding nothing amiss in them, we conclude that the hypothesis was not true; another hypothesis is then invented, another deduction inferred, and another experiment made; still no result is obtained. At this stage of the research, the inexperienced investigator is prone to abandon the pursuit; not so he who has successfully attempted to penetrate the secrets of nature. Undeterred by failure, he changes from time to

---

* See "Bulletin" of the society, vol. ii. p. 164. In the citation given, the words that emphasize the position here taken are italicized, the Italics being Professor Henry's only in the first instance.

time his hypothesis, makes new *guesses*, and again repeats the question as to their truth by means of experiment, until at length nature, as if wearied by his solicitations, grants him a new and positive result."

From this lucid exposition of the scientific method of experimentation, it must be clear to all that we have not yet reached a stage at which not only repeated trial but actual guess-work is not necessary to successful investigation. In the ordinary acceptation of the term, this is the very essence of empiricism.

What, then, is it that distinguishes science from empiricism?

It must be confessed that the only important characteristic which the former possesses, and which is absent from the latter, is the quality of being *systematic*. Science is methodical empiricism. Strictly speaking, science, as every one knows, is simply knowledge. More definitely, it is knowledge of the materials and laws of nature. In this wider sense it must precede art. Art is never the result of blind chance—of accident. It is always, however simple its form, the result of thought, of a recognition of the nature and reliableness of cause and effect, of the exercise of the inventive faculty in taking some advantage, however slight, of the natural forces. Even the least of such efforts, such as the selection of a well-shaped club from the broken sticks of a jungle, or the placing of fagots already prepared upon a forest fire, requires a degree of brain-power superior to that possessed by any wild animal. All the more essential useful arts were created long prior to the dawn of modern science, and each of these must have been preceded by a large amount of strictly scientific thought, accompanied by repeated trials of hypotheses, which were abandoned when unsuccessful, new ones being substituted, until success was attained. The method has always been the same as now, the faculty employed the same, the result the same. The real difference is that then every thing was partial and fragmentary; no whole field of knowledge had been mastered; the trials were all extremely specialized, and directed to the supply of immediate pressing wants. Empiricism may be called *intuitive science.* The laws comprehended are only the more obvious and superficial ones. With the deeper hidden laws no progress could at first be made, and all attempts to go below the surface of things resulted in failure. Hence, the arts were rude; but, fortunately, these rude arts were sufficient to give the race a complete supremacy on the globe. They consisted not merely in the ability to manufacture the appliances necessary to increase their means of subsistence, but in a higher degree in the skill acquired by their use, and in the pursuit of such means often wholly without artificial appliances. Mere cunning in securing such appointments and dispositions of occurrences known to be regular was an important quality of primitive art, and this, combined with labor in creating favorable combinations of circumstances, supplemented by that of devising the implements necessary to seize the greatest advantage of every thing thus, as it were, decoyed within reach, proved sufficient to multiply many hundred-fold the normal supply of nature.

From very early periods this method in art was adopted and successfully directed against all the departments of matter and force. As all subsistence, at least all alimentation, must be derived primarily from the vegetable kingdom, either directly or mediately through the animal, human ingenuity was directed toward inorganic matter and the physical forces chiefly in the creation of such artificial appliances as were found necessary to perform the required service in the organic kingdoms.

The great diversity now known to exist among the various low races of men still inhabiting certain parts of the globe has greatly shaken faith in the chronological order in which early writers assumed that man had successively sought his subsistence, viz., the existence of the hunting, pastoral, and agricultural stages. That the hunting, and particularly the fishing stage, has been a very early one with many races, there can be no doubt, but there is reason, both in the facts of ethnography and in fair deductions from the character of those animals from which biology teaches that man must have descended, to suppose that a purely vegetarian stage may have been the one during which the transition to manhood was effected and the infancy of the newly evolved race was spent.* But this can not be supposed to involve an acquaintance with agriculture in any proper sense, though doubtless skill, ingenuity, and a certain amount of artificial labor must have supplemented the spontaneous productions of nature. It is certainly natural to assume that human skill, art, and cunning were directed to the killing and capturing, in various ways, of different kinds of animals and fish, upon which to subsist, before it was directed to agriculture or to the domestication of animals.† We scarcely find either pastoral or agricultural tribes among true savages, although the interior of Africa seems to furnish some exceptions to this statement. These modes of life are usually associated with the social state which we call barbarism, or with the civilized state.

The chronological order of the development of these arts, however, concerns us less here than their special character as aids to human progress, the relative quality and quantity of brain-power required to produce them. Clearly the chase

* "The hunter state, which Montesquieu placed the first, was probably only the second stage at which mankind arrived; since so many arts must have been invented to catch a salmon or a deer, that society could no longer have been in its infancy when they came into use" (Brand's "Select Dissertations," from the "Amœn. Acad.," vol. i, p. 118; also, in Encycl. Brit., 6th ed., Suppl., vol. iii, 1824). See, also, Oscar Schmidt on the stage of "Uncultur," in the "Deutsche Rundschau," for November, 1878 (vol. xvii, S. 279).

† Humboldt lays much stress on the fact that none of the American aborigines domesticated animals for pastoral purposes, notwithstanding the abundance of the bison, llama, and other native species, which have been proved capable of becoming very useful to man. Such as passed to the agricultural stage, therefore, must have done so directly from the hunting stage. ("Kosmos," Bd. II, S. 313, 314, note 15 to page 210; also "Ansichten der Natur," S. 9, 35, 101.)

is the mode of subsistence which requires the least display of genius. Cunning, in learning the haunts and habits of game, and in devising various snares and ambushes for its capture, must, of course, be exercised in a high degree, while true ingenuity is called forth in this stage in the invention of various weapons by which more effectually to secure it. These qualities, sharpened by the constant spur of want, must have wrought a rapid development of the faculties required to be put to service. And, as it is the same faculties which are called into exercise in all forms of artificial contrivance, the genius of an Ericsson may have been foreshadowed in the inventor of the bow and arrow.

In the taming of wild animals, and their reduction to man's service in various ways, a somewhat different set of faculties was exercised. A larger degree of foresight was required. The successful efforts very early made to improve the breeds of animals required considerable reflection, although a large part of the progress thus made was doubtless due to accident.

But, of all the primitive modes of subsistence, that of agriculture called forth the greatest amount of intellectual effort, and demanded the most foresight. Here the indirect method must be exclusively applied, and the discipline of waiting an entire season for the rewards of labor had a most wholesome influence upon the development of mind and character. A larger number of utensils, too, were required for this class of labor than for either of the preceding, which stimulated the inventive powers, and led the way to the extension of the practical arts to all the departments of life.

The power to multiply in numbers and expand in local territory, which the exercise of a superior intellect gave to man, also contributed greatly to stimulate the progress of art. For, in his wanderings, he must soon find himself exposed to climates quite different from that of his native abode. He must have shelter from wind and storm and from extreme cold. It is easy to see how great a sharpener of the wits subjection to such vicissitudes must be. In those countries where population is now densest, the natural protection from cold is very slight. To realize this, it is only necessary to contemplate spending a winter in some large forest remote from civilization. Admitting that there be an abundant supply of food, to how large an extent would it be necessary to depend for comfort upon artificial means of shelter? To secure such means must have cost primitive man much close calculation.

The invention of clothing, too, afforded a great stimulus to art, since clothing must be manufactured; and, although at first it consisted of the skins of animals or the leaves of trees, still, as men advanced farther from the equator and improved in skill, it gradually led to the manufacture of cloth, than which no one commodity furnishes a greater amount of skilled and useful labor, or a higher or more substantial gratification when applied to its various uses. In the ancient world the loom and the distaff were the special emblems of industry, a fact which shows how important an art the manufacture of cloth must have been. The houses were then very poorly constructed, and many nations even in temperate latitudes dwelt in tents. Clothing was made a substitute for houses. It is only in comparatively recent times that the carpenter has been placed on an equal footing with the weaver.

It is amazing to contemplate the meagerness of the real physical comforts which were enjoyed during all the centuries down to the commencement of the modern epoch—the small extent to which iron was employed, the absence of glass for admitting light into houses, of paper for the transaction of business, of nearly all kinds of machinery, etc. The difference between the modern and ancient civilization in this respect is far greater than that which separates the latter from the most primitive state yet discovered among savages. The two epochs should, therefore, be considered separately. The modern epoch must be regarded as having been chiefly caused by the adoption of that systematic method of dealing with facts and phenomena which is distinguished as science, in contrast with the empiricism which underlay primitive art. A consideration of modern art, therefore, involves a review of modern science. The difference between man's early empirical applications of natural laws and his present analytical ones is not so radically great as might at first appear. For then he only knew observed effects—that is, phenomena—and phenomena are all he knows now. Still, the knowledge obtained by careful and thorough investigation and experiment has led him into a so much deeper, more minute, and more definite comprehension of Nature and her laws, that it seems to be a new and distinct department of human knowledge. It is not, then, so much the opening of a new channel as the widening and deepening of the old one. It is not so much the fact that men then began to discover truth as that they then learned a new and successful process for its discovery. It is not so much the quality of the truth evolved as the quantity which they have thus been enabled to evolve.

It is difficult to fix a period for the commencement of this era. There have been searchers after truth from the earliest ages, and every one who finds a truth is a scientific discoverer. From the times of Thales and Pythagoras, there have been many philosophers who delighted in the investigation of nature. In the fields of mathematics, astronomy, and natural history, considerable progress was made before the age of Bacon, Newton, Galileo, or Humboldt. Pythagoras, Euclid, Archimedes, ranged over a wide field in the domain of mathematics. Thales, Hipparchus, and Ptolemy went far in astronomy, while Aristotle and Pliny have left extensive treatises on natural history. Toward the close of the middle ages, not only was considerable interest again manifested in these departments of science, but the two sister sciences of physics and chemistry began to be sifted out of the chaff of demonism and alchemy. Still, in all this, little attempt was made by any of these writers to arrive at truth by investigation. They assumed truths, and with these they proceeded to elaborate other truths. These assumed truths were such as the popular mind universally or generally recognized, or such as a casual observation of things naturally suggested. For though, in the philosophy of Thales and others, an inductive method was pursued, yet the facts arrived at by this induction had never been put to a severe test by close inspection or elaborate experiment. It was, therefore, even inferior to those other systems which did not pretend to set out with any particular truths, but started from the broadest generalities, and deduced all specific truths by a strict course of reasoning upon these. And for the obvious reason that such generalities when assumed are more likely to be true than the particular propositions when only assumed. The fundamental error, therefore, had always been that of assuming any thing at all, and the world was a very long time in thoroughly freeing itself from this error. It was this that Bacon * sought to eradicate. He discovered that Nature possessed a vast storehouse of truths, every one of which was of great practical use to man, and he saw, moreover, what few had seen before him, that man was no more able to tell the contents of that storehouse, by gazing at its exterior, than he could tell those of a warehouse of goods by a similar process. He saw that it was necessary to seize the keys to the secret chambers of Nature's magazine, and to go in and examine the articles which she had thus been storing up and preserving during all time ; to handle them, expose them to the light, separate those that were mixed, test their qualities, and ascertain their constitution and their value. Conjecture would no longer answer. Nothing could properly be assumed as truth that had not been proved—not by logical syllogisms founded on assumed truths as premises, but proved by careful and repeated examination by the senses, the only

* For a statement of Bacon's claims to the title of " Founder of the Inductive Method," see vol. i, p. 140, note.

avenues of knowledge. Close observation, elaborate experiment, and repeated tactual and ocular tests, would alone suffice to establish a fact so as to justify its employment as a premise. It was very soon found that secondary truths thus obtained were of a nature calculated to sustain one another and lead to important practical results. From this point, then, we may most consistently date the scientific era. This new process, which Bacon advocated, was the precise reform needed to give an impetus to science. It was more in the nature of an art than of a science. It was to science what printing was to literature—a means of advancing it. Men have to learn how, before they can do any thing. They have to devise the means before they can accomplish any great object. And, when such means are proposed, the world is always ready to adopt them. I am disposed to exonerate the men of pre-scientific ages from the charges of idleness, negligence, and false dignity, which have been made against them, because they did not long before employ the laborious method of investigation and research now admitted to be so necessary, being convinced that they did not adopt this plan because it did not occur to them. They did not comprehend its importance or its necessity. They knew nothing of it. Some of the ancients did pursue it for some distance, but their successors did not appreciate the importance of continuing it. It required ages of failure in all other methods, and the consequences of that failure, at length to open the eyes even of the wisest.

I will not attempt to detail the results that followed the introduction of the scientific method. Less than three centuries have elapsed, and we see such an advance in science as could not have been dreamed of even by Bacon himself. It is true, other influences independent of this have conspired to accomplish this result. Of course, if it had not been for the invention of printing, comparatively little could have been done; and yet even this, unaccompanied by a sound principle to proceed upon, would have been likely to bring on another of those brilliant periods of useless speculation which characterized the literature of Greece and Rome, as well as that of the middle ages.

But, combined as these two influences were, they were eminently suited to the work which was then so greatly needed, viz., the reorganization of the civilizing forces of the world. No doubt, the world was ripe for this scientific reform, which would have soon come without Bacon, for contemporary with him in the last half of the sixteenth century we find a galaxy of great names, including those of Newton, Galileo, Leibnitz, and Descartes. The seventeenth century increased the number though not the eminence of the corps of scientific workers, and prepared the way for that of the eighteenth, during which the scientific method became fully established as the most potent agency of human progress.

It will thus be perceived that art, however viewed, is simply the application of science. What is called empiricism is the application of superficial truths, recognized in a loose, unsystematic way, to immediate and special needs; while science proper, considered with reference to art, consists in the application to the more general wants of mankind, both present and future, of the deeper and more general truths of the physical world which must have been unknown to the empiricist, and respecting which, if he possessed any ideas at all, he possessed erroneous ones, often conceiving them to be just the reverse of what they prove to be.

Very few fully realize to what extent modern civilized society depends upon practical, or inventive, art, or how thoroughly artificial civilization is. The erroneous idea which so extensively prevails of the essential inferiority of the artificial to the natural has already been analyzed and exposed (vol. i, p. 71 ; vol. ii, p. 86). This is the proper place to appreciate more fully the true scope of art in civilization.

The various objects which present themselves to the senses in the course of the experience of each individual

357

may be separated into two general groups, according to whether they seem to have assumed their present form by natural or by artificial processes. When we look at a mountain, we at once refer it to the first of these classes, and when we look at a house, we as readily refer it to the second. This distinction we preserve after we have learned that there was a time when the mountain did not exist as well as a time when the house did not exist, *i. e.*, when we have learned to regard both as the result of changes which have taken place in the materials of which they are composed. And we should recognize the distinction no less plainly though we were to regard all natural forms as the products of design, as well as all artificial forms. The former, we say, are *growths;* the latter, *manufactures.* The former are either the results of self-existent activities in the matter composing them, or they are the products of design independent of the human mind. The latter are certainly the products of human design.

But, between these two obviously distinct conditions, there is a third, or intermediate, class of objects. A house, a machine, or a watch, appears to be wholly the product of human design and labor, while a blade of grass or a wild buffalo is as clearly a natural product. But in a head of bald wheat and in a thorough-bred Durham cow we see the combined results of natural laws and of human calculation. Yet, if we look more closely at those objects which seem to be wholly artificial, we shall find that none of them are absolutely so. A mill is only an assemblage of material objects, so adjusted that they may be set in motion by the application of some natural force—it may be, the power of horses, of water, or of steam. In any case, man has only adapted material forms to natural forces, so that, together, results will follow which are advantageous to him. All machinery embodies this principle, while a house or any such object has a similar negative effect, and passively illustrates the same truth.

358

Viewing the matter from this stand-point, therefore, we may correctly regard that form of human agency which has accomplished the great improvements (from the point of view of human advantage) that have been effected in so many vegetable and animal forms, as a simple extension to organic objects of the power which man has exercised over inorganic objects, in so adjusting the circumstances that the natural forces to which they are subject will bring about results through them advantageous to him. This eliminates the apparent third class and restores the original classification; changed, however, in this: that the so-called artificial objects are only partially so, that only the adjustments are artificial, while the results wrought by means of such adjustments are as much the immediate consequence of natural forces as is the action of a volcano.

If, now, we contemplate these two classes of objects from a somewhat more practical point of view, we observe that what we call civilization is due almost exclusively to the increased proportion of the artificial over the natural objects in contact with man. As a rule—not, however, without exceptions—this proportion is a measure of civilization

Civilization, then, may be defined as the artificial adjustment of natural objects in such a manner that the natural forces will thereby produce results advantageous to man. Although human design and agency are most apparent in the domain of inorganic matter and physical force, whereby so great progress has been made in the material conditions by which society is now influenced, still, it may well be doubted whether such agency has not done even more to advance society in operating upon the more subtile organic objects and vital and psychic forces. For it must be remembered that agriculture, horticulture, and the breeding and domestication of animals, whether for service or for food, all rest upon this form of art. Upon whatever class of objects man has put his artificial stamp, he has at once elevated and ennobled it and transformed it into a servant and benefactor of the race. In a certain sense he has treated himself and society in this objective manner, and exercised a limited control over the moral, intellectual, and social forces. But, as this control can only be successful in proportion as his knowledge of the materials and forces dealt with is complete, his success in this direction has thus far been slight, and his failures numerous.

Civilization is essentially artificial, and by whatever agency we may suppose other objects created or developed, we find that very few of them are adapted to man's purposes until he so adapts them by his own thought and labor. But, as we have seen (*supra*, p. 175), there are not wanting those who deny the power of material civilization to make men happier. They assert that, notwithstanding all these new and convenient arrangements, these gigantic and complicated appliances, these novel and ingenious mechanisms, this lightning communication and almost lightning conveyance; notwithstanding the entire round of busy, nervous existence which science is enabling us to lead and hurrying us through —notwithstanding all this, they claim that man was happier before he had these things, and would be happier if he could return to his former calm, unruffled, and unconventional state; that such things only fire his brain and wear out his system. They admit that it is a fine thing to visit a friend a thousand miles away and return in a week or a fortnight, to receive communications from absent ones even beyond the ocean in a moment of time, to make the tour of the world in a single month. All this they agree is very wonderful, very desirable; but still they say we should be just as well off without it, should live just as long, feel just as well, and enjoy life all the same in other respects, and be spared a thousand excitements and disappointments. In short, they consider contentment the object to be sought, and justly observe that it is best obtained by a quiet, unemotional mode of life (*supra*, p. 175, note).

The answer to all this consists in carrying the argument

to its logical conclusion. Contentment is one thing; happiness quite another. The former results from the want of desire; the latter from its gratification. The one arises from the absence of pain; the other from the presence of pleasure. Contentment is, therefore, negative; happiness positive.

No one would go so far as to maintain that it is better to be without feeling than to experience agreeable feeling. No one denies that this civilization engenders great intensity of feeling. It must, therefore, be shown that more of it is disagreeable than agreeable; that there is more pain than pleasure, before it can be charged with detracting from the happiness of mankind. Such may have been the character of some of the false civilizations of the past when popular ignorance and superstition were combined with royal and sacerdotal supremacy, and worked the oppression and dejection of the many to gratify the pleasures and caprices of the few. But such is not the nature of the civilization which science inspires. On the contrary, it is wholly in the direction of relieving the burdens of men, of substituting mechanical for muscular force, of multiplying conveniences, cheapening and improving commodities, and thus of begetting and gratifying desires. It tends also to enlarge the views, elevate the thoughts, liberalize the sentiments, and extend universal charity and fraternal feeling.

Not only can we appeal to these general facts and considerations, but we can, to a considerable extent, support them by statistics. It has often been demonstrated that the actual casualties which result from the introduction of railway conveyance and travel are much less than those that formerly attended the use of stage-coaches for a given number of persons and a given distance. It is true, more people are injured and killed now than then, but it is because many times as many travel. The only point to be established is, whether in going a certain distance a person is most likely to incur danger by the one or the other conveyance. And the statistics show that in the railroad-car any one is far safer for the journey than in the stage-coach.*

It has recently been shown from reliable data, that there are ten chances of dying on the voyage across the Atlantic in a sailing-vessel to one in a steamship.† This refers to disease only, and does not include the risks of shipwreck, which, considering the greater length of voyage and the greater frailty of sailing-vessels, would probably at least double the danger. It has been proved also that the increase of knowledge respecting the laws of health, of physiology, and of ventilation, since the scientific epoch began, has both greatly diminished the amount of disease among men and increased the average length of human life.‡

* Mr. Charles Francis Adams, Jr., in his work entitled "Notes on Railroad Accidents" (p. 241), says: "During the four years 1875–'78, it will be remembered a single passenger only was killed on the railroads of Massachusetts in consequence of an accident to which he, by his own carelessness, in no way contributed. The average number of persons annually injured, not fatally, during these years was about five; yet during the year 1878, excluding all cases of mere injury, of which no account was made, no less than fifty-three persons came to their deaths in Boston from falling down-stairs, and thirty-seven more from falling out of windows; seven were scalded to death in 1878 alone. In the year 1874, seventeen were killed by being run over by teams in the streets. During the five years, 1874–'78, there were more persons murdered in the city of Boston alone than lost their lives as passengers through the negligence of all the railroad corporations in the whole State of Massachusetts during the nine years 1871–'78; although in these nine years were included both the Revere and the Wollaston disasters, the former of which resulted in the death of twenty-nine and the latter of twenty-one persons."

† See "Monthly Report of the United States Bureau of Statistics," No 19, Original Series (July 10, 1868), p. 14.

‡ See a paper by Dr. Edward Jarvis on the "Political Economy of Health," published in the "Fifth Annual Report of the Massachusetts Board of Health." Statistics collected by Mr. Baldwin Latham "show that, of seven leading towns and districts in England, such as Croydon, Ely, Salisbury, and others, where careful and thorough modes of sewerage prevail, the percentage of death-rates has been reduced from forty to twenty per cent." (From a paper by Dr. Andrew D. White, President of Cornell University, read before the "American Public Health Association" in 1873.) At the "Educational Conference," held in London in 1877, Mr. Thomas Bond, Assistant Surgeon to Westminster Hospital, asserted that on an average one half of the number of out-patients treated

In seeking to comprehend the real extent of the amelio-rative effect of artificial civilization, *i. e.*, of the civilization due to the arts, the problem is obscured by what may be de-nominated *latent amelioration*. This may be more specific-ally defined as progress which does not become perceptible in consequence of movements which it has alone rendered possible. The effect of this law is to increase the *quantity* of progress at the expense of its *degree*. Even this defini-tion, however, requires illustration. This quantitative prog-ress has taken place in two directions: first, toward increasing the number of individuals; and, second, toward increasing the local area occupied.

The fact that increased sagacity, which involves the fun-damental quality of mind that underlies all art, was the sole cause of man's ability to break over the barriers of the en-vironment which restrict all other animals to a circumscribed habitat, and prevent their multiplication beyond a certain degree of density fixed for each species, has been insisted upon, on numerous occasions (vol. i, Chapters VI and VII) as one of the fundamental truths of anthropology and sociol-ogy. This truth also illustrates with great clearness the principle above formulated. Notwithstanding the increased means devised by human sagacity for obtaining food, the human species found itself no better off than the remaining animals. The means of subsistence artificially created were applied to the increase of population hitherto impossible, and want still stared many individuals in the face as before. But in the animal state the mortality was far greater, since, while the reproductive forces were unchecked, and the same number were born as now, the friction of the environment was sufficient perfectly to equilibrate the deaths and births. In the new dynamic condition due to the exercise of a greater brain-power, there is a co-efficient of increase. If the in-

by a hospital surgeon suffer from diseases due primarily to a want of knowl-edge of the laws of health and cleanliness, chiefly in regard to dress, ablution, and ventilation ("Popular Science Monthly," vol. xii, p. 380).

creased means of subsistence could have been wholly applied to a number of survivors, sufficient only to keep the population stationary, the effect must have been to render these comparatively comfortable. But this real progressive effect, in consequence of the increase of population which it alone renders possible, is wholly lost to view, and may appropriately be called latent.

Again, a large amount of potential progress is locked up in migration. Unsatisfied to remain in one spot and enjoy the surplus which intelligent labor and skill compel nature to yield, men have ever been abandoning their mother-settlements, and pushing out into new and untried fields. This has not been accomplished without cost, and this cost has to be deducted from the sum total of enjoyment which the same effort would have yielded if wholly applied to that object.

These two powerful neutralizing influences have accompanied human society from its origin to the present day, and are as forcibly felt in the most advanced communities as they were in the primordial nucleus of society. The highly effective artificial appliances of science and inventive art are only made the means of more rapidly and thoroughly peopling the earth. The great advances made by literary and educational agencies are overslaughed by fresh additions to the illiterate classes of the population. The real progress of the world, which is immense, is being perpetually diluted by quantitative increments, leaving the apparent condition of society unchanged. As the world is now constituted, it requires constant renewals of the progressive impulses to maintain the stationary condition. Let science for a moment withdraw its daily re-enforcements, let popular education be relaxed for a single year, and the complicated machinery of civilization must come to a stop and social degeneracy set in.*

* The "hard times" occasioned by the financial crisis of 1873 produced a reaction in the States of Maine and Texas, which resulted in the repeal of an important part of the salutary educational legislation of those States, and the

364

The prevalent overweening faith in the necessary stability of the social system is unfounded. Renewed efforts at every moment, and the constant creation of new propelling agencies, are all that sustain it.

It is from this point of view, however, that the real influence of the four great progressive agencies—language, literature, art, and science—can best be appreciated, and the fallacy of the superiority of the natural to the artificial can most easily be exposed. The withdrawal of these influences, even now, would be followed by the rapid dwindling of the human race to a few sparse denizens of the earth, and their contraction within certain restricted territorial boundaries such as limit the various faunas of the globe.

PROGRESS.—PRIMARY MEANS.

It was doubtless this anomaly which prompted Kant to make the bold proposition to establish a science of *pure morals.** This proposition has not been responded to, however, and we can not be said to have any moral science yet.† But against the superficial treatment of the social phenomena there has been a strong reaction, and the principles of pure sociology have been in a great measure formulated. Like all reactions, however, this one has carried its advocates too far. In their intense sense of the lack of data and of laws, they have forgotten that these, when secured, are properly but the means to the same end which their opponents are vainly seeking to attain without them. And thus we have the singular spectacle presented in the field of social science of one class applying erroneous principles in ignorance of true ones, while insisting that this is all of social science; and another class collecting data and formulating laws while declaring that this constitutes the only true method of sociology. The one class insists that there can be no pure social science, the other that there can be no applied social science.

In one sense natural economic laws can not be controlled,

---

* " Kritik der reinen Vernunft," S. 340, 533.

† Mr. Spencer's " Data of Ethics," which has appeared since this was written, goes far to supply the want here designated, in pointing out clearly for the first time that morals, as popularly understood, consist of mere rules for healing a diseased condition. His " Absolute Ethics " must be regarded as the basis of the pure science.

i. e., they can not be arbitrarily created or destroyed; their essential nature can not be changed. In these respects, as in all others, they are identical with the physical, or mechanical, laws with which inventors have to deal. But in another sense the former as well as the latter can be controlled, *i. e.*, they can be guided by means of artificial devices into channels which they would not otherwise take, and made to expend themselves upon other objects than those upon which they would naturally expend themselves; they may be distributed, or divided into any number of parts, and thus diminished in their intensity or practically destroyed; or they may be condensed or intensified to any required degree. In short, whatever dispositions may be made of other natural forces by man and under the influence of intellectual insight, may in like manner be made of the social forces. Therefore, if government could be in the hands of social scientists instead of social empiricists, it might be elevated to the rank of an applied science, or the simple application of the scientific principles of social phenomena.

As a scientific investigator, the legislator would then set for himself the task of devising means to render harmless those forces now seen to be working evil results, and to render useful those now running to waste. Not only would the present prohibitive legislation, which seeks to accomplish its ends by the direct, or brute, method, be rapidly supplanted by attractive legislation accomplishing its purposes by the indirect, or intellectual, method, and thus fulfilling the protective functions of government at a saving of enormous loss through the friction of opposition, but the accommodative function would now be in condition to advance toward the position of a truly ameliorative one. Society, possessed for the first time of a completely integrated consciousness, could at last proceed to map out a field of independent operation for the systematic realization of its own interests, in the same manner that an intelligent and keen-sighted individual pursues his life-purposes. Not only would protection and

64

accommodation be secured without loss of liberty and at the least possible cost to society, but directly progressive measures would be adopted looking to the organization of human happiness. Fully realizing the character and mode of operation of the truly progressive agencies of society, government would not simply foster and protect these, but would increase and intensify them and their influence. No longer doubting that progress upon the whole must be in proportion to the degree and universality of intelligence, no effort or expense would be spared to impart to every citizen an equal and adequate amount of useful knowledge.

Briefly to formulate the underlying principles of this discussion, we may add in conclusion that, strictly speaking, no influence can be progressive which is not in itself a true art. Existing government, though artificial, is not itself an art. It can not, therefore, become a progressive institution until there are impressed upon it the marks which distinguish a true art. The arts are not merely conservative, but creative. They not only preserve, but produce. They do not leave matters where they find them, but carry them a stage higher. Conservative institutions, such as actual government, like the disturbances of the atmosphere or the tides of the ocean, after having gone through a cycle of changes, return to the same conditions as before they began. In creative institutions, such as are the inventive arts, the rhythm is an advancing one. By however little, the flood exceeds the ebb, and society moves. They are dynamical, not statical forces.

Moreover, whatever is not progressive must be retrogressive. There is no such thing as absolute rest. Conservative institutions, from their very nature, impose restraints upon progress. Conservation implies limitation. The forcible curbing of the centrifugal tendencies of progressive institutions involves great loss through friction, and this loss, however necessary to the existence of such institutions, is, considered in itself, an expense to progress.

367

Although her formal education was in the humanities, Ruth Benedict (1887-1948) was one of the pioneers of modern American cultural anthropology. Her work *Patterns of Culture*, first published in 1934, has become a classic introduction to this fascinating branch of the social sciences.

III

The Integration of Culture

THE diversity of cultures can be endlessly documented. A field of human behaviour may be ignored in some societies until it barely exists; it may even be in some cases unimagined. Or it may almost monopolize the whole organized behaviour of the society, and the most alien situations be manipulated only in its terms. Traits having no intrinsic relation one with the other, and historically independent, merge and become inextricable, providing the occasion for behaviour that has no counterpart in regions that do not make these identifications. It is a corollary of this that standards, no matter in what aspect of behaviour, range in different cultures from the positive to the negative pole. We might suppose that in the matter of taking life all peoples would agree in condemnation. On the contrary, in a matter of homicide, it may be held that one is blameless if diplomatic relations have been severed between neighbouring countries, or that one kills by custom his first two children, or that a husband has right of life and death over his wife, or that it is the duty of the child to kill his parents before they are old. It may be that those are killed who steal a fowl, or who cut their upper teeth first, or who are born on a Wednesday. Among some peoples a person suffers torments at having caused an accidental death; among others it is a matter of no conse-

From *Patterns of Culture* by Ruth Benedict. c.1934 by Ruth Benedict, c.renewed 1962 by Ruth Valentine. Reprinted by permission of Houghton Mifflin Co.

quence. Suicide also may be a light matter, the recourse of anyone who has suffered some slight rebuff, an act that occurs constantly in a tribe. It may be the highest and noblest act a wise man can perform. The very tale of it, on the other hand, may be a matter for incredulous mirth, and the act itself impossible to conceive as a human possibility. Or it may be a crime punishable by law, or regarded as a sin against the gods.

The diversity of custom in the world is not, however, a matter which we can only helplessly chronicle. Self-torture here, head-hunting there, prenuptial chastity in one tribe and adolescent licence in another, are not a list of unrelated facts, each of them to be greeted with surprise wherever it is found or wherever it is absent. The tabus on killing oneself or another, similarly, though they relate to no absolute standard, are not therefore fortuitous. The significance of cultural behaviour is not exhausted when we have clearly understood that it is local and man-made and hugely variable. It tends also to be integrated. A culture, like an individual, is a more or less consistent pattern of thought and action. Within each culture there come into being characteristic purposes not necessarily shared by other types of society. In obedience to these purposes, each people further and further consolidates its experience, and in proportion to the urgency of these drives the heterogeneous items of behaviour take more and more congruous shape. Taken up by a well-integrated culture, the most ill-assorted acts become characteristic of its peculiar goals, often by the most unlikely metamorphoses. The form that these acts take we can understand only by understanding first the emotional and intellectual mainsprings of that society.

Such patterning of culture cannot be ignored as if it

VII

The Nature of Society

THE three cultures of Zuñi, of Dobu, and of the Kwakiutl are not merely heterogeneous assortments of acts and beliefs. They have each certain goals toward which their behaviour is directed and which their institutions further. They differ from one another not only because one trait is present here and absent there, and because another trait is found in two regions in two different forms. They differ still more because they are oriented as wholes in different directions. They are travelling along different roads in pursuit of different ends, and these ends and these means in one society cannot be judged in terms of those of another society, because essentially they are incommensurable.

All cultures, of course, have not shaped their thousand items of behaviour to a balanced and rhythmic pattern. Like certain individuals, certain social orders do not subordinate activities to a ruling motivation. They scatter. If at one moment they seem to be pursuing certain ends, at another they are off on some tangent apparently inconsistent with all that has gone before, which gives no clue to activity that will come after.

This lack of integration seems to be as characteristic of certain cultures as extreme integration is of others. It is not everywhere due to the same circumstances. Tribes like those of the interior of British Columbia have incorporated traits from all the surrounding civilizations. They have taken their patterns for the manipulation of wealth from one culture area, parts of their religious practices from another, contradictory bits from still another. Their mythology is a hodge-podge of unco-ordinated accounts of culture heroes out of three different myth-cycles represented in areas around them. Yet in spite of such extreme hospitality to the institutions of others, their culture gives an impression of extreme poverty. Nothing is carried far enough to give body to the culture. Their social organization is little elaborated, their ceremonial is poorer than that in almost any other region of the world, their basketry and beading techniques give only a limited scope for activity in plastic arts. Like certain individuals who have been indiscriminately influenced in many different directions, their tribal patterns of behaviour are unco-ordinated and casual.

In these tribes of British Columbia the lack of integration appears to be more than a mere simultaneous presence of traits collected from different surrounding peoples. It seems to go deeper than that. Each facet of life has its own organization, but it does not spread to any other. At puberty great attention is paid to the magical education of children for the various professions and the acquisition of guardian spirits. On the western plains this vision practice saturates the whole complex of adult life, and the professions of hunting and warfare are dominated by correlated beliefs. But in British Columbia the vision quest is one organized activity and warfare is quite another. Similarly feasts and dances in British Columbia are strictly social. They are festive occasions at which the performers mimic animals for the amusement of the spectators. But it is strictly tabu to imitate animals who are counted as possible guardian spirits. The feasts do not have religious significance nor do they serve as opportunities for economic exchange. Every activity is segregated, as it were. It forms a complex of its own, and its motivations and goals are proper to its own limited field and are not extended to the whole life of the people. Nor does any characteristic psychological response appear to have arisen to dominate the culture as a whole.

It is not always possible to separate lack of cultural integration of this sort from that which is due more directly to exposure to contradictory influences. Lack of integration of this latter type occurs often on the borders of well-defined culture areas. These marginal regions are removed from close contact with the most characteristic tribes of their culture and are exposed to strong outside influences. As a result they may very often incorporate into their social organization or their art techniques most contradictory procedures. Sometimes they refashion the inharmonious material into a new harmony, achieving a result essentially unlike that of any of the well-established cultures with which they share so many items of behaviour. It may be that if we knew the past history of these cultures, we should see that, given a sufficient period of years, disharmonious borrowings tend to achieve harmony. Certainly in many cases they do. But in the cross-section of contemporary primitive cultures which is all that we can be sure of understanding, many marginal areas are conspicuous for apparent dissonance.

Other historical circumstances are responsible in other cases for a lack of integration in certain cultures. It is not only the marginal tribe whose culture may be uncoordinated, but the tribe that breaks off from its fellows and takes up its position in an area of different civilization.

In such cases the conflict that is most apparent is between the new influences brought to bear upon the people of the tribe and what we may call their indigenous behaviour. The same situation occurs also to a people who have stayed at home, when a tribe with either great prestige or great numbers is able to introduce major changes in an area to which they have newly come.

An intimate and understanding study of a genuinely disoriented culture would be of extraordinary interest. Probably the nature of the specific conflicts or of the facile hospitality to new influences would prove more important than any blanket characterizations of 'lack of integration,' but what such characterizations would be we cannot guess. Probably in even the most disoriented cultures it would be necessary to take account of accommodations that tend to rule out disharmonious elements and establish selected elements more securely. The process might even be the more apparent for the diversity of material upon which it operated.

THE NATURE OF SOCIETY

Facile generalizations about the integration of culture are most dangerous in field-work. When one is mastering the language and all the idiosyncrasies of behaviour of an esoteric culture, preoccupation with its configuration may well be an obstacle to a genuine understanding. The field-worker must be faithfully objective. He must chronicle all the relevant behaviour, taking care not to select according to any challenging hypothesis the facts that will fit a thesis. None of the peoples we have discussed in this volume were studied in the field with any preconception of a consistent type of behaviour which that culture illustrated. The ethnology was set down as it came, with no attempt to make it self-consistent. The total pictures are therefore much more convincing to the student. In theoretical discussions of culture, also, generalizations about the integration of culture will be empty in proportion as they are dogmatic and universalized. We need detailed information about contrasting limits of behaviour and the motivations that are dynamic in one society and not in another. We do not need a plank of configuration written into the platform of an ethnological school. On the other hand, the contrasted goods which different cultures pursue, the different intentions which are at the basis of their institutions, are essential to the understanding both of different social orders and of individual psychology.

The relation of cultural integration to studies of Western civilization and hence to sociological theory is easily misunderstood. Our own society is often pictured as an extreme example of lack of integration. Its huge complexity and rapid changes from generation to generation make inevitable a lack of harmony between its elements that does not occur in simpler societies. The lack of integration is exaggerated and misinterpreted, however, in

375

most studies because of a simple technical error. Primitive society is integrated in geographical units. Western civilization, however, is stratified, and different social groups of the same time and place live by quite different standards and are actuated by different motivations.

The effort to apply the anthropological culture area in modern sociology can only be fruitful to a very limited degree because different ways of living are today not primarily a matter of spatial distribution. There is a tendency among sociologists to waste time over the 'culture area concept.' There is properly no such 'concept.' When traits group themselves geographically, they must be handled geographically. When they do not, it is idle to make a principle out of what is at best a loose empirical category. In our civilization there is, in the anthropological sense, a uniform cosmopolitan culture that can be found in any part of the globe, but there is likewise unprecedented divergence between the labouring class and the Four Hundred, between those groups whose life centres in the church and those whose life centres on the race-track. The comparative freedom of choice in modern society makes possible important voluntary groups which stand for as different principles as the Rotary Clubs and Greenwich Village. The nature of the cultural processes is not changed with these modern conditions, but the unit in which they can be studied is no longer the local group.

The integration of culture has important sociological consequences and impinges upon several moot questions of sociology and social psychology. The first of these is the controversy over whether or not society is an organism. Most modern sociologists and social psychologists have argued elaborately that society is not and never can be anything over and above the individual minds that compose it. As part of their exposition they have vigorously attacked the 'group fallacy,' the interpretation which, they feel, would make thinking and acting a function of some mythical entity, the group. On the other hand, those who have dealt with diverse cultures, where the material shows plainly enough that all the laws of individual psychology are inadequate to explain the facts, have often expressed themselves in mystical phraseology. Like Durkheim they have cried, 'The individual does not exist,' or like Kroeber they have called in a force he calls the superorganic to account for the cultural process.

This is largely a verbal quarrel. No one of the so-called organicists really believes in any other order of mind than the minds of the individuals in the culture, and on the other hand even such a vigorous critic of the group-fallacy as Allport admits the necessity of the scientific study of groups, 'the province of the special science of sociology.' The argument between those who have thought it necessary to conceive of the group as more than the sum of its individuals and those who have not has been largely between students handling different kinds of data. Durkheim, starting from an early familiarity with the diversity of cultures and especially with the culture of Australia, reiterated, often in vague phraseology, the necessity of studies of culture. Sociologists, on the other hand, dealing rather with our own standardized culture, have attempted to demolish a methodology the need for which simply did not occur in their work.

It is obvious that the sum of all the individuals in Zuñi make up a culture beyond and above what those individuals have willed and created. The group is fed by tradition; it is 'time-binding.' It is quite justifiable to call it an organic whole. It is a necessary consequence of the animism embedded in our language that we speak of such a group as choosing its ends and having specific purposes; it should not be held against the student as an evidence of a mystic philosophy. These group phenomena must be studied if we are to understand the history of human behaviour, and individual psychology cannot of itself account for the facts with which we are confronted.

In all studies of social custom, the crux of the matter is that the behaviour under consideration must pass through the needle's eye of social acceptance, and only history in its widest sense can give an account of these social acceptances and rejections. It is not merely psychology that is in question, it is also history, and history is by no means a set of facts that can be discovered by introspection. Therefore those explanations of custom which derive our economic scheme from human competitiveness, modern war from human combativeness, and all the rest of the ready explanations that we meet in every magazine and modern volume, have for the anthropologist a hollow ring. Rivers was one of the first to phrase the issue vigorously. He pointed out that instead of trying to understand the blood feud from vengeance, it was necessary rather to understand vengeance from the institution of the blood feud. In the same way it is necessary to study jealousy from its conditioning by local sexual regulations and property institutions.

The difficulty with naïve interpretations of culture in terms of individual behaviour is not that these interpretations are those of psychology, but that they ignore history and the historical process of acceptance or rejection of traits. Any configurational interpretation of cultures also is an exposition in terms of individual psychology, but it depends upon history as well as upon psychology. It

378

holds that Dionysian behaviour is stressed in the institutions of certain cultures because it is a permanent possibility in individual psychology, but that it is stressed in certain cultures and not in others because of historical events that have in one place fostered its development and in others have ruled it out. At different points in the interpretation of cultural forms, both history and psychology are necessary; one cannot make the one do the service of the other.

This brings us to one of the most hotly debated of all the controversies which impinge upon configurational anthropology. This is the conflict as to the biological bases of social phenomena. I have spoken as if human temperament were fairly constant in the world, as if in every society a roughly similar distribution were potentially available, and as if the culture selected from these according to its traditional patterns and moulded the vast majority of individuals into conformity. Trance experience, for example, according to this interpretation, is a potentiality of a certain number of individuals in any population. When it is honoured and rewarded, a considerable proportion will achieve or simulate it, but in our civilization where it is a blot on the family escutcheon the number will dwindle and those individuals be classified with the abnormal.

But there is also another possible interpretation. It has been vigorously contended that traits are not culturally selected but biologically transmitted. According to this interpretation the distinction is racial, and the Plains Indians seek visions because this necessity is transmitted in the chromosomes of the race. Similarly, the Pueblo cultures pursue sobriety and moderation because such conduct is determined by their racial heredity. If the biological interpretation is true, it is not to history that we need to go to understand the behaviour of groups, but to physiology.

This biological interpretation, however, has never been given a firm scientific basis. In order to prove their point it would be necessary for those who hold this view to show physiological facts that account for even a small part of the social phenomena it is necessary to understand. It is possible that basal metabolism or the functioning of the ductless glands may differ significantly in different human groups and that such facts might give us insight into differences in cultural behaviour. It is not an anthropological problem, but when the physiologists and the geneticists have provided the material it may be of value to the students of cultural history.

The physiological correlations that the biologist may provide in the future, however, so far as they concern hereditary transmission of traits, cannot, at their best, cover all the facts as we know them. The North American Indians are biologically of one race, yet they are not all Dionysian in cultural behaviour. Zuñi is an extreme example of diametrically opposed motivations, and this Apollonian culture is shared by the other Pueblos, one group of which, the Hopi, are of the Shoshonean subgroup, a group which is widely represented among Dionysian tribes and to which the Aztec are said to be linguistically related. Another Pueblo group is the Tewa, closely related biologically and linguistically to the non-Pueblo Kiowa of the southern plains. Cultural configurations, therefore, are local and do not correlate with known relationships of the various groups. In the same way there is no biological unity in the western plains that sets these vision-seeking peoples off from other groups. The tribes who inhabit this region are drawn from the widespread Algonkian, Athabascan, and Siouan families, and each still retains the speech of their particular stock.[1] All these stocks include tribes who seek visions after the Plains fashion and tribes who do not. Only those who live within the geographical limits of the plains seek visions as an essential part of the equipment of every normal able-bodied man.

The environmental explanation is still more imperative, when instead of considering distribution in space, we turn to distribution in time. The most radical changes in psychological behaviour have taken place in groups whose biological constitution has not appreciably altered. This can be abundantly illustrated from our own cultural background. European civilization was as prone to mystic behaviour, to epidemics of psychic phenomena, in the Middle Ages, as it was in the nineteenth century to the most hard-headed materialism. The culture has changed its bias without a corresponding change in the racial constitution of the group.

Cultural interpretations of behaviour need never deny that a physiological element is also involved. Such a denial is based on a misunderstanding of scientific explanations. Biology does not deny chemistry, though chemistry is inadequate to explain biological phenomena. Nor is biology obliged to work according to chemical formulæ because it recognizes that the laws of chemistry underlie the facts it analyzes. In every field of science it is necessary to stress the laws and sequences that most adequately explain the situations under observation and nevertheless to insist that other elements are present, though they can be shown not to have had crucial importance in the final result. To

[1] The linguistic groupings in these cases correlate with biological relationship.

point out, therefore, that the biological bases of cultural behaviour in mankind are for the most part irrelevant is not to deny that they are present. It is merely to stress the fact that the historical factors are dynamic.

Experimental psychology has been forced to a similar emphasis even in studies dealing with our own culture. Recent important experiments dealing with personality traits have shown that social determinants are crucial even in the traits of honesty and leadership. Honesty in one experimental situation gave almost no indication whether the child would cheat in another. There turned out to be not honest-dishonest persons, but honest-dishonest situations. In the same way in the study of leaders there proved to be no uniform traits that could be set down as standard even in our own society. The rôle developed the leader, and his qualities were those that the situation emphasized. In these 'situational' results it has become more and more evident that social conduct even in a selected society is 'not simply the expression of a fixed mechanism that predetermines to a specific mode of conduct, but rather a set of tendencies aroused in variable ways by the specific problem that confronts us.'

When these situations that even in one society are dynamic in human behaviour are magnified into contrasts between cultures opposed to one another in goals and motivations to such a degree as Zuñi and the Kwakiutl, for instance, the conclusion is inescapable. If we are interested in human behaviour, we need first of all to understand the institutions that are provided in any society. For human behaviour will take the forms those institutions suggest, even to extremes of which the observer, deep-dyed in the culture of which he is a part, can have no intimation.

This observer will see the bizarre developments of behaviour only in alien cultures, not in his own. Nevertheless this is obviously a local and temporary bias. There is no reason to suppose that any one culture has seized upon an eternal sanity and will stand in history as a solitary solution of the human problem. Even the next generation knows better. Our only scientific course is to consider our own culture, so far as we are able, as one example among innumerable others of the variant configurations of human culture.

The cultural pattern of any civilization makes use of a certain segment of the great arc of potential human purposes and motivations, just as we have seen in an earlier chapter that any culture makes use of certain selected material techniques or cultural traits. The great arc along which all the possible human behaviours are distributed is far too immense and too full of contradictions for any one culture to utilize even any considerable portion of it. Selection is the first requirement. Without selection no culture could even achieve intelligibility, and the intentions it selects and makes its own are a much more important matter than the particular detail of technology or the marriage formality that it also selects in similar fashion.

THE NATURE OF SOCIETY

Or this one:

She pretends to be indifferent, not to love me, my true love, my
  dear.
My dear, you go too far, your good name is going down, my
  dear.
Friends, do not let us listen any longer to love songs that are
  sung by those who are out of sight.
Friends, it might be well if I took a new true love, a dear one.
I hope she will hear my love song when I cry to my new love,
  my dear one.

It is evident that grief turns easily into shame, but grief
nevertheless in certain limited situations is allowed expression. In the intimacies of Kwakiutl family life, also,
there is opportunity for the expression of warm affection
and the easy give-and-take of cheerful human relations.
Not all situations in Kwakiutl existence require equally
the motives that are most characteristic of their lives.

In Western civilization, as in Kwakiutl life, not all
aspects of life serve equally the will to power which is so
conspicuous in modern life. In Dobu and Zuñi, however,
it is not so easy to see what aspects of life are touched
lightly by their configurations. This may be due to the
nature of the cultural pattern, or it may be due to a genius
for consistency. At the present time it is not possible to
decide.

There is a sociological fact that must be taken into account in any understanding of cultural integration. This
is the significance of diffusion. A vast body of anthropological work has been devoted to plumbing the facts of
human imitativeness. The extent of the primitive areas
over which traits have diffused is one of the most startling
facts of anthropology. Traits of costume, of techniques,
of a ceremonial, of mythology, of economic exchange at

384

marriage, are spread over whole continents, and every tribe on one continent will often possess the trait in some form. Nevertheless, certain regions in these great areas have impressed distinctive goals and motivations upon this raw material. The Pueblos use the methods of agriculture, the magic devices, the widespread myths that belong to great sections of North America. An Apollonian culture on another continent would necessarily work with other raw material. The two cultures would have in common the direction in which they had modified the raw material that was available on each continent, but the available traits would be dissimilar. Comparable configurations in different parts of the world will therefore inevitably have different content. We can understand the direction in which Pueblo culture has moved by comparing it with other North American cultures, those which share the same elements but which use them in a different fashion. In a similar way we can best understand the Apollonian stress in Greek civilization by studying it in its local setting among the cultures of the eastern Mediterranean. Any clear understanding of the processes of cultural integration must take its point of departure from a knowledge of the facts of diffusion.

A recognition of these processes of integration, on the other hand, gives a quite different picture of the nature of widespread traits. The usual topical studies of marriage, or of initiation, or of religion, assume that each trait is a special area of behaviour which has generated its own motivations. Westermarck explains marriage as a situation of sex preference, and the usual interpretation of initiation procedures is that they are the result of puberty upheavals. Therefore all their thousand modifications are facts in a single series, and only ring the changes upon some one impulse or necessity that is implicit in the generic situation.

Very few cultures handle their great occasions in any such simple fashion. These occasions, whether of marriage or death or the invocation of the supernatural, are situations that each society seizes upon to express its characteristic purposes. The motivations that dominate it do not come into existence in the particular selected situation, but are impressed upon it by the general character of the culture. Marriage may have no reference to mating preferences, which are provided for in other ways, but accumulation of wives may be the current version of the accumulation of wealth. Economic practices may depart so far from their primary rôle of providing necessaries of food and clothing that all agricultural techniques may be directed toward piling up in lavish display many times the necessary food supply of the people and allowing it to rot ostentatiously for pride's sake.

The difficulty of understanding from the nature of the occasion even comparatively simple cultural responses has been clear over and over again in the description of the three cultures we have selected. Mourning, in terms of its occasion, is a grief or relief reaction to a loss situation. It happens that no one of the three cultures makes this type of response to its mourning institutions. The Pueblos come closest in that their rites treat the death of a relative as one of the important emergencies when society marshals its forces to put discomfort out of the way. Though grief is hardly institutionalized in their procedures, they recognize the loss situation as an emergency which it is necessary to minimize. Among the Kwakiutl, regardless of whether or not there may also be genuine sorrow, mourning institutions are special instances of a cultural paranoia

386

according to which they regard themselves as shamed by the death of their relatives and rouse themselves to get even. In Dobu the mourning institutions have much in common, but primarily they are punishments inflicted by the blood kin upon the spouse for having caused the death of one of their number. That is, the mourning institutions are again one of numberless occasions which Dobu interprets as treachery, and handles by selecting a victim whom it may punish.

It is an extraordinarily simple matter for tradition to take any occasion that the environment or the life-cycle provides and use it to channel purposes generically unrelated. The particular character of the event may figure so slightly that the death of a child from mumps involves the killing of a completely unimplicated person. Or a girl's first menstruation involves the redistribution of practically all the property of a tribe. Mourning, or marriage, or puberty rites, or economics are not special items of human behaviour, each with their own generic drives and motivations which have determined their past history and will determine their future, but certain occasions which any society may seize upon to express its important cultural intentions.

The significant sociological unit, from this point of view, therefore, is not the institution but the cultural configuration. The studies of the family, of primitive economics, or of moral ideas need to be broken up into studies that emphasize the different configurations that in instance after instance have dominated these traits. The peculiar nature of Kwakiutl life can never be clear in a discussion which singles out the family for discussion and derives Kwakiutl behaviour at marriage from the marriage situation. Similarly, marriage in our own civilization is a situation which can never be made clear as a mere variant on mating and domesticity. Without the clue that in our civilization at large man's paramount aim is to amass private possessions and multiply occasions of display, the modern position of the wife and the modern emotions of jealousy are alike unintelligible. Our attitudes toward our children are equally evidences of this same cultural goal. Our children are not individuals whose rights and tastes are casually respected from infancy, as they are in some primitive societies, but special responsibilities, like our possessions, to which we succumb or in which we glory, as the case may be. They are fundamentally extensions of our own egos and give a special opportunity for the display of authority. The pattern is not inherent in the parent-children situation, as we so glibly assume. It is impressed upon the situation by the major drives of our culture, and it is only one of the occasions in which we follow our traditional obsessions.

As we become increasingly culture-conscious, we shall be able to isolate the tiny core that is generic in a situation and the vast accretions that are local and cultural and man-made. The fact that these accretions are not inevitable consequences of the situation as such does not make them easier to change or less important in our behaviour. Indeed they are probably harder to change than we have realized. Detailed changes in the mother's nursery behaviour, for instance, may well be inadequate to save a neurotic child when he is trapped in a repugnant situation which is reinforced by every contact he makes and which will extend past his mother to his school and his business and his wife. The whole course of life which is presented to him emphasizes rivalry and ownership. Probably the child's way out lies through luck or detachment. In any case, the solution of the problem might well place less emphasis upon the difficulties inherent in the parent-child situation and more upon the forms taken in Western behaviour by ego-extension and the exploiting of personal relations.

The problem of social value is intimately involved in the fact of the different patternings of cultures. Discussions of social value have usually been content to characterize certain human traits as desirable and to indicate a social goal that would involve these virtues. Certainly, it is said, exploitation of others in personal relations and overweening claims of the ego are bad whereas absorption in group activities is good; a temper is good that seeks satisfaction neither in sadism nor in masochism and is willing to live and let live. A social order, however, which like Zuñi standardizes this 'good' is far from Utopian. It manifests likewise the defects of its virtues. It has no place, for instance, for dispositions we are accustomed to value highly, such as force of will or personal initiative or the disposition to take up arms against a sea of troubles. It is incorrigibly mild. The group activity that fills existence in Zuñi is out of touch with human life — with birth, love, death, success, failure, and prestige. A ritual pageant serves their purpose and minimizes more human interests. The freedom from any forms of social exploitation or of social sadism appears on the other side of the coin as endless ceremonialism not designed to serve major ends of human existence. It is the old inescapable fact that every upper has its lower, every right side its left.

The complexity of the problem of social values is exceptionally clear in Kwakiutl culture. The chief motive that the institutions of the Kwakiutl rely upon and which they share in great measure with modern society is the motive of rivalry. Rivalry is a struggle that is not centred upon the real objects of the activity but upon outdoing a competitor. The attention is no longer directed toward providing adequately for a family or toward owning goods that can be utilized or enjoyed, but toward outdistancing one's neighbours and owning more than anyone else. Everything else is lost sight of in the one great aim of victory. Rivalry does not, like competition, keep its eyes upon the original activity; whether making a basket or selling shoes, it creates an artificial situation: the game of showing that one can win out over others.

Rivalry is notoriously wasteful. It ranks low in the scale of human values. It is a tyranny from which, once it is encouraged in any culture, no man may free himself. The wish for superiority is gargantuan; it can never be satisfied. The contest goes on forever. The more goods the community accumulates, the greater the counters with which men play, but the game is as far from being won as it was when the stakes were small. In Kwakiutl institutions, such rivalry reaches its final absurdity in equating investment with wholesale destruction of goods. They contest for superiority chiefly in accumulation of goods, but often also, and without a consciousness of the contrast, in breaking in pieces their highest units of value, their coppers, and in making bonfires of their house-planks, their blankets and canoes. The social waste is obvious. It is just as obvious in the obsessive rivalry of *Middletown* where houses are built and clothing bought and entertainments attended that each family may prove that it has not been left out of the game.

It is an unattractive picture. In Kwakiutl life the rivalry is carried out in such a way that all success must be built upon the ruin of rivals; in *Middletown* in such a way that individual choices and direct satisfactions are reduced to a minimum and conformity is sought beyond all other human gratifications. In both cases it is clear that wealth is not sought and valued for its direct satisfaction of human needs but as a series of counters in the game of rivalry. If the will to victory were eliminated from the economic life, as it is in Zuñi, distribution and consumption of wealth would follow quite different 'laws.'

Nevertheless, as we can see in Kwakiutl society and in the rugged individualism of American pioneer life, the pursuit of victory can give vigor and zest to human existence. Kwakiutl life is rich and forceful in its own terms. Its chosen goal has its appropriate virtues, and social values in Kwakiutl civilization are even more inextricably mixed than they are in Zuñi. Whatever the social orientation, a society which exemplifies it vigorously will develop certain virtues that are natural to the goals it has chosen, and it is most unlikely that even the best society will be able to stress in one social order all the virtues we prize in human life. Utopia cannot be achieved as a final and perfect structure within which human life will reach a faultless flowering. Utopias of this sort should be recognized as pure day-dreaming. Real improvements in the social order depend upon more modest and more difficult discriminations. It is possible to scrutinize different institutions and cast up their cost in terms of social capital, in terms of the less desirable behaviour traits they stimulate, and in terms of human suffering and frustration. If any society wishes to pay that cost for its chosen and congenial traits, certain values will develop within this pattern, however 'bad' it may be. But the risk is great, and the social order may not be able to pay the price. It may break down beneath them with all the consequent wanton waste of revolution and economic and emotional disaster. In modern society this problem is the most pressing this generation has to face, and those who are obsessed with it too often imagine that an economic reorganization will give the world a Utopia out of their day-dreams, forgetting that no social order can separate its virtues from the defects of its virtues. There is no royal road to a real Utopia.

There is, however, one difficult exercise to which we may accustom ourselves as we become increasingly culture-conscious. We may train ourselves to pass judgment upon the dominant traits of our own civilization. It is difficult enough for anyone brought up under their power to recognize them. It is still more difficult to discount, upon necessity, our predilection for them. They are as familiar as an old loved homestead. Any world in which they do not appear seems to us cheerless and untenable. Yet it is these very traits which by the operation of a fundamental cultural process are most often carried to extremes. They overreach themselves, and more than any other traits they are likely to get out of hand. Just at the very point where there is greatest likelihood of the need of criticism, we are bound to be least critical. Revision comes, but it comes by way of revolution or of breakdown. The possibility of orderly progress is shut off because the generation in question could not make any appraisal of its overgrown institutions. It could not cast them up in terms of profit and loss because it had lost its power to look at them objectively. The situation had to reach a breaking-point before relief was possible.

Appraisal of our own dominant traits has so far waited till the trait in question was no longer a living issue. Religion was not objectively discussed till it was no longer the cultural trait to which our civilization was most deeply committed. Now for the first time the comparative study of religions is free to pursue any point at issue. It is not yet possible to discuss capitalism in the same way, and during wartime, warfare and the problems of international relations are similarly tabu. Yet the dominant traits of our civilization need special scrutiny. We need to realize that they are compulsive, not in proportion as they are basic and essential in human behaviour, but rather in the degree to which they are local and overgrown in our own culture. The one way of life which the Dobuan regards as basic in human nature is one that is fundamentally treacherous and safeguarded with morbid fears. The Kwakiutl similarly cannot see life except as a series of rivalry situations, wherein success is measured by the humiliation of one's fellows. Their belief is based on the importance of these modes of life in their civilizations. But the importance of an institution in a culture gives no direct indication of its usefulness or its inevitability. The argument is suspect, and any cultural control which we may be able to exercise will depend upon the degree to which we can evaluate objectively the favoured and passionately fostered traits of our Western civilization.

9

Henrik Ibsen,   AN ENEMY OF THE PEOPLE

1. Analyze the social and political structure of the
    town and decide which characters represent the
    various parts.

2. What pressures are exerted on Thomas Stockmann to
    conceal the truth about the battles? Which is the
    most difficult for him to resist? What is his con-
    clusion? Do you agree or disagree?

3. Do you agree with Stockmann's last great discovery:
    "that the strongest man in the world is the one
    who stands most alone"?

4. What seems to be Ibsen's opinion of modern democ-
    racy?

5. Is Thomas Stockmann an unblemished hero or does he
    display weaknesses and make mistakes that contrib-
    ute to his predicament?

6. Imagine a similar situation in your hometown, and
    speculate on the behavior of its citizens.

        Norwegian-born Henrik Ibsen (1828-1906) earned
for himself the epithet "Colossus of the North" as he
changed the course of modern drama. Because of the
realism of characterization and the relevance of the
dramatic situations, his plays have enjoyed a continuing popularity and critical acclaim. *An Enemy of the
People*, written in 1882, portrays man in conflict with
society.

AN ENEMY OF THE PEOPLE

DRAMATIS PERSONÆ

Dr. Thomas Stockmann, Medical Officer of the Municipal Baths.
Mrs. Stockmann, his wife.
Petra, their daughter, a teacher.
Ejlif
Morten } their sons (aged 13 and 10 respectively).
Peter Stockmann, the Doctor's elder brother; Mayor of the Town and Chief Constable, Chairman of the Baths' Committee, etc., etc.
Morten Kiil, a tanner (Mrs. Stockmann's adoptive father).
Hovstad, editor of the "People's Messenger."
Billing, sub-editor.
Captain Horster.
Aslaksen, a printer.
Men of various conditions and occupations, some few women, and a troop of schoolboys—the audience at a public meeting.

The action takes place in a coast town in southern Norway.

ACT I

(SCENE.—DR. STOCKMANN'S *sitting-room. It is evening. The room is plainly but neatly appointed and furnished. In the right-hand wall are two doors; the farther leads out to the hall, the nearer to the doctor's study. In the left-hand wall, opposite the door leading to the hall, is a door leading to the other rooms occupied by the family. In the middle of the same wall stands the stove, and, further forward, a couch with a looking-glass hanging over it and an oval table in front of it. On the table, a lighted lamp, with a lampshade. At the back of the room, an open door leads to the dining-room.* BILLING *is seen sitting at the dining table, on which a lamp is burning. He has a napkin tucked under his chin, and* MRS. STOCKMANN *is standing by the table handing him a large plate-full of roast beef. The other places at the table are empty, and the table somewhat in disorder, a meal having evidently recently been finished.*)

MRS. STOCKMANN. You see, if you come an hour late, Mr. Billing, you have to put up with cold meat.

BILLING (*as he eats*). It is uncommonly good, thank you —remarkably good.

MRS. STOCKMANN. My husband makes such a point of having his meals punctually, you know—

BILLING. That doesn't affect me a bit. Indeed, I almost think I enjoy a meal all the better when I can sit down and eat all by myself and undisturbed.

MRS. STOCKMANN. Oh well, as long as you are enjoying it—. (*Turns to the hall door, listening.*) I expect that is Mr. Hovstad coming too.

BILLING. Very likely.

(PETER STOCKMANN *comes in. He wears an overcoat and his official hat, and carries a stick.*)

PETER STOCKMANN. Good evening, Katherine.

MRS. STOCKMANN (*coming forward into the sitting-room*). Ah, good evening—is it you? How good of you to come up and see us!

PETER STOCKMANN. I happened to be passing, and so— (*looks into the dining-room*). But you have company with you, I see.

MRS. STOCKMANN (*a little embarrassed*). Oh, no—it was quite by chance he came in. (*Hurriedly.*) Won't you come in and have something, too?

PETER STOCKMANN. I! No, thank you. Good gracious— hot meat at night! Not with my digestion.

MRS. STOCKMANN. Oh, but just once in a way—

PETER STOCKMANN. No, no, my dear lady; I stick to my tea and bread and butter. It is much more wholesome in the long run—and a little more economical, too.

MRS. STOCKMANN (*smiling*). Now you mustn't think that Thomas and I are spendthrifts.

PETER STOCKMANN. Not you, my dear; I would never think that of you. (*Points to the Doctor's study.*) Is he not at home?

MRS. STOCKMANN. No, he went for a little turn after supper—he and the boys.

PETER STOCKMANN. I doubt if that is a wise thing to do. (*Listens.*) I fancy I hear him coming now.

MRS. STOCKMANN. No, I don't think it is he. (*A knock is heard at the door.*) Come in! (HOVSTAD *comes in from the hall.*) Oh, it is you, Mr. Hovstad!

HOVSTAD. Yes, I hope you will forgive me, but I was delayed at the printers. Good evening, Mr. Mayor.

PETER STOCKMANN (*bowing a little distantly*). Good evening. You have come on business, no doubt.

HOVSTAD. Partly. It's about an article for the paper.

PETER STOCKMANN. So I imagined. I hear my brother has become a prolific contributor to the "People's Messenger."

HOVSTAD. Yes, he is good enough to write in the "People's Messenger" when he has any home truths to tell.

MRS. STOCKMANN (*to* HOVSTAD). But won't you—? (*Points to the dining-room.*)

PETER STOCKMANN. Quite so, quite so. I don't blame him in the least, as a writer, for addressing himself to the quarters where he will find the readiest sympathy. And, besides that, I personally have no reason to bear any ill will to your paper, Mr. Hovstad.

HOVSTAD. I quite agree with you.

PETER STOCKMANN. Taking one thing with another, there is an excellent spirit of toleration in the town—an admirable municipal spirit. And it all springs from the fact of our having a great common interest to unite us—an interest that is in an equally high degree the concern of every right-minded citizen—

HOVSTAD. The Baths, yes.

PETER STOCKMANN. Exactly—our fine, new, handsome Baths. Mark my words, Mr. Hovstad—the Baths will become the focus of our municipal life! Not a doubt of it!

MRS. STOCKMANN. That is just what Thomas says.

PETER STOCKMANN. Think how extraordinarily the place has developed within the last year or two! Money has been flowing in, and there is some life and some business doing in the town. Houses and landed property are rising in value every day.

HOVSTAD. And unemployment is diminishing.

PETER STOCKMANN. Yes, that is another thing. The burden of the poor rates has been lightened, to the great relief of the propertied classes; and that relief will be even greater if only we get a really good summer this year, and lots of visitors— plenty of invalids, who will make the Baths talked about.

HOVSTAD. And there is a good prospect of that, I hear.

PETER STOCKMANN. It looks very promising. Enquiries about apartments and that sort of thing are reaching us every day.

HOVSTAD. Well, the doctor's article will come in very suitably.

PETER STOCKMANN. Has he been writing something just lately?

HOVSTAD. This is something he wrote in the winter; a recommendation of the Baths—an account of the excellent sanitary conditions here. But I held the article over, temporarily.

PETER STOCKMANN. Ah,—some little difficulty about it, I suppose?

HOVSTAD. No, not at all; I thought it would be better to wait till the spring, because it is just at this time that people begin to think seriously about their summer quarters.

PETER STOCKMANN. Quite right; you were perfectly right, Mr. Hovstad.

HOVSTAD. Yes, Thomas is really indefatigable when it is a question of the Baths.

PETER STOCKMANN. Well—remember, he is the Medical Officer to the Baths.

HOVSTAD. Yes, and what is more, they owe their existence to him.

PETER STOCKMANN. To him? Indeed! It is true I have heard from time to time that some people are of that opinion. At the same time I must say I imagined that I took a modest part in the enterprise.

398

MRS. STOCKMANN. Yes, that is what Thomas is always saying.

HOVSTAD. But who denies it, Mr. Stockmann? You set the thing going and made a practical concern of it; we all know that. I only meant that the idea of it came first from the doctor.

PETER STOCKMANN. Oh, ideas—yes! My brother has had plenty of them in his time—unfortunately. But when it is a question of putting an idea into practical shape, you have to apply to a man of different mettle, Mr. Hovstad. And I certainly should have thought that in this house at least—

MRS. STOCKMANN. My dear Peter—

HOVSTAD. How can you think that—?

MRS. STOCKMANN. Won't you go in and have something, Mr. Hovstad? My husband is sure to be back directly.

HOVSTAD. Thank you, perhaps just a morsel. (*Goes into the dining-room.*)

PETER STOCKMANN (*lowering his voice a little*). It is a curious thing that these farmers' sons never seem to lose their want of tact.

MRS. STOCKMANN. Surely it is not worth bothering about! Cannot you and Thomas share the credit as brothers?

PETER STOCKMANN. I should have thought so; but apparently some people are not satisfied with a share.

MRS. STOCKMANN. What nonsense! You and Thomas get on so capitally together. (*Listens.*) There he is at last, I think. (*Goes out and opens the door leading to the hall.*)

DR. STOCKMANN (*laughing and talking outside*). Look here—here is another guest for you, Katherine. Isn't that jolly! Come in, Captain Horster; hang your coat upon this peg. Ah, you don't wear an overcoat. Just think, Katherine; I met him in the street and could hardly persuade him to come up! (CAPTAIN HORSTER *comes into the room and greets* MRS. STOCKMANN. *He is followed by* DR. STOCKMANN.) Come along in, boys. They are ravenously hungry again, you know. Come along, Captain Horster; you must have a slice of beef. (*Pushes* HORSTER *into the dining-room.* EJLIF *and* MORTEN *go in after them.*)

MRS. STOCKMANN. But, Thomas, don't you see—?

DR. STOCKMANN (*turning in the doorway*). Oh, is it you, Peter? (*Shakes hands with him.*) Now that is very delightful.

PETER STOCKMANN. Unfortunately I must go in a moment—

DR. STOCKMANN. Rubbish! There is some toddy just coming in. You haven't forgotten the toddy, Katherine?

MRS. STOCKMANN. Of course not; the water is boiling now. (*Goes into the dining-room.*)

PETER STOCKMANN. Toddy too!

DR. STOCKMANN. Yes, sit down and we will have it comfortably.

PETER STOCKMANN. Thanks, I never care about an evening's drinking.

DR. STOCKMANN. But this isn't an evening's drinking.

PETER STOCKMANN. It seems to me—. (*Looks towards the dining-room.*) It is extraordinary how they can put away all that food.

DR. STOCKMANN (*rubbing his hands*). Yes, isn't it splendid to see young people eat? They have always got an appetite, you know! That's as it should be. Lots of food—to build up their strength! They are the people who are going to stir up the fermenting forces of the future, Peter.

PETER STOCKMANN. May I ask what they will find here to "stir up," as you put it?

DR. STOCKMANN. Ah, you must ask the young people that —when the times comes. We shan't be able to see it, of course. That stands to reason—two old fogies, like us—

PETER STOCKMANN. Really, really! I must say that is an extremely odd expression to—

DR. STOCKMANN. Oh, you mustn't take me too literally, Peter. I am so heartily happy and contented, you know. I think it is such an extraordinary piece of good fortune to be in the middle of all this growing, germinating life. It is a splendid time to live in! It is as if a whole new world were being created around one.

PETER STOCKMANN. Do you really think so?

DR. STOCKMANN. Ah, naturally you can't appreciate it as keenly as I. You have lived all your life in these surroundings, and your impressions have got blunted. But I, who have been buried all these years in my little corner up north, almost without ever seeing a stranger who might bring new ideas with him—well, in my case it has just the same effect as if I had been transported into the middle of a crowded city.

PETER STOCKMANN. Oh, a city—!

DR. STOCKMANN. I know, I know; it is all cramped enough here, compared with many other places. But there is life here —there is promise—there are innumerable things to work for and fight for; and that is the main thing. (*Calls.*) Katherine, hasn't the postman been here?

MRS. STOCKMANN (*from the dining-room*). No.

DR. STOCKMANN. And then to be comfortably off, Peter! That is something one learns to value, when one has been on the brink of starvation, as we have.

PETER STOCKMANN. Oh, surely—

DR. STOCKMANN. Indeed I can assure you we have often

been very hard put to it, up there. And now to be able to live like a lord! To-day, for instance, we had roast beef for dinner—and, what is more, for supper too. Won't you come and have a little bit? Or let me show it you, at any rate? Come here—

PETER STOCKMANN. No, no—not for worlds!

DR. STOCKMANN. Well, but just come here then. Do you see, we have got a table-cover?

PETER STOCKMANN. Yes, I noticed it.

DR. STOCKMANN. And we have got a lamp-shade too. Do you see? All out of Katherine's savings! It makes the room so cosy. Don't you think so? Just stand here for a moment—no, no, not there—just here, that's it! Look now, when you get the light on it altogether—I really think it looks very nice, doesn't it?

PETER STOCKMANN. Oh, if you can afford luxuries of this kind—

DR. STOCKMANN. Yes, I can afford it now. Katherine tells me I earn almost as much as we spend.

PETER STOCKMANN. Almost—yes!

DR. STOCKMANN. But a scientific man must live in a little bit of style. I am quite sure an ordinary civil servant spends more in a year than I do.

PETER STOCKMANN. I daresay. A civil servant—a man in a well-paid position—

DR. STOCKMANN. Well, any ordinary merchant, then! A man in that position spends two or three times as much as—

PETER STOCKMANN. It just depends on circumstances.

DR. STOCKMANN. At all events I assure you I don't waste money unprofitably. But I can't find it in my heart to deny myself the pleasure of entertaining my friends. I need that sort of thing, you know. I have lived for so long shut out of it all, that it is a necessity of life to me to mix with young, eager, ambitious men, men of liberal and active minds; and that describes every one of those fellows who are enjoying their supper in there. I wish you knew more of Hovstad—

PETER STOCKMANN. By the way, Hovstad was telling me he was going to print another article of yours.

DR. STOCKMANN. An article of mine?

PETER STOCKMANN. Yes, about the Baths. An article you wrote in the winter.

DR. STOCKMANN. Oh, that one! No, I don't intend that to appear just for the present.

PETER STOCKMANN. Why not? It seems to me that this would be the most opportune moment.

DR. STOCKMANN. Yes, very likely—under normal conditions. (*Crosses the room.*)

PETER STOCKMANN (*following him with his eyes*). Is there anything abnormal about the present conditions?

DR. STOCKMANN (*standing still*). To tell you the truth, Peter, I can't say just at this moment—at all events not to-night. There may be much that is very abnormal about the present conditions—and it is possible there may be nothing abnormal about them at all. It is quite possible it may be merely my imagination.

PETER STOCKMANN. I must say it all sounds most mysterious. Is there something going on that I am to be kept in ignorance of? I should have imagined that I, as Chairman of the governing body of the Baths—

DR. STOCKMANN. And I should have imagined that I—. Oh, come, don't let us fly out at one another, Peter.

PETER STOCKMANN. Heaven forbid! I am not in the habit of flying out at people, as you call it. But I am entitled to request most emphatically that all arrangements shall be made in a business-like manner, through the proper channels, and shall be dealt with by the legally constituted authorities. I can allow no going behind our backs by any roundabout means.

DR. STOCKMANN. Have I ever at any time tried to go behind your backs!

PETER STOCKMANN. You have an ingrained tendency to take your own way, at all events; and that is almost equally inadmissible in a well ordered community. The individual ought undoubtedly to acquiesce in subordinating himself to the community—or, to speak more accurately, to the authorities who have the care of the community's welfare.

DR. STOCKMANN. Very likely. But what the deuce has all this got to do with me?

PETER STOCKMANN. That is exactly what you never appear to be willing to learn, my dear Thomas. But, mark my words, some day you will have to suffer for it—sooner or later. Now I have told you. Good-bye.

DR. STOCKMANN. Have you taken leave of your senses? You are on the wrong scent altogether.

PETER STOCKMANN. I am not usually that. You must excuse me now if I—(*calls into the dining-room*). Good night, Katherine. Good night, gentlemen. (*Goes out.*)

MRS. STOCKMANN (*coming from the dining-room*). Has he gone?

DR. STOCKMANN. Yes, and in such a bad temper.

MRS. STOCKMANN. But, dear Thomas, what have you been doing to him again?

DR. STOCKMANN. Nothing at all. And, anyhow, he can't oblige me to make my report before the proper time.

MRS. STOCKMANN. What have you got to make a report to him about?

DR. STOCKMANN. Hm! Leave that to me, Katherine.—It is an extraordinary thing that the postman doesn't come.

(HOVSTAD, BILLING *and* HORSTER *have got up from the table and come into the sitting-room.* EJLIF *and* MORTEN *come in after them.*)

BILLING (*stretching himself*). Ah!—one feels a new man after a meal like that.

HOVSTAD. The mayor wasn't in a very sweet temper to-night, then.

DR. STOCKMANN. It is his stomach; he has a wretched digestion.

HOVSTAD. I rather think it was us two of the "People's Messenger" that he couldn't digest.

MRS. STOCKMANN. I thought you came out of it pretty well with him.

HOVSTAD. Oh yes; but it isn't anything more than a sort of truce.

BILLING. That is just what it is! That word sums up the situation.

DR. STOCKMANN. We must remember that Peter is a lonely man, poor chap. He has no home comforts of any kind; nothing but everlasting business. And all that infernal weak tea wash that he pours into himself! Now then, my boys, bring chairs up to the table. Aren't we going to have that toddy, Katherine?

MRS. STOCKMANN (*going into the dining-room*). I am just getting it.

DR. STOCKMANN. Sit down here on the couch beside me, Captain Horster. We so seldom see you—. Please sit down, my friends. (*They sit down at the table.* MRS. STOCKMANN *brings a tray, with a spirit-lamp, glasses, bottles, etc., upon it.*)

MRS. STOCKMANN. There you are! This is arrack, and this is rum, and this one is the brandy. Now every one must help themselves.

DR. STOCKMANN (*taking a glass*). We will. (*They all mix themselves some toddy.*) And let us have the cigars. Ejlif, you know where the box is. And you, Morten, can fetch my pipe. (*The two boys go into the room on the right.*) I have a suspicion that Ejlif pockets a cigar now and then!—but I take no notice of it. (*Calls out.*) And my smoking-cap too, Morten. Katherine, you can tell him where I left it. Ah, he has got it. (*The boys bring the various things.*) Now, my friends. I stick to my pipe, you know. This one has seen plenty of bad weather with me up north. (*Touches glasses with them.*)

Your good health! Ah, it is good to be sitting snug and warm here.

MRS. STOCKMANN (*who sits knitting*). Do you sail soon, Captain Horster?

HORSTER. I expect to be ready to sail next week.

MRS. STOCKMANN. I suppose you are going to America?

HORSTER. Yes, that is the plan.

MRS. STOCKMANN. Then you won't be able to take part in the coming election.

HORSTER. Is there going to be an election?

BILLING. Didn't you know?

HORSTER. No, I don't mix myself up with those things.

BILLING. But do you not take an interest in public affairs?

HORSTER. No, I don't know anything about politics.

BILLING. All the same, one ought to vote, at any rate.

HORSTER. Even if one doesn't know anything about what is going on?

BILLING. Doesn't know! What do you mean by that? A community is like a ship; every one ought to be prepared to take the helm.

HORSTER. May be that is all very well on shore; but on board ship it wouldn't work.

HOVSTAD. It is astonishing how little most sailors care about what goes on on shore.

BILLING. Very extraordinary.

DR. STOCKMANN. Sailors are like birds of passage; they feel equally at home in any latitude. And that is only an additional reason for our being all the more keen, Hovstad. Is there to be anything of public interest in tomorrow's "Messenger"?

HOVSTAD. Nothing about municipal affairs. But the day after to-morrow I was thinking of printing your article—

DR. STOCKMANN. Ah, devil take it—my article! Look here, that must wait a bit.

HOVSTAD. Really? We had just got convenient space for it, and I thought it was just the opportune moment—

DR. STOCKMANN. Yes, yes, very likely you are right; but it must wait all the same. I will explain to you later. (PETRA *comes in from the hall, in hat and cloak and with a bundle of exercise books under her arm.*)

PETRA. Good evening.

DR. STOCKMANN. Good evening, Petra; come along.

(*Mutual greetings;* PETRA *takes off her things and puts them down on a chair by the door.*)

PETRA. And you have all been sitting here enjoying yourselves, while I have been out slaving!

DR. STOCKMANN. Well, come and enjoy yourself too!

404

BILLING. May I mix a glass for you?

PETRA (*coming to the table*). Thanks, I would rather do it; you always mix it too strong. But I forgot, father—I have a letter for you. (*Goes to the chair where she has laid her things.*)

DR. STOCKMANN. A letter? From whom?

PETRA (*looking in her coat pocket*). The postman gave it to me just as I was going out—

DR. STOCKMANN (*getting up and going to her*). And you only give to me now!

PETRA. I really had not time to run up again. There it is!

DR. STOCKMANN (*seizing the letter*). Let's see, let's see, child! (*Looks at the address.*) Yes, that's all right!

MRS. STOCKMANN. Is it the one you have been expecting so anxiously, Thomas?

DR. STOCKMANN. Yes, it is. I must go to my room now and—. Where shall I get a light, Katherine? Is there no lamp in my room again?

MRS. STOCKMANN. Yes, your lamp is all ready lit on your desk.

DR. STOCKMANN. Good, good. Excuse me for a moment—. (*Goes into his study.*)

PETRA. What do you suppose it is, mother?

MRS. STOCKMANN. I don't know; for the last day or two he has always been asking if the postman has not been.

BILLING. Probably some country patient.

PETRA. Poor old dad!—he will overwork himself soon. (*Mixes a glass for herself.*) There, that will taste good!

HOVSTAD. Have you been teaching in the evening school again to-day?

PETRA (*sipping from her glass*). Two hours.

BILLING. And four hours of school in the morning—

PETRA. Five hours.

MRS. STOCKMANN. And you have still got exercises to correst, I see.

PETRA. A whole heap, yes.

HORSTER. You are pretty full up with work too, it seems to me.

PETRA. Yes—but that is good. One is so delightfully tired after it.

BILLING. Do you like that?

PETRA. Yes, because one sleeps so well then.

MORTEN. You must be dreadfully wicked, Petra.

PETRA. Wicked?

MORTEN. Yes, because you work so much. Mr. Rörlund says work is a punishment for our sins.

EJLIF. Pooh, what a duffer you are, to believe a thing like that!

MRS. STOCKMANN. Come, come, Ejlif!

BILLING (*laughing*). That's capital!

HOVSTAD. Don't you want to work as hard as that, Morten?

MORTEN. No, indeed I don't.

HOVSTAD. What do you want to be, then?

MORTEN. I should like best to be a Viking.

EJLIF. You would have to be a pagan then.

MORTEN. Well, I could become a pagan, couldn't I?

BILLING. I agree with you, Morten! My sentiments, exactly.

MRS. STOCKMANN (*signalling to him*). I am sure that is not true, Mr. Billing.

BILLING. Yes, I swear it is! I am a pagan, and I am proud of it. Believe me, before long we shall all be pagans.

MORTEN. And then shall be allowed to do anything we like?

BILLING. Well, you see, Morten—.

MRS. STOCKMANN. You must go to your room now, boys; I am sure you have some lessons to learn for to-morrow.

EJLIF. I should like so much to stay a little longer—

MRS. STOCKMANN. No, no; away you go, both of you. (*The boys say good night and go into the room on the left.*)

HOVSTAD. Do you really think it can do the boys any harm to hear such things?

MRS. STOCKMANN. I don't know; but I don't like it.

PETRA. But you know, mother, I think you really are wrong about it.

MRS. STOCKMANN. Maybe, but I don't like it—not in our own home.

PETRA. There is so much falsehood both at home and at school. At home one must not speak, and at school we have to stand and tell lies to the children.

HORSTER. Tell lies?

PETRA. Yes, don't you suppose we have to teach them all sorts of things that we don't believe?

BILLING. That is perfectly true.

PETRA. If only I had the means I would start a school of my own, and it would be conducted on very different lines.

BILLING. Oh, bother the means—!

HORSTER. Well if you are thinking of that, Miss Stockmann, I shall be delighted to provide you with a schoolroom. The great big old house my father left me is standing almost empty; there is an immense dining-room downstairs—

PETRA (*laughing*). Thank you very much; but I am afraid nothing will come of it.

HOVSTAD. No, Miss Petra is much more likely to take to

journalism, I expect. By the way, have you had time to do anything with that English story you promised to translate for us?

PETRA. No, not yet; but you shall have it in good time.

(DR. STOCKMANN *comes in from his room with an open letter in his hand.*)

DR. STOCKMANN (*waving the letter*). Well, now the town will have something new to talk about, I can tell you!

BILLING. Something new?

MRS. STOCKMANN. What is this?

DR. STOCKMANN. A great discovery, Katherine.

HOVSTAD. Really?

MRS. STOCKMANN. A discovery of yours?

DR. STOCKMANN. A discovery of mine. (*Walks up and down.*) Just let them come saying, as usual, that it is all fancy and a crazy man's imagination! But they will be careful what they say this time, I can tell you!

PETRA. But, father, tell us what it is.

DR. STOCKMANN. Yes, yes—only give me time, and you shall know all about it. If only I had Peter here now! It just shows how we men can go about forming our judgments, when in reality we are as blind as any moles—

HOVSTAD. What are you driving at, Doctor?

DR. STOCKMANN (*standing still by the table*). Isn't it the universal opinion that our town is a healthy spot?

HOVSTAD. Certainly.

DR. STOCKMANN. Quite an unusually healthy spot, in fact —a place that deserves to be recommended in the warmest possible manner either for invalids or for people who are well—

MRS. STOCKMANN. Yes, but my dear Thomas—

DR. STOCKMANN. And we have been recommending it and praising it—I have written and written, both in the "Messenger" and in pamphlets—

HOVSTAD. Well, what then?

DR. STOCKMANN. And the Baths—we have called them the "main artery of the town's life-blood," the "nerve-centre of our town," and the devil knows what else—

BILLING. "The town's pulsating heart" was the expression I once used on an important occasion—

DR. STOCKMANN. Quite so. Well, do you know what they really are, these great, splendid, much praised Baths, that have cost so much money—do you know what they are?

HOVSTAD. No, what are they?

MRS. STOCKMANN. Yes, what are they?

DR. STOCKMANN. The whole place is a pesthouse!

PETRA. The Baths, father?

MRS. STOCKMANN (*at the same time*). Our Baths!

HOVSTAD. But, Doctor—

BILLING. Absolutely incredible!

DR. STOCKMANN. The whole Bath establishment is a whited, poisoned sepulchre, I tell you—the gravest possible danger to the public health! All the nastiness up at Mölledal, all that stinking filth, is infecting the water in the conduit-pipes leading to the reservoir; and the same cursed, filthy poison oozes out on the shore too—

HORSTER. Where the bathing-place is?

DR. STOCKMANN. Just there.

HOVSTAD. How do you come to be so certain of all this, Doctor?

DR. STOCKMANN. I have investigated the matter most conscientiously. For a long time past I have suspected something of the kind. Last year we had some very strange cases of illness among the visitors—typhoid cases, and cases of gastric fever—

MRS. STOCKMANN. Yes, that is quite true.

DR. STOCKMANN. At the time, we supposed the visitors had been infected before they came; but later on, in the winter, I began to have a different opinion; and so I set myself to examine the water, as well as I could.

MRS. STOCKMANN. Then that is what you have been so busy with?

DR. STOCKMANN. Indeed I have been busy, Katherine. But here I had none of the necessary scientific apparatus; so I sent samples, both of the drinking-water and of the sea-water, up to the University, to have an accurate analysis made by a chemist.

HOVSTAD. And have you got that?

DR. STOCKMANN (*showing him the letter*). Here it is! It proves the presence of decomposing organic matter in the water—it is full of infusoria. The water is absolutely dangerous to use, either internally or externally.

MRS. STOCKMANN. What a mercy you discovered it in time.

DR. STOCKMANN. You may well say so.

HOVSTAD. And what do you propose to do now, Doctor?

DR. STOCKMANN. To see the matter put right—naturally.

HOVSTAD. Can that be done?

DR. STOCKMANN. It must be done. Otherwise the Baths will be absolutely useless and wasted. But we need not anticipate that; I have a very clear idea what we shall have to do.

MRS. STOCKMANN. But why have you kept this all so secret, dear?

DR. STOCKMANN. Do you suppose I was going to run about the town gossiping about it, before I had absolute proof? No, thank you. I am not such a fool.

PETRA. Still, you might have told us—

DR. STOCKMANN. Not a living soul. But to-morrow you may run around to the old Badger—

MRS. STOCKMANN. Oh, Thomas! Thomas!

DR. STOCKMANN. Well, to your grandfather, then. The old boy will have something to be astonished at! I know he thinks I am cracked—and there are lots of other people think so too, I have noticed. But now these good folks shall see—they shall just see—! (*Walks about, rubbing his hands.*) There will be a nice upset in the town, Katherine; you can't imagine what it will be. All the conduit-pipes will have to be relaid.

HOVSTAD (*getting up*). All the conduit-pipes—?

DR. STOCKMANN. Yes, of course. The intake is too low down; it will have to be lifted to a position much higher up.

PETRA. Then you were right after all.

DR. STOCKMANN. Ah, you remember, Petra—I wrote opposing the plans before the work was begun. But at that time no one would listen to me. Well, I am going to let them have it, now! Of course I have prepared a report for the Baths Committee; I have had it ready for a week, and was only waiting for this to come. (*Shows the letter.*) Now it shall go off at once. (*Goes into his room and comes back with some papers.*) Look at that! Four closely written sheets!—and the letter shall go with them. Give me a bit of paper, Katherine —something to wrap them up in. That will do! Now give it to—to—(*stamps his foot*)—what the deuce is her name?— give it to the maid, and tell her to take it at once to the Mayor.

(MRS. STOCKMANN *takes the packet and goes out through the dining-room.*)

PETRA. What do you think uncle Peter will say, father?

DR. STOCKMANN. What is there for him to say? I should think he would be very glad that such an important truth has been brought to light.

HOVSTAD. Will you let me print a short note about your discovery in the "Messenger"?

DR. STOCKMANN. I shall be very much obliged if you will.

HOVSTAD. It is very desirable that the public should be informed of it without delay.

DR. STOCKMANN. Certainly.

MRS. STOCKMANN (*coming back*). She has just gone with it.

BILLING. Upon my soul, Doctor, you are going to be the foremost man in the town!

DR. STOCKMANN (*walking about happily*). Nonsense! As a

409

matter of fact I have done nothing more than my duty. I have only made a lucky find—that's all. Still, all the same—

BILLING. Hovstad, don't you think the town ought to give Dr. Stockmann some sort of testimonial?

HOVSTAD. I will suggest it, anyway.

BILLING. And I will speak to Aslaksen about it.

DR. STOCKMANN. No, my good friends, don't let us have any of that nonsense. I won't hear of anything of the kind. And if the Baths Committee should think of voting me an increase of salary, I will not accept it. Do you hear, Katherine?—I won't accept it.

MRS. STOCKMANN. You are quite right, Thomas.

PETRA (*lifting her glass*). Your health, father!

HOVSTAD and BILLING. Your health, Doctor! Good health!

HORSTER (*touches glasses with* DR. STOCKMANN). I hope it will bring you nothing but good luck.

DR. STOCKMANN. Thank you, thank you, my dear fellows! I feel tremendously happy! It is a splendid thing for a man to be able to feel that he has done a service to his native town and to his fellow-citizens. Hurrah, Katherine! (*He puts his arms round her and whirls her round and round, while she protests with laughing cries. They all laugh, clap their hands, and cheer the* DOCTOR. *The boys put their heads in at the door to see what is going on.*)

ACT II

(Scene—*The same. The door into the dining-room is shut.
It is morning.* Mrs. Stockmann, *with a sealed letter in her
hand, comes in from the dining-room, goes to the door of the*
Doctor's *study, and peeps in.*)

Mrs. Stockmann. Are you in, Thomas?

Dr. Stockmann (*from within his room*). Yes, I have just
come in. (*Comes into the room.*) What is it?

Mrs. Stockmann. A letter from your brother.

Dr. Stockmann. Aha, let us see! (*Opens the letter and
reads:*) "I return herewith the manuscript you sent me"—
(*reads on in a low murmur*) Hm!—

Mrs. Stockmann. What does he say?

Dr. Stockmann (*putting the papers in his pocket*). Oh,
he only writes that he will come up here himself about
midday.

Mrs. Stockmann. Well, try and remember to be at home
this time.

Dr. Stockmann. That will be all right; I have got through
all my morning visits.

Mrs. Stockmann. I am extremely curious to know how he
takes it.

Dr. Stockmann. You will see he won't like it's having been
I, and not he, that made the discovery.

Mrs. Stockmann. Aren't you a little nervous about that?

Dr. Stockmann. Oh, he really will be pleased enough, you
know. But, at the same time, Peter is so confoundedly afraid
of anyone's doing any service to the town except himself.

Mrs. Stockmann. I will tell you what, Thomas—you
should be good natured, and share the credit of this with him.
Couldn't you make out that it was he who set you on the
scent of this discovery?

411

DR. STOCKMANN. I am quite willing. If only I can get the thing set right. I—

(MORTEN KIIL *puts his head in through the door leading from the hall, looks round in an enquiring manner, and chuckles.*)

MORTEN KIIL (*slyly*). Is it—is it true?

MRS. STOCKMANN (*going to the door*). Father!—is it you?

DR. STOCKMANN. Ah, Mr. Kiil—good morning, good morning!

MRS. STOCKMANN. But come along in.

MORTEN KIIL. If it is true, I will; if not, I am off.

DR. STOCKMANN. If what is true?

MORTEN KIIL. This tale about the water supply. Is it true?

DR. STOCKMANN. Certainly it is true. But how did you come to hear it?

MORTEN KIIL (*coming in*). Petra ran in on her way to the school—

DR. STOCKMANN. Did she?

MORTEN KIIL. Yes; and she declares that—. I thought she was only making a fool of me, but it isn't like Petra to do that.

DR. STOCKMANN. Of course not. How could you imagine such a thing!

MORTEN KIIL. Oh well, it is better never to trust anybody; you may find you have been made a fool of before you know where you are. But it is really true, all the same?

DR. STOCKMANN. You can depend upon it that it is true. Won't you sit down? (*Settles him on the couch.*) Isn't it a real bit of luck for the town—

MORTEN KIIL (*suppressing his laughter*). A bit of luck for the town?

DR. STOCKMANN. Yes, that I made the discovery in good time.

MORTEN KIIL (*as before*). Yes, yes, yes!—But I should never have thought you the sort of man to pull your own brother's leg like this!

DR. STOCKMANN. Pull his leg!

MRS. STOCKMANN. Really, father dear—

MORTEN KIIL (*resting his hands and his chin on the handle of his stick and winking slyly at the* DOCTOR). Let me see, what was the story? Some kind of beast that had got into the water-pipes, wasn't it?

DR. STOCKMANN. Infusoria—yes.

MORTEN KIIL. And a lot of these beasts had got in, according to Petra—a tremendous lot.

DR. STOCKMANN. Certainly; hundreds of thousands of them, probably.

MORTEN KIIL. But no one can see them—isn't that so?

DR. STOCKMANN. Yes; you can't see them.

MORTEN KIIL (*with a quiet chuckle*). Damme—it's the finest story I have ever heard!

DR. STOCKMANN. What do you mean?

MORTEN KIIL. But you will never get the Mayor to believe a thing like that.

DR. STOCKMANN. We shall see.

MORTEN KIIL. Do you think he will be fool enough to—?

DR. STOCKMANN. I hope the whole town will be fools enough.

MORTEN KIIL. The whole town! Well, it wouldn't be a bad thing. It would just serve them right, and teach them a lesson. They think themselves so much cleverer than we old fellows. They hounded me out of the council; they did, I tell you— they hounded me out. Now they shall pay for it. You pull their legs too, Thomas!

DR. STOCKMANN. Really, I—

MORTEN KIIL. You pull their legs! (*Gets up.*) If you can work it so that the Mayor and his friends all swallow the same bait, I will give ten pounds to a charity—like a shot!

DR. STOCKMANN. That is very kind of you.

MORTEN KIIL. Yes, I haven't got much money to throw away, I can tell you; but if you can work this, I will give five pounds to a charity at Christmas.

(HOVSTAD *comes in by the hall door.*)

HOVSTAD. Good morning! (*Stops.*) Oh, I beg your pardon—

DR. STOCKMANN. Not at all; come in.

MORTEN KIIL (*with another chuckle*). Oho!—is he in this too?

HOVSTAD. What do you mean?

DR. STOCKMANN. Certainly he is.

MORTEN KIIL. I might have known it! It must get into the papers. You know how to do it, Thomas! Set your wits to work. Now I must go.

DR. STOCKMANN. Won't you stay a little while?

MORTEN KIIL. No, I must be off now. You keep up this game for all it is worth; you won't repent it, I'm damned if you will!

(*He goes out;* MRS. STOCKMANN *follows him into the hall.*)

DR. STOCKMANN (*laughing*). Just imagine—the old chap doesn't believe a word of all this about the water supply.

HOVSTAD. Oh that was it, then?

DR. STOCKMANN. Yes, that was what we were talking about. Perhaps it is the same thing that brings you here?

ACT II

HOVSTAD. Yes, it is. Can you spare me a few minutes, Doctor?

DR. STOCKMANN. As long as you like, my dear fellow.

HOVSTAD. Have you heard from the Mayor yet?

DR. STOCKMANN. Not yet. He is coming here later.

HOVSTAD. I have given the matter a great deal of thought since last night.

DR. STOCKMANN. Well?

HOVSTAD. From your point of view, as a doctor and a man of science, this affair of the water-supply is an isolated matter. I mean, you do not realise that it involves a great many other things.

DR. STOCKMANN. How, do you mean?—Let us sit down, my dear fellow. No, sit here on the couch. (HOVSTAD *sits down on the couch,* DR. STOCKMANN *on a chair on the other side of the table.*) Now then. You mean that—?

HOVSTAD. You said yesterday that the pollution of the water was due to impurities in the soil.

DR. STOCKMANN. Yes, unquestionably it is due to that poisonous morass up at Mölledal.

HOVSTAD. Begging your pardon, doctor, I fancy it is due to quite another morass altogether.

DR. STOCKMANN. What morass?

HOVSTAD. The morass that the whole life of our town is built on and is rotting in.

DR. STOCKMANN. What the deuce are you driving at, Hovstad?

HOVSTAD. The whole of the town's interests have, little by little, got into the hands of a pack of officials.

DR. STOCKMANN. Oh, come!—they are not all officials.

HOVSTAD. No, but those that are not officials are at any rate the officials' friends and adherents; it is the wealthy folk, the old families in the town, that have got us entirely in their hands.

DR. STOCKMANN. Yes, but after all they are men of ability and knowledge.

HOVSTAD. Did they show any ability or knowledge when they laid the conduit-pipes where they are now?

DR. STOCKMANN. No, of course that was a great piece of stupidity on their part. But that is going to be set right now.

HOVSTAD. Do you think that will be all such plain sailing?

DR. STOCKMANN. Plain sailing or no, it has got to be done, anyway.

HOVSTAD. Yes, provided the press takes up the question.

DR. STOCKMANN. I don't think that will be necessary, my dear fellow, I am certain my brother—

414

HOVSTAD. Excuse me, doctor; I feel bound to tell you I am inclined to take the matter up.

DR. STOCKMANN. In the paper?

HOVSTAD. Yes, When I took over the "People's Messenger" my idea was to break up this ring of self-opinionated old fossils who had got hold of all the influence.

DR. STOCKMANN. But you know you told me yourself what the result had been; you nearly ruined your paper.

HOVSTAD. Yes, at the time we were obliged to climb down a peg or two, it is quite true; because there was a danger of the whole project of the Baths coming to nothing if they failed us. But now the scheme has been carried through, and we can dispense with these grand gentlemen.

DR. STOCKMANN. Dispense with them, yes; but we owe them a great debt of gratitude.

HOVSTAD. That shall be recognised ungrudgingly. But a journalist of my democratic tendencies cannot let such an opportunity as this slip. The bubble of official infallibility must be pricked. This superstition must be destroyed, like any other.

DR. STOCKMANN. I am whole-heartedly with you in that, Mr. Hovstad; if it is a superstition, away with it!

HOVSTAD. I should be very reluctant to bring the Mayor into it, because he is your brother. But I am sure you will agree with me that truth should be the first consideration.

DR. STOCKMANN. That goes without saying. (*With sudden emphasis.*) Yes, but—but—

HOVSTAD. You must not misjudge me. I am neither more self-interested nor more ambitious than most men.

DR. STOCKMANN. My dear fellow—who suggests anything of that kind?

HOVSTAD. I am of humble origin, as you know; and that has given me opportunities of knowing what is the most crying need in the humbler ranks of life. It is that they should be allowed some part in the direction of public affairs, Doctor. That is what will develop their faculties and intelligence and self respect—

DR. STOCKMANN. I quite appreciate that.

HOVSTAD. Yes—and in my opinion a journalist incurs a heavy responsibility if he neglects a favourable opportunity of emancipating the masses—the humble and oppressed. I know well enough that in exalted circles I shall be called an agitator, and all that sort of thing; but they may call what they like. If only my conscience doesn't reproach me, then—

DR. STOCKMANN. Quite right! Quite right, Mr. Hovstad. But all the same—devil take it! (*A knock is heard at the door.*) Come in!

(ASLAKSEN *appears at the door. He is poorly but decently dressed, in black, with a slightly crumpled white neck-cloth; he wears gloves and has a felt hat in his hand.*)

ASLAKSEN (*bowing*). Excuse my taking the liberty, Doctor—

DR. STOCKMANN (*getting up*). Ah, it is you, Aslaksen!

ASLAKSEN. Yes, Doctor.

HOVSTAD (*standing up*). Is it me you want, Aslaksen?

ASLAKSEN. No; I didn't know I should find you here. No, it was the Doctor I—

DR. STOCKMANN. I am quite at your service. What is it?

ASLAKSEN. Is what I heard from Mr. Billing true, sir— that you mean to improve our water-supply?

DR. STOCKMANN. Yes, for the Baths.

ASLAKSEN. Quite so, I understand. Well, I have come to say that I will back that up by every means in my power.

HOVSTAD (*to the* DOCTOR). You see!

DR. STOCKMANN. I shall be very grateful to you, but—

ASLAKSEN. Because it may be no bad thing to have us small tradesmen at your back. We form, as it were, a compact majority in the town—if we choose. And it is always a good thing to have the majority with you, Doctor.

DR. STOCKMANN. This is undeniably true; but I confess I don't see why such unusual precautions should be necessary in this case. It seems to me that such a plain, straightforward thing—

ASLAKSEN. Oh, it may be very desirable, all the same. I know our local authorities so well; officials are not generally very ready to act on proposals that come from other people. That is why I think it would not be at all amiss if we made a little demonstration.

HOVSTAD. That's right.

DR. STOCKMANN. Demonstration, did you say? What on earth are you going to make a demonstration about?

ASLAKSEN. We shall proceed with the greatest moderation, Doctor. Moderation is always my aim; it is the greatest virtue in a citizen—at least, I think so.

DR. STOCKMANN. It is well known to be a characteristic of yours, Mr. Aslaksen.

ASLAKSEN. Yes, I think I may pride myself on that. And this matter of the water-supply is of the greatest importance to us small tradesmen. The Baths promise to be a regular gold-mine for the town. We shall all make our living out of them, especially those of us who are householders. That is why we will back up the project as strongly as possible. And as I am at present Chairman of the Householders' Association—

DR. STOCKMANN. Yes—?

ASLAKSEN. And, what is more, local secretary of the Temperance Society—you know, sir, I suppose, that I am a worker in the temperance cause?

DR. STOCKMANN. Of course, of course.

ASLAKSEN. Well, you can understand that I come into contact with a great many people. And as I have the reputation of a temperate and law-abiding citizen—like yourself, Doctor—I have a certain influence in the town, a little bit of power, if I may be allowed to say so.

DR. STOCKMANN. I know that quite well, Mr. Aslaksen.

ASLAKSEN. So you see it would be an easy matter for me to set on foot some testimonial, if necessary.

DR. STOCKMANN. A testimonial?

ASLAKSEN. Yes, some kind of an address of thanks from the townsmen for your share in a matter of such importance to the community. I need scarcely say that it would have to be drawn up with the greatest regard to moderation, so as not to offend the authorities—who, after all, have the reins in their hands. If we pay strict attention to that, no one can take it amiss, I should think!

HOVSTAD. Well, and even supposing they didn't like it—

ASLAKSEN. No, no, no; there must be no discourtesy to the authorities, Mr. Hovstad. It is no use falling foul of those upon whom our welfare so closely depends. I have done that in my time, and no good ever comes of it. But no one can take exception to a reasonable and frank expression of a citizen's views.

DR. STOCKMANN (*shaking him by the hand*). I can't tell you, dear Mr. Aslaksen, how extremely pleased I am to find such hearty support among my fellow-citizens. I am delighted —delighted! Now, you will take a small glass of sherry, eh?

ASLAKSEN. No, thank you; I never drink alcohol of that kind.

DR. STOCKMANN. Well, what do you say to a glass of beer, then?

ASLAKSEN. Nor that either, thank you, Doctor. I never drink anything as early as this. I am going into town now to talk this over with one or two householders, and prepare the ground.

DR. STOCKMANN. It is tremendously kind of you, Mr. Aslaksen; but I really cannot understand the necessity for all these precautions. It seems to me that the thing should go of itself.

ASLAKSEN. The authorities are somewhat slow to move, Doctor. Far be it from me to seem to blame them—

HOVSTAD. We are going to stir them up in the paper to-morrow, Aslaksen.

ASLAKSEN. But not violently, I trust, Mr. Hovstad. Proceed with moderation, or you will do nothing with them. You may take my advice; I have gathered my experience in the school of life. Well, I must say good-bye, Doctor. You know now that we small tradesmen are at your back at all events, like a solid wall. You have the compact majority on your side, Doctor.

DR. STOCKMANN. I am very much obliged, dear Mr. Aslaksen. (*Shakes hands with him.*) Good-bye, good-bye.

ASLAKSEN. Are you going my way, towards the printing-office, Mr. Hovstad?

HOVSTAD. I will come later; I have something to settle up first.

ASLAKSEN. Very well. (*Bows and goes out;* STOCKMANN *follows him into the hall.*)

HOVSTAD (*as* STOCKMANN *comes in again*). Well, what do you think of that, Doctor? Don't you think it is high time we stirred a little life into all this slackness and vacillation and cowardice?

DR. STOCKMANN. Are you referring to Aslaksen?

HOVSTAD. Yes, I am. He is one of those who are floundering in a bog—decent enough fellow though he may be, other-wise. And most of the people here are in just the same case—see-sawing and edging first to one side and then to the other, so overcome with caution and scruple that they never dare to take any decided step.

DR. STOCKMANN. Yes, but Aslaksen seemed to me so thoroughly well-intentioned.

HOVSTAD. There is one thing I esteem higher than that; and that is for a man to be self-reliant and sure of himself.

DR. STOCKMANN. I think you are perfectly right there.

HOVSTAD. That is why I want to seize this opportunity, and try if I cannot manage to put a little virility into these well-intentioned people for once. The idol of Authority must be shattered in this town. This gross and inexcusable blunder about the water-supply must be brought home to the mind of every municipal voter.

DR. STOCKMANN. Very well; if you are of opinion that it is for the good of the community, so be it. But not until I have had a talk with my brother.

HOVSTAD. Anyway, I will get a leading article ready; and if the Mayor refuses to take the matter up—

DR. STOCKMANN. How can you suppose such a thing possible?

HOVSTAD. It is conceivable. And in that case—

DR. STOCKMANN. In that case I promise you—. Look here, in that case you may print my report—every word of it.

HOVSTAD. May I? Have I your word for it?

DR. STOCKMANN (*giving him the MS.*). Here it is; take it with you. It can do no harm for you to read it through, and you can give it back to me later on.

HOVSTAD. Good, good! That is what I will do. And now good-bye, Doctor.

DR. STOCKMANN. Good-bye, good-bye. You will see everything will run quite smoothly, Mr. Hovstad—quite smoothly.

HOVSTAD. Hm!—we shall see. (*Bows and goes out.*)

DR. STOCKMANN (*opens the dining-room door and looks in*). Katherine! Oh, you are back, Petra?

PETRA (*coming in*). Yes, I have just come from the school.

MRS. STOCKMANN (*coming in*). Has he not been here yet?

DR. STOCKMANN. Peter? No. But I have had a long talk with Hovstad. He is quite excited about my discovery. I find it has a much wider bearing than I at first imagined. And he has put his paper at my disposal if necessity should arise.

MRS. STOCKMANN. Do you think it will?

DR. STOCKMANN. Not for a moment. But at all events it makes me feel proud to know that I have the liberal-minded independent press on my side. Yes, and—just imagine—I have had a visit from the Chairman of the Householders' Association!

MRS. STOCKMANN. Oh! What did he want?

DR. STOCKMANN. To offer me his support too. They will support me in a body if it should be necessary. Katherine—do you know what I have got behind me?

MRS. STOCKMANN. Behind you? No, what have you got behind you?

DR. STOCKMANN. The compact majority.

MRS. STOCKMANN. Really? Is that a good thing for you Thomas?

DR. STOCKMANN. I should think it was a good thing. (*Walks up and down rubbing his hands.*) By Jove, it's a fine thing to feel this bond of brotherhood between oneself and one's fellow citizens!

PETRA. And to be able to do so much that is good and useful, father!

DR. STOCKMANN. And for one's own native town into the bargain, my child!

MRS. STOCKMANN. That was a ring at the bell.

DR. STOCKMANN. It must be he, then. (*A knock is heard at the door.*) Come in!

419

PETER STOCKMANN (*comes in from the hall*). Good morning.

DR. STOCKMANN. Glad to see you, Peter!

MRS. STOCKMANN. Good morning, Peter. How are you?

PETER STOCKMANN. So so, thank you. (*To* DR. STOCKMANN.) I received from you yesterday, after office hours, a report dealing with the condition of the water at the Baths.

DR. STOCKMANN. Yes. Have you read it?

PETER STOCKMANN. Yes, I have.

DR. STOCKMANN. And what have you to say to it?

PETER STOCKMANN (*with a sidelong glance*). Hm!—

MRS. STOCKMANN. Come along, Petra. (*She and* PETRA *go into the room on the left.*)

PETER STOCKMANN (*after a pause*). Was it necessary to make all these investigations behind my back?

DR. STOCKMANN. Yes, because until I was absolutely certain about it—

PETER STOCKMANN. Then you mean that you are absolutely certain now?

DR. STOCKMANN. Surely you are convinced of that.

PETER STOCKMANN. Is it your intention to bring this document before the Baths Committee as a sort of official communication?

DR. STOCKMANN. Certainly. Something must be done in the matter—and that quickly.

PETER STOCKMANN. As usual, you employ violent expressions in your report. You say, amongst other things, that what we offer visitors in our Baths is a permanent supply of poison.

DR. STOCKMANN. Well, can you describe it any other way, Peter? Just think—water that is poisonous, whether you drink it or bathe in it! And this we offer to the poor sick folk who come to us trustfully and pay us at an exorbitant rate to be made well again!

PETER STOCKMANN. And your reasoning leads you to this conclusion, that we must build a sewer to draw off the alleged impurities from Mölledal and must relay the water-conduits.

DR. STOCKMANN. Yes. Do you see any other way out of it? I don't.

PETER STOCKMANN. I made a pretext this morning to go and see the town engineer, and, as if only half seriously, broached the subject of these proposals as a thing we might perhaps have to take under consideration some time later on.

DR. STOCKMANN. Some time later on!

PETER STOCKMANN. He smiled at what he considered to be my extravagance, naturally. Have you taken the trouble to consider what your proposed alterations would cost? According to the information I obtained, the expenses would probably mount up to fifteen or twenty thousand pounds.

DR. STOCKMANN. Would it cost so much?

PETER STOCKMANN. Yes; and the worst part of it would be that the work would take at least two years.

DR. STOCKMANN. Two years? Two whole years?

PETER STOCKMANN. At least. And what are we to do with the Baths in the meantime? Close them? Indeed we should be obliged to. And do you suppose any one would come near the place after it had got about that the water was dangerous?

DR. STOCKMANN. Yes but, Peter, that is what it is.

PETER STOCKMANN. And all this at this juncture—just as the Baths are beginning to be known. There are other towns in the neighbourhood with qualifications to attract visitors for bathing purposes. Don't you suppose they would immediately strain every nerve to divert the entire stream of strangers to themselves? Unquestionably they would; and then where should we be? We should probably have to abandon the whole thing, which has cost us so much money—and then you would have ruined your native town.

DR. STOCKMANN. I—should have ruined—!

PETER STOCKMANN. It is simply and solely through the Baths that the town has before it any future worth mentioning. You know that just as well as I.

DR. STOCKMANN. But what do you think ought to be done, then?

PETER STOCKMANN. Your report has not convinced me that the condition of the water at the Baths is as bad as you represent it to be.

DR. STOCKMANN. I tell you it is even worse!—or at all events it will be in summer, when the warm weather comes.

PETER STOCKMANN. As I said, I believe you exaggerate the matter considerably. A capable physician ought to know what measures to take—he ought to be capable of preventing injurious influences or of remedying them if they become obviously persistent.

DR. STOCKMANN. Well? What more?

PETER STOCKMANN. The water supply for the Baths is now an established fact, and in consequence must be treated as such. But probably the Committee, at its discretion, will not be disinclined to consider the question of how far it might be possible to introduce certain improvements consistently with a reasonable expenditure.

DR. STOCKMANN. And do you suppose that I will have anything to do with such a piece of trickery as that?

PETER STOCKMANN. Trickery! !

DR. STOCKMANN. Yes, it would be a trick—a fraud, a lie, a downright crime towards the public, towards the whole community!

PETER STOCKMANN. I have not, as I remarked before, been able to convince myself that there is actually any imminent danger.

DR. STOCKMANN. You have! It is impossible that you should not be convinced. I know I have represented the facts absolutely truthfully and fairly. And you know it very well, Peter, only you won't acknowledge it. It was owing to your action that both the Baths and the water-conduits were built where they are; and that is what you won't acknowledge—that damnable blunder of yours. Pooh!—do you suppose I don't see through you?

PETER STOCKMANN. And even if that were true? If I perhaps guard my reputation somewhat anxiously, it is in the best interests of the town. Without moral authority I am powerless to direct public affairs as seems, to my judgment, to be best for the common good. And on that account—and for various other reasons too—it appears to me to be a matter of importance that your report should not be delivered to the Committee. In the interests of the public, you must withhold it. Then, later on, I will raise the question and we will do our best, privately; but nothing of this unfortunate affair—not a single word of it—must come to the ears of the public.

DR. STOCKMANN. I am afraid you will not be able to prevent that now, my dear Peter.

PETER STOCKMANN. It must and shall be prevented.

DR. STOCKMANN. It is no use, I tell you. There are too many people that know about it.

PETER STOCKMANN. That know about it? Who? Surely you don't mean those fellows on the "People's Messenger"?

DR. STOCKMANN. Yes, they know. The liberal-minded independent press is going to see that you do your duty.

PETER STOCKMANN (after a short pause). You are an extraordinarily independent man, Thomas. Have you given no thought to the consequences this may have for yourself?

DR. STOCKMANN. Consequences?—for me?

PETER STOCKMANN. For you and yours, yes.

DR. STOCKMANN. What the deuce do you mean?

PETER STOCKMANN. I believe I have always behaved in a brotherly way to you—have always been ready to oblige or to help you?

DR. STOCKMANN. Yes, you have, and I am grateful to you for it.

PETER STOCKMANN. There is no need. Indeed, to some

extent I was forced to do so—for my own sake. I always hoped that, if I helped to improve your financial position, I should be able to keep some check on you.

DR. STOCKMANN. What! ! Then it was only for your own sake—!

PETER STOCKMANN. Up to a certain point, yes. It is painful for a man in an official position to have his nearest relative compromising himself time after time.

DR. STOCKMANN. And do you consider that I do that?

PETER STOCKMANN. Yes, unfortunately, you do, without even being aware of it. You have a restless, pugnacious, rebellious disposition. And then there is that disastrous propensity of yours to want to write about every sort of possible and impossible thing. The moment an idea comes into your head, you must needs go and write a newspaper article or a whole pamphlet about it.

DR. STOCKMANN. Well, but is it not the duty of a citizen to let the public share in any new ideas he may have?

PETER STOCKMANN. Oh, the public doesn't require any new ideas. The public is best served by the good, old-established ideas it already has.

DR. STOCKMANN. And that is your honest opinion?

PETER STOCKMANN. Yes, and for once I must talk frankly to you. Hitherto I have tried to avoid doing so, because I know how irritable you are; but now I must tell you the truth, Thomas. You have no conception what an amount of harm you do yourself by your impetuosity. You complain of the authorities, you even complain of the government— you are always pulling them to pieces; you insist that you have been neglected and persecuted. But what else can such a cantankerous man as you expect?

DR. STOCKMANN. What next! Cantankerous, am I?

PETER STOCKMANN. Yes, Thomas, you are an extremely cantankerous man to work with—I know that to my cost. You disregard everything that you ought to have consideration for. You seem completely to forget that it is me you have to thank for your appointment here as medical officer to the Baths—

DR. STOCKMANN. I was entitled to it as a matter of course!— I and nobody else! I was the first person to see that the town could be made into a flourishing watering-place, and I was the only one who saw it at that time. I had to fight single-handed in support of the idea for many years; and I wrote and wrote—

PETER STOCKMANN. Undoubtedly. But things were not ripe for the scheme then—though, of course, you could not judge of that in your out-of-the-way corner up north. But as soon as the opportune moment came I—and the others—took the matter into our hands—

DR. STOCKMANN. Yes, and made this mess of all my beautiful plan. It is pretty obvious now what clever fellows you were!

PETER STOCKMANN. To my mind the whole thing only seems to mean that you are seeking another outlet for your combativeness. You want to pick a quarrel with your superiors —an old habit of yours. You cannot put up with any authority over you. You look askance at anyone who occupies a superior official position; you regard him as a personal enemy, and then any stick is good enough to beat him with. But now I have called your attention to the fact that the town's interests are at stake—and, incidentally, my own too. And therefore I must tell you, Thomas, that you will find me inexorable with regard to what I am about to require you to do.

DR. STOCKMANN. And what is that?

PETER STOCKMANN. As you have been so indiscreet as to speak of this delicate matter to outsiders, despite the fact that you ought to have treated it as entirely official and confidential, it is obviously impossible to hush it up now. All sorts of rumours will get about directly, and everybody who has a grudge against us will take care to embellish these rumours. So it will be necessary for you to refute them publicly.

DR. STOCKMANN. I! How? I don't understand.

PETER STOCKMANN. What we shall expect is that, after making further investigations, you will come to the conclusion that the matter is not by any means as dangerous or as critical as you imagined in the first instance.

DR. STOCKMANN. Oho!—so that is what you expect!

PETER STOCKMANN. And, what is more, we shall expect you to make public profession of your confidence in the Committee and in their readiness to consider fully and conscientiously what steps may be necessary to remedy any possible defects.

DR. STOCKMANN. But you will never be able to do that by patching and tinkering at it—never! Take my word for it, Peter; I mean what I say, as deliberately and emphatically as possible.

PETER STOCKMANN. As an officer under the Committee, you have no right to any individual opinion.

DR. STOCKMANN (*amazed*). No right?

PETER STOCKMANN. In your official capacity, no. As a private person, it is quite another matter. But as a subordinate member of the staff of the Baths, you have no right to express any opinion which runs contrary to that of your superiors.

DR. STOCKMANN. This is too much! I, a doctor, a man of science, have no right to—!

PETER STOCKMANN. The matter in hand is not simply a scientific one. It is a complicated matter, and has its economic as well as its technical side.

DR. STOCKMANN. I don't care what it is! I intend to be free to express my opinion on any subject under the sun.

PETER STOCKMANN. As you please—but not on any subject concerning the Baths. That we forbid.

DR. STOCKMANN (*shouting*). You forbid—! You! A pack of—

PETER STOCKMANN. *I* forbid it—I, your chief; and if I forbid it, you have to obey.

DR. STOCKMANN (*controlling himself*). Peter—if you were not my brother—

PETRA (*throwing open the door*). Father, you shan't stand this!

MRS. STOCKMANN (*coming in after her*). Petra, Petra!

PETER STOCKMANN. Oh, so you have been eavesdropping.

MRS. STOCKMANN. You were talking so loud, we couldn't help—

PETRA. Yes, I was listening.

PETER STOCKMANN. Well, after all, I am very glad—

DR. STOCKMANN (*going up to him*). You were saying something about forbidding and obeying?

PETER STOCKMANN. You obliged me to take that tone with you.

DR. STOCKMANN. And so I am to give myself the lie, publicly?

PETER STOCKMANN. We consider it absolutely necessary that you should make some such public statement as I have asked for.

DR. STOCKMANN. And if I do not—obey?

PETER STOCKMANN. Then we shall publish a statement ourselves to reassure the public.

DR. STOCKMANN. Very well; but in that case I shall use my pen against you. I stick to what I have said; I will show that I am right and that you are wrong. And what will you do then?

PETER STOCKMANN. Then I shall not be able to prevent your being dismissed.

DR. STOCKMANN. What—?

PETRA. Father—dismissed!

MRS. STOCKMANN. Dismissed!

PETER STOCKMANN. Dismissed from the staff of the Baths. I shall be obliged to propose that you shall immediately be given notice, and shall not be allowed any further participation in the Baths' affairs.

DR. STOCKMANN. You would dare to do that!

PETER STOCKMANN. It is you that are playing the daring game.

PETRA. Uncle, that is a shameful way to treat a man like father!

MRS. STOCKMANN. Do hold your tongue, Petra!

PETER STOCKMANN (*looking at* PETRA). Oh, so we volunteer our opinions already, do we? Of course. (*To* MRS. STOCKMANN.) Katherine, I imagine you are the most sensible person in this house. Use any influence you may have over your husband, and make him see what this will entail for his family as well as—

DR. STOCKMANN. My family is my own concern and nobody else's!

PETER STOCKMANN. —for his own family, as I was saying, as well as for the town he lives in.

DR. STOCKMANN. It is I who have the real good of the town at heart! I want to lay bare the defects that sooner or later must come to the light of day. I will show whether I love my native town.

PETER STOCKMANN. You, who in your blind obstinacy want to cut off the most important source of the town's welfare?

DR. STOCKMANN. The source is poisoned, man! Are you mad? We are making our living by retailing filth and corruption! The whole of our flourishing municipal life derives its sustenance from a lie!

PETER STOCKMANN. All imagination—or something even worse. The man who can throw out such offensive insinuations about his native town must be an enemy to our community.

DR. STOCKMANN (*going up to him*). Do you dare to—!

MRS. STOCKMANN (*throwing herself between them*). Thomas!

PETRA (*catching her father by the arm*). Don't lose your temper, father!

PETER STOCKMANN. I will not expose myself to violence. Now you have had a warning; so reflect on what you owe to yourself and your family. Good-bye. (*Goes out.*)

DR. STOCKMANN (*walking up and down*). Am I to put up with such treatment as this? In my own house, Katherine! What do you think of that!

MRS. STOCKMANN. Indeed it is both shameful and absurd, Thomas—

PETRA. If only I could give uncle a piece of my mind—

426

DR. STOCKMANN. It is my own fault. I ought to have flown out at him long ago!—shown my teeth!—bitten! To hear him call me an enemy to our community! Me! I shall not take that lying down, upon my soul!

MRS. STOCKMANN. But, dear Thomas, your brother has power on his side—

DR. STOCKMANN. Yes, but I have right on mine, I tell you.

MRS. STOCKMANN. Oh yes, right—right. What is the use of having right on your side if you have not got might?

PETRA. Oh, mother!—how can you say such a thing!

DR. STOCKMANN. Do you imagine that in a free country it is no use having right on your side? You are absurd, Katherine. Besides, haven't I got the liberal-minded independent press to lead the way, and the compact majority behind me? That is might enough, I should think!

MRS. STOCKMANN. But, good heavens, Thomas, you don't mean to—?

DR. STOCKMANN. Don't mean to what?

MRS. STOCKMANN. To set yourself up in opposition to your brother.

DR. STOCKMANN. In God's name, what else do you suppose I should do but take my stand on right and truth?

PETRA. Yes, I was just going to say that.

MRS. STOCKMANN. But it won't do you any earthly good. If they won't do it, they won't.

DR. STOCKMANN. Oho, Katherine! Just give me time, and you will see how I will carry the war into their camp.

MRS. STOCKMANN. Yes, you carry the war into their camp, and you get your dismissal—that is what you will do.

DR. STOCKMANN. In any case I shall have done my duty towards the public—towards the community. I, who am called its enemy!

MRS. STOCKMANN. But towards your family, Thomas? Towards your own home! Do you think that is doing your duty towards those you have to provide for?

PETRA. Ah, don't think always first of us, mother.

MRS. STOCKMANN. Oh, it is easy for you to talk; you are able to shift for yourself, if need be. But remember the boys, Thomas; and think a little too of yourself, and of me—

DR. STOCKMANN. I think you are out of your senses, Katherine! If I were to be such a miserable coward as to go on my knees to Peter and his damned crew, do you suppose I should ever know an hour's peace of mind all my life afterwards?

MRS. STOCKMANN. I don't know anything about that; but God preserve us from the peace of mind we shall have, all the same, if you go on defying him! You will find yourself

427

again without the means of subsistence, with no income to count upon. I should think we had had enough of that in the old days. Remember that, Thomas; think what that means.

DR. STOCKMANN (*collecting himself with a struggle and clenching his fists*). And this is what this slavery can bring upon a free, honourable man! Isn't it horrible, Katherine?

MRS. STOCKMANN. Yes, it is sinful to treat you so, it is perfectly true. But, good heavens, one has to put up with so much injustice in this world.—There are the boys, Thomas! Look at them! What is to become of them? Oh, no, you can never have the heart—. (EJLIF *and* MORTEN *have come in while she was speaking, with their school books in their hands.*)

DR. STOCKMANN. The boys—! (*Recovers himself suddenly.*) No, even if the whole world goes to pieces, I will never bow my neck to this yoke! (*Goes towards his room.*)

MRS. STOCKMANN (*following him*). Thomas—what are you going to do!

DR. STOCKMANN (*at his door*). I mean to have the right to look my sons in the face when they are grown men. (*Goes into his room.*)

MRS. STOCKMANN (*bursting into tears*). God help us all!

PETRA. Father is splendid! He will not give in.

(*The boys look on in amazement;* PETRA *signs to them not to speak.*)

ACT III

(SCENE.—*The editorial office of the "People's Messenger."
The entrance door is on the left-hand side of the back wall;
on the right-hand side is another door with glass panels
through which the printing-room can be seen. Another door
in the right-hand wall. In the middle of the room is a large
table covered with papers, newspapers and books. In the
foreground on the left a window, before which stands a desk
and a high stool. There are a couple of easy chairs by the
table, and other chairs standing along the wall. The room is
dingy and uncomfortable; the furniture is old, the chairs
stained and torn. In the printing-room the compositors are
seen at work, and a printer is working a hand-press.* HOVSTAD
is sitting at the desk, writing. BILLING *comes in from the right
with* DR. STOCKMANN'S *manuscript in his hand.*)

BILLING. Well, I must say!

HOVSTAD (*still writing*). Have you read it through?

BILLING (*laying the MS. on the desk*). Yes, indeed I have.

HOVSTAD. Don't you think the Doctor hits them pretty
hard?

BILLING. Hard? Bless my soul, he's crushing! Every word
falls like—how shall I put it?—like the blow of a sledge-
hammer.

HOVSTAD. Yes, but they are not the people to throw up the
sponge at the first blow.

BILLING. That is true; and for that reason we must strike
blow upon blow until the whole of this aristocracy tumbles to
pieces. As I sat there reading this, I almost seemed to see a
revolution in being.

HOVSTAD (*turning round*). Hush!—Speak so that Aslaksen
cannot hear you.

BILLING (*lowering his voice*). Aslaksen is a chicken-hearted
chap, a coward; there is nothing of the man in him. But this

429

time you will insist on your own way, won't you? You will
put the Doctor's article in?

HOVSTAD. Yes, and if the Mayor doesn't like it—

BILLING. That will be the devil of a nuisance.

HOVSTAD. Well, fortunately we can turn the situation to
good account, whatever happens. If the Mayor will not fall
in with the Doctor's project, he will have all the small tradesmen down on him—the whole of the Householders' Association and the rest of them. And if he does fall in with it, he
will fall out with the whole crowd of large shareholders in the
Baths, who up to now have been his most valuable supporters—

BILLING. Yes, because they will certainly have to fork out
a pretty penny—

HOVSTAD. Yes, you may be sure they will. And in this
way the ring will be broken up, you see, and then in every
issue of the paper we will enlighten the public on the Mayor's
incapability on one point and another, and make it clear that
all the positions of trust in the town, the whole control of
municipal affairs, ought to be put in the hands of the Liberals.

BILLING. That is perfectly true! I see it coming—I see it
coming; we are on the threshold of a revolution!

(*A knock it heard at the door.*)

HOVSTAD. Hush! (*Calls out.*) Come in! (DR. STOCKMANN
comes in by the street door. HOVSTAD *goes to meet him.*) Ah,
it is you, Doctor! Well?

DR. STOCKMANN. You may set to work and print it, Mr.
Hovstad!

HOVSTAD. Has it come to that, then?

BILLING. Hurrah!

DR. STOCKMANN. Yes, print away. Undoubtedly it has come
to that. Now they must take what they get. There is going
to be a fight in the town, Mr. Billing!

BILLING. War to the knife, I hope! We will get our knives
to their throats, Doctor!

DR. STOCKMANN. This article is only a beginning. I have
already got four or five more sketched out in my head. Where
is Aslaksen?

BILLING (*calls into the printing-room*). Aslaksen, just come
here for a minute!

HOVSTAD. Four or five more articles, did you say? On the
same subject?

DR. STOCKMANN. No—far from it, my dear fellow. No,
they are about quite another matter. But they all spring from
the question of the water-supply and the drainage. One thing
leads to another, you know. It is like beginning to pull down
an old house, exactly.

BILLING. Upon my soul, it's true; you find you are not done till you have pulled all the old rubbish down.

ASLAKSEN (*coming in*). Pulled down? You are not thinking of pulling down the Baths surely, Doctor?

HOVSTAD. Far from it, don't be afraid.

DR. STOCKMANN. No, we meant something quite different. Well, what do you think of my article, Mr. Hovstad?

HOVSTAD. I think it is simply a masterpiece—

DR. STOCKMANN. Do you really think so? Well, I am very pleased, very pleased.

HOVSTAD. It is so clear and intelligible. One need have no special knowledge to understand the bearing of it. You will have every enlightened man on your side.

ASLAKSEN. And every prudent man too, I hope?

BILLING. The prudent and the imprudent—almost the whole town.

ASLAKSEN. In that case we may venture to print it.

DR. STOCKMANN. I should think so!

HOVSTAD. We will put it in to-morrow morning.

DR. STOCKMANN. Of course—you must not lose a single day. What I wanted to ask you, Mr. Aslaksen, was if you would supervise the printing of it yourself.

ASLAKSEN. With pleasure.

DR. STOCKMANN. Take care of it as if it were a treasure! No misprints—every word is important. I will look in again a little later; perhaps you will be able to let me see a proof. I can't tell you how eager I am to see it in print, and see it burst upon the public—

BILLING. Burst upon them—yes, like a flash of lightning!

DR. STOCKMANN. —and to have it submitted to the judgment of my intelligent fellow-townsmen. You cannot imagine what I have gone through to-day. I have been threatened first with one thing and then with another; they have tried to rob me of my most elementary rights as a man—

BILLING. What! Your rights as a man!

DR. STOCKMANN. —they have tried to degrade me, to make a coward of me, to force me to put personal interests before my most sacred convictions—

BILLING. That is too much—I'm damned if it isn't.

HOVSTAD. Oh, you mustn't be surprised at anything from that quarter.

DR. STOCKMANN. Well, they will get the worst of it with me; they may assure themselves of that. I shall consider the "People's Messenger" my sheet-anchor now, and every single day I will bombard them with one article after another, like bomb-shells—

ASLAKSEN. Yes, but—

431

BILLING. Hurrah!—it is war, it is war!

DR. STOCKMANN. I shall smite them to the ground—I shall crush them—I shall break down all their defences, before the eyes of the honest public! That is what I shall do!

ASLAKSEN. Yes, but in moderation, Doctor—proceed with moderation—

BILLING. Not a bit of it, not a bit of it! Don't spare the dynamite!

DR. STOCKMANN. Because it is not merely a question of water-supply and drains now, you know. No—it is the whole of our social life that we have got to purify and disinfect—

BILLING. Spoken like a deliverer!

DR. STOCKMANN. All the incapables must be turned out, you understand—and that in every walk of life! Endless vistas have opened themselves to my mind's eye to-day. I cannot see it all quite clearly yet, but I shall in time. Young and vigorous standard-bearers—those are what we need and must seek, my friends; we must have new men in command at all our outposts.

BILLING. Hear, hear!

DR. STOCKMANN. We only need to stand by one another, and it will all be perfectly easy. The revolution will be launched like a ship that runs smoothly off the stocks. Don't you think so?

HOVSTAD. For my part I think we have now a prospect of getting the municipal authority into the hands where it should lie.

ASLAKSEN. And if only we proceed with moderation, I cannot imagine that there will be any risk.

DR. STOCKMANN. Who the devil cares whether there is any risk or not! What I am doing, I am doing in the name of truth and for the sake of my conscience.

HOVSTAD. You are a man who deserves to be supported, Doctor.

ASLAKSEN. Yes, there is no denying that the Doctor is a true friend to the town—a real friend to the community, that he is.

BILLING. Take my word for it, Aslaksen, Dr. Stockmann is a friend of the people.

ASLAKSEN. I fancy the Householders' Association will make use of that expression before long.

DR. STOCKMANN (*affected, grasps their hands*). Thank you, thank you, my dear staunch friends. It is very refreshing to me to hear you say that; my brother called me something quite different. By Jove, he shall have it back, with interest! But now I must be off to see a poor devil—. I will come back, as I said. Keep a very careful eye on the manuscript, Aslaksen, and don't for worlds leave out any of my notes of exclamation! Rather put one or two more in! Capital, capital! Well, good-bye for the present—good-bye, good-bye!

(*They show him to the door, and bow him out.*)

HOVSTAD. He may prove an invaluably useful man to us.

ASLAKSEN. Yes, so long as he confines himself to this matter of the Baths. But if he goes farther afield, I don't think it would be advisable to follow him.

HOVSTAD. Hm!—that all depends—

BILLING. You are so infernally timid, Aslaksen!

ASLAKSEN. Timid? Yes, when it is a question of the local authorities, I am timid, Mr. Billing; it is a lesson I have learnt in the school of experience, let me tell you. But try me in higher politics, in matters that concern the government itself, and then see if I am timid.

BILLING. No, you aren't, I admit. But this is simply contradicting yourself.

ASLAKSEN. I am a man with a conscience, and that is the whole matter. If you attack the government, you don't do the community any harm, anyway; those fellows pay no attention to attacks, you see—they go on just as they are, in spite of them. But *local* authorities are different; they *can* be turned out, and then perhaps you may get an ignorant lot into office who may do irreparable harm to the householders and everybody else.

HOVSTAD. But what of the education of citizens by self government—don't you attach any importance to that?

ASLAKSEN. When a man has interests of his own to protect, he cannot think of everything, Mr. Hovstad.

HOVSTAD. Then I hope I shall never have interests of my own to protect!

BILLING. Hear, hear!

ASLAKSEN (*with a smile*). Hm! (*Points to the desk.*) Mr. Sheriff Stensgaard was your predecessor at that editorial desk.

BILLING (*spitting*). Bah! That turncoat.

HOVSTAD. I am not a weathercock—and never will be.

ASLAKSEN. A politician should never be too certain of anything, Mr. Hovstad. And as for you, Mr. Billing, I should think it is time for you to be taking in a reef or two in your sails, seeing that you are applying for the post of secretary to the Bench.

BILLING. I—!

HOVSTAD. Are you, Billing?

BILLING. Well, yes—but you must clearly understand I am only doing it to annoy the bigwigs.

ASLAKSEN. Anyhow, it is no business of mine. But if I am to be accused of timidity and of inconsistency in my principles, this is what I want to point out: my political past is an open book. I have never changed, except perhaps to become a little more moderate, you see. My heart is still with the people; but I don't deny that my reason has a certain bias towards the authorities—the local ones, I mean. (*Goes into the printing-room.*)

BILLING. Oughtn't we to try and get rid of him, Hovstad?

HOVSTAD. Do you know anyone else who will advance the money for our paper and printing bill?

BILLING. It is an infernal nuisance that we don't possess some capital to trade on.

HOVSTAD (*sitting down at his desk*). Yes, if we only had that, then—

BILLING. Suppose you were to apply to Dr. Stockmann?

HOVSTAD (*turning over some papers*). What is the use? He has got nothing.

BILLING. No, but he has got a warm man in the background, old Morten Kiil—"the Badger," as they call him.

HOVSTAD (*writing*). Are you so sure *he* has got anything?

BILLING. Good Lord, of course he has! And some of it must come to the Stockmanns. Most probably he will do something for the children, at all events.

HOVSTAD (*turning half round*). Are you counting on that?

BILLING. Counting on it? Of course I am not counting on anything.

HOVSTAD. That is right. And I should not count on the secretaryship to the Bench either, if I were you; for I can assure you—you won't get it.

BILLING. Do you think I am not quite aware of that? My object is precisely *not* to get it. A slight of that kind stimulates a man's fighting power—it is like getting a supply of fresh bile—and I am sure one needs that badly enough in a hole-and-corner place like this, where it is so seldom anything happens to stir one up.

HOVSTAD (*writing*). Quite so, quite so.

BILLING. Ah, I shall be heard of yet!—Now I shall go and write the appeal to the Householders' Association. (*Goes into the room on the right.*)

HOVSTAD (*sitting at his desk, biting his penholder, says slowly*). Hm!—that's it, is it. (*A knock is heard.*) Come in! (*PETRA comes in by the outer door. HOVSTAD gets up.*) What, you!—here?

PETRA. Yes, you must forgive me—

HOVSTAD (*pulling a chair forward*). Won't you sit down?

PETRA. No, thank you; I must go again in a moment.

HOVSTAD. Have you come with a message from your father, by any chance?

434

PETRA. No, I have come on my own account. (*Takes a book out of her coat pocket.*) Here is the English story.

HOVSTAD. Why have you brought it back?

PETRA. Because I am not going to translate it.

HOVSTAD. But you promised me faithfully—

PETRA. Yes, but then I had not read it. I don't suppose you have read it either?

HOVSTAD. No, you know quite well I don't understand English; but—

PETRA. Quite so. That is why I wanted to tell you that you must find something else. (*Lays the book on the table.*) You can't use this for the "People's Messenger."

HOVSTAD. Why not?

PETRA. Because it conflicts with all your opinions.

HOVSTAD. Oh, for that matter—

PETRA. You don't understand me. The burden of this story is that there is a supernatural power that looks after the so-called good people in this world and makes everything happen for the best in their case—while all the so-called bad people are punished.

HOVSTAD. Well, but that is all right. That is just what our readers want.

PETRA. And are you going to be the one to give it to them? For myself, I do not believe a word of it. You know quite well that things do not happen so in reality.

HOVSTAD. You are perfectly right; but an editor cannot always act as he would prefer. He is often obliged to bow to the wishes of the public in unimportant matters. Politics are the most important thing in life—for a newspaper, anyway; and if I want to carry my public with me on the path that leads to liberty and progress, I must not frighten them away. If they find a moral tale of this sort in the serial at the bottom of the page, they will be all the more ready to read what is printed above it; they feel more secure, as it were.

PETRA. For shame! You would never go and set a snare like that for your readers; you are not a spider!

HOVSTAD (*smiling*). Thank you for having such a good opinion of me. No; as a matter of fact that is Billing's idea and not mine.

PETRA. Billing's!

HOVSTAD. Yes; anyway he propounded that theory here one day. And it is Billing who is so anxious to have that story in the paper; I don't know anything about the book.

PETRA. But how can Billing, with his emancipated views—

HOVSTAD. Oh, Billing is a many-sided man. He is applying for the post of secretary to the Bench, too, I hear.

PETRA. I don't believe it, Mr. Hovstad. How could he possibly bring himself to do such a thing?

HOVSTAD. Ah, you must ask him that.

PETRA. I should never have thought it of him.

HOVSTAD (*looking more closely at her*). No? Does it really surprise you so much?

PETRA. Yes. Or perhaps not altogether. Really, I don't quite know—

HOVSTAD. We journalists are not much worth, Miss Stockmann.

PETRA. Do you really mean that?

HOVSTAD. I think so sometimes.

PETRA. Yes, in the ordinary affairs of everyday life, perhaps; I can understand that. But now, when you have taken a weighty matter in hand—

HOVSTAD. This matter of your father's, you mean?

PETRA. Exactly. It seems to me that now you must feel you are a man worth more than most.

HOVSTAD. Yes, to-day I do feel something of that sort.

PETRA. Of course you do, don't you? It is a splendid vocation you have chosen—to smooth the way for the march of unappreciated truths, and new and courageous lines of thought. If it were nothing more than because you stand fearlessly in the open and take up the cause of an injured man—

HOVSTAD. Especially when that injured man is—ahem!—I don't rightly know how to—

PETRA. When that man is so upright and so honest, you mean?

HOVSTAD (*more gently*). Especially when he is your father, I meant.

PETRA (*suddenly checked*). That?

HOVSTAD. Yes, Petra—Miss Petra.

PETRA. Is it *that*, that is first and foremost with you? Not the matter itself? Not the truth?—not my father's big generous heart?

HOVSTAD. Certainly—of course—that too.

PETRA. No, thank you; you have betrayed yourself, Mr. Hovstad, and now I shall never trust you again in anything.

HOVSTAD. Can you really take it so amiss in me that it is mostly for your sake—?

PETRA. What I am angry with you for, is for not having been honest with my father. You talked to him as if the truth and the good of the community were what lay nearest to your heart. You have made fools of both my father and me. You are not the man you made yourself out to be. And that I shall never forgive you—never!

436

HOVSTAD. You ought not to speak so bitterly, Miss Petra —least of all now.

PETRA. Why not now, especially?

HOVSTAD. Because your father cannot do without my help.

PETRA (*looking him up and down*). Are you that sort of man too? For shame!

HOVSTAD. No, no, I am not. This came upon me so unexpectedly—you must believe that.

PETRA. I know what to believe. Good-bye.

ASLAKSEN (*coming from the printing-room, hurriedly and with an air of mystery*). Damnation, Hovstad!—(*Sees* PETRA.) Oh, this is awkward—

PETRA. There is the book; you must give it to some one else. (*Goes towards the door.*)

HOVSTAD (*following her*). But, Miss Stockmann—

PETRA. Good-bye. (*Goes out.*)

ASLAKSEN. I say—Mr. Hovstad—

HOVSTAD. Well, well!—what is it?

ASLAKSEN. The Mayor is outside in the printing-room.

HOVSTAD. The Mayor, did you say?

ASLAKSEN. Yes, he wants to speak to you. He came in by the back door—didn't want to be seen, you understand.

HOVSTAD. What can he want? Wait a bit—I will go myself. (*Goes to the door of the printing-room, opens it, bows and invites* PETER STOCKMANN *in.*) Just see, Aslaksen, that no one—

ASLAKSEN. Quite so. (*Goes into the printing-room.*)

PETER STOCKMANN. You did not expect to see me here, Mr. Hovstad?

HOVSTAD. No, I confess I did not.

PETER STOCKMANN (*looking round*). You are very snug in here—very nice indeed.

HOVSTAD. Oh—

PETER STOCKMANN. And here I come, without any notice, to take up your time!

HOVSTAD. By all means, Mr. Mayor. I am at your service. But let me relieve you of your— (*takes* STOCKMANN'S *hat and stick and puts them on a chair*). Won't you sit down?

PETER STOCKMANN (*sitting down by the table*). Thank you. (HOVSTAD *sits down.*) I have had an extremely annoying experience to-day, Mr. Hovstad.

HOVSTAD. Really? Ah well, I expect with all the various business you have to attend to—

PETER STOCKMANN. The Medical Officer of the Baths is responsible for what happened to-day.

HOVSTAD. Indeed? The Doctor?

PETER STOCKMANN. He has addressed a kind of report to

the Baths Committee on the subject of certain supposed defects in the Baths.

HOVSTAD. Has he indeed?

PETER STOCKMANN. Yes—has he not told you? I thought he said—

HOVSTAD. Ah, yes—it is true he did mention something about—

ASLAKSEN (*coming from the printing-room*). I ought to have that copy—

HOVSTAD (*angrily*). Ahem!—there it is on the desk.

ASLAKSEN (*taking it*). Right.

PETER STOCKMANN. But look there—that is the thing I was speaking of!

ASLAKSEN. Yes, that is the Doctor's article, Mr. Mayor.

HOVSTAD. Oh, is *that* what you were speaking about?

PETER STOCKMANN. Yes, that is it. What do you think of it?

HOVSTAD. Oh, I am only a layman—and I have only taken a very cursory glance at it.

PETER STOCKMANN. But you are going to print it?

HOVSTAD. I cannot very well refuse a distinguished man—

ASLAKSEN. I have nothing to do with editing the paper, Mr. Mayor—

PETER STOCKMANN. I understand.

ASLAKSEN. I merely print what is put into my hands.

PETER STOCKMANN. Quite so.

ASLAKSEN. And so I must— (*moves off towards the printing-room*).

PETER STOCKMANN. No, wait a moment, Mr. Aslaksen. You will allow me, Mr. Hovstad?

HOVSTAD. If you please, Mr. Mayor.

PETER STOCKMANN. You are a discreet and thoughtful man, Mr. Aslaksen.

ASLAKSEN. I am delighted to hear you think so, sir.

PETER STOCKMANN. And a man of very considerable influence.

ASLAKSEN. Chiefly among the small tradesmen, sir.

PETER STOCKMANN. The small tax-payers are the majority —here as everywhere else.

ASLAKSEN. That is true.

PETER STOCKMANN. And I have no doubt you know the general trend of opinion among them, don't you?

ASLAKSEN. Yes I think I may say I do, Mr. Mayor.

PETER STOCKMANN. Yes. Well, since there is such a praiseworthy spirit of self-sacrifice among the less wealthy citizens of our town—

ASLAKSEN. What?

HOVSTAD. Self-sacrifice?

PETER STOCKMANN. It is pleasing evidence of a public-spirited feeling, extremely pleasing evidence. I might almost say I hardly expected it. But you have a closer knowledge of public opinion than I.

ASLAKSEN. But, Mr. Mayor—

PETER STOCKMANN. And indeed it is no small sacrifice that the town is going to make.

HOVSTAD. The town?

ASLAKSEN. But I don't understand. Is it the Baths—?

PETER STOCKMANN. At a provisional estimate, the alterations that the Medical Officer asserts to be desirable will cost somewhere about twenty thousand pounds.

ASLAKSEN. That is a lot of money, but—

PETER STOCKMANN. Of course it will be necessary to raise a municipal loan.

HOVSTAD (*getting up*). Surely you never mean that the town must pay—?

ASLAKSEN. Do you mean that it must come out of the municipal funds?—out of the ill-filled pockets of the small tradesmen?

PETER STOCKMANN. Well, my dear Mr. Aslaksen, where else is the money to come from?

ASLAKSEN. The gentlemen who own the Baths ought to provide that.

PETER STOCKMANN. The proprietors of the Baths are not in a position to incur any further expense.

ASLAKSEN. Is that absolutely certain, Mr. Mayor.

PETER STOCKMANN. I have satisfied myself that it is so. If the town wants these very extensive alterations, it will have to pay for them.

ASLAKSEN. But, damn it all—I beg your pardon—this is quite another matter, Mr. Hovstad!

HOVSTAD. It is, indeed.

PETER STOCKMANN. The most fatal part of it is that we shall be obliged to shut the Baths for a couple of years.

HOVSTAD. Shut them? Shut them altogether?

ASLAKSEN. For two years?

PETER STOCKMANN. Yes, the work will take as long as that —at least.

ASLAKSEN. I'm damned if we will stand that, Mr. Mayor! What are we householders to live upon in the meantime?

PETER STOCKMANN. Unfortunately that is an extremely difficult question to answer, Mr. Aslaksen. But what would you have us do? Do you suppose we shall have a single visitor in the town, if we go about proclaiming that our water is polluted, that we are living over a plague spot, that the entire town—

ASLAKSEN. And the whole thing is merely imagination?

PETER STOCKMANN. With the best will in the world, I have not been able to come to any other conclusion.

ASLAKSEN. Well then I must say it is absolutely unjustifiable of Dr. Stockmann—I beg your pardon, Mr. Mayor—

PETER STOCKMANN. What you say is lamentably true, Mr. Aslaksen. My brother has unfortunately always been a headstrong man.

ASLAKSEN. After this, do you mean to give him your support, Mr. Hovstad?

HOVSTAD. Can you suppose for a moment that I—?

PETER STOCKMANN. I have drawn up a short *résumé* of the situation as it appears from a reasonable man's point of view. In it I have indicated how certain possible defects might suitably be remedied without out-running the resources of the Baths Committee.

HOVSTAD. Have you got it with you, Mr. Mayor.

PETER STOCKMANN (*fumbling in his pocket*). Yes, I brought it with me in case you should—

ASLAKSEN. Good Lord, there he is!

PETER STOCKMANN. Who? My brother?

HOVSTAD. Where? Where?

ASLAKSEN. He has just gone through the printing-room.

PETER STOCKMANN. How unlucky! I don't want to meet him here, and I had still several things to speak to you about.

HOVSTAD (*pointing to the door on the right*). Go in there for the present.

PETER STOCKMANN. But—?

HOVSTAD. You will only find Billing in there.

ASLAKSEN. Quick, quick, Mr. Mayor—he is just coming.

PETER STOCKMANN. Yes, very well; but see that you get rid of him quickly. (*Goes out through the door on the right, which* ASLAKSEN *opens for him and shuts after him.*)

HOVSTAD. Pretend to be doing something, Aslaksen. (*Sits down and writes.* ASLAKSEN *begins foraging among a heap of newspapers that are lying on a chair.*)

DR. STOCKMANN (*coming in from the printing-room*). Here I am again. (*Puts down his hat and stick.*)

HOVSTAD (*writing*). Already, Doctor? Hurry up with what we were speaking about, Aslaksen. We are very pressed for time to-day.

DR. STOCKMANN (*to* ASLAKSEN). No proof for me to see yet, I hear.

ASLAKSEN (*without turning round*). You couldn't expect it yet, Doctor.

DR. STOCKMANN. No, no; but I am impatient, as you can

understand. I shall not know a moment's peace of mind till I
see it in print.

HOVSTAD. Hm!—It will take a good while yet, won't it,
Aslaksen?

ASLAKSEN. Yes, I am almost afraid it will.

DR. STOCKMANN. All right, my dear friends; I will come
back. I do not mind coming back twice if necessary. A matter
of such great importance—the welfare of the town at stake—
it is no time to shirk trouble. (*Is just going, but stops and
comes back.*) Look here—there is one thing more I want to
speak to you about.

HOVSTAD. Excuse me, but could it not wait till some other
time?

DR. STOCKMANN. I can tell you in half a dozen words. It is
only this. When my article is read to-morrow and it is realised
that I have been quietly working the whole winter for the
welfare of the town—

HOVSTAD. Yes but, Doctor—

DR. STOCKMANN. I know what you are going to say. You
don't see how on earth it was any more than my duty—my
obvious duty as a citizen. Of course it wasn't; I know that as
well as you. But my fellow citizens, you know—! Good Lord,
think of all the good souls who think so highly of me—!

ASLAKSEN. Yes, our townsfolk have had a very high
opinion of you so far, Doctor.

DR. STOCKMANN. Yes, and that is just why I am afraid
they—. Well, this is the point; when this reaches them, especially the poorer classes, and sounds in their ears like a sum-
mons to take the town's affairs into their own hands for the
future—

HOVSTAD (*getting up*). Ahem! Doctor, I won't conceal
from you the fact—

DR. STOCKMANN. Ah!—I knew there was something in the
wind! But I won't hear a word of it. If anything of that sort
is being set on foot—

HOVSTAD. Of what sort?

DR. STOCKMANN. Well, whatever it is—whether it is a
demonstration in my honour, or a banquet, or a subscription
list for some presentation to me—whatever it is, you must
promise me solemnly and faithfully to put a stop to it. You
too, Mr. Aslaksen; do you understand?

HOVSTAD. You must forgive me, Doctor, but sooner or later
we must tell you the plain truth—

(*He is interrupted by the entrance of* MRS. STOCKMANN,
who comes in from the street door.)

MRS. STOCKMANN (*seeing her husband*). Just as I thought!

HOVSTAD (*going towards her*). You too, Mrs. Stockmann?

DR. STOCKMANN. What on earth do *you* want here, Katherine?

MRS. STOCKMANN. I should think you know very well what I want.

HOVSTAD. Won't you sit down? Or perhaps—

MRS. STOCKMANN. No, thank you; don't trouble. And you must not be offended at my coming to fetch my husband; I am the mother of three children, you know.

DR. STOCKMANN. Nonsense!—we know all about that.

MRS. STOCKMANN. Well, one would not give you credit for much thought for your wife and children to-day; if you had had that, you would not have gone and dragged us all into misfortune.

DR. STOCKMANN. Are you out of your senses, Katherine! Because a man has a wife and children, is he not to be allowed to proclaim the truth—is he not to be allowed to be an actively useful citizen—is he not to be allowed to do a service to his native town!

MRS. STOCKMANN. Yes, Thomas—in reason.

ASLAKSEN. Just what I say. Moderation in everything.

MRS. STOCKMANN. And that is why you wrong us, Mr. Hovstad, in enticing my husband away from his home and making a dupe of him in all this.

HOVSTAD. I certainly am making a dupe of no one—

DR. STOCKMANN. Making a dupe of me! Do you suppose *I* should allow myself to be duped!

MRS. STOCKMANN. It is just what you do. I know quite well you have more brains than anyone in the town, but you are extremely easily duped, Thomas. (*To Hovstad.*) Please to realise that he loses his post at the Baths if you print what he has written—

ASLAKSEN. What!

HOVSTAD. Look here, Doctor—

DR. STOCKMANN (*laughing*). Ha—ha!—just let them try! No, no—they will take good care not to. I have got the compact majority behind me, let me tell you!

MRS. STOCKMANN. Yes, that is just the worst of it—your having any such horrid thing behind you.

DR. STOCKMANN. Rubbish, Katherine!—Go home and look after your house and leave me to look after the community. How can you be so afraid, when I am so confident and happy? (*Walks up and down, rubbing his hands.*) Truth and the People will win the fight, you may be certain! I see the whole of the broad-minded middle class marching like a victorious army—! (*Stops beside a chair.*) What the deuce is that lying there?

ASLAKSEN. Good Lord!

HOVSTAD. Ahem!

DR. STOCKMANN. Here we have the topmost pinnacle of authority! (*Takes the Mayor's official hat carefully between his finger-tips and holds it up in the air.*)

MRS. STOCKMANN. The Mayor's hat!

DR. STOCKMANN. And here is the staff of office too. How in the name of all that's wonderful—?

HOVSTAD. Well, you see—

DR. STOCKMANN. Oh, I understand. He has been here trying to talk you over. Ha—ha!—he made rather a mistake there! And as soon as he caught sight of me in the printing-room—. (*Bursts out laughing.*) Did he run away, Mr. Aslaksen?

ASLAKSEN (*hurriedly*). Yes, he ran away, Doctor.

DR. STOCKMANN. Ran away without his stick or his—. Fiddlesticks! Peter doesn't run away and leave his belongings behind him. But what the deuce have you done with him? Ah!—in there, of course. Now you shall see, Katherine!

MRS. STOCKMANN. Thomas—please don't—!

ASLAKSEN. Don't be rash, Doctor.

(DR. STOCKMANN *has put on the Mayor's hat and taken his stick in his hand. He goes up to the door, opens it, and stands with his hand to his hat at the salute.* PETER STOCKMANN *comes in, red with anger.* BILLING *follows him.*)

PETER STOCKMANN. What does this tomfoolery mean?

DR. STOCKMANN. Be respectful, my good Peter. I am the chief authority in the town now. (*Walks up and down.*)

MRS. STOCKMANN (*almost in tears*). Really, Thomas!

PETER STOCKMANN (*following him about*). Give me my hat and stick.

DR. STOCKMANN (*in the same tone as before*). If you are chief constable, let me tell you that I am the Mayor—I am the master of the whole town, please understand!

PETER STOCKMANN. Take off my hat, I tell you. Remember it is part of an official uniform.

DR. STOCKMANN. Pooh! Do you think the newly awakened lion-hearted people are going to be frightened by an official hat? There is going to be a revolution in the town to-morrow, let me tell you. You thought you could turn me out; but now I shall turn you out—turn you out of all your various offices. Do you think I cannot? Listen to me. I have triumphant social forces behind me. Hovstad and Billing will thunder in the "People's Messenger," and Aslaksen will take the field at the head of the whole Householders' Association—

ASLAKSEN. That I won't, Doctor.

DR. STOCKMANN. Of course you will—

PETER STOCKMANN. Ah!—may I ask then if Mr. Hovstad intends to join this agitation.

HOVSTAD. No, Mr. Mayor.

ASLAKSEN. No, Mr. Hovstad is not such a fool as to go and ruin his paper and himself for the sake of an imaginary grievance.

DR. STOCKMANN (*looking round him*). What does this mean?

HOVSTAD. You have represented your case in a false light, Doctor, and therefore I am unable to give you my support.

BILLING. And after what the Mayor was so kind as to tell me just now, I—

DR. STOCKMANN. A false light! Leave that part of it to me. Only print my article; I am quite capable of defending it.

HOVSTAD. I am not going to print it. I cannot and will not and dare not print it.

DR. STOCKMANN. You dare not? What nonsense!—you are the editor; and an editor controls his paper, I suppose!

ASLAKSEN. No, it is the subscribers, Doctor.

PETER STOCKMANN. Fortunately, yes.

ASLAKSEN. It is public opinion—the enlightened public—householders and people of that kind; they control the newspapers.

DR. STOCKMANN (*composedly*). And I have all these influences against me?

ASLAKSEN. Yes, you have. It would mean the absolute ruin of the community if your article were to appear.

DR. STOCKMANN. Indeed.

PETER STOCKMANN. My hat and stick, if you please. (DR. STOCKMANN *takes off the hat and lays it on the table with the stick.* PETER STOCKMANN *takes them up.*) Your authority as mayor has come to an untimely end.

DR. STOCKMANN. We have not got to the end yet. (*To* HOVSTAD.) Then it is quite impossible for you to print my article in the "People's Messenger"?

HOVSTAD. Quite impossible—out of regard for your family as well.

MRS. STOCKMANN. You need not concern yourself about his family, thank you, Mr. Hovstad.

PETER STOCKMANN (*taking a paper from his pocket*). It will be sufficient, for the guidance of the public, if this appears. It is an official statement. May I trouble you?

HOVSTAD (*taking the paper*). Certainly; I will see that it is printed.

DR. STOCKMANN. But not mine. Do you imagine that you can silence me and stifle the truth! You will not find it so easy as you suppose. Mr. Aslaksen, kindly take my manuscript at once and print it as a pamphlet—at my expense. I will have four hundred copies—no, five—six hundred.

ASLAKSEN. If you offered me its weight in gold, I could not lend my press for any such purpose, Doctor. It would be flying in the face of public opinion. You will not get it printed anywhere in the town.

DR. STOCKMANN. Then give it back to me.

HOVSTAD (giving him the MS.). Here it is.

DR. STOCKMANN (taking his hat and stick). It shall be made public all the same. I will read it out at a mass meeting of the townspeople. All my fellow-citizens shall hear the voice of truth!

PETER STOCKMANN. You will not find any public body in the town that will give you the use of their hall for such a purpose.

ASLAKSEN. Not a single one, I am certain.

BILLING. No, I'm damned if you will find one.

MRS. STOCKMANN. But this is too shameful! Why should every one turn against you like that?

DR. STOCKMANN (angrily). I will tell you why. It is because all the men in this town are old women—like you; they all think of nothing but their families, and never of the community.

MRS. STOCKMANN (putting her arm into his). Then I will show them that an—an old woman can be a man for once. I am going to stand by you, Thomas!

DR. STOCKMANN. Bravely said, Katherine! It shall be made public—as I am a living soul! If I can't hire a hall, I shall hire a drum, and parade the town with it and read it at every street-corner.

PETER STOCKMANN. You are surely not such an arrant fool as that!

DR. STOCKMANN. Yes, I am.

ASLAKSEN. You won't find a single man in the whole town to go with you.

BILLING. No, I'm damned if you will.

MRS. STOCKMANN. Don't give in, Thomas. I will tell the boys to go with you.

DR. STOCKMANN. That is a splendid idea!

MRS. STOCKMANN. Morten will be delighted; and Ejlif will do whatever he does.

DR. STOCKMANN. Yes, and Petra!—and you too, Katherine!

MRS. STOCKMANN. No, I won't do that; but I will stand at the window and watch you, that's what I will do.

DR. STOCKMANN (puts his arms round her and kisses her). Thank you, my dear! Now you and I are going to try a fall,

445

my fine gentlemen! I am going to see whether a pack of cowards can succeed in gagging a patriot who wants to purify society! (*He and his wife go out by the street door.*)

PETER STOCKMANN (*shaking his head seriously*). Now he has sent *her* out of her senses, too.

ACT IV

(SCENE.—*A big old-fashioned room in* CAPTAIN HORSTER'S *house. At the back folding-doors, which are standing open, lead to an ante-room. Three windows in the left-hand wall. In the middle of the opposite wall a platform has been erected. On this is a small table with two candles, a water-bottle and glass, and a bell. The room is lit by lamps placed between the windows. In the foreground on the left there is a table with candles and a chair. To the right is a door and some chairs standing near it. The room is nearly filled with a crowd of townspeople of all sorts, a few women and schoolboys being amongst them. People are still streaming in from the back, and the room is soon filled.*)

1ST CITIZEN (*meeting another*). Hullo, Lamstad! You here too?

2ND CITIZEN. I go to every public meeting, I do.

3RD CITIZEN. Brought your whistle too, I expect!

2ND CITIZEN. I should think so. Haven't you?

3RD CITIZEN. Rather! And old Evensen said he was going to bring a cow-horn, he did.

2ND CITIZEN. Good old Evensen! (*Laughter among the crowd.*)

4TH CITIZEN (*coming up to them*). I say, tell me what is going on here to-night.

2ND CITIZEN. Dr. Stockmann is going to deliver an address attacking the Mayor.

4TH CITIZEN. But the Mayor is his brother.

1ST CITIZEN. That doesn't matter; Dr. Stockmann's not the chap to be afraid.

3RD CITIZEN. But he is in the wrong; it said so in the "People's Messenger."

2ND CITIZEN. Yes, I expect he must be in the wrong this time, because neither the Householders' Association nor the Citizens' Club would lend him their hall for his meeting.

1ST CITIZEN. He couldn't even get the loan of the hall at the Baths.

2ND CITIZEN. No, I should think not.

A MAN IN ANOTHER PART OF THE CROWD. I say—who are we to back up in this?

ANOTHER MAN, BESIDE HIM. Watch Aslaksen, and do as he does.

BILLING (*pushing his way through the crowd, with a writing-case under his arm*). Excuse me, gentlemen— do you mind letting me through? I am reporting for the "People's Messenger." Thank you very much! (*He sits down at the table on the left.*)

A WORKMAN. Who was that?

SECOND WORKMAN. Don't you know him? It's Billing, who writes for Aslaksen's paper.

(CAPTAIN HORSTER *brings in* MRS. STOCKMANN *and* PETRA *through the door on the right.* EJLIF *and* MORTEN *follow them in.*)

HORSTER. I thought you might all sit here; you can slip out easily from here, if things get too lively.

MRS. STOCKMANN. Do you think there will be a disturbance?

HORSTER. One can never tell—with such a crowd. But sit down, and don't be uneasy.

MRS. STOCKMANN (*sitting down*). It was extremely kind of you to offer my husband the room.

HORSTER. Well, if nobody else would—

PETRA (*who has sat down beside her mother*). And it was a plucky thing to do, Captain Horster.

HORSTER. Oh, it is not such a great matter as all that.

(HOVSTAD *and* ASLAKSEN *make their way through the crowd.*)

ASLAKSEN (*going up to* HORSTER). Has the Doctor not come yet?

HORSTER. He is waiting in the next room. (*Movement in the crowd by the door at the back.*)

HOVSTAD. Look—here comes the Mayor!

BILLING. Yes, I'm damned if he hasn't come after all!

(PETER STOCKMANN *makes his way gradually through the crowd, bows courteously, and takes up a position by the wall on the left. Shortly afterwards* DR. STOCKMANN *comes in by the right-hand door. He is dressed in a black frock-coat, with a white tie. There is a little feeble applause, which is hushed down. Silence is obtained.*)

DR. STOCKMANN (*in an undertone*). How do you feel, Katherine?

MRS. STOCKMANN. All right, thank you. (*Lowering her voice.*) Be sure not to lose your temper, Thomas.

DR. STOCKMANN. Oh, I know how to control myself. (*Looks at his watch, steps on to the platform, and bows.*) It is a quarter past—so I will begin. (*Takes his MS. out of his pocket.*)

ASLAKSEN. I think we ought to elect a chairman first.

DR. STOCKMANN. No, it is quite unnecessary.

SOME OF THE CROWD. Yes—yes!

PETER STOCKMANN. I certainly think too that we ought to have a chairman.

DR. STOCKMANN. But I have called this meeting to deliver a lecture, Peter.

PETER STOCKMANN. Dr. Stockmann's lecture may possibly lead to a considerable conflict of opinion.

VOICES IN THE CROWD. A chairman! A chairman!

HOVSTAD. The general wish of the meeting seems to be that a chairman should be elected.

DR. STOCKMANN (*restraining himself*). Very well—let the meeting have its way.

ASLAKSEN. Will the Mayor be good enough to undertake the task?

THREE MEN (*clapping their hands*). Bravo! Bravo!

PETER STOCKMANN. For various reasons, which you will easily understand, I must beg to be excused. But fortunately we have amongst us a man who I think will be acceptable to you all. I refer to the President of the Householders' Association, Mr. Aslaksen!

SEVERAL VOICES. Yes—Aslaksen! Bravo Aslaksen!

(DR. STOCKMANN *takes up his MS. and walks up and down the platform.*)

ASLAKSEN. Since my fellow-citizens choose to entrust me with this duty, I cannot refuse.

(*Loud applause.* ASLAKSEN *mounts the platform.*)

BILLING (*writing*). "Mr. Aslaksen was elected with enthusiasm."

ASLAKSEN. And now, as I am in this position, I should like to say a few brief words. I am a quiet and peaceable man, who believes in discreet moderation, and—and—in moderate discretion. All my friends can bear witness to that.

SEVERAL VOICES. That's right! That's right, Aslaksen!

ASLAKSEN. I have learnt in the school of life and experience that moderation is the most valuable virtue a citizen can possess—

PETER STOCKMANN. Hear, hear!

ASLAKSEN. —And moreover that discretion and moderation

are what enable a man to be of most service to the community. I would therefore suggest to our esteemed fellow-citizen, who has called this meeting, that he should strive to keep strictly within the bounds of moderation.

A MAN BY THE DOOR. Three cheers for the Moderation Society!

A VOICE. Shame!

SEVERAL VOICES. Sh!—Sh!

ASLAKSEN. No interruptions, gentlemen, please! Does anyone wish to make any remarks?

PETER STOCKMANN. Mr. Chairman.

ASLAKSEN. The Mayor will address the meeting.

PETER STOCKMANN. In consideration of the close relationship in which, as you all know, I stand to the present Medical Officer of the Baths, I should have preferred not to speak this evening. But my official position with regard to the Baths and my solicitude for the vital interests of the town compel me to bring forward a motion. I venture to presume that there is not a single one of our citizens present who considers it desirable that unreliable and exaggerated accounts of the sanitary condition of the Baths and the town should be spread abroad.

SEVERAL VOICES. No, no! Certainly not! We protest against it!

PETER STOCKMANN. Therefore I should like to propose that the meeting should not permit the Medical Officer either to read or to comment on his proposed lecture.

DR. STOCKMANN (*impatiently*). Not permit—! What the devil—!

MRS. STOCKMANN (*coughing*). Ahem!—ahem!

DR. STOCKMANN (*collecting himself*). Very well. Go ahead!

PETER STOCKMANN. In my communication to the "People's Messenger," I have put the essential facts before the public in such a way that every fair-minded citizen can easily form his own opinion. From it you will see that the main result of the Medical Officer's proposals—apart from their constituting a vote of censure on the leading men of the town—would be to saddle the ratepayers with an unnecessary expenditure of at least some thousands of pounds.

(*Sounds of disapproval among the audience, and some cat-calls.*)

ASLAKSEN (*ringing his bell*). Silence, please, gentlemen! I beg to support the Mayor's motion. I quite agree with him that there is something behind this agitation started by the Doctor. He talks about the Baths; but it is a revolution he is aiming at—he wants to get the administration of the town put into new hands. No one doubts the honesty of the Doctor's intentions—no one will suggest that there can be any two opinions as to that. I myself am a believer in self-government for the people, provided it does not fall too heavily on the ratepayers. But that would be the case here; and that is why I will see Dr. Stockmann damned—I beg your pardon—before I go with him in the matter. You can pay too dearly for a thing sometimes; that is my opinion.

(*Loud applause on all sides.*)

HOVSTAD. I, too, feel called upon to explain my position. Dr. Stockmann's agitation appeared to be gaining a certain amount of sympathy at first, so I supported it as impartially as I could. But presently we had reason to suspect that we had allowed ourselves to be misled by misrepresentation of the state of affairs—

DR. STOCKMANN. Misrepresentation—!

HOVSTAD. Well, let us say a not entirely trustworthy representation. The Mayor's statement has proved that. I hope no one here has any doubt as to my liberal principles; the attitude of the "People's Messenger" towards important political questions is well known to every one. But the advice of experienced and thoughtful men has convinced me that in purely local matters a newspaper ought to proceed with a certain caution.

ASLAKSEN. I entirely agree with the speaker.

HOVSTAD. And, in the matter before us, it is now an undoubted fact that Dr. Stockmann has public opinion against him. Now, what is an editor's first and most obvious duty, gentlemen? Is it not to work in harmony with his readers? Has he not received a sort of tacit mandate to work persistently and assiduously for the welfare of those whose opinions he represents? Or is it possible I am mistaken in that?

VOICES FROM THE CROWD. No, no! You are quite right!

HOVSTAD. It has cost me a severe struggle to break with a man in whose house I have been lately a frequent guest—a man who till to-day has been able to pride himself on the undivided goodwill of his fellow-citizens—a man whose only, or at all events whose essential failing, is that he is swayed by his heart rather than his head.

A FEW SCATTERED VOICES. That is true! Bravo, Stockmann!

HOVSTAD. But my duty to the community obliged me to break with him. And there is another consideration that impels me to oppose him, and, as far as possible, to arrest him on the perilous course he has adopted; that is, consideration for his family—

DR. STOCKMANN. Please stick to the water-supply and drainage!

HOVSTAD. —consideration, I repeat, for his wife and his children for whom he has made no provision.

MORTEN. Is that us, mother?

MRS. STOCKMANN. Hush!

ASLAKSEN. I will now put the Mayor's proposition to the vote.

DR. STOCKMANN. There is no necessity! To-night I have no intention of dealing with all that filth down at the Baths. No; I have something quite different to say to you.

PETER STOCKMANN (aside). What is coming now?

A DRUNKEN MAN (by the entrance door). I am a rate-payer! And therefore I have a right to speak too! And my entire—firm—inconceivable opinion is—

A NUMBER OF VOICES. Be quiet, at the back there!

OTHERS. He is drunk! Turn him out! (They turn him out.)

DR. STOCKMANN. Am I allowed to speak?

ASLAKSEN (ringing his bell). Dr. Stockmann will address the meeting.

DR. STOCKMANN. I should like to have seen anyone, a few days ago, dare to attempt to silence me as has been done to-night! I would have defended my sacred rights as a man, like a lion! But now it is all one to me; I have something of even weightier importance to say to you. (The crowd presses nearer to him, MORTEN KIIL conspicuous among them.)

DR. STOCKMANN (continuing). I have thought and pondered a great deal, these last few days—pondered over such a variety of things that in the end my head seemed too full to hold them—

PETER STOCKMANN (with a cough). Ahem!

DR. STOCKMANN. —but I got them clear in my mind at last, and then I saw the whole situation lucidly. And that is why I am standing here to-night. I have a great revelation to make to you, my fellow-citizens! I will impart to you a discovery of a far wider scope than the trifling matter that our water-supply is poisoned and our medicinal Baths are standing on pestiferous soil.

A NUMBER OF VOICES (shouting). Don't talk about the Baths! We won't hear you! None of that!

DR. STOCKMANN. I have already told you that what I want to speak about is the great discovery I have made lately—the discovery that all the sources of our *moral* life are poisoned and that the whole fabric of our civic community is founded on the pestiferous soil of falsehood.

VOICES OF DISCONCERTED CITIZENS. What is that he says?

PETER STOCKMANN. Such an insinuation—!

ASLAKSEN (*with his hand on his bell*). I call upon the speaker to moderate his language.

DR. STOCKMANN. I have always loved my native town as a man only can love the home of his youthful days. I was not old when I went away from here; and exile, longing and memories cast as it were an additional halo over both the town and its inhabitants. (*Some clapping and applause.*) And there I stayed, for many years, in a horrible hole far away up north. When I came into contact with some of the people that lived scattered about among the rocks, I often thought it would of been more service to the poor half-starved creatures if a veterinary doctor had been sent up there, instead of a man like me. (*Murmurs among the crowd.*)

BILLING (*laying down his pen*). I'm damned if I have ever heard—!

HOVSTAD. It is an insult to a respectable population!

DR. STOCKMANN. Wait a bit! I do not think anyone will charge me with having forgotten my native town up there. I was like one of the eider-ducks brooding on its nest, and what I hatched was—the plans for these Baths. (*Applause and protests.*) And then when fate at last decreed for me the great happiness of coming home again—I assure you, gentlemen, I thought I had nothing more in the world to wish for. Or rather, there was one thing I wished for—eagerly, untiringly, ardently—and that was to be able to be of service to my native town and the good of the community.

PETER STOCKMANN (*looking at the ceiling*). You chose a strange way of doing it—ahem!

DR. STOCKMANN. And so, with my eyes blinded to the real facts, I revelled in happiness. But yesterday morning—no, to be precise, it was yesterday afternoon—the eyes of my mind were opened wide, and the first thing I realised was the colossal stupidity of the authorities—. (*Uproar, shouts and laughter.* MRS. STOCKMANN *coughs persistently.*)

PETER STOCKMANN. Mr. Chairman!

ASLAKSEN (*ringing his bell*). By virtue of my authority—!

DR. STOCKMANN. It is a pretty thing to catch me up on a word, Mr. Aslaksen. What I mean is only that I got scent of the unbelievable piggishness our leading men had been responsible for down at the Baths. I can't stand leading men at any price!—I have had enough of such people in my time. They are like billy-goats in a young plantation; they do mischief everywhere. They stand in a free man's way, whichever way he turns, and what I should like best would be to see them exterminated like any other vermin—. (*Uproar.*)

PETER STOCKMANN. Mr. Chairman, can we allow such expressions to pass?

ASLAKSEN (*with his hand on his bell*). Doctor—!

DR. STOCKMANN. I cannot understand how it is that I have only now acquired a clear conception of what these gentry are, when I had almost daily before my eyes in this town such an excellent specimen of them—my brother Peter—slow-witted and hide-bound in prejudice—. (*Laughter, uproar and hisses.* MRS. STOCKMANN *sits coughing assiduously.* ASLAKSEN *rings his bell violently.*)

THE DRUNKEN MAN (*who has got in again*). Is it me he is talking about? My name's Petersen, all right—but devil take me if I—

ANGRY VOICES. Turn out that drunken man! Turn him out. (*He is turned out again.*)

PETER STOCKMANN. Who was that person?

1ST CITIZEN. I don't know who he is, Mr. Mayor.

2ND CITIZEN. He doesn't belong here.

3RD CITIZEN. I expect he is a navvy from over at—(*the rest is inaudible*).

ASLAKSEN. He had obviously had too much beer.—Proceed, Doctor; but please strive to be moderate in your language.

DR. STOCKMANN. Very well, gentlemen, I will say no more about our leading men. And if anyone imagines, from what I have just said, that my object is to attack these people this evening, he is' wrong—absolutely wide of the mark. For I cherish the comforting conviction that these parasites—all these venerable relics of a dying school of thought—are most admirably paving the way for their own extinction; they need no doctor's help to hasten their end. Nor is it folk of that kind who constitute the most pressing danger to the community. It is not they who are most instrumental in poisoning the sources of our moral life and infecting the ground on which we stand. It is not they who are the most dangerous enemies of truth and freedom amongst us.

SHOUTS FROM ALL SIDES. Who then? Who is it? Name! Name!

DR. STOCKMANN. You may depend upon it I shall name them! That is precisely the great discovery I made yesterday. (*Raises his voice.*) The most dangerous enemy of truth and freedom amongst us is the compact majority—yes, the damned compact Liberal majority—that is it! Now you know! (*Tremendous uproar. Most of the crowd are shouting, stamping and hissing. Some of the older men among them exchange stolen glances and seem to be enjoying themselves.* MRS.

STOCKMANN *gets up, looking anxious.* EJLIF *and* MORTEN *advance threateningly upon some schoolboys who are playing pranks.* ASLAKSEN *rings his bell and begs for silence.* HOV-STAD *and* BILLING *both talk at once, but are inaudible. At last quiet is restored.)*

ASLAKSEN. As chairman, I call upon the speaker to withdraw the ill-considered expressions he has just used.

DR. STOCKMANN. Never, Mr. Aslaksen! It is the majority in our community that denies me my freedom and seeks to prevent my speaking the truth.

HOVSTAD. The majority always has right on its side.

BILLING. And truth too, by God!

DR. STOCKMANN. The majority *never* has right on its side. Never, I say! That is one of these social lies against which an independent, intelligent man must wage war. Who is it that constitute the majority of the population in a country? Is it the clever folk or the stupid? I don't imagine you will dispute the fact that at present the stupid people are in an absolutely overwhelming majority all the world over. But, good Lord! —you can never pretend that it is right that the stupid folk should govern the clever ones! (*Uproar and cries.*) Oh, yes— you can shout me down, I know! but you cannot answer me. The majority has *might* on its side—unfortunately; but *right* it has *not.* I am in the right—I and a few other scattered individuals. The minority is always in the right. (*Renewed uproar.*)

HOVSTAD. Aha!—so Dr. Stockmann has become an aristocrat since the day before yesterday!

DR. STOCKMANN. I have already said that I don't intend to waste a word on the puny, narrow-chested, short-winded crew whom we are leaving astern. Pulsating life no longer concerns itself with them. I am thinking of the few, the scattered few amongst us, who have absorbed new and vigorous truths. Such men stand, as it were, at the outposts, so far ahead that the compact majority has not yet been able to come up with them; and there they are fighting for truths that are too newly-born into the world of consciousness to have any considerable number of people on their side as yet.

HOVSTAD. So the Doctor is a revolutionary now!

DR. STOCKMANN. Good heavens—of course I am, Mr. Hovstad! I propose to raise a revolution against the lie that the majority has the monopoly on the truth. What sort of truths are they that the majority usually supports? They´are truths that are of such advanced age that they are beginning to break up. And if a truth is as old as that, it is also in a fair way to become a lie, gentlemen. (*Laughter and mocking cries.*) Yes, believe me or not, as you like; but truths are by no means as long-lived at Methuselah—as some folks imagine. A normally constituted truth lives, let us say, as a rule seventeen or eighteen, or at most twenty years; seldom longer. But truths as aged as that are always worn frightfully thin, and nevertheless it is only then that the majority recognises them and recommends them to the community as wholesome moral nourishment. There is no great nutritive value in that sort of fare, I can assure you; and, as a doctor, I ought to know. These "majority truths" are like last year's cured meat—like rancid, tainted ham; and they are the origin of the moral scurvy that is rampant in our communities.

ASLAKSEN. It appears to me that the speaker is wandering a long way from his subject.

PETER STOCKMANN. I quite agree with the Chairman.

DR. STOCKMANN. Have you gone clean out of your senses, Peter? I am sticking as closely to my subject as I can; for my subject is precisely this, that it is the masses, the majority—this infernal compact majority—that poisons the sources of our moral life and infects the ground we stand on.

HOVSTAD. And all this because the great, broad-minded majority of the people is prudent enough to show deference only to well-ascertained and well-approved truths?

DR. STOCKMANN. Ah, my good Mr. Hovstad, don't talk nonsense about well-ascertained truths! The truths of which the masses now approve are the very truths that the fighters at the outposts held to in the days of our grandfathers. We fighters at the outposts nowadays no longer approve of them; and I do not believe there is any other well-ascertained truth except this, that no community can live a healthy life if it is nourished only on such old marrowless truths.

HOVSTAD. But instead of standing there using vague generalities, it would be interesting if you would tell us what these old marrowless truths are, that we are nourished on.

(*Applause from many quarters.*)

DR. STOCKMANN. Oh, I could give you a whole string of such abominations; but to begin with I will confine myself to one well-approved truth, which at bottom is a foul lie, but upon which nevertheless Mr. Hovstad and the "People's Messenger" and all the "Messenger's" supporters are nourished.

HOVSTAD. And that is—?

DR. STOCKMANN. That is, the doctrine you have inherited from your forefathers and proclaim thoughtlessly far and wide—the doctrine that the public, the crowd, the masses, are the essential part of the population—that they constitute the People—that the common folk, the ignorant and incomplete

456

element in the community, have the same right to pronounce judgment and to approve, to direct and to govern, as the isolated, intellectually superior personalities in it.

BILLING. Well, damn me if ever I—

HOVSTAD (*at the same time, shouting out*). Fellow-citizens, take good note of that!

A NUMBER OF VOICES (*angrily*). Oho!—we are not the People! Only the superior folk are to govern, are they!

A WORKMAN. Turn the fellow out, for talking such rubbish!

ANOTHER. Out with him!

ANOTHER (*calling out*). Blow your horn, Evensen!

(*A horn is blown loudly, amidst hisses and an angry uproar.*)

DR. STOCKMANN (*when the noise has somewhat abated*). Be reasonable! Can't you stand hearing the voice of truth for once? I don't in the least expect you to agree with me all at once; but I must say I did expect Mr. Hovstad to admit I was right, when he had recovered his composure a little. He claims to be a freethinker—

VOICES (*in murmurs of astonishment*). Freethinker, did he say? Is Hovstad a freethinker?

HOVSTAD (*shouting*). Prove it, Dr. Stockmann! When have I said so in print?

DR. STOCKMANN (*reflecting*). No, confound it, you are right!—you have never had the courage to. Well, I won't put you in a hole, Mr. Hovstad. Let us say it is I that am the freethinker, then. I am going to prove to you, scientifically, that the "People's Messenger" leads you by the nose in a shameful manner when it tells you that you—that the common people, the crowd, the masses, are the real essence of the People. That is only a newspaper lie, I tell you! The common people are nothing more than the raw material of which a People is made. (*Groans, laughter and uproar.*) Well, isn't that the case. Isn't there an enormous difference between a well-bred and an ill-bred strain of animals? Take, for instance, a common barn-door hen. What sort of eating do you get from a shrivelled up old scrag of a fowl like that? Not much, do you! And what sort of eggs does it lay? A fairly good crow or a raven can lay pretty nearly as good an egg. But take a well-bred Spanish or Japanese hen, or a good pheasant or a turkey—then you will see the difference. Or take the case of dogs, with whom we humans are on such intimate terms. Think first of an ordinary common cur—I mean one of the horrible, coarse-haired, low-bred curs that do nothing but run about the streets and befoul the walls of the houses. Compare one of these curs with a poodle whose sires for many generations have been bred in a gentleman's house, where they have had the best of food and had the opportunity of hearing soft voices and music. Do you not think that the poodle's brain is developed to quite a different degree from that of the cur? Of course it is. It is puppies of well-bred poodles like that, that showmen train to do incredibly clever tricks—things that a common cur could never learn to do even if it stood on its head. (*Uproar and mocking cries.*)

A CITIZEN (*calls out*). Are you going to make out we are dogs, now?

ANOTHER CITIZEN. We are not animals, Doctor!

DR. STOCKMANN. Yes but, bless my soul, we *are*, my friend! It is true we are the finest animals anyone could wish for; but, even amongst us, exceptionally fine animals are rare. There is a tremendous difference between poodle-men and cur-men. And the amusing part of it is, that Mr. Hovstad quite agrees with me as long as it is a question of four-footed animals—

HOVSTAD. Yes, it is true enough as far as they are concerned.

DR. STOCKMANN. Very well. But as soon as I extend the principle and apply it to two-legged animals, Mr. Hovstad stops short. He no longer dares to think independently, or to pursue his ideas to their logical conclusion; so he turns the whole theory upside down and proclaims in the "People's Messenger" that it is the barn-door hens and street curs that are the finest specimens in the menagerie. But that is always the way, as long as a man retains the traces of common origin and has not worked his way up to intellectual distinction.

HOVSTAD. I lay no claim to any sort of distinction. I am the son of humble countryfolk, and I am proud that the stock I come from is rooted deep among the common people he insults.

VOICES. Bravo, Hovstad! Bravo! Bravo!

DR. STOCKMANN. The kind of common people I mean are not only to be found low down in the social scale; they crawl and swarm all around us—even in the highest social positions. You have only to look at your own fine, distinguished Mayor! My brother Peter is every bit as plebian as anyone that walks in two shoes—(*laughter and hisses*).

PETER STOCKMANN. I protest against personal allusions of this kind.

DR. STOCKMANN (*imperturbably*).—and that, not because he is, like myself, descended from some old rascal of a pirate from Pomerania or thereabouts—because that is who we are descended from—

PETER STOCKMANN. An absurd legend. I deny it!

DR. STOCKMANN. —but because he thinks what his superiors think and holds the same opinions as they. People who do that are, intellectually speaking, common people; and that is why my magnificent brother Peter is in reality so very far from any distinction—and consequently also so far from being liberal-minded.

PETER STOCKMANN. Mr. Chairman—!

HOVSTAD. So it is only the distinguished men that are liberal-minded in this country? We are learning something quite new! (*Laughter.*)

DR. STOCKMANN. Yes, that is part of my new discovery too. And another part of it is that broad-mindedness is almost precisely the same thing as morality. That is why I maintain that it is absolutely inexcusable in the "People's Messenger" to proclaim, day in and day out, the false doctrine that it is the masses, the crowd, the compact majority, that have the monopoly of broad-mindedness and morality—and that vice and corruption and every kind of intellectual depravity are the result of culture, just as all the filth that is draining into our Baths is the result of the tanneries up at Mölledal! (*Uproar and interruptions.* DR. STOCKMANN *is undisturbed, and goes on, carried away by his ardour, with a smile.*) And yet this same "People's Messenger" can go on preaching that the masses ought to be elevated to higher conditions of life! But, bless my soul, if the "Messenger's" teaching is to be depended upon, this very raising up the masses would mean nothing more or less than setting them straightway upon the paths of depravity! Happily the theory that culture demoralises is only an old falsehood that our forefathers believed in and we have inherited. No, it is ignorance, poverty, ugly conditions of life, that do the devil's work! In a house which does not get aired and swept every day—my wife Katherine maintains that the floor ought to be scrubbed as well, but that is a debatable question—in such a house, let me tell you, people will lose within two or three years the power of thinking or acting in a moral manner. Lack of oxygen weakens the conscience. And there must be a plentiful lack of oxygen in very many houses in this town, I should think, judging from the fact that the whole compact majority can be unconscientious enough to wish to build the town's prosperity on a quagmire of falsehood and deceit.

ASLAKSEN. We cannot allow such a grave accusation to be flung at a citizen community.

A CITIZEN. I move that the Chairman direct the speaker to sit down.

VOICES (*angrily*). Hear, hear! Quite right! Make him sit down!

DR. STOCKMANN (*losing his self-control*). Then I will go and shout the truth at every street corner! I will write it in other towns' newspapers! The whole country shall know what is going on here!

HOVSTAD. It almost seems as if Dr. Stockmann's intention were to ruin the town.

DR. STOCKMANN. Yes, my native town is so dear to me that I would rather ruin it than see it flourishing upon a lie.

ASLAKSEN. This is really serious. (*Uproar and cat-calls. MRS. STOCKMANN coughs, but to no purpose; her husband does not listen to her any longer.*)

HOVSTAD (*shouting above the din*). A man must be a public enemy to wish to ruin a whole community!

DR. STOCKMANN (*with growing fervour*). What does the destruction of a community matter, if it lives on lies! It ought to be razed to the ground, I tell you! All who live by lies ought to be exterminated like vermin! You will end by infecting the whole country; you will bring about such a state of things that the whole country will deserve to be ruined. And if things come to that pass, I shall say from the bottom of my heart: Let the whole country perish, let all these people be exterminated!

VOICES FROM THE CROWD. That is talking like an out-and-out enemy of the people!

BILLING. There sounded the voice of the people, by all that's holy!

THE WHOLE CROWD (*shouting*). Yes, yes! He is an enemy of the people! He hates his country! He hates his own people!

ASLAKSEN. Both as a citizen and as an individual, I am profoundly disturbed by what we have had to listen to. Dr. Stockmann has shown himself in a light I should never have dreamed of. I am unhappily obliged to subscribe to the opinion which I have just heard my estimable fellow-citizens utter; and I propose that we should give expression to that opinion in a resolution. I propose a resolution as follows: "This meeting declares that it considers Dr. Thomas Stockmann, Medical Officer of the Baths, to be an enemy of the people." (*A storm of cheers and applause. A number of men surround the DOCTOR and hiss him. MRS. STOCKMANN and PETRA have got up from their seats. MORTEN and EJLIF are fighting the other schoolboys for hissing; some of their elders separate them.*)

DR. STOCKMANN (*to the men who are hissing him*). Oh, you fools! I tell you that—

ASLAKSEN (*ringing his bell*). We cannot hear you now,

Doctor. A formal vote is about to be taken; but, out of regard for personal feelings, it shall be by ballot and not verbal. Have you any clean paper, Mr. Billing?

BILLING. I have both blue and white here.

ASLAKSEN (*going to him*). That will do nicely; we shall get on more quickly that way. But it up into small strips—yes, that's it. (*To the meeting.*) Blue means no; white means yes. I will come round myself and collect votes. (PETER STOCKMANN *leaves the hall.* ASLAKSEN *and one or two others go round the room with the slips of paper in their hats.*)

1ST CITIZEN (*to* HOVSTAD). I say, what has come to the Doctor? What are we to think of it?

HOVSTAD. Oh, you know how headstrong he is.

2ND CITIZEN (*to* BILLING). Billing, you go to their house —have you ever noticed if the fellow drinks?

BILLING. Well I'm hanged if I know what to say. There are always spirits on the table when you go.

3RD CITIZEN. I rather think he goes quite off his head sometimes.

1ST CITIZEN. I wonder if there is any madness in his family?

BILLING. I shouldn't wonder if there were.

4TH CITIZEN. No, it is nothing more than sheer malice; he wants to get even with somebody for something or other.

BILLING. Well certainly he suggested a rise in his salary on one occasion lately, and did not get it.

THE CITIZENS (*together*). Ah!—then it is easy to understand how it is!

THE DRUNKEN MAN (*who has got amongst the audience again*). I want a blue one, I do! And I want a white one too!

VOICES. It's that drunken chap again! Turn him out!

MORTEN KIIL (*going up to* DR. STOCKMANN). Well, Stockmann, do you see what these monkey tricks of yours lead to?

DR. STOCKMANN. I have done my duty.

MORTEN KIIL. What was that you said about the tanneries at Mölledal?

DR. STOCKMANN. You heard well enough. I said they were the source of all the filth.

MORTEN KIIL. My tannery too?

DR. STOCKMANN. Unfortunately your tannery is by far the worst.

MORTEN KIIL. Are you going to put that in the papers?

DR. STOCKMANN. I shall conceal nothing.

MORTEN KIIL. That may cost you dear, Stockmann. (*Goes out.*)

A STOUT MAN (*going up to* CAPTAIN HORSTER, *without taking any notice of the ladies*). Well, Captain, so you lend your house to enemies of the people?

HORSTER. I imagine I can do what I like with my own possessions, Mr. Vik.

THE STOUT MAN. Then you can have no objection to my doing the same with mine.

HORSTER. What do you mean, sir?

THE STOUT MAN. You shall hear from me in the morning. (*Turns his back on him and moves off.*)

PETRA. Was that not your owner, Captain Horster?

HORSTER. Yes, that was Mr. Vik the ship-owner.

ASLAKSEN (*with the voting-papers in his hands, gets up on to the platform and rings his bell*). Gentlemen, allow me to announce the result. By the votes of every one here except one person—

A YOUNG MAN. That is the drunk chap!

ASLAKSEN. By the votes of every one here except a tipsy man, this meeting of citizens declares Dr. Thomas Stockmann to be an enemy of the people. (*Shouts and applause.*) Three cheers for our ancient and honourable citizen community! (*Renewed applause.*) Three cheers for our able and energetic Mayor, who has so loyally suppressed the promptings of family feeling! (*Cheers.*) The meeting is dissolved. (*Gets down.*)

BILLING. Three cheers for the Chairman!

THE WHOLE CROWD. Three cheers for Aslaksen! Hurrah!

DR. STOCKMANN. My hat and coat, Petra! Captain, have you room on your ship for passengers to the New World?

HORSTER. For you and yours we will make room, Doctor.

DR. STOCKMANN (*as PETRA helps him into his coat*). Good. Come, Katherine! Come, boys!

MRS. STOCKMANN (*in an undertone*). Thomas, dear, let us go out by the back way.

DR. STOCKMANN. No back ways for me, Katherine. (*Raising his voice.*) You will hear more of this enemy of the people, before he shakes the dust off his shoes upon you! I am not so forgiving as a certain Person; I do not say: "I forgive you, for ye know not what ye do."

ASLAKSEN (*shouting*). That is a blasphemous comparison, Dr. Stockmann!

BILLING. It is, by God! It's dreadful for an earnest man to listen to.

A COARSE VOICE. Threatens us now, does he!

OTHER VOICES (*excitedly*). Let's go and break his windows! Duck him in the fjord!

ANOTHER VOICE. Blow your horn, Evensen! Pip, pip!

(*Horn-blowing, hisses, and wild cries. DR. STOCKMANN goes out through the hall with his family, HORSTER elbowing a way for them.*)

462

THE WHOLE CROWD (*howling after them as they go*).
Enemy of the People! Enemy of the People!

BILLING (*as he puts his papers together*). Well, I'm damned
if I go and drink toddy with the Stockmanns to-night!

(*The crowd press towards the exit. The uproar continues
outside; shouts of "Enemy of the People!" are heard
from without.*)

ACT V

(SCENE.—DR. STOCKMANN'S *study. Bookcases, and cabinets containing specimens, line the walls. At the back is a door leading to the hall; in the foreground on the left, a door leading to the sitting-room. In the right-hand wall are two windows, of which all the panes are broken. The* DOCTOR'S *desk, littered with books and papers, stands in the middle of the room, which is in disorder. It is morning.* DR. STOCKMANN *in dressing-gown, slippers and a smoking-cap, is bending down and raking with an umbrella under one of the cabinets. After a little while he rakes out a stone.*)

DR. STOCKMANN (*calling through the open sitting-room door*). Katherine, I have found another one.

MRS. STOCKMANN (*from the sitting-room*). Oh, you will find a lot more yet, I expect.

DR. STOCKMANN (*adding the stone to a heap of others on the table*). I shall treasure these stones as relics. Ejlif and Morten shall look at them every day, and when they are grown up they shall inherit them as heirlooms. (*Rakes about under a bookcase.*) Hasn't—what the deuce is her name?— the girl, you know—hasn't she been to fetch the glazier yet?

MRS. STOCKMANN (*coming in*). Yes, but he said he didn't know if he would be able to come to-day.

DR. STOCKMANN. You will see he won't dare to come.

MRS. STOCKMANN. Well, that is just what Randine thought —that he didn't dare to, on account of the neighbours. (*Calls into the sitting-room.*) What is it you want, Randine? Give it to me. (*Goes in, and comes out again directly.*) Here is a letter for you, Thomas.

DR. STOCKMANN. Let me see it. (*Opens and reads it.*) Ah! —of course.

MRS. STOCKMANN. Who is it from?

DR. STOCKMANN. From the landlord. Notice to quit.

MRS. STOCKMANN. Is it possible? Such a nice man—

DR. STOCKMANN (*looking at the letter*). Does not dare do otherwise, he says. Doesn't like doing it, but dare not do otherwise—on account of his fellow-citizens—out of regard for public opinion. Is in a dependent position—dare not offend certain influential men—

MRS. STOCKMANN. There, you see, Thomas!

DR. STOCKMANN. Yes, yes, I see well enough; the whole lot of them in the town are cowards; not a man among them dares do anything for fear of the others. (*Throws the letter on to the table.*) But it doesn't matter to us, Katherine. We are going to sail away to the New World, and—

MRS. STOCKMANN. But, Thomas, are you sure we are well advised to take this step?

DR. STOCKMANN. Are you suggesting that I should stay here, where they have pilloried me as an enemy of the people —branded me—broken my windows! And just look here, Katherine—they have torn a great rent in my black trousers too!

MRS. STOCKMANN. Oh, dear!—and they are the best pair you have got!

DR. STOCKMANN. You should never wear your best trousers when you go out to fight for freedom and truth. It is not that I care so much about the trousers, you know; you can always sew them up again for me. But that the common herd should dare to make this attack on me, as if they were my equals— that is what I cannot, for the life of me, swallow!

MRS. STOCKMANN. There is no doubt they have behaved very ill to you, Thomas; but is that sufficient reason for our leaving our native country for good and all?

DR. STOCKMANN. If we went to another town, do you suppose we should not find the common people just as insolent as they are here? Depend upon it, there is not much to choose between them. Oh, well, let the curs snap—that is not the worst part of it. The worst is that, from one end of this country to the other, every man is the slave of his Party. Although, as far as that goes, I daresay it is not much better in the free West either; the compact majority, and liberal public opinion, and all that infernal old bag of tricks are probably rampant there too. But there things are done on a larger scale, you see. They may kill you, but they won't put you to death by slow torture. They don't squeeze a free man's soul in a vice, as they do here. And, if need be, one can live in solitude. (*Walks up and down.*) If only I knew where there was a virgin forest or a small South Sea island for sale, cheap—

MRS. STOCKMANN. But think of the boys, Thomas!

DR. STOCKMANN (*standing still*). What a strange woman you are, Katherine! Would you prefer to have the boys grow up in a society like this? You saw for yourself last night that half the population are out of their minds; and if the other half have not lost their senses, it is because they are mere brutes, with no sense to lose.

MRS. STOCKMANN. But, Thomas dear, the imprudent things you said had something to do with it, you know.

DR. STOCKMANN. Well, isn't what I said perfectly true? Don't they turn every idea topsy-turvy? Don't they make a regular hotch-potch of right and wrong? Don't they say that the things I know are true, are lies? The craziest part of it all is the fact of these "liberals," men of full age, going about in crowds imagining that they are the broad-minded party? Did you ever hear anything like it, Katherine!

MRS. STOCKMANN. Yes, yes, it's mad enough of them, certainly; but—(PETRA comes in from the sitting-room). Back from school already?

PETRA. Yes. I have been given notice of dismissal.

MRS. STOCKMANN. Dismissal?

DR. STOCKMANN. You too?

PETRA. Mrs. Busk gave me my notice; so I thought it was best to go at once.

DR. STOCKMANN. You were perfectly right, too!

MRS. STOCKMANN. Who would have thought Mrs. Busk was a woman like that!

PETRA. Mrs. Busk isn't a bit like that, mother; I saw quite plainly how it hurt her to do it. But she didn't dare do otherwise, she said; and so I got my notice.

DR. STOCKMANN (laughing and rubbing his hands). She didn't dare do otherwise, either! It's delicious!

MRS. STOCKMANN. Well, after the dreadful scenes last night—

PETRA. It was not only that. Just listen to this, father!

DR. STOCKMANN. Well?

PETRA. Mrs. Busk showed me no less than three letters she received this morning—

DR. STOCKMANN. Anonymous, I suppose?

PETRA. Yes.

DR. STOCKMANN. Yes, because they didn't dare to risk signing their names, Katherine!

PETRA. And two of them were to the effect that a man, who has been our guest here, was declaring last night at the Club that my views on various subjects are extremely emancipated—

DR. STOCKMANN. You did not deny that, I hope?

PETRA. No, you know I wouldn't. Mrs. Busk's own views are tolerably emancipated, when we are alone together; but now that this report about me is being spread, she dare not keep me on any longer.

MRS. STOCKMANN. And some one who had been a guest of ours! That shows you the return you get for your hospitality, Thomas!

DR. STOCKMANN. We won't live in such a disgusting hole any longer. Pack up as quickly as you can, Katherine; the sooner we can get away, the better.

MRS. STOCKMANN. Be quiet—I think I hear some one in the hall. See who it is, Petra.

PETRA (*opening the door*). Oh, it's you, Captain Horster! Do come in.

HORSTER (*coming in*). Good morning. I thought I would just come in and see how you were.

DR. STOCKMANN (*shaking his hand*). Thanks—that is really kind of you.

MRS. STOCKMANN. And thank you, too, for helping us through the crowd, Captain Horster.

PETRA. How did you manage to get home again?

HORSTER. Oh, somehow or other. I am fairly strong, and there is more sound than fury about these folk.

DR. STOCKMANN. Yes, isn't their swinish cowardice astonishing? Look here, I will show you something! There are all the stones they have thrown through my windows. Just look at them! I'm hanged if there are more than two decently large bits of hardstone in the whole heap; the rest are nothing but gravel—wretched little things. And yet they stood out there bawling and swearing that they would do me some violence; but as for *doing* anything—you don't see much of that in this town.

HORSTER. Just as well for you this time, Doctor!

DR. STOCKMANN. True enough. But it makes one angry all the same; because if some day it should be a question of a national fight in real earnest, you will see that public opinion will be in favour of taking to one's heels, and the compact majority will turn tail like a flock of sheep, Captain Horster. That is what is so mournful to think of; it gives me so much concern, that—. No, devil take it, it is ridiculous to care about it! They have called me an enemy of the people, so an enemy of the people let me be!

MRS. STOCKMANN. You will never be that, Thomas.

DR. STOCKMANN. Don't swear to that, Katherine. To be called an ugly name may have the same effect as a pin-scratch in the lung. And that hateful name—I can't get quit of it. It is sticking here in the pit of my stomach, eating into me like a corrosive acid. And no magnesia will remove it.

PETRA. Bah!—you should only laugh at them, father.

HORSTER. They will change their minds some day, Doctor.

467

MRS. STOCKMANN. Yes, Thomas, as sure as you are standing here.

DR. STOCKMANN. Perhaps, when it is too late. Much good may it do them! They may wallow in their filth then and rue the day when they drove a patriot into exile. When do you sail, Captain Horster?

HORSTER. Hm!—that was just what I had come to speak about—

DR. STOCKMANN. Why, has anything gone wrong with the ship?

HORSTER. No; but what has happened is that I am not to sail in it.

PETRA. Do you mean that you have been dismissed from your command?

HORSTER (*smiling*). Yes, that's just it.

PETRA. You too.

MRS. STOCKMANN. There, you see, Thomas!

DR. STOCKMANN. And that for the truth's sake! Oh, if I had thought such a thing possible—

HORSTER. You mustn't take it to heart; I shall be sure to find a job with some ship-owner or other, elsewhere.

DR. STOCKMANN. And that is this man Vik—a wealthy man, independent of every one and everything—! Shame on him!

HORSTER. He is quite an excellent fellow otherwise; he told me himself he would willingly have kept me on, if only he had dared—

DR. STOCKMANN. But he didn't dare? No, of course not.

HORSTER. It is not such an easy matter, he said, for a party man—

DR. STOCKMANN. The worthy man spoke the truth. A party is like a sausage machine; it mashes up all sorts of heads together into the same mincemeat—fatheads and blockheads, all in one mash!

MRS. STOCKMANN. Come, come, Thomas dear!

PETRA (*to* HORSTER). If only you had not come home with us, things might not have come to this pass.

HORSTER. I do not regret it.

PETRA (*holding out her hand to him*). Thank you for that!

HORSTER (*to* DR. STOCKMANN). And so what I came to say was that if you are determined to go away, I have thought of another plan—

DR. STOCKMANN. That's splendid!—if only we can get away at once.

MRS. STOCKMANN. Hush!—wasn't that some one knocking?

PETRA. That is uncle, surely.

DR. STOCKMANN. Aha! (*Calls out.*) Come in!

468

MRS. STOCKMANN. Dear Thomas, promise me definitely—.
(PETER STOCKMANN *comes in from the hall.*)

PETER STOCKMANN. Oh, you are engaged. In that case,
I will—

DR. STOCKMANN. No, no, come in.

PETER STOCKMANN. But I wanted to speak to you alone.

MRS. STOCKMANN. We will go into the sitting-room in the
meanwhile.

HORSTER. And I will look in again later.

DR. STOCKMANN. No, go in there with them, Captain
Horster; I want to hear more about—.

HORSTER. Very well, I will wait, then. (*He follows* MRS.
STOCKMANN *and* PETRA *into the sitting-room.*)

DR. STOCKMANN. I daresay you find it rather draughty
here to-day. Put your hat on.

PETER STOCKMANN. Thank you, if I may. (*Does so.*) I
think I caught cold last night; I stood and shivered—

DR. STOCKMANN. Really? I found it warm enough.

PETER STOCKMANN. I regret that it was not in my power to
prevent those excesses last night.

DR. STOCKMANN. Have you anything particular to say to
me besides that?

PETER STOCKMANN (*taking a big letter from his pocket*). I
have this document for you, from the Baths Committee.

DR. STOCKMANN. My dismissal?

PETER STOCKMANN. Yes, dating from to-day. (*Lays the
letter on the table.*) It gives us pain to do it; but, to speak
frankly, we dared not do otherwise on account of public
opinion.

DR. STOCKMANN (*smiling*). Dared not? I seem to have
heard that word before, to-day.

PETER STOCKMANN. I must beg you to understand your
position clearly. For the future you must not count on any
practice whatever in the town.

DR. STOCKMANN. Devil take the practice! But why are you
so sure of that?

PETER STOCKMANN. The Householders' Association is cir-
culating a list from house to house. All right-minded citizens
are being called upon to give up employing you; and I can
assure you that not a single head of a family will risk refusing
his signature. They simply dare not.

DR. STOCKMANN. No, no; I don't doubt it. But what then?

PETER STOCKMANN. If I might advise you, it would be best
to leave the place for a little while—

DR. STOCKMANN. Yes, the propriety of leaving the place *has*
occurred to me.

PETER STOCKMANN. Good. And then, when you have had

six months to think things over, if, after mature consideration, you can persuade yourself to write a few words of regret, acknowledging your error—

DR. STOCKMANN. I might have my appointment restored to me, do you mean?

PETER STOCKMANN. Perhaps. It is not at all impossible.

DR. STOCKMANN. But what about public opinion, then? Surely you would not dare to do it on account of public feeling.

PETER STOCKMANN. Public opinion is an extremely mutable thing. And, to be quite candid with you, it is a matter of great importance to us to have some admission of that sort from you in writing.

DR. STOCKMANN. Oh, that's what you are after, is it! I will just trouble you to remember what I said to you lately about foxy tricks of that sort!

PETER STOCKMANN. Your position was quite different then. At that time you had reason to suppose you had the whole town at your back—

DR. STOCKMANN. Yes, and now I feel I have the whole town *on* my back—(*flaring up*). I would not do it if I had the devil and his dam on my back—! Never—never, I tell you!

PETER STOCKMANN. A man with a family has no right to behave as you do. You have no right to do it, Thomas.

DR. STOCKMANN. I have no right! There is only one single thing in the world a free man has no right to do. Do you know what that is?

PETER STOCKMANN. No.

DR. STOCKMANN. Of course you don't, but I will tell you. A free man has no right to soil himself with filth; he has no right to behave in a way that would justify his spitting in his own face.

PETER STOCKMANN. This sort of thing sounds extremely plausible, of course; and if there were no other explanation for your obstinacy—. But as it happens that there is.

DR. STOCKMANN. What do you mean?

PETER STOCKMANN. You understand very well what I mean. But, as your brother and as a man of discretion, I advise you not to build too much upon expectations and prospects that may so very easily fail you.

DR. STOCKMANN. What in the world is all this about?

PETER STOCKMANN. Do you really ask me to believe that you are ignorant of the terms of Mr. Kiil's will?

DR. STOCKMANN. I know that the small amount he possesses is to go to an institution for indigent old workpeople. How does that concern me?

PETER STOCKMANN. In the first place, it is by no means a

470

small amount that is in question. Mr. Kiil is a fairly wealthy man.

DR. STOCKMANN. I had no notion of that!

PETER STOCKMANN. Hm!—hadn't you really? Then I suppose you had no notion, either, that a considerable portion of his wealth will come to your children, you and your wife having a life-rent of the capital. Has he never told you so?

DR. STOCKMANN. Never, on my honour! Quite the reverse; he has consistently done nothing but fume at being so unconscionably heavily taxed. But are you perfectly certain of this, Peter?

PETER STOCKMANN. I have it from an absolutely reliable source.

DR. STOCKMANN. Then, thank God, Katherine is provided for—and the children too! I must tell her this at once—(*calls out*) Katherine, Katherine!

PETER STOCKMANN (*restraining him*). Hush, don't say a word yet!

MRS. STOCKMANN (*opening the door*). What is the matter?

DR. STOCKMANN. Oh, nothing, nothing; you can go back. (*She shuts the door.* DR. STOCKMANN *walks up and down in his excitement.*) Provided for!—Just think of it, we are all provided for! And for life! What a blessed feeling it is to know one is provided for!

PETER STOCKMANN. Yes, but that is just exactly what you are not. Mr. Kiil can alter his will any day he likes.

DR. STOCKMANN. But he won't do that, my dear Peter. The "Badger" is much too delighted at my attack on you and your wise friends.

PETER STOCKMANN (*starts and looks intently at him*). Ah, that throws a light on various things.

DR. STOCKMANN. What things?

PETER STOCKMANN. I see that the whole thing was a combined manœuvre on your part and his. These violent, reckless attacks that you have made against the leading men of the town, under the pretence that it was in the name of truth—

DR. STOCKMANN. What about them?

PETER STOCKMANN. I see that they were nothing else than the stipulated price for that vindictive old man's will.

DR. STOCKMANN (*almost speechless*). Peter—you are the most disgusting plebeian I have ever met in all my life.

PETER STOCKMANN. All is over between us. Your dismissal is irrevocable—we have a weapon against you now. (*Goes out.*)

DR. STOCKMANN. For shame! For shame! (*Calls out.*) Katherine, you must have the floor scrubbed after him! Let

—what's her name—devil take it, the girl who has always got soot on her nose—

MRS. STOCKMANN (*in the sitting-room*). Hush, Thomas, be quiet!

PETRA (*coming to the door*). Father, grandfather is here, asking if he may speak to you alone.

DR. STOCKMANN. Certainly he may. (*Going to the door.*) Come in, Mr. Kiil. (MORTEN KIIL *comes in.* DR. STOCKMANN *shuts the door after him.*) What can I do for you? Won't you sit down?

MORTEN KIIL. I won't sit. (*Looks around.*) You look very comfortable here to-day, Thomas.

DR. STOCKMANN. Yes, don't we!

MORTEN KIIL. Very comfortable—plenty of fresh air. I should think you have got enough to-day of that oxygen you were talking about yesterday. Your conscience must be in splendid order to-day, I should think.

DR. STOCKMANN. It is.

MORTEN KIIL. So I should think. (*Taps his chest.*) Do you know what I have got here?

DR. STOCKMANN. A good conscience, too, I hope.

MORTEN KIIL. Bah!—No, it is something better than that. (*He takes a thick pocket-book from his breast-pocket, opens it, and displays a packet of papers.*)

DR. STOCKMANN (*looking at him in astonishment*). Shares in the Baths?

MORTEN KIIL. They were not difficult to get to-day.

DR. STOCKMANN. And you have been buying—?

MORTEN KIIL. As many as I could pay for.

DR. STOCKMANN. But, my dear Mr. Kiil—consider the state of the Baths' affairs!

MORTEN KIIL. If you behave like a reasonable man, you can soon set the Baths on their feet again.

DR. STOCKMANN. Well, you can see for yourself that I have done all I can, but—. They are all mad in this town!

MORTEN KIIL. You said yesterday that the worst of this pollution came from my tannery. If that is true, then my grandfather and my father before me, and I myself, for many years past, have been poisoning the town like three destroying angels. Do you think I am going to sit quiet under that reproach?

DR. STOCKMANN. Unfortunately I am afraid you will have to.

MORTEN KILL. No, thank you. I am jealous of my name and reputation. They call me "the Badger," I am told. A badger is a kind of pig, I believe; but I am not going to give them the right to call me that. I mean to live and die a clean man.

DR. STOCKMANN. And how are you going to set about it?

MORTEN KIIL. You shall cleanse me, Thomas.

DR. STOCKMANN. I!

MORTEN KIIL. Do you know what money I have bought these shares with? No, of course you can't know—but I will tell you. It is the money that Katherine and Petra and the boys will have when I am gone. Because I have been able to save a little bit after all, you know.

DR. STOCKMANN (*flaring up*). And you have gone and taken Katherine's money for *this*!

MORTEN KIIL. Yes, the whole of the money is invested in the Baths now. And now I just want to see whether you are quite stark, staring mad, Thomas! If you still make out that these animals and other nasty things of that sort come from my tannery, it will be exactly as if you were to flay broad strips of skin from Katherine's body, and Petra's, and the boys'; and no decent man would do that—unless he were mad.

DR. STOCKMANN (*walking up and down*). Yes, but I *am* mad; I *am* mad!

MORTEN KIIL. You cannot be so absurdly mad as all that, when it is a question of your wife and children.

DR. STOCKMANN (*standing still in front of him*). Why couldn't you consult me about it, before you went and bought all that trash?

MORTEN KIIL. What is done cannot be undone.

DR. STOCKMANN (*walks about uneasily*). If only I were not so certain about it—! But I am absolutely convinced that I am right.

MORTEN KIIL (*weighing the pocket-book in his hand*). If you stick to your mad idea, this won't be worth much, you know. (*Puts the pocket-book in his pocket.*)

DR. STOCKMANN. But, hang it all! it might be possible for science to discover some prophylactic, I should think—or some antidote of some kind—

MORTEN KIIL. To kill these animals, do you mean?

DR. STOCKMANN. Yes, or to make them innocuous.

MORTEN KIIL. Couldn't you try some rat's-bane?

DR. STOCKMANN. Don't talk nonsense! They all say it is only imagination, you know. Well, let it go at that! Let them have their own way about it! Haven't the ignorant, narrow-minded curs reviled me as an enemy of the people?—and haven't they been ready to tear the clothes off my back too?

MORTEN KIIL. And broken all your windows to pieces!

DR. STOCKMANN. And then there is my duty to my family. I must talk it over with Katherine; she is great on those things.

473

ACT V

MORTEN KIIL. That is right; be guided by a reasonable woman's advice.

DR. STOCKMANN (*advancing towards him*). To think you could do such a preposterous thing! Risking Katherine's money in this way, and putting me in such a horribly painful dilemma! When I look at you, I think I see the devil himself—.

MORTEN KIIL. Then I had better go. But I must have an answer from you before two o'clock—yes or no. If it is no, the shares go to a charity, and that this very day.

DR. STOCKMANN. And what does Katherine get?

MORTEN KIIL. Not a halfpenny. (*The door leading to the hall opens, and* HOVSTAD *and* ASLAKSEN *make their appearance.*) Look at those two!

DR. STOCKMANN (*staring at them*). What the devil!—have *you* actually the face to come into my house?

HOVSTAD. Certainly.

ASLAKSEN. We have something to say to you, you see.

MORTEN KIIL (*in a whisper*). Yes or no—before two o'clock.

ASLAKSEN (*glancing at* HOVSTAD). Aha! (MORTEN KIIL *goes out.*)

DR. STOCKMANN. Well, what do you want with me? Be brief.

HOVSTAD. I can quite understand that you are annoyed with us for our attitude at the meeting yesterday—

DR. STOCKMANN. Attitude, do you call it? Yes, it was a charming attitude! I call it weak, womanish—damnably shameful!

HOVSTAD. Call it what you like, we could not do otherwise.

DR. STOCKMANN. You *dared* not do otherwise—isn't that it?

HOVSTAD. Well, if you like to put it that way.

ASLAKSEN. But why did you not let us have word of it beforehand?—just a hint to Mr. Hovstad or to me?

DR. STOCKMANN. A hint? Of what?

ASLAKSEN. Of what was behind it all.

DR. STOCKMANN. I don't understand you in the least.

ASLAKSEN (*with a confidential nod*). Oh yes, you do, Dr. Stockmann.

HOVSTAD. It is no good making a mystery of it any longer.

DR. STOCKMANN (*looking first at one of them and then at the other*). What the devil do you both mean?

ASLAKSEN. May I ask if your father-in-law is not going round the town buying up all the shares in the Baths?

DR. STOCKMANN. Yes, he has been buying Baths shares to-day; but—

ASLAKSEN. It would have been more prudent to get some one else to do it—some one less nearly related to you.

HOVSTAD. And you should not have let your name appear in the affair. There was no need for anyone to know that the attack on the Baths came from you. You ought to have consulted me, Dr. Stockmann.

DR. STOCKMANN (*looks in front of him; then a light seems to dawn on him and he says in amazement:*) Are such things conceivable? Are such things possible?

ASLAKSEN (*with a smile*). Evidently they are. But it is better to use a little *finesse*, you know.

HOVSTAD. And it is much better to have several persons in a thing of that sort; because the responsibility of each individual is lessened, when there are others with him.

DR. STOCKMANN (*composedly*). Come to the point, gentlemen. What do you want?

ASLAKSEN. Perhaps Mr. Hovstad had better—

HOVSTAD. No, you tell him, Aslaksen.

ASLAKSEN. Well, the fact is that, now we know the bearings of the whole affair, we think we might venture to put the "People's Messenger" at your disposal.

DR. STOCKMANN. Do you dare do that now? What about public opinion? Are you not afraid of a storm breaking upon our heads?

HOVSTAD. We will try to weather it.

ASLAKSEN. And you must be ready to go off quickly on a new tack, Doctor. As soon as your invective has done its work—

DR. STOCKMANN. Do you mean, as soon as my father-in-law and I have got hold of the shares at a low figure?

HOVSTAD. Your reasons for wishing to get the control of the Baths are mainly scientific, I take it.

DR. STOCKMANN. Of course; it was for scientific reasons that I persuaded the old "Badger" to stand in with me in the matter. So we will tinker at the conduit-pipes a little, and dig up a little bit of the shore, and it shan't cost the town a sixpence. That will be all right—eh?

HOVSTAD. I think so—if you have the "People's Messenger" behind you.

ASLAKSEN. The Press is a power in a free community, Doctor.

DR. STOCKMANN. Quite so. And so is public opinion. And you, Mr. Aslaksen—I suppose you will be answerable for the Householders' Association?

ASLAKSEN. Yes, and for the Temperance Society. You may rely on that.

DR. STOCKMANN. But, gentlemen—I really am ashamed to ask the question—but, what return do you—?

HOVSTAD. We should prefer to help you without any return

whatever, believe me. But the "People's Messenger" is in rather a shaky condition; it doesn't go really well; and I should be very unwilling to suspend the paper now, when there is so much work to do here in the political way.

DR. STOCKMANN. Quite so; that would be a great trial to such a friend of the people as you are. (*Flares up.*) But I am an enemy of the people, remember! (*Walks about the room.*) Where have I put my stick? Where the devil is my stick?

HOVSTAD. What's that?

ASLAKSEN. Surely you never mean—?

DR. STOCKMANN (*standing still*). And suppose I don't give you a single penny of all I get out of it? Money is not very easy to get out of us rich folk, please to remember!

HOVSTAD. And you please to remember that this affair of the shares can be represented in two ways!

DR. STOCKMANN. Yes, and you are just the man to do it. If I don't come to the rescue of the "People's Messenger," you will certainly take an evil view of the affair; you will hunt me down, I can well imagine—pursue me—try to throttle me as a dog does a hare.

HOVSTAD. It is a natural law; every animal must fight for its own livelihood.

ASLAKSEN. And get its food where it can, you know.

DR. STOCKMANN (*walking about the room*). Then you go and look for yours in the gutter; because I am going to show you which is the strongest animal of us three! (*Finds an umbrella and brandishes it above his head.*) Ah, now—!

HOVSTAD. You are surely not going to use violence!

ASLAKSEN. Take care what you are doing with that umbrella.

DR. STOCKMANN. Out of the window with you, Mr. Hovstad!

HOVSTAD (*edging to the door*). Are you quite mad!

DR. STOCKMANN. Out of the window, Mr. Aslaksen! Jump, I tell you! You will have to do it, sooner or later.

ASLAKSEN (*running round the writing-table*). Moderation, Doctor—I am a delicate man—I can stand so little—(*calls out*) help, help!

(MRS. STOCKMANN, PETRA *and* HORSTER *come in from the sitting-room.*)

MRS. STOCKMANN. Good gracious, Thomas! What is happening?

DR. STOCKMANN (*brandishing the umbrella*). Jump out, I tell you! Out into the gutter!

HOVSTAD. An assault on an unoffending man! I call you to witness, Captain Horster. (*Hurries out through the hall.*)

ASLAKSEN (*irresolutely*). If only I knew the way about here—. (*Steals out through the sitting-room.*)

MRS. STOCKMANN (*holding her husband back*). Control yourself, Thomas!

DR. STOCKMANN (*throwing down the umbrella*). Upon my soul, they have escaped after all.

MRS. STOCKMANN. What did they want you to do?

DR. STOCKMANN. I will tell you later on; I have something else to think about now. (*Goes to the table and writes something on a calling-card.*) Look there, Katherine; what is written there?

MRS. STOCKMANN. Three big *Noes*; what does that mean.

DR. STOCKMANN. I will tell you that too, later on. (*Holds out the card to* PETRA.) There, Petra; tell sooty-face to run over to the "Badger's" with that, as quick as she can. Hurry up! (PETRA *takes the card and goes out to the hall.*)

DR. STOCKMANN. Well, I think I have had a visit from every one of the devil's messengers to-day! But now I am going to sharpen my pen till they can feel its point; I shall dip it in venom and gall; I shall hurl my ink-pot at their heads!

MRS. STOCKMANN. Yes, but we are going away, you know, Thomas.

(PETRA *comes back.*)

DR. STOCKMANN. Well?

PETRA. She has gone with it.

DR. STOCKMANN. Good.—Going away, did you say? No, I'll be hanged if we are going away! We are going to stay where we are, Katherine!

PETRA. Stay here?

MRS. STOCKMANN. Here, in the town?

DR. STOCKMANN. Yes, here. This is the field of battle—this is where the fight will be. This is where I shall triumph! As soon as I have had my trousers sewn up I shall go out and look for another house. We must have a roof over our heads for the winter.

HORSTER. That you shall have in my house.

DR. STOCKMANN. Can I?

HORSTER. Yes, quite well. I have plenty of room, and I am almost never at home.

MRS. STOCKMANN. How good of you, Captain Horster!

PETRA. Thank you!

DR. STOCKMANN (*grasping his hand*). Thank you, thank you! That is one trouble over! Now I can set to work in earnest at once. There is an endless amount of things to look through here, Katherine! Luckily I shall have all my time at my disposal; because I have been dismissed from the Baths, you know.

MRS. STOCKMANN (*with a sigh*). Oh yes, I expected that.

DR. STOCKMANN. And they want to take my practice away from me too. Let them! I have got the poor people to fall back upon, anyway—those that don't pay anything! and, after all, they need me most, too. But, by Jove, they will have to listen to me; I shall preach to them in season and out of season, as it says somewhere.

MRS. STOCKMANN. But, dear Thomas, I should have thought events had showed you what use it is to preach.

DR. STOCKMANN. You are really ridiculous, Katherine. Do you want me to let myself be beaten off the field by public opinion and the compact majority and all that deviltry? No, thank you! And what I want to do is so simple and clear and straightforward. I only want to drum into the heads of these curs the fact that the liberals are the most insidious enemies of freedom—that party programmes strangle every young and vigorous truth—that considerations of expediency turn morality and justice upside down—and that they will end by making life here unbearable. Don't you think, Captain Horster, that I ought to be able to make people understand that?

HORSTER. Very likely; I don't know much about such things myself.

DR. STOCKMANN. Well, look here—I will explain! It is the party leaders that must be exterminated. A party leader is like a wolf, you see—like a voracious wolf. He requires a certain number of smaller victims to prey upon every year, if he is to live. Just look at Hovstad and Aslaksen! How many smaller victims have they not put an end to—or at any rate maimed and mangled until they are fit for nothing except to be householders or subscribers to the "People's Messenger"! (*Sits down on the edge of the table.*) Come here, Katherine—look how beautifully the sun shines to-day! And this lovely spring air I am drinking in!

MRS. STOCKMANN. Yes, if only we could live on sunshine and spring air, Thomas.

DR. STOCKMANN. Oh, you will have to pinch and save a bit —then we shall get along. That gives me very little concern. What is much worse is, that I know of no one who is liberal-minded and high-minded enough to venture to take up my work after me.

PETRA. Don't think about that, father; you have plenty of time before you.—Hullo, here are the boys already!

(EJLIF *and* MORTEN *come in from the sitting-room.*)

MRS. STOCKMANN. Have you got a holiday?

AN ENEMY OF THE PEOPLE

MORTEN. No; but we were fighting with the other boys between lessons—

EJLIF. That isn't true; it was the other boys were fighting with us.

MORTEN. Well, and then Mr. Rörlund said we had better stay at home for a day or two.

DR. STOCKMANN (*snapping his fingers and getting up from the table*). I have it! I have it, by Jove! You shall never set foot in the school again!

THE BOYS. No more school!

MRS. STOCKMANN. But, Thomas—

DR. STOCKMANN. Never, I say. I will educate you myself; that is to say, you shan't learn a blessed thing—

MORTEN. Hooray!

DR. STOCKMANN. —but I will make liberal-minded and high-minded men of you. You must help me with that, Petra.

PETRA. Yes, father, you may be sure I will.

DR. STOCKMANN. And my school shall be in the room where they insulted me and called me an enemy of the people. But we are too few as we are; I must have at least twelve boys to begin with.

MRS. STOCKMANN. You will certainly never get them in this town.

DR. STOCKMANN. We shall. (*To the boys.*) Don't you know any street urchins—regular ragamuffins—?

MORTEN. Yes, father, I know lots!

DR. STOCKMANN. That's capital! Bring me some specimens of them. I am going to experiment with curs, just for once; there may be some exceptional heads amongst them.

MORTEN. And what are we going to do, when you have made liberal-minded and high-minded men of us?

DR. STOCKMANN. Then you shall drive all the wolves out of the country, my boys!

(EJLIF *looks rather doubtful about it;* MORTEN *jumps about crying* "Hurrah!")

MRS. STOCKMANN. Let us hope it won't be the wolves that will drive you out of the country, Thomas.

DR. STOCKMANN. Are you out of your mind, Katherine? Drive me out! Now—when I am the strongest man in the town!

MRS. STOCKMANN. The strongest—now?

DR. STOCKMANN. Yes, and I will go so far as to say that now I am the strongest man in the whole world.

MORTEN. I say!

DR. STOCKMANN (*lowering his voice*). Hush! You mustn't say anything about it yet; but I have made a great discovery.

MRS. STOCKMANN. Another one?

479

DR. STOCKMANN. Yes. (*Gathers them round him, and says confidentially:*) It is this, let me tell you—that the strongest man in the world is he who stands most alone.

MRS. STOCKMANN (*smiling and shaking her head*). Oh, Thomas, Thomas!

PETRA (*encouragingly, as she grasps her father's hands*). Father!